BECOMING WOMEN

The Embodied Self in Image Culture

In a culture where beauty is currency, women's bodies are often perceived as measures of value and worth. The search for visibility and self-acceptance can be daunting, especially for those on the margins of conventional Western notions of beauty.

Becoming Women offers a thoughtful examination of the search for identity in an image-oriented world. That search is told through the experiences of a group of women who came of age in the wake of second- and third-wave feminism, and focuses especially on voices from marginalized and misrepresented groups.

Carla Rice pairs images from popular culture with personal narratives to expose the "culture of contradiction" where exhortations for body acceptance have been matched by even more restrictive feminine image ideals and norms. Drawing on insights gained from her advisory role with the Dove Campaign for Real Beauty, Rice exposes the beauty industry's colonization of women's bodies, and examines why "the beauty myth" persists.

CARLA RICE is the Canada Research Chair in Care, Gender, and Relationships in the College of Social and Applied Human Sciences at the University of Guelph. She has more than twenty years of experience as a clinician, researcher, and media consultant on body image and beauty culture.

CARLA RICE

Becoming Women

The Embodied Self in Image Culture

UNIVERSITY OF TORONTO PRESS
Toronto Buffalo London

ISBN 978-1-4426-4043-6 (cloth)
ISBN 978-1-4426-1005-7 (paper)

∞

Printed on acid-free, 100% post-consumer recycled paper with
vegetable-based inks.

Library and Archives Canada Cataloguing in Publication

Rice, Carla, author
Becoming women : the embodied self in image culture / Carla Rice.

Includes bibliographical references.
ISBN 978-1-4426-4043-6 (bound). – ISBN 978-1-4426-1005-7 (pbk.)

1. Body image in women – Social aspects.   2. Body image in girls –
Social aspects.   3. Beauty, Personal – Social aspects.
4. Feminine beauty (Aesthetics) – Social aspects.   I. Title.

HQ1219.R53 2014   306.4'613   C2013-906769-8

This book has been published with the help of a grant from the Canadian
Federation for the Humanities and Social Sciences, through the Awards
to Scholarly Publications Program, using funds provided by the Social
Sciences and Humanities Research Council of Canada.

University of Toronto Press acknowledges the financial assistance to its
publishing program of the Canada Council for the Arts and the Ontario Arts
Council.

Canada Council   Conseil des Arts
for the Arts   du Canada

University of Toronto Press acknowledges the financial support of the
Government of Canada through the Canada Book Fund for its publishing
activities.

Contents

Illustrations and Tables

Illustrations

Tables

Acknowledgments

No writer can hope to endure the lonely journey of writing a book without a supportive circle to guide her.

I wish first to thank my spouse, Susan Dion, whose belief in me has proved far greater than my disbelief. Without your formidable intellect, love, and faith I could *never* have completed this task. I express profound gratitude to my parents, Mabel Mingarelli Rice and Ian Stanley Briar Rice, who endured my absence at family events with understanding and approbation, and whose sense of identity and place have given me a far stronger foundation than I can acknowledge or even know.

Among my friends, I offer a special thanks to Eva Karpinski, whose vital dose of confidence at a critical moment enabled me to craft the story of becoming women; Elisabeth Harrison, whose intellectual brilliance helped me navigate the challenging and rewarding world of feminist theory; and Eliza Chandler, whose insights into the representational history of disability were a revelation. I am lucky to count you as colleagues, friends, and supporters. I owe a deep debt of gratitude to my mentors, my thesis supervisor Nancy Mandell, and committee members Virginia Rock and Lorraine Code, for facilitating my process of becoming. Acknowledgments are due to Marg Hobbs for shouldering my worries and qualms, and Noelani Rodriguez for teaching me how to trust and to wonder.

This book has been published with the help of a grant from the Federation for the Humanities and Social Sciences, through the Awards to Scholarly Publications Program, using funds provided by the Social Sciences and Humanities Research Council of Canada. Grants from the Ontario Graduate Scholarship Program, the Social Sciences and Humanities Research Council of Canada Doctoral Fellowship Program, and Women's College Hospital also helped to fund the research. I thank the Graduate Program in Women's Studies, York University, the Department of Gender and Women's Studies, Trent University, and the College of Social and Applied Human Sciences, University of Guelph for the gift of time to incubate the ideas developed in this book. Finally, I offer my sincere thanks to Elizabeth Rooney and Jacqueline Larson for their careful copy-editing; Gina MacDonald for her efficient facilitation of the image permissions; Doug Hildebrand and Anne Laughlin for their conscientious and responsive management at critical moments of the project; Wangechi Mutu, Susan Dion, Lindsay Fisher, John Harrison, Holly Norris, Jes Sachse, and Jenny Saville for permission to use their images; and the anonymous reviewers whose perceptive comments contributed substantively to strengthening ideas developed in this book.

This book is dedicated to the generation of women whose stories are told between its covers and especially those who generously agreed to participate in the research, from whom I have learned so much. It is also dedicated to the generations that have followed, as an invitation to take up feminism's unfinished work and to move its visions forward.

BECOMING WOMEN

The Embodied Self in Image Culture

Introduction: Searching for Identity in Image Culture

Jillian: Mostly my body image is negative. I bet that's true for many women: our chief relationship with our bodies is what we don't like.

Rose: Beauty ideals are racist. [But] most of what I read is only a white woman's point of view. They exclude the minority.

Elizabeth: For a lot of people with facial disfigurements, it's not about being beautiful, it's about blending in and being accepted.

Leila: I want my point made public. I'm a fantastic person, but nobody could see past the fat. It angers me more than it hurts me. But it hurts.

For girls coming of age in consumerist, individualist, and media-driven cultures, the body has become an important identity project. A key medium of self-making, many girls and women also experience their body as a significant obstacle and a source of distress. Studies conducted in wealthy nations show how girls as young as six already express dissatisfaction with their bodies (Irving, 2000; Ricciardelli & McCabe, 2001). More and more adolescents in the Western world suffer from eating problems, including 27 per cent of Canadian middle-school girls who report disordered eating (Jones, Bennett, Olmsted, Lawson, & Rodin, 2001) and 60 per cent who have tried dieting (McVey, Pepler, Davis, Flett, & Abdolell, 2002). Most recently, some 40 per cent of girls think they're too fat and 20 per cent feel depressed about their lives and pessimistic about the future (Freeman, King, Pickett, Craig, Elgar, Janssen, & Klinger, 2011). Worldwide, millions of women worry about image understanding that appearance shapes their self-esteem, social status, and life chances (Etcoff, Orbach, Scott, & D'Agostino, 2004). A psychologically sophisticated, highly profitable, globalizing beauty/dieting industry has colonized and capitalized on women's most intimate wishes and worries about their bodies in order to sell a dizzying array of products to expanding consumer markets. As a result, millions are affected by a growing global trade in harmful skin-lightening products, by a rapidly spreading culture of cosmetic surgery, and by mounting fears about an obesity epidemic said to threaten public health.

This book examines the reach of cultural misrepresentations and their wide-ranging consequences for ordinary Canadian women. It explores the ways that girls become women in response to the messages they receive and how they work to create a sense of bodily self through and against the images and narratives the culture hands to them. It's now almost a cliché to say that the body has become a consuming project for girls growing up in image culture, but women *are not* simply dupes of manipulative marketers or of a pervasive beauty myth. For close to one hundred women with whom I spoke, something else is at stake. Rather than vanity or superficiality, their body projects and problems stem from deeper doubts about their personhood and value. Coming of age in a body categorized as female and often otherwise as different, their body concerns represent, rather than individual flaws or failings, their search for identity in an image-oriented world.

Most books about bodies focus either on cultural imagery or on personal narrative. This book synthesizes both. It highlights the stories of women aged twenty to forty-five from all walks of life, the first generation to grow up in an image-saturated world replete with visual technologies like cameras, scales, and movies as well as methods for modifying their appearance such as skin-lightening products and cosmetic surgery. Since research largely looks at white, middle-class girls, I include under-researched groups falling outside the bounds of "idealized femininity": those from different social classes and racial backgrounds, of diverse body types, and with and without disabilities and physical differences. (Profiles of participants, including their pseudonym, age, self-identified ethnicity, disability, sexuality, education, class, and body size are listed alphabetically in appendix A.) I situate their stories not only within the context of popular media but also school curricula, health campaigns, and government policies on multiculturalism. By locating their stories in the social milieu, this book reframes, from a critical feminist perspective, how diverse women respond to a barrage of messages in their attempt to create an acceptable identity and affirm a self.

Most women I interviewed came of age between the late 1970s and the early 1990s. (Since I conducted this research at the end of the millennium, the cohort is now aged approximately 30 to 55.) They grew up wedged between two intense periods of vigorous action to end sexism – the first running from the late 1960s to the late 1970s, and the second from the early 1990s to the early 2000s. Important books documenting the history of women's organizing in Canada during the peaks of feminism's second and third waves (Mitchell, Rundle, & Karaian, 2001; Rebick, 2005) have contributed to our collective memory. But I was curious about the unnamed cohort that came of age *between* these crests: women who had little opportunity to take part in second-wave organizing and who missed out on third-wave media strategies of culture jamming, 'zine making, and other creative responses to controlling standards. I was also intent on hearing the voices of those missing from the story of North American feminism: women who grew up in geographic, social, and cultural spaces that gave them little access to feminist ideas and organizing. By focusing on these women, the book captures a historical moment of transition for a generation overlooked by writers more concerned with the experiences and activities of those at feminism's crests and centres. I am concerned about how the cohort caught between the peaks of activism negotiated image culture because I am a member of it, and because I witnessed and experienced many of the issues that emerged as significant to this hidden generation.

Although inspired by my observations, this project was guided by a deeper intention: to grasp, without collapsing, women's experiences of differences. Thus, I carefully distinguish the accounts of those I interviewed in multiple ways, including by race, size, disability, and age. For example, how do messages about femininity and beauty differ based on a woman's race and physical ability? What life-shaping lessons about bodies do those with disabilities and physical differences learn in medical systems? And why do younger women in this cohort tell much more positive menstruation stories than older ones? The life stories show that while everyone felt pressures to embody restrictive standards, they did not experience these in the same way. The diversity of women's perspectives resonates with current feminist intersectional approaches that highlight the importance of power and difference in understanding experiences. *Intersectionality* describes the idea that people live multiple layered identities and encounter shifting privileges and oppressions (Canadian Research Institute for the Advancement of Women [CRIAW], 2006). Instead of focusing solely on gender, it attends to the "indivisibility and interaction" of people's identities and situations (Freedman, 2002, p. 6). For example, all women are judged according to beauty codes, but young thin white women are more likely to be seen as the epitome of beauty; disabled women as undesirable and sexless; Black women as wild and aggressive; Asian or South Asian women as meek and mysterious; and poor women as loud and lewd. These standards and stereotypes overlap in participants' stories in complicated, distressing, and, ultimately, limiting ways.

As I talked with diverse storytellers, their narratives became a chorus of distinct yet harmonized voices. Through their rich descriptions and difficult disclosures, I learned that beauty ideals are shadowed by other images, phantoms of the abject body that also haunt these women's bodily selves. Fearing negative responses to fat, ethnic distinctiveness, disability, and other attributes regarded as unusual or anomalous, many describe how they altered or concealed the unacceptable to avoid judgment and rejection. While feminists in the past have argued that women diet, undergo surgery, and otherwise modify their bodies to live up to impossible ideals, women's desire to fit in and find approval was often the major motivator. In our body-conscious society where any small difference is highlighted, women's efforts were about trying to make themselves physically acceptable and recognizable in an attempt to reverse in/visibility and "othering." I wanted to understand the role of abject images in giving rise to a generation's fantasies and fears, and ultimately in shaping their bodily experiences.

Why Women Worry about Their Bodies

The Uneasy Primacy of Image

In Western culture, women are identified socially with our bodies. How the culture values or devalues our physical features, sizes, and capacities has a significant impact on our sense of body and self. Feminist critics have long been interested in representations of female bodies because women looking at these often have had a hard time recognizing themselves (Hearn, 2007; Mulvey, 1975). When they looked at images, critics quickly came to see how women were positioned as "objects" of a male gaze. As cultural critic John Berger (1972) said of the ways that women have been depicted in Western art and advertising: "Women are to be looked at" and men do the looking. For many participants in this study, being looked at was an everyday occurrence in their lives: "No one verbalizes it. It becomes the norm. 'He was looking at my tits.' 'He was looking at my ass'" (Sheila). In sexist visual society, where men as a group are handed greater power to determine women's desirability and value, girls grow up with varying degrees of insecurity about the beholder's assessment: "I see girls who are competent yet they fall apart because a guy walks in the door" (Andrea). Gendered looking relations that position female bodies as objects of evaluative looks not only affected how the women surveyed their bodies, but by teaching them certain ideals and norms of femininity and femaleness, also taught them to police the boundaries of their gendered and sexed embodiment.

It can be difficult to develop a critical perspective on the gendered looking relations that Berger and the women I spoke to describe because we live inside them. Values and assumptions that are naturalized in art, advertising, and popular culture can be difficult to question. Immersed as we are in these conventions, they appear as normal. (I use the pronoun "we" not to refer to any one group of people but to include imagined and intended readers who may identify with and/or recognize the issues and dynamics described.) Making the conventions strange can make us see them better. Modern-day Japanese "appropriation" artist Yasumasa Morimura (2008) remakes classical nudes by altering his features through make-up, costume, and digital-image manipulation, and then inserting himself in the place of the idealized female figures in famous paintings such as Manet's *Olympia*. (View his work at http://www.luhringaugustine.com/artists/yasu masa-morimura#.) By putting himself, as a Japanese man, in place of iconic beauty ideals, Morimura draws our attention to gendered looking relations, challenging the Western convention of seeing female bodies as objects to be looked at and especially of seeing white women's bodies as desirable objects.

Pervasive throughout the history of Western art, these looking relations continue in today's media. When women look at visual media, we learn to identify with actual or imagined spectators looking at the ideal woman depicted in the image. In this way, we become conscious of potential or actual others looking at us. These gazes have become even more complex in today's commercial culture, as women are encouraged to find pleasure in looking at each other's bodies. While this may appear less sexist, cultural theorist Rosalind Gill argues that the shift from an "external, male judging gaze" to an internal "self policing" gaze may represent deeper manipulation, since it invites female audiences to become more adept at scrutinizing themselves (2007b, p. 151).

All the women in this study were conscious that their bodies were to be looked at. Yet the dynamics of the gaze varied depending on who was being surveyed and who was casting the look. Those who had the experience of being regarded as an object of desire found that this could be an exciting aspect of their sexualities. While being gazed upon could be a source of pleasure and power, intrusive looks, stares, and glares carried negatively charged emotions and meanings. The work of Polish artist Katarzyna Kozyra explores the invasive looks that women seen as abject encounter such as those undergoing treatment for cancer. Rather than posing as an idealized female figure in her version of Manet's *Olympia*, Kozyra, after confronting her own diagnosis with cancer, evokes the ideal's dreaded, abject other by presenting herself lying naked on a hospital bed under the watchful gaze of a medic. (View her work at: http://katarzynakozyra.pl/main/10/olympia/.) Like Kozyra, women with disabilities and visible differences described the fearful and fascinated "stare" of non-disabled others: "There's a human fascination with difference. People want the gory details of disability because they want to feel that they are better off" (Harriet). For many racialized women, cultural stereotypes often informed and validated hyper-sexualizing looks onto their bodies: "From a lot of white men, I get sexual fascination: I'm the wild Black woman, with pronounced buttocks and thighs" (Marcia).

Nearly every woman I spoke with recognized the controlling influence of these cultural gazes. As a result, all described degrees of dissatisfaction with image, from distress as an insistent alarm to discomfort as background noise. Despite the currency and power of people's looks, none were absolute or unchanging in their assessments of the mirror's image: "Some days I feel so ugly. The other days I feel great" (Kate). When they reflected further, even those for whom body distress was the dominant state uncovered contradictory emotions and attitudes: "What interested me in this study was also: what's our larger relationship with our body? How *else* do we feel?" (Jillian). In her charcoal-drawn image *Mirror* (see figure 0.1), British painter Jenny Saville vividly captures these kinds of ambiguities by drawing and then partially rubbing out iconic beauties from famous paintings (such as Manet's *Olympia*), referencing the long tradition in Western art of seeing women as the object of the gaze. On top of these traces, she stretches fragments of her own body as a way of evoking the fluid, fleshy, multi-sensory experience of embodiment from the subjective viewpoint of the woman in the body. Mirroring Saville's artistic insights, contradiction and fluctuation were

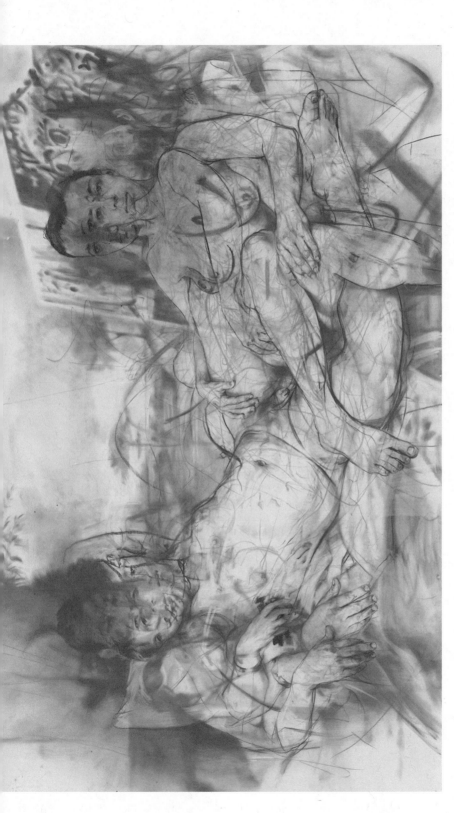

Figure 0.1. *Mirror*: British artist Jenny Saville intervenes in the representational history of female bodies by layering iconic images of beautiful women from famous Western paintings with sketches of her own embodied experience. Her dynamic drawing captures the contradictions and fluctuations in embodiment experienced by many women: that of inhabiting our bodies while being observed and observer. By Jenny Saville, *Mirror, 2011 – 2012*, Charcoal on paper, 71 1/8 × 109 13/16 × 3 inches / 180.5 × 279 × 7.5 cm (framed) © Jenny Saville. Courtesy Gagosian Gallery.

in evidence everywhere in women's narratives. The majority felt most divided from their bodies and distressed about image during adolescence: "If I was still a teenager there's no way in hell I'd be here disclosing this painful problem" (Gayle). Many struggled to find resolution in the adult years once they could seek alternative possibilities of embodiment and preferred accounts of selves: "In some ways, I've come to terms with my body: I have good days and bad days. It's not the all-consuming focus of my life" (Gayle).

Gathering Fleshy Stories

This study involved a wide range of storytellers. Because most body image research focuses on white, average-sized, and non-disabled women's weight problems, I sought to attract diversely embodied individuals to shed light on similarities and differences in experiences. However, when I disseminated flyers to organizations, media outlets, and other venues asking, "Would you like to talk about body image and beauty?" mostly white, middle-class women responded. I knew through my work as a counsellor that women from diverse walks of life struggled with image. I wondered at first whether the skewed response was related to the phrase *body image*, which conjures up stereotypes of affluent spoiled white girls – self-absorbed and obsessed with appearance. Perplexed by the homogeneity of responders, I soon learned that socially powerful groups (those who are white, straight, and have good incomes and a post-secondary education) answer invitations to take part in research in greater numbers than those from marginalized ones. And generic calls soliciting *all* women instead appeal to so-called *ordinary* ones, or those untouched by differences such as disability and race. So, to engage a diversity of voices and viewpoints, I created announcements for specific communities, including African, South Asian, and Asian Canadian women, and those living with disabilities.[1]

By addressing difference directly, using questions such as "Do you identify as a Black, African Canadian, or multiracial woman? Would you like to talk about body image and beauty?" I drew the rich medley of voices I sought. Participants included a mix of those typically featured in body image research and those excluded from the dialogue. After a write-up about the study appeared in a national women's

---

1   While I interviewed two Aboriginal women for this project, I did not gather a sample large enough to write about them as a distinct group. I have come to realize that this was a significant omission on my part.

magazine, I received calls from over three hundred women across Canada. Following consultations with those who contacted me, I conducted telephone interviews with some, asked others to fill out questionnaires, and held intimate open-ended, semi-structured interviews with close to a hundred. (Samples of flyers along with my *Body Image Interview Guide* can be found in appendix B.) My approach evolved to combine snowball (where women came to participate through ads and word of mouth) and strategic (where I asked specific groups to join in the dialogue) sampling. Face-to-face, telephone, and written contact reflected women's chosen or the most pragmatic modes of communication. I chose to exclude women over forty five because I wanted to capture the experiences of the first generation coming of age in an image-replete world. I see a focus on women aging in image culture as a story of "undoing" womanhood, which opens up fascinating terrain for future writing but it is not the emphasis here. Participants were interviewed between 1997 and 2001. Though many called Toronto home at the time of the interviews, women from across the country also took part. Since the study looks at how girls become women in image culture, I posed questions that invited interviewees to reflect on messages they received about their bodies while growing up and into their adult lives. Taken together, their words build a convincing case for moving the discussion beyond weight towards understanding how our physical ideals and stereotypes shape women's embodied identities and contribute to their image struggles.

The words of those interviewed do not appear in this book exactly as they were spoken. I condensed and culled for clarity and space reasons. Although editing quotes is not common in research informed by grounded theory, which is the mainstay of qualitative research, it's fairly common in research informed by other traditions such as postmodern and creative ones, which acknowledge that people's descriptions of reality are socially shaped. Hence, my editing of participants' narratives was guided by two principles: (a) respecting their voices, and (b) representing them in ways that condensed and clarified their thoughts and feelings. Where they repeated the same idea or experience to emphasize its significance, digressed by telling stories within stories that took us off topic (the interviews covered a lot of territory, so storytellers often referred back to earlier events), and used interjections such "uhm," "ah," and "like," I edited these out. While I recognize that there is sometimes a reason to include these (and I would agree were I doing an analysis of language), what was important for my purposes was achieving brevity and clarity of thought that I believed was most respectful to participants and to readers. Speaking and writing are two different modes of communication – in the context of a research interview, people are often generating their thoughts as they speak, so repetitions, interjections, and digestions are to be expected. In fact, after reviewing their transcripts, some interviewees wanted to edit these out. Taking my cues from them, I sought to turn their conversational speech into the written word while staying "true" to their intended meaning. I acknowledge that any mistakes are mine, and hope that my approach helped to distil, not obscure or alter, their perspectives and experiences.

Why Women Wanted to Talk

Coming of age in image culture, most women, regardless of their appearances or difference(s), saw their bodies as measures of their value and worth as women and, even further, as integral to their very sense of self. They decided to join in the conversation for a variety of reasons. Some wanted a non-judgmental space to tell their stories. For others, interviews offered a chance to discuss their body-modification dilemmas: "I'm going in for a breast reduction so I think it's important for me to talk as much as possible" (Anne Marie). Many wanted to contemplate the consequences of the "body beautiful" for themselves and women in general. While most wished to explore beauty ideals, some, like Hannah, welcomed the chance to work out why they sometimes subjected themselves to injurious practices: "In my life, it's a control issue and it's important to look at the reasons women feel a lack of control, where the body becomes a playground or battleground for this to get worked out." Acceptance of one's difference(s) was another motivating factor. As Sophia put it: "Being a woman of colour, it's hard to get media representation. It has been a struggle to come to the realization that we are different body types and races. Accepting me, the whole package."

For most, the interviews became opportunities to understand the consequences of their perceptions for themselves and those they cared about, including daughters and friends. Some hoped that they could find ways to avoid passing on problems and so protect the next generation from a negative image: "I don't have a very good impression of myself and I don't want my daughter to think like that. I want her to have a better outlook" (Maya). Most storytellers puzzled about the impact of their self-criticisms on friendships with women. In contrast, some worried about how *other* women's attitudes were affecting *their* image: "It's frustrating to be around friends who are still very critical of their bodies. I run up against walls when I listen to them" (Christian). Their friends' criticisms not only fuelled image problems, but also contributed to secretiveness, separation, and spoken and unspoken competition based on looks and beauty. As Erum described it, "I see my friends struggling and competing. They compete with me and I compete with them! I feel bad about it. I know they feel it too." If appearance-based competition undermined relationships, some hoped their wisdom, hard-won as a result of past struggles, might actually assist others: "If there's something that I've gone through that can help other women, that's what made me call" (Fredericka).

Virtually all recited the widely acknowledged truth that beauty culture causes body damage. Those who worked in the beauty business saw their participation as one way of speaking back to the perfected images they helped to create and disseminate: "I ran a women's magazine, so I've encountered so many problems. You're not going to stop putting these women in magazines, but it's something to participate in this study" (Yolanda). Alarmingly, some also talked about ways that feminist messages had adversely affected their own self-images. Growing up at the tail end or after the peak of second-wave feminism in the late 1970s, 1980s, and early 1990s, many had internalized feminist ideas about how women should feel about their bodies. A sizable minority had read Naomi Wolf's *The Beauty Myth* along with other feminist books on beauty and image. While an earlier generation hoped the manifesto of body acceptance would emancipate women from the yoke of oppressive ideals, this cohort revealed how second-wave activism inadvertently created additional pressures that left them feeling failed as a feminine, or flawed as a feminist, woman. Not only did the beauty industry make them feel bad about their bodies, but the popularized feminist platform also made them feel bad about feeling bad! As Marianne put it: "I thought I was Miss Rebel but I totally bought into this stupid society. I can tell my friends and myself, 'You are absolutely beautiful the way you are.' But then I look at myself and say, 'You're so fat! You're disgusting!'" This type of contradiction left many feeling caught between cultural standards that sanctioned body appraisal and alternative feminist values that obliged acceptance of bodies devalued by society. Melissa described the energy that adopting either set of values entailed: "My women friends talk about the stress that we're under – fighting against or falling into it. You get tired."

Seeing Difference Differently

Women marginalized in research and media reporting joined the dialogue because they wanted to re-vision conventional accounts and enrich understanding about the implications of difference. Leigh hoped to fill a gap in popular magazines and studies that focused solely on white or American women: "Women's magazines don't cover diverse viewpoints. We need research relevant to the racial make-up of Canadians." Treated as marginal in feminist writing on beauty that addresses mainly white women's issues, women of colour enrolled as a way of advocating for greater inclusion and representation: "I was reading this feminist book and the person who had read it before me had written in the margins, 'This is only a white woman's point of view.' So I'd like to give my perspective" (Rose). Even when books or articles stress experiences of Black or Asian women, authors still tend to take an ethnocentric approach by looking at issues primarily from a single group's vantage point. For multiracial women who see themselves as having many identities (being Black, Asian, and female, for example), the ethnocentric perspective is inadequate to capture the nuances of their embodiment: "I found books focusing on Caucasian or Black women only. I didn't find books that understood women with multiracial backgrounds. They weren't relevant to me" (Ada).

Racialized women in this research did *not* see their concerns as identical to white women's. (The term "racialized" refers the social process of viewing non-dominant racial groups according to pre-existing racial categories and stereotypes, which reproduces the categories as significant identities and sources of inequalities). Many sought to move the conversation beyond size to include issues of hair and hue: "It wasn't so much size, it was also colour. In my family, I'm lighter so kids at school would tease me. I realized then that people judged based on colour" (Sharon). As a result of living in a country where citizens are imagined to be white and where other groups are divided into ethnic and racial silos, many confronted barriers to belonging that negatively affected their embodied being: "I am a multiracial woman who's had a hard time accepting myself because I don't belong to one community. On top of that I was always searching to be Canadian, Canadian, Canadian. I didn't fit in any one ethnic group and I didn't fit in the broader society" (Anita). Some women sought to increase awareness about how European colonialism brought a hierarchy of beauty to colonized peoples that imposed Western ideals of whiteness, in part through creating visual stereotypes about racial difference. "Women in the Caribbean community are supposed to be bigger so I have been harassed for being skinny. At the same time, Western society wants you to be thin" (Rhonda). While fitting a racial stereotype could create conflict when the stereotype clashes with Western ideals, *not* fitting this moulded image also caused distress: "Asian women are tinier than average. Because I am 5'8" without heels, the petite image works against me and I grew up with a huge case of low self-esteem" (Leigh). These women wanted to explain how racist body stereotypes colliding with white beauty ideals have fuelled their insecurities and dissatisfactions.

Just as some received the message that they failed as feminists if they aspired to the body beautiful, women of colour got sent the moralizing message that they'd failed at being Black, Asian, or Aboriginal enough if they modified their features to avoid stereotyping and stigma. Although civil rights and anti-colonial movements have generated ideals of ethnic looks to promote people's pride in their identities and the beauty of their bodies, many women felt trapped by the message that embracing their racial identity necessarily meant *not* altering their appearance. As Rebecca expressed it: "I get the message that I'm not Black enough if I straighten my hair. Sorry, to be Black, your hair's got to be natural." Some racialized women wanted space free of moralizing messages that framed them as self-hating victims or "race traitors" for modifying their features. For many, body modification was motivated more by a desire to reverse invisibility than reject their race in a society where all women are judged on looks. They hoped to stimulate dialogue about being caught between beauty ideals that featured long flowing hair and light skin as the epitome of femininity, and alternative values that advocated adopting a narrow, "untainted" version of natural ethnic beauty, which dramatically increased their vulnerability to stereotyping.

Women with disabilities and physical differences joined the dialogue to challenge the lack of disability-positive imagery and the widespread stereotypes that have a profound effect on disabled women's lives. Due to impossible ideals of beauty and negative evaluations of bodily differences, many conveyed how they live at the intersection of two "minority" identities: a woman and a person with a disability. As Fatima put it: "People with disabilities are forced into the medical system, which views your body as an object. Body image is a big issue for anyone with a disability but more so for women with disabilities. We are looked at as asexual and as imperfect, and our bodies are viewed as being damaged and not worthy of love." Similarly, women perceived as fat spoke passionately about the significance of size to their sense of self. For many, telling their story was one way to impart how fat has joined race and disability as an embodied difference that affects people's life chances in powerful ways: "What I felt as a fat kid must be similar to what kids of colour experience. The hate and rage people direct towards you is discrimination, especially for women" (Iris).

A Cultural Story of Becoming through Images

These women's narratives, taken together, tell a "collective ethnography" – a cultural story of becoming women in an image-saturated world. Since I was working with many voices, I decided not to approach each as a discrete oral history. As much as I came to respect informants' subjectivities, I didn't want to focus on them as individuals. Rather, I wanted to tell a collective story of a cohort's search for selfhood. As a member of this group, I also wanted to include myself as one of the chorus. This study came to be a historically specific, grounded exploration of a generation of women caught between second- and third-wave feminism as well as an ethnographic analysis of "becoming women" against an intensifying barrage of cultural images. The women I interviewed had a range of views on feminism. Some identified as feminist. Many did not. At the same time, all were affected by feminist ideas and efforts. Insights of the second wave brought about a new level of self- and social consciousness among women growing up in the late 1960s, 1970s, and 1980s that women in the 1940s and 1950s did not have. The cohort I interviewed benefited from these understandings, but they were also the first generation faced with an onslaught of hegemonic (authoritative) messages from visual culture. Since overtly political strategies for resisting oppressive media images were not yet being elaborated by the third wave, responders tended to express resistance in individualized ways in the intimate contexts of their lives (e.g., by becoming nerds, engaging in passive resistance, refusing to be a woman, etc.).

A key question I pose is how participants, in the face of controlling body standards, search and strive for an acceptable self. By "search for self" I mean that the self is not a fixed destination but an ongoing project. Each chapter presents evidence of storytellers' striving for selfhood: where they find, create, lose, and re-create themselves in interactions with their surroundings in a process that is never fully coherent or complete. This is what I mean by "becoming." Despite the messages they receive, they craft a bodily self (albeit an open-ended and changing one) through their own creativity and the agency of their bodies. This takes place in their negotiation of gender, their responses to the medical gaze, their resistance to puberty, and their diverse body projects. In our media-driven world, "the search for self" frequently occurs in and through bodies, which operate as a key site of women's self-making for the reasons detailed between these covers. The body, according to philosopher Maurice Merleau-Ponty (1962, p. 82), is our "vehicle of being," the instrument through which we explore, interact with, and understand the world. The self is not entirely about body experience (it obviously has intellectual, relational, creative, political, and spiritual dimensions), but neither can the two be separated. They are integral. Thus, the "embodied self" is an important concept because it recognizes the inseparability of physicality from psyche – how selves are expressed/materialized through bodies and how meanings given to bodies inevitably shape selves. At the same time, I distinguish between *embodiment*, which connotes a multifaceted and intwined experience of our bodily selves, and *body image*, which suggests the narrower experience of how we understand and make sense of our bodily perceptions, including appearance. This distinction is critical because it recognizes that while the self is embodied, image isn't everything. Rather, it is one site that has become laden for girls becoming women in visual culture today. My use of the "embodied self" further speaks to how interviewees seek a sense of self that is not split off from their bodies. They struggle against the Western tradition of the mind-body split as well as against constraints imposed on female bodies in our media- and market-driven world. Desiring neither to transcend nor be reduced to bodies, they strive to negotiate meaningful, affirming relationships with their bodies in a world of evaluative looks and idealized and abject images.

What Scholarship Tells Us about Women's Body Images

The amount of psychological research and of feminist scholarship on the body is vast, reflecting rapidly growing interest in physical appearance and pressures placed on people to fit norms and ideals. Hits on Google for "body image" now exceed 12 million and the number of academic references to the phrase in one popular Canadian university library database is close to 250,000. To find my way through this massive literature, I begin with the stories of diversely embodied women living in Canada. Recognizing that the North American context is not the same as the European or Australian one, I bring into dialogue with the women's narratives the contributions of key Australian and British psychologists, feminist thinkers transnationally, and relevant developmental researchers.

Psychology Envisions the Body

The phrase *body image* is used most frequently in psychology to refer to issues relating to appearance satisfaction (Smolak & Thompson, 2009; Thompson, Penner, & Altabe, 1990), but it has been applied in a variety of other ways. Since the early 1900s, the term has been used to describe body perceptions in people with acquired nervous system impairments (who have lost a limb or had a stroke, for example) (Fisher, 1990; Heinberg, 1996; Thompson, Heinberg, Altabe, & Tantleff-Dunn, 1999), as well as children and adults over the course of their development (Bernstein, 1990; McCloskey, 1976). Some early researchers referred to such physical perception as "body schema" – the body sense produced by neurological processes that register our body's presence and position in space (Fisher, 1990; Newell, 2000; Shontz, 1990) – and this remains the preferred term today. Beginning in the 1950s, theories of body perception moved beyond biology to consider the impact of psyche and society on people's body images (Grogan, 2008). Research has since tended to focus on body-image problems, and especially on eating disorders among girls and women (Pruzinsky, 1990; Smolak & Cash, 2011; Thompson, Penner, & Altabe, 1990). For instance, psychiatrist Hilde Bruch's path-breaking work on eating disorders placed body image concerns at the centre of anorexia and bulimia's development and maintenance (Bruch, 1974, 1978; Thompson, 1990; Rosen 1990). However, researchers have also noted that body dissatisfaction may be "normative," affecting most women, rather than only those labelled with disordered eating (McKinley, 2011; Rodin, Silberstein, & Striegel-Moore, 1984; Yates, 1989).

Despite the explosion of scholarly work on body image in recent decades (Cash & Smolak, 2011), relatively little has changed in understanding the concept, except in accordance with general trends in psychology as a whole. For instance, when psychoanalytic theories dominated, body image problems tended to be explained in relation to Freudian theories of psychosexual development (Cash & Smolak,

2011). In the 1970s, the shift towards social psychology led to an increased recognition of society and culture's role in psychological functioning (Goodley & Lawthom, 2006), although mainstream psychology has yet to consider the implications of this shift for defining body image "disturbance" (Thompson, 1990). Beginning in the 1980s, "biopsychosocial" or "multidimensional" models came into prominence as an explanatory framework for problems with eating and image (Garfinkel & Garner, 1982; Heinberg, 1996). These have retained a dominant position in the field (Cash & Smolak, 2011; Thompson et al., 1999). While multidimensional models posit that a mix of biological, psychological, and social factors cause psychological distress, they tend to view individuals' vulnerabilities and sensitivities as ultimately responsible for who develops body-image and eating concerns, and who does not (Grogan, 2008; McKinley, 2011). As critical psychologist Sylvia Blood has put it, "society is seen as an external force that works on the vulnerable minds of individual women" (2005, p. 2). Despite the rapid increase in body-image research over the last century, underlying approaches to understanding the issues and concepts remain largely unchanged.

The recent rise of obesity-related research has led to a proliferation of psychological studies on body image and weight aimed at curbing the apparent "obesity epidemic" (Latner & Wilson, 2011; Neumark-Sztainer, 2011; Smolak & Thompson, 2009). Further, the scope of research has broadened to account for the experiences of diversely situated groups, including racialized women, boys and men, people with visible differences, older people, and sexual minorities (Altabe, 1996; Cash & Smolak, 2011; Gillen & Lefkowitz, 2011; Reel & Bucciere, 2010; Rumsey & Harcourt, 2011; Sheldon, Renwich, & Yoshida, 2011). In all these cases, body-image problems tend to be understood as existing primarily within the individual and as measurable in levels of individual "distortion" or disturbance, and the individual is still understood as the focus of intervention. The experiences of disabled people have been central to body-image scholarship from its inception as a line of inquiry investigating the body perceptions of people with nervous system impairments (Shontz, 1990). But as in body-image research generally, studies of disabled people typically interpret body-image problems to be the result of individual disturbance (Ittyerah & Kumar, 2007; Lawrence & Fauerbach, 2011; Newell, 2000), arising from the impairment itself, rather than from a society that rejects disability. The same holds for research on race, which often downplays the constitutive role of social forces such as skin colour prejudice in shaping people's bodily self-images. As critical psychologists Dan Goodley and Rebecca Lawthom (2006) stress, while many regard psychology as individualizing and apolitical, the field is extremely diverse. Feminist, critical, and community psychology have all developed theories that acknowledge the social conditions implicated in body-image problems faced by diverse groups. Unfortunately, these remain marginal in psychology as a whole.

Feminism Re-visions the Body

Although concepts of body image and embodiment have remained relatively static in psychology in recent years, feminist analyses have undergone major shifts. Feminists exploring the significance of image to female identity have subjected the concept itself to debate. During the second wave, writers developed a political understanding of idealized femininity, which they saw as limiting possibilities for women's lives and contributing to sexual inequality (Brownmiller, 1984; Greer, 1972). Clinicians' and activists' concerns mounted throughout the 1980s, when the rise of eating problems led many to focus attention on the profound psychosocial consequences of sexist body standards for girls and young women (Schoenfielder & Wieser, 1983; Székely, 1988). In *Fat Is a Feminist Issue*, published in 1979, feminist therapist Susie Orbach argued that body image and eating problems were a direct response to the political status of women, and could be improved only by working to change social conditions. As Orbach later wrote, "Eating problems are charged with bearing the burden of a political exclusion" (1993, p. xix), in that they reflected women's acceptance of, and protest against, a subordinate social position in patriarchal society. The role of representation has since been a major concern of feminists, in terms of understanding both the origins and functions of idealized images (Bordo, 1993; Frost, 2001) and how such imagery influences women's identities and selves (Coleman, 2009; Weiss, 1999).

When social constructionist theories began to be accepted in the 1990s, feminists moved away from the idea that women develop body-image problems as a result of pervasive sexism and started to focus on how women use cultural images to shape their bodily self-images (Butler, 1990; De Lauretis, 1987; Ussher, 1997). Social constructionist perspectives emphasize the role of power in the creation of knowledge and values in society (Markula, Burns, & Riley, 2008). Just as the term suggests, theorists analyse how language and taken-for-granted truths "construct" people's experiences and understandings of reality, including their perceptions of the body. Mainstream studies of body image typically approach the body as an objectively knowable entity separate from the psyche. Yet such objectivity is impossible to assume, since people are always embodied and embedded in social contexts that influence their image. Within social constructionism, the connection between cultural images and actual bodies (and our body images) varies: either bodies and body images are seen as shaped by the social contexts in which they are situated, as many theorists understand it (Bordo, 1993; Ussher, 1989); or bodies and body images are not directly accessible to us without being mediated by culture and language as others argue (Butler, 1990, 1993; Oudshoorn, 1994). The first group posits that cultural messaging orients people to modify their bodies by manipulating their desires and perceptions in socially preferred ways (e.g. to desire thinness). For the second, cultural bias is impossible to eradicate since scientists must translate their observations into words and pictures in order to make meaning. Belief systems inevitably seep in via researchers' choice of language and metaphor.

According to historian Londa Schiebinger, social constructionist theories of embodiment are important because they seek to "break the stranglehold of arguments from nature" (2000, p. 2) by showing how the meanings given to sex, race, and other differences are socially and historically variable. For critical psychologists Sylvia Blood (2005), Helen Malson (2009), and Jane Ussher (1989, 1997), social constructionism offers a much-needed critique of labels such as "body image disturbance" and "eating disorders," since these diagnoses often reinforce harmful assumptions. For example, mainstream psychology typically privileges personal over social explanations of image-related problems, thus regarding individuals who experience such difficulties as deviant. Mainstream models further download responsibility for problems onto individuals by failing to consider how their distress may be socially produced and by recommending that they correct problem behaviours in themselves (Blood, 2005; Malson & Burns, 2009). Finally, by treating the body as separate from the mind, conventional theories reduce bodies to images – to how they *look* – and discourage women from attending to more multifaceted experiences of embodiment (such as touch and movement).

Since the late 1990s, social constructionism has been challenged by two theories about bodies and embodiment. These are body becoming theory (Battersby, 1998), an offshoot of feminist philosophy on the body (Coleman, 2009; Weiss, 1999); and the new materialism, which has derived, in part, from feminist studies of science (Hird, 2004). Unlike social constructionism, which analyses how bodies are portrayed and talked about, these theories attend to lived experience and to the biology of bodies. Body becoming theorists do not see bodies as bounded, stable entities, but as fluid forms that come to be through relations with natural and cultural forces that surround them. In this view, the unexpected, accidental, and everything that befalls people – from insults and injuries to technologies and pleasures – become new ingredients in their bodies' history and development (Grosz, 1999, 2008). Instead of predicting or proscribing what bodies will be, theorists ask how particular biological, environmental, and cultural forces expand or limit possibilities for what they become. Like body becoming theory, the new materialism conceptualizes the physical body as a source of knowledge in itself and understands matter to have agency independent of people's perceptions or manipulations of it (Barad, 2003). This means that all matter – from rocks and birds to blood and finger nails – has agency through the energy it possesses at an atomic level and through the ways it affects, and is affected by, the matter that surrounds it. Theorists see the becoming of bodies is a relatively open process that cannot be predicted or determined in advance (Coole & Frost, 2010) and seek to explain how the natural and the cultural affect and transform each other to jointly construct our common world (Alaimo & Hekman, 2008). Body-becoming and new materialist theories converge in theorizing bodies as emergent systems that materialize as a result of their own agency and other forces acting upon them. Since cultural contexts, physical and social environments, and personal habits shape each person's physical being, no one can predict with one hundred percent certainty what any body will become. Thus within these frames, bodies do not come to be before their interactions but emerge through interacting. These recent theoretical shifts are important because they recognize the roles of physicality, process, unpredictability, and creativity in understanding the human body and embodiment.

Re-visioning Development as Becoming

Body becoming theories do more than challenge taken-for-granted ideas about bodies. They contribute to our understanding of selves by disputing the conventional story of human psychological change.

There is a long history of psychological theorizing about human (mostly male) development and a shorter history of feminist theorizing about female development. Since the 1970s, feminists have challenged the canon of developmental theory for (a) assuming attributes associated with white, middle-class, and Westernized men to be the norm and (b) mistakenly approaching development as a progression from inferior child- and female-associated qualities of connection and dependency towards superior adult- and male-coded attributes of autonomy, separation, and mastery. In response to the field's bias, psychologists Jean Baker Miller (1976) and Carol Gilligan (1982) famously proposed girl- and woman-centred theories that stress the centrality of relationships to female development. Their "relational" approach made a major contribution in unearthing how women form a sense of self in relationships (Jordan, 2010) and in analysing what happens when girls move from the relative freedom of childhood to the restrictions of adolescence imposed by sexist society (Brown & Gilligan, 1992). While offering a unique take on female development as a relational process that resonates with many women, some feminists today argue that relational accounts, like mainstream ones, remain untouched by recent critiques of the idea of "development" itself.

According to critical theorists Sheila Greene (2003), Erica Burman (1997, 2008), and Allison James (1995, 2000), most psychological theories err in seeing human development as universal, unidirectional, and past-oriented: (a) universal in that all people are assumed to go through similar preset stages of change and to progress from an unformed child to fully formed adult in a predictable way; (b) unidirectional in that these changes are thought to occur in one direction only, either from innate processes occurring within the person or from external forces acting upon them; and (c) past-oriented in that researchers search through the history of the person to explain change, assuming that "early events cause later events to be as they are," and failing to acknowledge the influence of the present and imagined future on a person's self (Greene, p. 4). The term *development*, they argue, may not accurately describe the human life course, since it implies that psychological change follows a predictable pathway with a specific end-point – mature adulthood – assumed to be superior to its starting point – immature childhood (James, 1995). The problem with the "progress" narrative is that it interprets human lives according to an evolutionary model that values children primarily for their future contributions, and undervalues who they are and what they know now (like their sophisticated understanding of play and insights about the social world) (Greene, 2003; James, 2000). Mainstream theory privileges ideas about progress by implying that people should be advancing as they age instead of seeing merit in who individuals are now or acknowledging that they face gains and losses at every age (Burman, 2008; James, 2000). By assuming that genes or early experiences predetermine what a person can be, the theory further fails to recognize people's capacities to revise themselves and initiate change *throughout* their lives (Greene, 2003). According to Greene, even feminist relational psychologists do not adequately take into account the "self directing, self creating power" of our psyches or the randomness of life events that shape who we become (p. 5).

Rather than abandon a developmental perspective, Greene asks us to rethink development *in time*, as an open-ended process that is "constrained rather than determined, emergent not given, historically and culturally contingent not universal, more constructed than natural" (p. 18). Time is integral to human development in four respects. First, a person's life course is strongly influenced by the conditions and events occurring during the historical period through which s/he lives, making one's cohort an important social identity. Second, all cultures impose socially created phases such as childhood or adolescence onto the life course. As a result of such periodization, people confront socially shared value judgments about the best time to have sex, get married, or come out that profoundly influence their sense of normalcy and difference. Third, our sense of self comes into being through memory and imagination, through the interplay of past experiences with future possibilities made available to us by our culture. Fourth, as biological organisms, we have an "on-going irreversible relationship" with time, since "it defines the ultimate rhythm and patterns of our life, its beginning and its end" (Greene, p. 133). The inevitability of death imposes obvious constraints on our being, but because what happens to us in time cannot be determined in advance, we are always becoming in unexpected ways. Greene's approach is promising because it captures the predictable patterns along with the conditions of flux that influence our embodied psyches. It also considers how expectations based on our social location intersect with past experiences to contour our becoming. By approaching developmental processes (like acquiring gender) as patterned rather than predictable, becoming theories can account for new ways of being to emerge (such as being transgendered) without labelling them as abnormal or diseased.

Becoming Women: How Bodies Come to Be Gendered and Sexed

For years I have looked for a suitable theoretical approach to interpret women's body histories. Within feminism, social constructionist perspectives offered critical insights into how cultural ideas circulate and are taken up by individuals, and thus how culture itself is reproduced. But I also found constructionism lacking because it leaves out embodied experience and the biological body. I also didn't feel that a psychological approach that universalizes and individualizes self-development and bodily experience fit with my cultural and historical understanding either. I aimed instead to develop a critical framework that builds on the contributions of constructionist and psychological perspectives but does not reduce experience to the psychological or the social/cultural alone. Theoretically, I came to align with becoming theory and the new materialism, which recognize the agency of the psyche and the physical body, and to theorize how they play a part in the embodied person's becoming. Throughout this book, I point out the validity and limitations of various perspectives for understanding body image and embodiment, *including* the shortcomings of feminist social constructionist positions, which fail to account for the body's materiality or the self-directing capacity of the person. An important corrective to earlier approaches, body becoming theory provides a promising framework for analysing women's embodiment narratives.

This book offers a unique take on issues related to body image and embodiment in four respects: (1) it introduces readers to the rich corpus of feminist body and image theory by presenting it in a nuanced yet accessible way; (2) it locates women's body perceptions and practices historically, culturally, socially, and economically, and foregrounds the stories of women of colour and women with disabilities, which have been neglected in feminist and psychological research; (3) it introduces body becoming and new materialist theoretical frameworks as correctives to earlier feminist approaches; and finally (4) it proposes a new critical theory of embodied becoming that challenges conventional theories of human development. Extrapolating from individuals' unique experiences, I craft a collective story of becoming gendered and sexed in visual culture that reveals how becoming a woman is inextricably a biological, psychological, *and* a cultural process. Cultural images of idealized and abject bodies have intensified and diversified for women coming of age in contemporary culture. Although challenged by two successive waves of feminism, idealized femininity and beauty remain problematic because bodies have become ever more critical markers of status in our commercialized media-focused world. The most blatant forms of sexism and racism are no longer permissible in North America. People instead become preoccupied with managing their appearance in a context where individuals and institutions reproduce sex, race, and body inequalities under the guise of aesthetics, personal taste, desirability, self-care, health, and choice. Throughout this book, diverse women's stories bring attention to an underlining, pressing issue: the ways in which our relationships to our bodies – hence, our sense of ourselves as embodied – are increasingly mediated by commercial media. Unfortunately, this issue is as socially significant in 2013 as it was for earlier generations.

In *Becoming Women*, the women interviewed are continually negotiating with a media culture that attempts to objectify their bodies and render them abject. While negative experiences often overshadow the pleasures of embodiment in their accounts, their stories of resistance and action, delight and desire, resolve and recuperation are also woven throughout the book. These convey a sense of becoming as a process that is constrained, but not determined, by images. Their resistance and agency tend to be expressed in highly individualized, often internal, ways. Perhaps one reason they describe responding and acting in individualized modes is that children and young people lack voice, resources, and power in this society, which limits their capacity to intervene in changing the surrounding social relations and cultural scripts. But they still protest their situations in surprising and creative ways. The women I interviewed also express agency in individualized forms because they were caught between the second and third waves of feminism and, hence, had fewer frameworks and tools at hand for elaborating discontent. Second-wave feminism gave many North American women, whether they called themselves feminist or not, a greater consciousness of their second-class status and otherness in gender and sexual relations. Precisely because participants came of age in the wake of feminist revolution but were situated on its cusps, they did not have access to the more collective and self-consciously political strategies for resistance that the third wave elaborated. They inherited second-wave discourse about the body as a site of constraint but lacked access to the playfully defiant language such as "girl power" and "riot girls," as well as the media savvy of third wavers and young globally minded feminist activists who have succeeded them. Although feminist discussions about the body as a source of possibility and pleasure were occurring when I conducted my interviews, they were not yet available to many informants. Hence women's analysis reflects the kinds of experiences and ways of interpreting reality available to them at the time.

The book follows a developmental pathway that starts with participants' earliest memories and traces their becoming into young adulthood. However, it is not written from the premises of conventional socialization theory or linear, staged models of human development. Participants do not "progress" from being unformed children to fully formed adults or make this journey in some universal predictable way where they pass through preset developmental stages. Neither do their body journeys fit neatly into psychology's theories of embodiment that suggest a preset pathway: that girls possess a positive embodiment in early childhood (when they are "at one" with their bodies and have physical freedom and little consciousness of outsider judgments); that they experience disembodiment at puberty when their bodies become sites of vulnerability, constraint, and scrutiny; and, finally, that they learn to reconnect with their bodies in adulthood through navigating their bodily realities and the social world (Piran, Carter, et al., 2002). Though initially I framed the accounts in this way (see Rice, 1997), I've come to see that the women's journeys were more unpredictable and variable than a single developmental story could capture. For example, some told how foundational experiences of sexual or medical abuse and, later, body-based harassment at school erased or interrupted any early sense of bodily connectedness far *before* puberty. Others reported how they struggled with body issues for most of their lives or, conversely, how they managed to maintain a positive body sense despite the imposition of norms and ideals.

This book draws on body becoming theory to develop a *critical developmental* or *body becoming account of embodiment*. It approaches the becoming of participants' embodied selves as ongoing and open ended, as historically and socially constructed, and as determined by many forces, including their own psychic creativity and the biological agency of their bodies. Taking my cues from them, I locate the source of women's body-related conflicts and disconnections not in the home, school, or the media. Neither physical differences nor age-related changes like puberty generated distress. No single person, entity, or biological process was responsible for their disembodiment or development of image concerns. Instead, the women tell how their bodily distresses and disruptions emerged through messages received from diverse contexts and connections over the course of their lives. In tracing messages they received about, from, and through their bodies from earliest childhood to young adulthood, my book tells the story of women's search for an embodied self in image culture. Beginning with their diverse body narratives, it also proposes a new becoming theory of embodiment that bridges mainstream developmental psychology (which offers a universal, unidirectional, and past-oriented model of development), with critical theory (which theorizes the embodied self and its emergent relationship with society), to craft an *open-ended context-sensitive* story of bodily self-becoming in contemporary culture.

I begin with the story of difference. Although most people recognize that our ideas about beauty are socially shaped, few grasp how concepts of difference are likewise constructed. Relating a cultural history of differences, chapter 1 sheds light on the ideas that have cast a shadow over the images of storytellers in this study. Moving from the broad sweep of history to the intimate stories of individual women, chapter 2 explores the process the women identified as pivotal in shaping their earliest sense of body: becoming gendered. While almost all vividly remember moments of playing with gender, they also relate the serious work of coming to know their gendered selves – the frustrating, unfunny, and weighty ways they worked at embodying an acceptable gender. In answer to the questions "who am I?" and "who do I want to be?" many looked to cultural icons and influential others to give them a first glimpse of womanhood.

Chapter 3 focuses on the experiences of women often marginalized in image research: those with disabilities and differences. Their childhood experiences in medically oriented systems reveal how women with body differences became "invisible in full view." This occurred when their bodies became the primary focus of others' attention, and their personhood remained overlooked and unseen. Chapter 4 then looks at women's experiences in school, a place where perceptions of appearance and difference shaped belonging and status. Body standards were communicated everywhere in schools, from textbooks and classroom instruction to school uniforms and student placement in class pictures. Although all women received lessons about their bodies as students, racialized women and women perceived as fat felt keenly the social consequences of being different.

At the heart of the study, chapters 5 and 6 focus on puberty – a central drama in the social process of becoming a woman. Analysing the dominant story of maturation, I uncover how official accounts frame puberty in ways that do not serve young women's interests or support them in the transition to womanhood. Despite adults' concerns about the supposed risks puberty poses to girls, our culture's coupling of puberty with sex and sexuality, rather than the physical maturation process itself, creates many of the emotional and social problems associated with puberty in girls. Chapter 6 turns to puberty experiences and illuminates how many women moved through adolescence with a deep sense of difference. Body dissatisfaction emerged or peaked between ages 9 and 16 when each encountered negative attributions given to developing differences along with mounting pressures to appear desirable. The chapter weaves examples from puberty and sex education to illustrate the ways that cultural texts have encouraged women to see their bodies as measures of womanhood.

Chapter 7 illustrates how commercial culture is deeply implicated in women's body projects. In a consumerist visual society, research participants dealt with the disparity between their differences and ideals of desirability by imagining their "best possible" body and self. Messages in contemporary beauty industries echo women's efforts to close the gap between their body differences and ideals of desirability by aspiring to their best body. This sophisticated self-making strategy has also become a marketing strategy since it pulls diverse audiences into image-related concerns and, thereby, into consumerism. The conclusion moves beyond individual struggles to spotlight participants' resistance and broader responses to body standards. I analyse the transformative possibilities, contradictions, and limitations of making change from within commercial capitalism itself by reflecting on my involvement with the "Dove Campaign for Real Beauty." Turning to media work by women pushed to the margins of beauty culture, I highlight the tremendous potential and promising avenues that exist through new media for our creative expression and collective action.

Chapter One

In the Shadow of Difference

Most people assume that sex is a biological feature of bodies whereas gender is a psychic feature of selves interacting with societies. Yet the "becoming of woman" is a complex cultural story. To tell it, this chapter offers a cultural mini-narrative of how "woman" was created in Western history through processes of othering as well as through sexing and gendering bodies.

The Abject Body

Julia Kristeva, a French feminist philosopher, calls the abject the "twisted braid" (1982, p. 3) of fear and fascination that people feel when they encounter bodily fluids, serious illness, open wounds, and even corpses. According to Kristeva, these things evoke revulsion and horror even as they compel our attention, not because they are inherently disgusting or fascinating but because they remind us of the ever-present dangers the world poses to our survival and sense of self. Physical features or functions seen as abject remind us of our bodies' unknowability and uncontainability, our vulnerability to disease, and the certainty of our death. For scholar Deborah Covino (2000), abjection captures undesirable dimensions of embodiment that people want to push away (pain, disease) as well as the scapegoating of groups associated with those experiences. Picking up on this concept, artists have created "abject art" that explores features of bodies deemed inappropriate for public viewing. Cindy Sherman, for example, depicts the refuse of human life – half-eaten food, vomit, dead bodies – and constructs strange mannequin-like figures using mismatched body parts obtained from medical catalogues.

The current popularity of the corpse in horror movies and crime shows such as *CSI, Criminal Minds, Dexter, Walking Dead,* and *True Blood* suggests a cultural preoccupation with images of death and dying. One way to explain their audience appeal is to note how the genre invites viewers to look on the dead body as an image of both repulsion and attraction. In many of these shows, viewers tend to be frightened and sickened by the recurring image of the bloody or decaying corpse, but at the same time, they're fixated on it. They can't look away. For Kristeva, the corpse is the ultimate exemplar of the abject because it graphically reminds us of our fragility and mortality. On abjection, she writes:

> It is something rejected from which one does not part, from which one does not protect oneself as from an object. Imaginary uncanniness and real threat, it beckons to us and ends up engulfing us. It is thus not lack of cleanliness or health that causes abjection but what disturbs identity, system, order. What does not respect borders, positions, rules. The in-between, the ambiguous, the composite. (1982, p. 4)

Kristeva argues that people feel twisted or ambivalent emotions of fear and fixation, awe and shock, terror and fascination, not just in the face of objects or others that call to mind their loss of life, but also when confronted by what conjures the loss of self. She thus understands abjection as something more than the push and pull individuals feel when encountering graphic reminders of death. People reject and push away things (and other people) that challenge or undermine the integrity of their identities and selves. We can read Kristeva's theory as an embodied way of understanding identity formation.[1] Babies come into the world with bodies before they have a sense of self. As children develop, they continuously establish the borders of their identity through ejecting what they define as other. At first, they form ideas about what is "me" through taking in and physically expelling what is "not me," namely, fluids such as their mother's milk and later, solid food and other objects. To keep hold of and maintain the boundaries of

---

1   This is how one student, Elisabeth Harrison, interpreted Kristeva in a class I taught a few years ago. I am indebted to Elisabeth for her brilliant insights into Kristeva's work; to Sharon Caldwell for her poetic interpretations of images of the corpse in popular culture; and to Stacey Dinelle for her diligent questioning of a difficult theorist.

their physical selves, they learn to expel not only fluids or objects but also those they come to regard as others – first mothers as their primary caregivers, then other people. Since the fledgling person depends on the maternal body, a child must make its mother abject to form a self. Gradually, children learn to "expel" those whom their families, communities, and societies define as different. The concept is germane to understanding embodiment because it shows the body's significance to human development and social relationships, and because it offers a useful explanation for discrimination based on physical difference. The theory helps to illuminate why people with anomalous bodies and those seen as racially distinct are often viewed as frightening and other: people want to banish what is unfamiliar because it disturbs their identities and selves. Since no one's sense of self is ever completely settled or secure, the abject continues to haunt our consciousness by making us vigilant against anything that might jeopardize the boundaries of our being.

Kristeva's theory offers important insight into why people reject the unfamiliar. Yet it fails to clarify why attributes subject to abjection vary from culture to culture or why some societies fear unwanted or unknown aspects of embodiment more than others. Why do certain cultures deny bodily difference and suffering while others accept vulnerability and mortality? And why have people celebrated and denigrated the same body features in different time periods and places? Fatness, for instance, has been seen as a sign of wealth, health, and advantage in some societies but a symbol of disease, downtroddenness, and undesirability in others. In North American society, the abject has come to include any difference that resists our desires to control our bodies. This includes physical anomalies and processes that defy expectations of how bodies should look and how they should function. It means transgendered and intersexed bodies that challenge clear distinctions between male and female and bodily fluids and fleshiness such as menstrual blood, milk, and fat that signify lack of containment and control of the body, and permeable boundaries between self and other. Finally, the abject includes bodies marked as ethnically distinct from the dominant unmarked norm. These examples suggest that we seek to contain, control, and exclude bodies, or parts of bodies, that unsettle our notion of the "proper" bodily self – the invulnerable, autonomous self so highly valued in Western culture (Zitzelsberger, 2010).

Media images continually play on our fear of abjection and desire to embody ideals by showing us "rejected" *before* and "perfected" *after* pictures of people who undergo extreme weight loss or other body makeovers (Covino, 2004). For example, cosmetic surgery advertisements often claim that surgery will restore a person's "real" self hidden in the wrong body. Here people's external appearances are seen to reflect their inner selves so body alteration is sold as the ticket to a more authentic or improved identity. Ads claim that girls will "blossom" with breast implants; vaginal surgery will enhance women's sexual pleasure and "restore" their virginity; eyelid surgery will "uplift and open" Asian eyes; skin lightening will enable a lighter, prettier self to emerge from a darkened, diseased body; and straightened hair will transform an unhappy, unkempt individual into someone professional and put-together. This popular formula of attempting to alter one's body so that it matches one's ideal self has a long history in the West that dates back to Plato (ca. 427–ca. 347 BCE; Cooper & Hutchinson, 1997). Abjection of the female body also has its roots in Western thought, especially in the ways science and culture have viewed women's bodies as different and deviant.

Imagining the Other: Women's Bodies in Science and Culture

In Western cultural history, women's bodies have habitually been seen as different from and inferior to men's. Yet the ways that women have been understood as being different have varied across time and place. In the Western world, many people believe that one's biology, not one's socialization or psychology, makes men and women distinct. This essentialist view understands difference as a natural, fixed, and unchanging property of bodies. But gender and sex theorists have shown how the biology of sex differences itself has a history. Through tracing how culture informs scientific ideas about male and female bodies, they have developed the social constructionist view, or the idea that cultural meanings always infuse our interpretations of biology.

In her influential book *Sexing the Body*, feminist biologist Anne Fausto-Sterling shows that research into sex differences is not value free (2000). Our two-sex model – our shared belief that there are only two sexes, male and female – is a socially created idea. One reason the "two sex" model is problematic is that it pathologizes bodies that do not conform to it. In other words, it excludes the one in a thousand people who are born with bodies that don't fit the typical definitions of female or male (Chase, 1998). Babies with variances such as a large clitoris, small penis, or parts of both male and female genitalia undergo surgeries to make their genitals "fit" conventional male or female bodies. Many people with such conditions argue that the problem lies not with their bodies but with a culture that forces people to fit into its rigid ideas about sex. We uphold our belief in the "two sex" model by labelling as abnormal all those who don't measure up. This includes intersexed people (a broad term that includes people whose genital, chromosomal, or hormonal features don't fit typical definitions of male or female) and those who identify as trans (another umbrella term including transsexuals, transgendered people, drag queens, and anyone who transgresses our sex-gender categories). People whose gender identity contravenes the sexed body into which they were born (e.g., a person born into a male body who identifies as a woman) are labelled as suffering from a psychiatric disorder (American Psychiatric Association, 2000). Yet most trans people don't believe they are mentally ill. Rather, the sickness lies in a society that believes people's genitals must match their gender for them to be considered "normal."

Sex differences have been used for centuries to justify the subjugation of women and deny recognition to bodies that don't fit sex and gender binaries, like intersex and transgender bodies. Thus, our two-sex system not only rejects or pathologizes (and attempts to correct) those whose bodies don't fit. It allows our society to rationalize sexual inequality by appealing to biology – justifying sexism through the argument that women are ruled by their body's rhythms or reproductive processes. The two-sex system tends to create a hierarchical relationship between the sexes – seeing one sex as normal and usual, and the other as different and deviant. Over the past five hundred years, as Western science became powerful and widespread in Europe and the colonized world, it played an increasingly pivotal role in the abjection of certain embodiments.

Conceptions of male and female bodies were radically different during pre-modern times – a period spanning from ancient Greece to the fifteenth century (Cadden, 1995). A one-sex model dominated, where women were not viewed as biologically different but rather as lesser or inferior versions of a male norm (Laqueur, 1990). Our modern ideas were made when scientific and social revolutions in Europe between the fifteenth and the eighteenth centuries dramatically altered people's ideas about male and female bodies. This is when the two-sex model – the idea that there are two polar-opposite yet complementary sexes – emerged. During the same period, biology gained authority as the model for defining these and other bodily differences, such as race and disability. Although conceptions of female bodies changed radically over this time, one critical thing remained constant: in a patriarchal world, men's bodies were still envisioned as the standard while women's bodies were imagined as anomalous and other.

To understand pre-modern views of women's bodies, we must return to the ideas of ancient Greek and Roman scholars. Many ancient philosophers and physicians interpreted the female body as a defective or inferior copy of the male norm. This is what historian Thomas Laqueur (1990) has famously called the one-sex model – the idea that the male was the original and superior sex and the female was an imperfect copy. Aristotle (384–322 BCE) was the first thinker to create a hierarchy of life that naturalized women's inferiority. Of the female body, he wrote: "Females are weaker and colder in nature, and we must look upon the female character as being a sort of natural deficiency" (2007, book 4, section 6, para. 3). Aristotle argued that a female was similar to an immature or impotent male because she supplied only the raw flesh for generation (reproduction), while the man provided the form or soul. Although Aristotle described women's menstrual discharge and men's semen as similar, he also argued that male fluid was superior: "The female is as it were a deformed male; and the menstrual discharge is semen, though in an impure condition; i.e., it lacks one constituent … the principle of Soul" (Aristotle & Peck, 1943, p. 175). In his view, women's natural "deficiency" explained and justified their social subordination.

Influenced by classical texts passed down from one generation to the next, European physicians in the Middle Ages believed women, being supposedly cold and excessively moist, were inferior to men, who were hot and relatively dry. For example, the ancient Roman healer Galen (ca. 130–ca. 200 CE) put forward his famous theory of the four humours – yellow bile, black bile, phlegm, and blood – body fluids that he believed determined health and temperament. In his view, women were associated with the depressed humour, black bile, and the moist, cold humour, phlegm. Men, in contrast, he associated with the anger-inducing humour, yellow bile, as well as the cheerful, optimistic humour, blood. Because heat was more conducive to life than cold, Galen argued that men must be superior: "The man is more perfect than the woman … her workmanship is necessarily more imperfect … as she is colder than he … The parts of the female cannot escape to the outside … She accumulates an excess of useful nutriment and has imperfect semen and a hollow instrument to receive the perfect semen" (Galen & May, 1968, vol. 2, pp. 630–2; to read Galen's comparison of male and female anatomy go to http://www.stoa.org/diotima/anthology/wlgr/wlgr-medicine351.shtml).

According to Galen, a woman's organs were an inverted version of a man's – her genitals were a smaller and less-developed version of his. Following Galen, many physicians in the Middle Ages saw the woman's uterus, cervix, and vagina as an internal penis and her ovaries as testes (E. Martin, 1992; Oudshoorn, 1994). Women's genitals were also thought to be retained inside the body because of their so-called lesser heat. This conception of sex saw the female body not as fundamentally different, but as a lesser version of the male body. In Galen's version of the one-sex model, sex differences were located not in the genitals but in the body's degree of fluids and heat.

Anatomists generally used male bodies to represent the human body in medieval anatomical texts. They thus viewed the male body as the standard, and the female body as the "other." When women's bodies were drawn, they usually were depicted with fetuses, examination centring on their reproductive capacities. Images of the womb often symbolized its mysterious and potentially monstrous power. Commonly illustrated with small ears or horns that probably represented the ovaries of the reproductive system, the uterus was frequently drawn to evoke ominous associations (of an animal or a demon). (See Carmichael & Ratzan, 1991, for examples, including a ninth-century illustration from *Gynecology*, by Soranus of Ephesus, p. 21.) This suggests that male physicians looked on the female reproductive system with intense curiosity and fear, as having strange, even sinister, properties. Many medieval physicians adopted the beliefs of Plato, who likened the uterus to an animal:

> The womb is an animal which longs to generate children. When it remains barren too long after puberty, it is distressed and sorely disturbed, and straying about in the body and cutting off the passages of the breath, it impedes respiration and brings the sufferer into the extremest anguish and provokes all manner of diseases besides. Such is the nature of women and all that is female. (as cited in Bernheimer, 1990, p. 3)

To summarize, medieval conceptions of sex were very different from our own. Philosophers and scientists saw women's bodies as (a) similar to but lesser versions of men's bodies (e.g., having an inverted penis); (b) differentiated from men's bodies by degrees of body fluid and of heat (different humours); and (c) monstrous other (animal-like with ears or horns). While pre-modern conceptions of the female body varied considerably, depictions were mostly negative, reflecting women's subordinate place in the cosmic and social orders (Cadden, 1995).

Beginning in the sixteenth century, conceptions of the human body were remade as part of the scientific revolution. Scientists began to believe that dissecting bodies would reveal radical new truths about human beings. By the end of eighteenth century, the body was no longer seen as a magical part of a mysterious universe, but as a discoverable object of scientific study (Duden, 1991). Scientists for the first time rejected the theories passed down from ancient philosophers. Instead, they argued that people could come to know and understand the world only by observing it with the rational mind, which they thought to be distinct and detachable from the impluses of the unruly, untrustworthy body. While this idea was enormously valuable in giving birth to the scientific method of discovery, it also marked the beginning of what feminists now call "the mind-body split." According to philosopher Margrit Shildrick (1997), the new view of the body as separate from the mind elevated the mind as the portal to knowledge as it downgraded the body as an obstacle to reason and objectivity. Male scientists of the period associated men with the mind, and saw women as exemplifying and manifesting the dangers that bodily urges posed to science and society. Not only did women's assumed greater physicality and emotionalism threaten to overwhelm men's reasoning capacities, but their unique role in reproduction left them unable to rise above their bodies. Pregnancy, with its lack of clear boundaries between fetus and mother, called into question women's capacities to control and contain their bodies (Battersby, 1998). Rather than throwing out a theory that denied the bodily experiences of most women, scientists saw women's bodies as deviant and fearsome. According to Shildrick, the male-dominated world imagined women to be more embodied than men and envisioned the female form to be more fluid and less contained than the male form. Women, with their assumed greater physicality and more permeable boundaries, were now seen to inhabit what she (1997) has dubbed "leaky bodies."

Despite a newfound belief in empirical observation, anatomists who dissected bodies continued to depict the female body as an inferior version of the male body (Oudshoorn, 1994). Emphasizing body similarities over differences, they used the same names for female as for male reproductive organs (Laqueur, 1990). For example, Berengario (1522), one of first anatomists committed to "an anatomy of what could be seen," labelled the uterus and associated vessels to make correspondences between male and female organs clear (ibid., pp. 74–5). In his drawings, he called the ovaries "female testes" and the fallopian tubes, "female spermatic ducts." Here the one-sex model – the idea that women's bodies were biologically similar but inferior versions of men's bodies – prevailed. (See figure 1.1 for examples [from Bartolomeo Eustachi, 1520–1574]. These are illustrations not of male genitalia but of female reproduction organs.)

Old theories were so deeply entrenched that anatomists did not explore further the question of sexual differences. Instead, they continued to illustrate female reproductive anatomy as an inverted version of male anatomy. Even Andreas Vesalius (1543), considered the founder of modern anatomy, drew phallus-like female reproductive organs. Although Vesalius rejected the authority of the ancients and resolved to tell the truth about the "Fabric of the Human Body," he continued to see women as inverted men in his detailed depictions of anatomy (Thomas Fisher, Landon, & Oldfield, 2006).

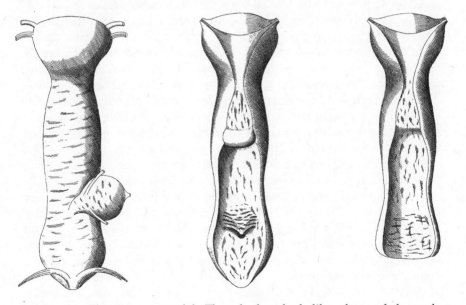

Figure 1.1. The one-sex model: Though they look like plates of the male reproductive system, these are female reproductive organs. From Bartolomeo Eustachi, 1520–1574.

Historian Nellie Oudshoorn (1994) argues that anatomists' disregard for sex differences was not a consequence of their ignorance. They dissected women's bodies as part of their anatomical practice and expressed scientific commitment to accurately interpret what they saw. Anatomists were incorporating cultural views about men and women into their interpretations of male and female bodies. In a male public world, woman was a lesser version of man, therefore female genitalia were seen as inferior versions of male genitals. Dissection was important, not because it could distinguish men from women, but because it affirmed the power of science to master truths about the body, as well as the power of men to reveal mysteries inherent in the fear-inspiring female womb.

It was not until the seventeeth and eighteenth centuries that scientists began to develop a concept of sex similar to our present-day two-sex model (Laqueur, 1990). Gradually, they came to interpret men's and women's reproductive organs as fundamentally different. For example, a significant change occurred in the depiction of the female body with Regnier de Graaf (Graaf & Officinâ Hackiana, 1672), who discovered the ovarian follicle (a sac in the ovary enclosing a developing egg). This discovery provided a biological basis for modern models of sexual difference. Once labelled an inverted penis, the womb became the uterus. Seen as analogous to male testicles for over a thousand years, the female testes now became ovaries. Does this mean that scientists finally discovered the truth about the female body? That they finally represented sex differences accurately? Not exactly. Instead, they used these new discoveries as further physiological "proof" of women's deviant nature. The medieval horns disappeared, but illustrations and descriptions still emphasized women's reproductive organs and associated their bodies with the irrational, animalistic, and abnormal.

Ideas about women's bodies as animal-like and monstrous continue to circulate in popular culture. One tongue-in-cheek depiction of the monstrous female body is found in the horror film *Teeth* (2007). After being raped, a young Christian woman who had pledged virginity grows vaginal teeth to exact her revenge. The film plays on the age-old cautionary tale about the *vagina dentata* or the toothed vagina, which was used to warn men against the dangers of sex with strange women. Feminists have argued that the *vagina dentata* myth reflects male fears of devouring women who threaten men with castration and emasculation. Some of my students have suggested that the killer shark in the horror movie *Jaws* (1975) is a contemporary example of the *vagina dentata*, given that throughout the film, the shark is repeatedly referred to as "she." In other classic films such as *Alien* (1979) and *Rosemary's Baby* (1968), the pregnant body is a frightening vessel from which malevolent forces erupt. Arguably, these films play on deep-seated fears in the Western psyche – of women's vaginas and pregnant bodies as sources, not of human creation, but rather, of its destruction.

According to historian Londa Schiebinger (1993), the new biology searched for biological differences between men and women as a new way to justify women's subordination. Why did scientists need new biological evidence to rationalize women's subordination in the eighteenth century? The answer is found in politics. For the first time, the spread of democratic ideas during the French and American Revolutions politicized people who did not have basic rights by causing them to question their lack of liberty. In the face of people's demands for change, scientists looked to the "laws of nature" to defend inequitable laws of society (Schiebinger, 1993). In Schiebinger's view, women emerged from this struggle, not with greater political or economic freedom, but with a different body equipped for their new social role: motherhood. Seen as being ruled by their reproductive processes, women were now regarded as morally and intellectually immature persons who did not deserve the vote, education, or other privileges of adult citizen status. Instead, they were now viewed as biologically built for maternity only. As one physician wrote in 1813 of female nature: "Women, in all civilizations, have the management of domestic affairs, and it is very proper that they should, as nature has made them less fit for the more active and laborious employments" (Buchan & Buchan, 1813, p. 410; also cited in Mitchinson, 1987). Whereas the old science imagined the female as a deficient version of the male, the new science saw women as different but no less defective in relation to the male standard. In this way, the two-sex model took hold.

The new biology searched for biological differences not only between men and women, but also between the races. Western science turned observed physical differences into inequalities that appeared to be grounded in scientific "facts" about the body. For example, the origins of the now disproved concept of race as a biological concept can be traced to the eighteenth century. This is when Europeans needed a convincing justification for slavery and colonial exploitation because such practices contradicted emerging political theories of universal human rights (Gould, 1993; Schiebinger, 1993). Western scientists created a hierarchy of races based on physical traits, which governments then used to justify continued racial oppression. Petrus Camper (1794) was the first of many eighteenth-century scientists who claimed that the skulls of African people most clearly resembled those of apes, justifying slavery and colonialism. Skulls were used to forge racial and sexual hierarchies because anatomists believed that skull measurements would reveal a group's intelligence. In Europe, America, and the whole of the colonized world, where the capacity to reason had become the decisive factor for citizenship, bogus biological theories of racial and sexual intelligence were used to rationalize social inequalities (Gould, 1992).

When women's bodies were compared across races, anatomists used pelvis size as the main measure of womanliness. Pelvis size was thought to determine a woman's capacity to carry out her maternal role successfully. Many medical men argued that African, Asian, and Aboriginal women had pelvises that were inferior to white European women's (Schiebinger, 1993). They also ranked women based on other physical traits thought to be markers of femininity such as hair, breasts, and genital size. For example, Black women's bodies became targets of European science and society when Saartje Baartman, a San woman from South Africa, was exhibited in Europe as "The Hottentot Venus" from 1810 until her death in 1815 (Hobson, 2005). Her white owners displayed her caged and almost naked on fairgrounds and in freak shows, making her genitalia and buttocks objects of public aversion and attraction. While Baartman's body was by all accounts average in relation to other San women's bodies, her buttocks and genitals were larger or shaped differently than those of most white women. For white audiences, her differences became visual proof of the animalistic sexuality of African women against the more contained, civilized sexuality ascribed to white Europeans. Not recognized as a human being in life, her abjection continued after death. According to feminist scholar Janell Hobson, when Baartman died, her corpse was dissected by an anatomist who stored her genitals in a Paris Museum as physical evidence of Black women's natural deficiency and hyper-sexuality (2005).

Another disturbing example of the devaluation of racialized female bodies is Julia Pastrana, who was exhibited throughout the United States and Europe as "The Ugliest Woman in the World" and as "Ape" and "Dog" woman (Browne & Messenger, 2003; Garland-Thomson, 1997). Of Aboriginal Mexican descent, Pastrana, like Baartman, became the object of public wonder and horror due to her excess facial and body hair (caused by a rare condition called hypertrichosis), which her handlers contrasted with the sexually suggestive garments she was made to wear on stage (see figure 1.2; Miles, 1974). Disability studies scholar Rosemarie

Figure 1.2. Julia Pastrana: Indigenous Mexican freak-show performer Julia Pastrana, billed the "The Ugliest Woman in the World" and as "Ape" and "Dog" woman, became the object of public wonder and horror in the nineteenth century due to her excess facial hair (caused by a rare condition called hypertrichosis).

Garland-Thomson (1997) notes that advertisers attracted audiences to their sideshow with suggestive images that emphasized Julia's sexuality and exaggerated her female, male, and supposedly ape-like features. Just as Baartman's genitals remained on display after her death, Pastrana's body was preserved (Browne & Messenger, 2003) to confirm theories about racialized women's aberrant bodies and sexualities. Visible markers of racial difference, whether in the absence or presence of a disability, were enough for white audiences to justify their gaze upon racialized women's bodies while denying the women their personhood (Clare, 2009). These examples demonstrate that the new ideal of women as sexless mothers did not extend to racialized women or white women perceived to have disabilities (Kudlick, 2005). Instead, they became the abject to the white European ideal – women who were imagined not only as less civilized but also as more sexual, abnormal, and frightful.

In case you think that the depiction of racialized women as hairy and masculine is a racist practice relegated to our colonial past, consider a recent controversy surrounding the Art Gallery of Ontario (AGO) exhibition dubbed *Passion, Politics, and Painting* featuring the work of famous Mexican artists Frida Kahlo and Diego Rivera. Believing that audiences knew little about Kahlo save for her iconic "unibrow," AGO marketers initiated a scheme inviting patrons to take self-portraits sporting stick-on unibrows in photo booths installed in front of the gallery for the show. (Go to Sarah Mortimer's account for more information on these events: http://www.shamelessmag.com/blog/2012/11/an-open-letter-to-the-ago-about-frida-kahlos-unib/.) The resulting photos of people with felt unibrows making funny faces, later printed in local newspapers (see figure 1.3), suggest that rather than raising awareness, the gimmick provoked public ridicule because it drew on old ideas about Indigenous women as unfeminine and ugly. The AGO tried to defend its stunt by asserting that Kahlo aggressively challenged these associations in her art. However, I question whether the gallery would promote an exhibition featuring a revered white male artist that poked fun of attributes similarly weighted with historical meanings, such as his small skull or penis. (Read the AGO's position here at http://artmatters.ca/wp/2012/11/our-director-of-marketing-weighs-in-on-the-frida-unibrow-debate/.) In the wake of recent bullying-related suicides in Canada and an anti-bullying law passed by the Legislative Assembly of Ontario, it seems particularly ironic that one of the province's major cultural institutions would initiate a marketing scheme which teaches children it is permissible to mock others' bodily differences.

Figure 1.3. Family wearing unibrows at Art Gallery of Ontario Frida Kahlo photo booth: Controversy surrounding the "unibrow" campaign sponsored by the AGO to bring people into an exhibition featuring the artwork of Indigenous Mexican artist Frida Kahlo suggests that notions of racialized women as hairy and masculine still have currency in our cultural imagination.

Although circuses and freak shows featuring people with unusual appearances are now considered unacceptable, casting individuals with different bodies as other continues today. Consider television programs like *My Shocking Story*, *Big Medicine*, *My Strange Addiction*, *My 600lb Life*, and *The Biggest Loser* that depict such people in stigmatizing ways. Millions of viewers in North America have access to these shows virtually on demand, making ominous images and narratives of people with bodily differences more widespread now than they were in the nineteenth or early twentieth century. Often, people featured on these programs are not shown to be full human beings and typically their voices are ignored or silenced in favour of expert opinion. Audiences are invited to collude with seeing differences as abject when we watch these programs. We might feel troubled by the unusual appearances of featured people, but at the same time, safe in the knowledge that we are not one of them.

In the eighteenth century, anatomists also became fascinated with physical variations violating their ideas of human perfection. The quest to discover the origins of disabilities centred on the female uterus (not sperm), as anatomists debated whether disabilities were preordained by God or created by the woman whose womb provided a field for the fetus. The mind-body split gave experts greater permission to gaze and experiment on bodies – female, anomalous, and racialized – to isolate causes of difference. Initially, they focused on babies born with ambiguous sex organs, whom they called hermaphrodites (Dreger, 1998; Gilman, 1989). (Today many people with intersex conditions consider the word *hermaphrodite* to be insulting.) Over time, they rejected biological variations that did not fit their definition of a normal, healthy body. They began to treat the different-looking body in much the same way they treated the sexually different one, as a threat to the fitness and wellness of society. In the nineteenth century, when statisticians began to calculate averages in ability and appearance within populations, they called on governments to reduce or eliminate variances below the normal range (L.J. Davis, 1995). Since then, physicians have been charged with the job of restoring the broken body and mind to a "normal" state. Although there are situations in which cures for mental and physical disabilities may be possible, this is not always the case. Many disabilities and differences are not modifiable or reversible. In addition, we know that health is enhanced through holistic concern with a whole person rather than through exclusive focus on the biological body.

The new imperative for individuals to achieve norms in mobility, sight, hearing, affect, and intelligence was based on a drive to eradicate disabilities. Francis Galton, a cousin of Charles Darwin, first championed the pseudo-science of eugenics in the 1870s. Galton argued that if a country wanted to improve its economic competitiveness and military might, it had to intervene in people's reproductive lives (L.J. Davis, 1995). Following Galton, eugenicists claimed that by encouraging the "best" citizens to have children and preventing others from reproducing (either voluntarily or by force), they could improve the competitiveness of nations. Leading eugenicists created pedigree charts to prove that problems as diverse as alcoholism and tuberculosis were inherited. These gave the impression that vague behaviours and wide-ranging illnesses were genetic traits. In reality they showed nothing about heredity. If the sexuality of racialized women was seen as deviant, as in the case of Saartjie Baartman and Julia Pastrana, the sexuality of women with vague labels (such as poor, shifty, mentally weak) came to be regarded as similarly problematic. Perceived as lacking the capacity to create healthy citizens, women so categorized were sent the message that their sexuality and reproductivity were illegitimate. By the early twentieth century, eugenics, despite its highly questionable claims and aims, became a broad social movement. To improve social health, eugenicists charged women with the special task of ensuring that they produced strong, able-bodied offspring.

Male thinkers who privileged the intellectual over the physical created a two-tiered system in which those groups assumed to be tied to their bodies were seen as incapable of reasoning and, therefore, as unfit citizens. Scientists played an important role in creating hierarchies of sex, race, and ability by developing theories of difference that appealed to biology to defend inequitable society. Although all women were measured against a male standard, some women were seen as more deficient than others. White, non-disabled women were charged with the task of upholding a fit, fair-skinned, feminine ideal against which other women were unfavourably compared. This included racialized women and women with disabilities, who were regarded either as asexual or inappropriately sexual and lacking in maternal capacity. Dominant discourses reduced those with differences to a few undesirable characteristics, thus turning the woman into an abject image that discounted her personhood.

Gendering and Sexing Bodies

The West has problematized embodiments seen as threatening to its identities and institutions. Tracing this history is vital because it helps us to understand the ideas that still inform women's embodied experiences today. While we assume that antiquated views about "woman as other" have faded into a distant sexist, racist, and ablist past, cultural messages about the ideal and abject body – about breasts, fat, and vaginas, about hair and hips, and about other characteristics unique to female-sexed bodies – continue to feature in girls' body and self-images. Looking back at this dominant story helps us to grasp the counter-story told by feminists and gender theorists in response to its legacy. Unmasking the myth of the gendered and sexed woman enables us to compose an alternative theory of "woman" that challenges conventional accounts.

Sex and Gender: Same or Different?

Rethinking gender and sex began in the 1960s, when second-wave feminists first questioned inequalities and challenged rigid gender roles and relations. Many argued that gender was a socially created category distinct from sex, which they saw as biological. Psychiatrists such as Robert Stoller (1968) first articulated this distinction to advance psychosocial theories of gender (the idea that early relationships shape a child's gender). Feminists drew on his distinction to refute biological determinism, or the prevailing belief that biology determined all human behaviour. They hoped to challenge theories of women's biological inferiority that had been used for centuries to rationalize women's second-class status. To counter the old "biology as destiny" mindset, they argued that (a) sex is a biological concept distinct from socially created gender, and (b) most differences between men and women arise from culture, not biology (Rubin, 1975; Unger, 1979). In an effort to create a third gender, some borrowed from psychology the concept of androgyny to describe people who combined masculine and feminine traits. Although this notion granted women permission to refuse the straightjacket idea of femininity and gave men leave to reject rigid masculine roles, it was short-lived as a feminist ideal. Because androgyny depended on integrating clichéd masculine and feminine traits into an androgynous being, it left gender stereotypes unquestioned. It also tended to favour more socially valued masculine traits over less valued feminine traits. Famous women known for their androgyny – such as k.d. lang – are more butch than femme, suggesting that the very category of androgyny implicitly favours masculine-coded attributes over feminine ones.

The sex-gender distinction helped feminists to make the case that inequality between the sexes was due less to biology than to society. In terms of the nature-nurture debates, they favoured nurture by stressing how our social roles and relations reproduced our gender hierarchy. This position ultimately failed to discredit biological determinism – if feminists could claim that gender roles and relations created women's subordination, then social conservatives and traditionalists could counter that claim by arguing that innate sex differences were the root cause of women's lesser social status. In the nature-nurture debate, traditionalists alleged that nature not nurture was at the heart of gender disparities. During the 1980s, conservatives, who were becoming increasingly fearful of feminist agendas such as pay equity and universal child care, used sex-based research into the brain to mobilize against progressive change. Some began to blame girls' apparent lack of math ability on differences presumed to be hard-wired into our brains.

Harvard University president Larry Summers made media headlines in 2005 when he suggested that "intrinsic aptitude" partially explained why women were underrepresented in top-level science jobs (Bombardieri, 2005; Summers, 2005). In 1992, Mattel Toys also got into hot water when they marketed talking Barbie, whose first words were, "Math class is tough!" ("Mattel says," 1992). Although Mattel thought they were expressing the sentiments of many school-aged girls, math-phobic Barbies (like female scientist-phobic Larry Summers) created controversy because they drew on age-old disputes and deep-seated stereotypes about sex differences in math and science ability. As progressive educators have shown, we continue to debate highly speculative biology-as-destiny theories despite mounting studies showing that class, nationality, and geographic location are much greater predictors of children's math scores than sex or gender (Wellesley College & American Association of University Women, 1992). The recent rash of popular books (such as Gurian, 1996; Sax, 2005) that focus on why schools are failing boys is just the latest in a long history of biologically based arguments that seek to justify gender inequalities using pseudo-science. Despite simplistic claims made by the proponents of "brain sex," much research indicates that the majority of people combine "masculine" and "feminine" traits rather than displaying one set or the other (Marecek, 2001); and most research has found no significant gender differences in intelligence, cognitive abilities, or learning styles (Hyde & McKinley, 1997). This has led prominent scholar R.W. Connell (2002) to argue that we should call such research "sex similarity" rather than "sex difference" research!

For some American feminist activists already upset with Barbie's anorexic figure and excessive consumerism, hearing about a talking Barbie who giggled, "Math class is tough!" "I love shopping!" and "Will we ever have enough clothes?" proved to be the final straw. In 1993, they decided to form the Barbie Liberation Organization (BLO) to "liberate" Barbie from her stereotypic gender role. The BLO's first act was to abscond with and switch the electric voice boxes of several hundred talking Barbies and talking G.I. Joes found in the group's local toy stores. They then returned altered dolls to the toy store shelves, which sold Barbies who yelled, "Vengeance is mine!" and G.I. Joes who cooed, "Let's plan our dream wedding!" To make media headlines, they placed "Call your local TV news" stickers on the back of the doll packages hoping kids would phone. The group followed up on their "culture jamming" action with an underground film also called *BLO*. (For more information on this "event," go to http://sniggle.net/barbie.php.)

Simplistic appeals to biology have proved tempting because they provide easy explanations for complex differences and inequalities. Throughout the 1980s and 1990s, feminist writers responded to vexing biological justifications for gender inequality by developing stronger cultural understandings. In their landmark essay "Doing Gender," sociologists Candace West and Don Zimmerman explained how individuals "do gender" as a "recurring accomplishment" (1987, p. 126). Feminist philosopher Judith Butler subsequently used the concept of "performance" as a way of thinking about the cultural constitution of gender. In her now classic *Gender Trouble* (1990), Butler argues that gender is an act of becoming (something we continually aspire to) rather than an innate identity. We become gendered – out of desire and under duress – through speech and other everyday acts of performing gender. In Butler's view, gender is something done to us and also something that we do. It is "a stylization of the body, a set of repeated acts within highly rigid regulatory frame that congeals over time to produce the appearance of substance, of a natural sort of being" (1988, p. 33). Because innumerable authorities assign and re-inscribe gender, people come to experience it as innate. And because failure to embody gender norms has extreme consequences (ostracism, violence), many come to see their conformity as natural and necessary. Butler argues that drag, cross-dressing, and butch-femme roles "trouble" us (hence the title of her book) because they parody gender norms by exposing them as unnatural.

Like earlier feminists, Butler claims that gender is a construction. What separates her thinking from that of previous writers is her contention that sex, too, is a construction and, even more, that it's a culturally created *outcome* of gender. She develops this idea using her concept of "the heterosexual matrix" which she defines as a grid of culturally powerful ideas about sex, gender, and desire that lead us to assume "there must be a stable sex expressed through a stable gender" (1990, p. 151). Belief in the biology of sex is deeply engrained in our society but her concept can be thought about in this way: in order to be recognized as a legitimate person in society, we must fit exclusively into the category of male or female, our gender expression must match our sexed body, and we must express sexual desire for only the "opposite" sex. We thus learn to regulate our sex, gender, and desire according to a heterosexual matrix. People come with a range of biological differences in hormones, physiologies, and genetics. Yet our gendered language and social organization force us into one or another category. We must be either male or female. Given our vast anatomical variations – from those of us with penises and high-pitched voices to those with vaginas and facial hair – why do our genitals alone determine sex? And why do sex organs matter so much more than other attributes in determining who we are? According to Butler, the Western idea that sex is inherent *in* the body is the product of preconceived gender and sex norms imposed *onto* bodies. The dualistic sex-gender-sexuality system is so powerful that it shapes scientific truths about bodies and desires. But biology alone cannot provide definitive answers to the question of what makes people distinct because cultural beliefs always infuse our interpretations of biology.

Butler's theory rings true, in part, because it explains why our society marginalizes, pathologizes, and even brutalizes those who don't fit our two-gender, two-sex system. This includes trans and intersex people. Although gender variance and sexed body diversity have existed historically and cross-culturally, the Western paradigm of two genders based on two sexes began to prevail only in the past four hundred years (Dreger, 1998). In North America today, gender-variant people face widespread fear and abhorrence (Namaste, 2000; Wilchins, 2004). Trans communities have some of the highest murder and hate-crime rates of all groups in North America (Stotzer, 2009). Trans people regularly face abuse ranging from harassment to rape at the hands of the very people who are supposed to protect them: the police (Amnesty International USA, 2005). It is a common occurrence for trans patients to be refused medical treatment due to care providers' discomfort with gender variance, and psychiatry still considers gender nonconformity a mental illness (American Psychiatric Association, 2000). The documentary *Southern Comfort* (2001) powerfully illustrates the medical mistreatment of one female-to-male trans man named Robert Eads, who died of ovarian cancer after he couldn't find a doctor to treat him.

Unlike trans people who are denied care, infants born with intersex conditions often face a surfeit of unnecessary medical interventions. According to Cheryl Chase (1998) of the Intersex Society of North America, these include genital surgeries intended to make their bodies fit sex categories that our society considers "natural" (for more information go to http://www.isna.org). Studies estimate that one in a hundred babies are born with variations in sex anatomy that differ from standard male or female, and one in a thousand will receive surgery to "correct" their condition (Blackless, Charuvastra, Derryck, Fausto-Sterling et al., 2000). Most intersex people say that treatments (like removing a girl's clitoris if it's deemed too large at birth or changing a boy into a girl in infancy if his penis is judged to be too small) have hugely adverse effects on individuals' capacities to experience sexual pleasure and feel comfortable in their bodies (Bloom, 2002). The Intersex Society of North America recommends that such surgeries not be performed (other than in cases of medical necessity) until children can make informed decisions about their genitals. But medicine does not hold a monopoly on mistreatment of the intersexed. In 2009, track star Caster Semenya was banned from competitive running for almost a year while officials investigated speculations about her sex (Rubenstein, 2010). Her case raises troubling questions about the ethics of forcing intersex athletes to undergo humiliating public scrutiny and intrusive medical verification just to compete. In addition to folks who identify as gender- or sex-variant, many people grapple with the pressures to conform to our two-sex system, including those of us who undergo costly and painful interventions such as electrolysis or cosmetic surgery to fit standards of a normal womanly or manly body.

Feminism's radical re-visioning of sex and gender has sparked two decades of critical debate. Is sex natural? Or is it just as socially constructed as gender? Transsexual people who feel betrayed by their birth bodies and seek hormone therapy and sex reassignment surgery to become their desired bodies are proof that sex is malleable (Schrock, Reid, & Boyd, 2005). Intersex people prove that sex is more varied than we care to admit, and both groups support the argument that the two-sex system is a social configuration. But this does not mean sex and gender should be thought of as the same. Following Butler, who contributed to erasing the sex-gender distinction by claiming that sex categories are cultural by-products of gender ideologies, many academics have replaced the concept *sex* with the catch-all term *gender*. Many use *gender* as a "proxy" or substitute for the biological, the social, or some combination of the two (Auerbach, 1999, p. 701; Carr, 2005; Kessler & McKenna, 2000). Adding to this confusion, most people in everyday speech still take *gender* to mean psychosocial masculinity and femininity, and sex to denote biological maleness and femaleness. Others simply use the term *gender* interchangeably with *sex* without thinking about what either word means. However, most feminists who study sex and gender would probably agree that they are not synonymous. Since in our society we are all in some ways sexed and gendered – we are assigned a sex based on our genitals and a gender based on our appearance, interests, and occupations – people experience these as connected yet distinct aspects of identity.

In this book, I do not use the word *gender* interchangeably with, or instead of, the term *sex*. By *sex* I mean the sexed body and not sexuality or sexual acts. I concur with writers who argue that collapsing sex into gender ignores the lived body and erases people's distinct experiences of their gender and their sex (Chambers, 2007). The women in my study, for example, did not speak of experiencing gender and sex as the same thing but talked about the ways that they formed their sense of gender and sex at different ages and in different contexts. I also do not revive the second-wave formula of approaching gender as social fiction and sex as biological fact. Trans people, who experience the assigned labels as incompatible with their preferred sex and gender, have taught feminists and gender theorists not to repeat that mistake. Instead, by *gender* I mean people's felt sense of themselves as masculine, feminine, or some other combination. In contrast, sex is their sense of themselves as male, female, or another sex. Sexed identity speaks to how people see themselves as male or female, an inner conviction that can mirror or conflict with meanings given to outward anatomy. While Butler understands gender and sex as co-creating, I separate these terms here because this was how participants described working out gender and sex in their lives. Certain assumptions about sexuality and sex were conveyed and expressed via their gender learning and play in childhood, but the women weren't expected to figure out or elaborate these as *identities* until puberty, when others responded to their changing bodies as sexed and as sexual. I thus approach both sex and gender as outcomes of biology, psyche, and society in interaction. Applying "body becoming" theory, I view them as distinct but entwined experiences of our bodily selves generated at different life stages through the interplay of our bodies, selves, and culture.

The Body Becoming

While many feminists have critiqued the "biology as destiny" formula, they also note that even when biology is *not* used to rationalize sexism, any effort to define women according to physical features remains problematic. For example, if we accepted biology as the litmus test for femaleness, would breast or ovarian cancer survivors count as women? How about those who have never been pregnant? In addition to excluding many women, the physiological definition forcibly includes transsexual men and rejects transsexual women. Our culture's belief in the sex-as-biology equation helps to explain the carnival sideshow that greeted Thomas Beatie (a transsexual man) when he publicly announced his pregnancy in 2008 (Trebay, 2008). People had trouble comprehending that Thomas's anatomy did not define his sex but tried to categorize him as female despite his legal claim and inner conviction that he was a man. These examples illustrate how biological definitions of *woman*, because they impose narrow norms on bodies and fail to consider people's lived experiences of sex, must be rejected as inadequate and limiting.

In the past fifty years, feminists have provided alternative conceptions of *woman* that challenge taken-for-granted accounts. Simone de Beauvoir first began this inquiry by famously writing "one is not born, but rather becomes, a woman" (1974, p. 301). She argued that women's bodies are central to this process – through media, schools, medical systems, and beauty culture we learn how to alter our bodies to create our sex. In her now classic work *The Second Sex*, de Beauvoir makes the case that women throughout Western history have been defined as the second or other sex: not only as different but also as deviant from the male norm. While pre-adolescent boys and girls aren't treated so very differently, puberty emerges as pivotal to sexual othering because it marks girls' move from the relative freedom of an androgynous child's body to the more closely regulated body of a young woman. Of this process, de Beauvoir writes:

> For the young woman ... there is a contradiction between her status as a real human being and her vocation as female. And just here is to be found the reason why adolescence is for a woman so difficult and decisive a moment. Up to this time she has been an autonomous individual: now she must renounce her sovereignty. Not only is she torn ... between the past and the future, but in addition a conflict breaks out between her original claim to be a subject, active, free, and, on the other hand, the erotic urges and the social pressure to accept herself as passive object ... Such is the painful dilemma with which the woman-to-be must struggle. Oscillating between desire and disgust, between hope and fear ... she lingers in suspense between the time of childish independence and that of womanly submission. (De Beauvoir, 1974, pp. 376–7)

For de Beauvoir, the bodily changes that mark a child as a woman cannot account for the difficulties girls confront at puberty. Puberty in itself has no meaning. It takes on meaning in a culture where development demarcates the female body as different from, and other than, the male norm. As their bodies mature, girls are forced into a negative awareness of the changes by messages about women that bombard them everywhere. It is not sexual development that makes a girl other – because womanly bodies are cast as other the changes come to be experienced as difficult and troublesome. De Beauvoir concludes that without the imposition of sexual otherness no one can know what girls might become.

Building on de Beauvoir's statement that one is not born but becomes a woman, Judith Butler has argued that the category of *woman* is itself a social creation, "a term in process, a becoming, a constructing that cannot rightfully be said to originate or end" (1990, p. 33). Like de Beauvoir, Butler challenges biological accounts of sex difference. Unlike de Beauvoir, who theorizes bodily experience, Butler focuses on the sex/gender distinction. Feminists before Butler tended to see sex (being male or female) as the biological given on which gender (becoming masculine or feminine) is socially created. Butler's insight was to invert the relationship between these categories so that we can begin to see sex as an *outcome* of gender – how our two-gender system limits sexed bodies by imposing dichotomy (or twoness) on potential diversity. In her view, girls become women by compelling their bodies to conform to a historical idea of woman – a construct so pervasive that individuals come to think of it as physiological rather than ideological (1988).

Social constructivism has been crucial to the development of feminist theories of sex. By showing how cultural beliefs contribute to scientific models of sex differences, theorists have disputed biological determinism. Yet some have argued that the focus on facts as socially constructed alone ignores the role of biology in making bodies what they become (Birke, 2000a). In a theoretical move described by sociologist Myra Hird (2003b, p. 187) as the "new materialism" (see introduction), they have proposed going back to the biological but returning in a new way: to more holistic accounts that capture the complexity of living things and the inseparability of the biological from the social (Asberg & Birke, 2010; Barad, 1998). Instead of seeing bodies as fixed, static, and passive, new materialists and body becoming theorists view them as open-ended emergent systems that "become" as a result of their own agency and other forces acting on them (Hird, 2003a, 2003b).

Body becoming theory emphasizes how physiology, psyche, and society each play a part in the body's dynamic process of becoming (Birke, 2000a). According to this framework, biology and culture are not polar opposites. Rather, our bodies are lived in social contexts: they change constantly in relation to social, psychological, physical, and other stimuli and, thus, they can be understood only in relation to the contexts in which they are embedded. Philosopher Elizabeth Grosz believes that biological processes provide the raw material for human development but that our bodily selves, without a human society and culture, will not be moulded into recognizable form (1994). She uses the Möbius strip as a visual image to convey how body, mind, and culture can be thought of as continuous (see figure 1.4). A Möbius strip is a continuous loop made by twisting a strip of paper then taping the two ends.

Figure 1.4. The Möbius strip: Philosopher Elizabeth Grosz employs the Möbius strip as her metaphor for the dynamic, open-ended relationship among body, psyche, and society. Photo courtesy of John Harrison.

If you were to walk along the length of this strip, you would return to your starting point having traversed both sides of the strip, without ever crossing an edge. For Grosz, the body, like the Möbius strip, has no clear distinction between inside and outside; instead, the outside and inside (like society, psyche, and body) fold into each other. Transcending the nature-versus-nurture debate, her approach invites us to explore how social meaning through our psyches becomes embodied – literally incorporated into our physical being.

Feminist biologist Anne Fausto-Sterling (2000) likewise uses Russian nesting dolls to visualize the various layers that make up human beings – from the cellular, to the psyche, to the social and historical (see figure 1.5). Because layers of the nesting doll, like the human body in context, have to fit together properly for the whole system to work, changes at one level require the entire interlinked system to change – changes in the body change culture, changes in psyche change the body, and so on. These models offer visual images that can help us understand how human biology and psychology are inherently social, and have no innate origin outside of culture. The concept of the body's open-ended becoming, whether from the philosophy of Grosz or the new materialism of Fausto-Sterling, speaks back to older, more deterministic ways of understanding the body. (Determinist models posit

Figure 1.5. Russian nesting dolls: Biologist Anne Fausto-Sterling illustrates her new materialist theory of sex and sexuality development using Russian nesting dolls. Photo courtesy of John Harrison.

that bodily attributes are shaped either by biological factors, such as behaviour and genetic make-up, or by social ones, such as institutions and built environments.) The body becoming approach does not discount the biological or the psychical but is non-determinist in theorising opened-ended "rhizomatous" trajectories for what bodies can become.

Since the second wave, feminist scientists (Hubbard, 1990) have shed light on the ways that science has been harnessed for sexist purposes by naturalizing sexual differences to rationalize inequality. Building on this scholarship, new materialist thinkers have moved beyond critique, drawing on the lessons of biology to demonstrate how sex variances "trouble" our two-sex model (Fausto-Sterling, 2000). Myra Hird, for instance, uses biological research to reveal how neither genitals nor chromosomes provide definitive markers of sex. The human body itself is intersexed, since all cells have "female" and "male" chromosomes except those that make up sperm and eggs; and even our sex chromosomes are not dichotomous, but have many variations including xxx, xxxy, and xxyy (Hird, 2003b, pp. 194–6). Further, women with polycystic ovarian syndrome (who have large amounts of facial hair and male-pattern hair loss) or vaginal agenesis (those with no vagina or a shortened vagina) do not fit conventional female bodies. Because biology itself challenges the naturalness of the two-sex model, our theories of sex difference cannot emerge from nature. Instead, according to Hird, we make meaning by "superimpos[ing] dichotomies onto a world of variability" (2003b, p. 195), thus confirming our belief in sexual dualism. By pointing out the high frequency of intersex (sex-combining) and transex (sex-changing) life forms – ranging from barnacles and earth worms to some species of snails and butterflies and most plants and fungi – these critical science scholars invite us to consider the positive implications of sexual diversity in nature for explaining and embracing sex variance in humans (Hird, 2006; Lane, 2009).

The new materialism does not simply challenge the two-sex story. It also sees biology as an ally in crafting more inclusive accounts. These possibilities are carefully explored in the critically acclaimed film XXY (2007), which tells the story of an intersex teen named Alex who is taking hormones to suppress her male sex characteristics (beard) and to facilitate her growth of female ones (breasts). As a child, she was able to hide her difference, but at puberty, passing has become impossible. Despite her parents' best efforts to protect her, others' curiosity and cruelty intrude as she faces pressures to undergo surgery and is nearly raped by local punks. In a world that requires her to choose one sex or the other and where even caring adults attempt to force this choice, Alex furiously refuses. The film draws on new materialist thinking through her marine biologist father, who uses his knowledge of nature's diversity to support Alex in her decisions to stop hormone treatment and resist sex-assignment surgery and, more importantly, in her deeper impulses to become sexed outside the categories. The theme of nature's diversity recurs in lingering shots of Alex's aquarium filled with hermaphroditic fish. Hybrid possibilities for her body are further illustrated in Alex's collection of dolls, complete with penises she has attached. While many of us take for granted that we transition from girl to woman or boy to man, why are these so much more acceptable than the change Alex undergoes? Discomfort with Alex's ambiguity may expose our culture's deeper difficulties with relating to bodies that violate the binary of male and female, and perhaps reflect a more profound unease with the uncertainty and ambiguity that is the basis of all life.

XXY is compelling because it doesn't reproduce the binaries but challenges us to imagine sexed bodies beyond male or female. Alex doesn't know what the future holds – life as a woman, a man, or another – and we as viewers can't know the answer either. By refusing categories of male or female, she evades others' control over her sexed body and carves out space to begin exploring what she might otherwise become. Her struggle enables us to consider how biology, psyche, and sociality are implicated in our becoming. According to constructionist theory, it is our culture's reading of biology, not biology itself, that creates dualistic sex differences. From a new materialist/body becoming perspective, however, biology also plays an influential role, interweaving with the social and the psychological to shape a person's sex. While biology has long been used to justify the subordination of women and sex-variant people under a two-sex system, new materialist theory does not hold to such oppressive norms because it stresses the body's *open-ended* becoming. Thus, it enables us to see how people become sexed through the interplay of cultural meanings with their psyches and physical bodies – how biology influences but does not determine what their bodies can be. By capturing the inseparability of the biological and social in sexual development, the theory deepens our insight into Alex's struggle. While the culture wants to pathologize her body and enforce her conformity to the two-sex system, her father's close proximity to nature's diversity enables him to support Alex in becoming sexed beyond the binary. By opening up possibilities for sexed bodies premised on diversity rather than dichotomy, his new materialist thinking gives Alex a more inclusive model for becoming a uniquely sexed self.

New materialism and body becoming perspectives layer our thinking because they expose the limitations of the two-sex model, calling into question theories of sexual difference premised on male superiority and creating possibilities for sexed bodies beyond the binary. These theories offer non-oppressive ways to bring the *biological* body back in, but they do not shed light on the *lived* female body. Despite theoretical developments that have shaken sexual dualism, our capacity to qualify as women (or men) still has profound consequences for our lives. When de Beauvoir posed the question "What is a woman?" she argued that biology did not make one a woman; rather one became a woman through initiation into an identity. Following her, philosopher Toril Moi (1999) has maintained that studying the lived body can give insight into what it means to be a woman without reducing sex to biology because our lived bodies are always embedded in contexts and subjected to culture. Participants' narratives shed light on this process by illuminating diverse trajectories and strategies for embodying and challenging the mythical norm of the natural woman. By giving us invitation to question arbitrary standards of femininity and the female body, their stories also open up space to imagine new ways of being and becoming gendered and sexed.

Chapter Two

In a Girl's Body

When recalling early memories, most women in this study described how bodies were vehicles for their active exploration of the world. While all remembered playing with gender, they also related the serious work of coming to know their gendered selves. For many, the spontaneity and freedom-to-be (captured in figures 2.1 and 2.2) were eclipsed, even in childhood, by messages about the type of girl they could be. This chapter relies on women's accounts to make visible something that seems so natural most people don't call it into question: how the social process of *becoming gendered* enlists girls to act on their bodies and adopt ways of being in response to the cultural demand to be gendered. In interactions with others, women discovered their bodies to be visible markers of identity, and they learned to view themselves in relation to the bodies they saw favoured for girls in this culture. All of them describe the painful work that accompanied the pleasurable play of gender: the fun of imagining their future selves and the fear of failing to fit the culture's standards. Becoming gendered emerged as a common thread in the stories they told. Yet they also became aware of differences in size, skin colour, and physicality through learning opposing values assigned to variations in bodies – such as white/Black, thin/fat, fit/unfit, and so on – with the first part of the binary often signifying "good" and the second "bad." Gender interacting with these differences defined the kinds of girls they could become. Gendered meanings imposed on bodies shaped their sense of self, even when they were children, and this aspect of their stories provides insight into the pivotal role of image in girls' self-making.

Figure 2.1. Playing dress-up: This girl is playing dress-up with her mother's cast-off clothes and costume jewellery. The image captures the pleasures she feels in trying on femininity, a moment unfettered by the demand for conformity to norms or ideals, a time before she, like many in our culture, becomes conscious of how her body compares to other girls' and to outside standards. I like the image because it evokes memories of a former, less weighed-down self. This girl was me. Photo courtesy of author.

Figure 2.2. Freedom to be: This image evokes the spirit of curiosity and adventure that many girls find in tomboyism. When she looks at the photo, the woman who was the girl in the picture recalls searching the path ahead and picking up fallen leaves while listening to the murmuring voices of the adults who follow behind her. As they call to take her picture, she remembers wanting to get her position and expression just right. Mostly she loves the photo because it represents her earliest memory of the freedom-to-be she felt that day. Photo courtesy of Susan D. Dion.

Grappling with Gender

Gender includes the meanings and relations of femininity, masculinity, and other related categories that people create and reproduce in their daily lives, regardless of the sex of their bodies (Spade & Valentine, 2011). In North American society, gender is central to self-identity. As children acquire English, they learn that to speak of others, or be spoken of themselves, they must use the words *he* and *she* "correctly" in a language lacking gender-neutral pronouns to refer to human beings. While language plays a critical role in constraining people to conform to male or female in order to have a recognizable human identity, gendering processes are also physical and social. People assign gender based on bodily attributes from the earliest moments of infants' lives, making it a massively externally imposed way of identifying people compared with other identities (Jenkins, 1996). Children as young as age three learn to label bodies as male or female and to split attributes into categories of masculine or feminine to establish identities in the world (Davies, 2003). Beyond being opposites, gender groupings are typically hierarchical. More than an identity, gender is an inequality built into the institutions and meanings that shape children's lives. Qualities categorized as masculine – such as active and strong – not only are *opposite* to those deemed feminine – including soft, yielding, and kind – but masculine-labelled traits are viewed as *superior*. In spite of this hierarchy, most children eventually embody the "correct" gender as integral to their sense of self.

Those who dispute the idea that gender is fundamental to self-identity fail to consider how they would navigate the world without it. Without a recognizable gender, how would you fill out forms such as a driver's licence application? In public places, where would you go to the bathroom? What pronouns would you use when speaking about yourself? Some readers might recall the gender-ambiguous character called Pat on the comedy show *Saturday Night Live* (1975–) who made audiences laugh because nobody could figure out whether Pat was a boy or a girl. This joke worked because it poked fun at a fundamental truth about gender: our ability to read someone as male or female is essential to our ability to interact with them (Jhally, 2009). If we think about common ways people identify gender, using phrases such as "acts like a man" or "runs like a girl," we begin to grasp how gender is not simply imposed on us but something we embody – incorporating gender through how we look, move, speak, and act. Gender becomes part of who we are physically and psychologically. Girls in our culture confront pressure to conform to "the body beautiful" as a measure of femininity. Many learn to minimize the physical space they occupy by adopting feminine-coded body movements (such as throwing like a girl; Young, 1990). While feminists (Brownmiller, 1984; Greer, 1972) once looked upon femininity as a mental and physical straightjacket for women, many now recognize its positive aspects. Playing with clothing and appearance can be sensuous and fun. Some traits categorized as feminine, such as sensitivity and attunement to others, may be assigned little value in Westernized cultures, but these are vital skills. For many women, femininity is a meaningful dimension of self-definition.

Gender is something we *become*. We become gendered by modifying our bodies and behaviours to match how we feel inside with the messages that we get from outside. Since gender is constrained by norms, taboos, and expectations that originate outside of our selves, we do not create our gender freely. Instead, through reproducing and reinventing norms, we become gendered. Unlike Pat, the character from *Saturday Night Live*, most people achieve gender clarity because we learn rules that teach us how to present ourselves in the socially correct way. We incorporate gender codes – shorthand, taken-for-granted, instantly recognizable ways of communicating gender – into our body language and ways of being to such an extent that they come to feel natural (Jhally, 2009). The association of pink with girls and blue with boys is the most recognizable gender code in Westernized societies, but there are many others. Children send and receive innumerable messages about condoned gender expression, including that tomboy girls are more readily accepted than boys perceived to be "crybabies" or "sissies." We all have experienced being typecast into circumscribed categories, yet the shades and complexities of our genders might vary as widely as our human diversity.

Immersed as we are in an inequitable gender system that underpins all social institutions, from families to schools and workplaces, it can be difficult to see how gender structures and regulates our lives. One way to grasp the regulating power of gender is to consider what happens when people break the rules. In the French film *Ma vie en rose* (1997), a young boy named Ludovic breaches our culture's gender codes by wanting to be a girl. Convinced that she's the product of misplaced chromosomes (she imagines that a stork has mixed up her genetic material), she sets about righting the mistake by experimenting with lipstick and make-up, wearing skirts and high heels, and anxiously awaiting the start of menses. An otherwise friendly suburban community is horrified by Ludo's gender expression, but the film tenderly explores how intolerant adults struggle to come to terms with her felt gender. *Ma vie en rose* is a touching story of gender variance with a hopeful outcome. Not so for *Boys Don't Cry* (1999), a film based on the real-life story of a trans man named Brandon Teena (who was born with a female body, but whose preferred gender and sex were masculine and male). The film unsentimentally depicts how Brandon's efforts to transcend gender boundaries and sex differences to live as a man ended abruptly in tragedy in 1993. When Brandon's supposed friends discover his female anatomy, they rape and murder him.

These films show how our society rejects those who don't fit conventions of male and female, whose preferred gender and sex don't mesh with the labels assigned at birth. They also reveal some of the ways gender inequalities operate. In *Ma vie en rose*, a rough-and-tumble tomboy character Christine is introduced to show how, unlike sissy-boy Ludovic, tomboys are tolerated in our culture. Perhaps we accept tough girls because they embody the gender deemed superior while we reject sissy boys because they personify subordinate femininity. We expect girls to grow out of tomboy ways as soon as their estrogen kicks into higher gear. What happens to girls who refuse to give up their masculinity? The violence done to Brandon Teena indicates that an anatomical woman who successfully passes as a man may challenge our stubborn belief in the innateness of gender and sex, and may offend and insult men's assumed rights to the privileges of masculinity.

The gender system has negative consequences for many of us, whether we identify as gender variant or not, because it downplays *similarities between* genders and erases *differences within* each gender, so that there is only one way to be feminine and one way to be masculine. According to gender scholar Raewyn Connell (2002), so much effort goes into reinforcing gender differences because these help to sustain inequalities that benefit men as a group. Men still earn more income than women in virtually every society and are still massively over-represented among the world's elite in politics, business, and science. Volumes of data show that what we perceive as natural is rooted in the unequal and asymmetrical life experiences, resources, and power of men compared to women (Connell, 2002). Although such inequalities are the result of social forces, gender identities are deeply felt by individuals. As women's stories here can attest, the cultural story of gender puts tremendous pressure on people to conform because the consequences of nonconformity can be severe.

Body becoming theory has important implications for understanding how we embody gender. It tracks how people come to be gendered and sexed without relegating sex to biology or seeing gender as wholly social. It allows us to analyse the interplay of biology and society in the body's becoming via the psyche – how individuals learn to identify with and embody gender and sex throughout their lives. Women I met acquired gender early when they faced the demand to create gendered selves. As their bodies began to change, women told of how they intervened in the physical processes of puberty (e.g., by controlling their weight and removing body hair) to fit with our culture's idea of a properly sexed female form. Thus, their gendered embodiment in childhood preceded sexed embodiment in puberty. The eighty-one study participants represent the diversity of women in today's Canada. Their narratives reveal how they worked to accomplish gender and sex while contending with other visible differences – race, ability, and size – and the interplay of these with their *learning* and *doing* gender (and later, sex).

The Serious Work of Gender Play

In her classic work on gender in childhood, sociologist Barrie Thorne developed the concept of "gender play" to understand the social processes through which children construct gender (1993). According to Thorne, our top-down, adult-to-child socialization theories err by ignoring how children actively create gender in response to the roles into which adults try to socialize them. While her work is helpful, Thorne herself acknowledges that the idea of play falls short of capturing the serious consequences of our two-gender system in children's lives (reproducing inequalities, punishing those who don't conform, etc.). Building on Thorne's metaphor of play, I use "the serious work of gender play" to stress how participants, when confronted with the cultural demand to recognize gender in others and to claim a gender for themselves, played *and* worked at that task. While Thorne focuses on the ways children perform gender through peer relationships and popular culture, she purposely leaves out one context women here identified as highly significant: families. Families loomed large as the contexts in which women gained access to multiple gender stories. Rather than characterizing parents as primary transmitters, their narratives suggest an alternative story of families as influential, but not exclusive, arbiters of cultural knowledge about gender. Before exploring what participants learned in families, my story begins with what they learned through everyday objects of material culture: mirrors and toys, especially dolls.

When students in my classes first encounter the idea that children *actively* construct gender, they often mistake it to mean that children *freely* create it. Many then jump to the conclusion that we can transform gender norms and inequalities simply by teaching children to reject stereotypes. One group of feminists who tried to tackle gender in this way was cultural activists. In the 1970s, they aimed to expand gender roles available to children by creating a television special called *Free to Be … You and Me* (1974). Because it challenged gender stereotypes such as boys don't cry and girls can't be athletes, the show became a beloved classic. Despite its educational and entertainment value, *Free to Be … You and Me* perpetuated the myth that casting off gender stereotypes would free children to pursue their talents and dreams. It overlooked how changing systems of inequality involves more than simply correcting misconceptions. The women I interviewed, for example, describe how gender is a physical process of body training that over time becomes deeply engrained. At every turn and in all spheres of influence, they confronted and responded to the requirement to become gendered.

Beyond brushing off stereotypes, altering this system requires broader and deeper changes at social, psychological, and physical levels, such as changing our language, institutions, relationships, and our sense of our bodies and selves. Because it was the product of its time, *Free to Be … You and Me* left the gender dichotomy intact. Today, a new generation of children's books such as *Gender Now* (Gonzalez, 2010) and cartoons like Karleen Pendleton Jiménez's *Tomboy* (2008) (to view go to: http://vimeo.com/10772672) aim to promote greater body and gender diversity (being intersex or trans) for young children and their caregivers. By opening up multiple possibilities for gender, these resources challenge both the rigidity of the dualistic categories and the hierarchical relationship between them.

Instrument to Image

Women gained awareness of their body images and ideals of femininity through cultural meanings that were conveyed early – they used these to gender their bodies and selves. Yet, when recalling their earliest memories (which mostly involved play), a majority described experiences of their bodies that were *not* image based. Instead, they (74 out of 81) remembered how bodies were fun, playful vehicles for their spirited exploration of the world. (The minority of women who recalled feeling distressed about and divided from their bodies in childhood had experienced sexual abuse at young ages.) When women gave accounts of first grasping the world through their senses – touch, smell, taste, hearing, balance, motion, and sight – vision was neither the first nor the most important faculty for experiencing their bodies. Before sight became a dominant way of perceiving, they related to bodies spontaneously (without thinking about them) as they engaged with their surroundings. This included those born with differences and disabilities, who registered their difference even as they experienced their bodies as vehicles of exploration and connection.

> Joanne: I used to have this "crazy car" [a plastic car that you sit in and use your arms to turn the wheels]. I would get out of my wheelchair into the crazy car and I would be just like the rest of the kids. Some of the kids didn't know I had a disability until I got out. It was great because I could build my arm muscles and I could go everywhere and not have to rely on anybody. What comes to mind is how much freedom there was with that.

> Elizabeth: One of my favourite things my mom did was to make "roads" on my face. She would take her finger and trace all along my face. She didn't have to say anything, because that normalized my facial difference. It was her way of saying, "Your face is still lovable and I accept you the way you are." In her manner was always unconditional love.

Most women describe a brief period in their early years when their bodies were *sensed* rather than seen – before visual culture got its grip on them. If they thought about bodies at all, many considered their mothers' and caretakers' bodies, which they perceived in terms of capacity for comfort and love rather than according to visual attributes like fat or thin. Strikingly, some recounted how their caregivers' patient grooming and affirming gaze helped them to build a positive sense of body. This was especially important for racialized girls and those with body differences growing up in predominantly white and non-disabled contexts. Their narratives suggest that a caregiver's loving touch and gaze gave them a reservoir of positive body memories from which they could draw when their attributes were being devalued.

Zoë: I remember kissing my mother all the time. She had the softest skin on her arms and I would put my head on her tummy because I loved all the gurgling sounds it would make. I would say, "It's time for tummy talk!" Because she is full bodied she would laugh and her whole body would vibrate and I thought that was wonderful.

Nicole: My grandmother has unconditional love. Any time I would go visit her it would be a fantastic experience. She didn't go out of her way to say anything but she would give hugs and kisses and she wouldn't be impatient combing my hair. That means a lot. She might not say anything but she would look in the mirror with me and give me a kiss. Actions speak louder than words sometimes. It was a gift. So empowering.

These accounts suggest that smell, sound, and touch might offer a different experience of our bodies in the world than vision does. The acclaimed science fiction writer Octavia Butler imagines these different experiences in *Lilith's Brood* (2000), her award-winning trilogy. *Lilith's Brood* explores contact between human beings and the Oankali, a fictional race with three genders: male, female, and intermediate. The Oankali travel in an interstellar ship made entirely of living tissue, and manipulate the genetic material of other living beings with whom they make contact. Driven to heal other sentient life, they rescue a post–nuclear-holocaust Earth by merging genetically with humankind. In Butler's trilogy touch emerges as the privileged sense through which the Oankali explore, understand, and transform their worlds. Butler imagines gender and sex beyond our visually oriented, two-gender system and considers the untapped possibilities of touch as an alternative, perhaps more highly developed, method of knowing our world than sight.

The power of visual images was imposed early on the storytellers in this study. Many pondered ways in which the presence of mirrors shaped how they perceived their bodies. For most, someone else's objectification of their appearance interrupted their prior unity with their spontaneously lived bodies. During the second wave, feminists viewed *sexual objectification* (turning women into objects for men's sexual pleasure) and, later, *body objectification* (reducing women to their bodies by valuing them for their looks) as key mechanisms of sexist subordination (Bordo, 1993; Dworkin, 1974). In our contemporary visually oriented culture that embraces an idealized aesthetic and imposes negative meanings on bodies that don't fit, girls and women face the demand to present themselves in accordance with a narrow range of acceptable bodies. According to Sandra Bartky (1990), pressure to conform to these standards is pervasive throughout Westernized cultures and reinforced everywhere in social interactions. Because of the ubiquity of imagery that positions women as to be looked at, girls learn to survey their bodies from an outsider's perspective and regard such scrutiny as voluntary. Although this is thought to lay the foundation for women's image problems, some writers have challenged the idea that objectification is always harmful, arguing that taking pleasure in one's appearance can be an enjoyable, sensual part of bodily life.

In childhood, virtually every participant became conscious that being looked at was associated with being female and that relating to one's body as an image was foundational to femininity. Through self-scrutiny and watching others look at them, all experienced their bodies as visual emblems of themselves and as subject to outside standards. This was not wholly negative. Many recalled the pleasures of gazing on their girl bodies and the possibilities of imagining their future female selves. At the same time, they described how such objectification could cause damage by instilling a vulnerability to outsider looks. Growing up in a world of reflecting surfaces and observing eyes, these women suggested that sight eclipsed other experiences of bodies – especially touch and movement – which were the bases for their first tangible reality. Yet none except Shirley could say how images overshadowed other perceptions. Because Shirley spent her early years on a farm in rural Jamaica, she had no consciousness of her body as an image until she moved to the city.

> Shirley: Moving from rural to urban was huge. I remember shopping because for the first time I could choose what looked flattering. I began to think, "You can look nice in clothes." I felt better because I could choose what to wear. Before I became conscious of what I looked like, my grandmother made my clothes. There was no concept of shopping and looking at yourself in the mirror. All that despairing didn't enter my mind.

Most of those interviewed developed body consciousness through the many cultural mirrors in their daily lives: other people. For close to 80 per cent, family members first imparted the cultural significance of physical features through body-based comparisons with sisters, cousins, and female friends. Teasing and taunting mainly by fathers and brothers had a particularly powerful impact on their developing bodily self-images. As a result of comparisons and criticisms, all became conscious of unequal values given to differences in size, hair texture, skin colour, and appearance.

> Claudia: There was this hierarchy of how you look. My Dad would say, "It's great that you're tall." It made me feel proud of being tall. Although sometimes it worked against my sisters because they weren't as tall as me.

> Nicole: My Dad used to say that I had an ugly smile ... When you are really young and they tell you that you're ugly, it really sticks. It's funny, because I never really thought about it 'til now. But he set me up from a very young age to not like myself.

Gendered looking relations tend to be naturalized in Western art and media. But recently commercial capitalism, in its quest for sales, has also been positioning men as to-be-looked-at (Bordo, 1999a). This trend has led people to conclude that sexist objectification must be a thing of the past. Although some men may be succumbing to the feminine-coded preoccupation of needing to look good in order to feel good, it's worth asking whether boys and men are valued primarily for their looks, or experience the same degree of visual scrutiny as women do in our society. If the answer is "no," then inequalities in ways of looking still must be operating. This doesn't mean that wanting to be looked at is necessarily bad; rather, it may well be the degree of control we have over the conditions of looking – who looks at us, how we are looked at – that ultimately determines our experiences of objectification.

Fantasies of Femininity

Over the twentieth century, commercial culture has emerged as a powerful force in children's lives. As a result of proliferating media and sophisticated marketing strategies, advertisers spend $16 billion a year to reach North American children, a group whose buying power recently topped $30 billion (Schor, 2004). To understand the extent to which commercial culture has colonized children's play, we need only think about kids in our lives. How much time do they spend engaged with electronic media like television, computers, and videos? How often do they play with media-linked toys such as those based on movies or TV shows? Although many people regard toys as simple playthings, our $26 billion North American toy industry ("Toys and games," 2010) does serious gender work. Under the guise of fun and creativity, toys influence children's desires and values, teach them how boys and girls behave, and give prescribed versions of adult roles (Linn, 2009). Providing the tools that structure what is possible in play, toys assist children in the process of becoming and defining themselves in relation to the world. By looking at one popular toy marketed to the women I interviewed, Barbie, I analyse the messages about gender and race that she sent to those who played with her. This invites us to consider the meanings about gender and race that toys today carry and how children might reproduce – and resist – those messages in their play.

Feminists have long observed how toymakers reinforce gender by making toys that promote feminine- or masculine-coded activities and identities (Wagner-Ott, 2002). By encouraging girls to imagine themselves in their doll's image, fashion dolls in particular transport girls into the realm of idealized femininity, wealth, and success (DuCille, 1996). By far, the girl's toy most accused of pushing narrow notions of feminine beauty is the blond, blue-eyed, 1950s bombshell, Barbie. Ruth Handler, co-founder of Mattel, created Barbie (after a sexy German novelty doll and comic strip character named Lilli) when she noticed that her daughter loved to act out scenes from adult women's lives as she dressed and undressed her paper dolls (Talbot, 2006). For girls growing up in the 1960s and later, Barbie enabled them to roleplay a sexually mature ideal of femininity that went beyond the mothering roles previous doll play allowed. The fashion icon thus gave girls a model to fantasize their future selves even as she set high standards against which, subsequently, many have come to judge their own bodies. With her blond hair, white skin, super-human shape, and glamorous wardrobe, Barbie represents an impossible ideal. According to Attfield (1996), because Barbie was originally created to model clothing, her designers saw no need to construct more than five movable body parts. In contrast, the designers of G.I. Joe gave that doll twenty-one body movements. These doll designs, by creating different (and unequal) capacities for movement, literally construct female bodies as passive and male bodies as active. Attfield argues that toys do not determine children's actions, but nonetheless, girls and boys often use them to try out culturally favoured ways of being.

Hidden under the frills and sparkles, Barbie promotes a narrow range of identities and bodies. Theorists have uncovered the invisible operations not only of gender but also of race in the doll's making and marketing. According to Barbie scholar Ann DuCille (1996), it was not until 1968 that Mattel made its first Black fashion doll, Christie, who was essentially a white doll painted brown. Cast from the same moulds as the blond, blue-eyed archetype, Christie preserved a white ideal because she implied that Black women could be beautiful only insofar as they looked white. Since the 1990s, multicultural Barbies have come in a rainbow of colours and ethnicities, yet almost all of them still look like the prototypical white Barbie save for their different dye jobs and wardrobe changes (DuCille, 1996). For example, most of Mattel's "Dolls of the World" resemble blond Barbie dolled up in a stereotypic costume from the ethnic group or nation they supposedly represent. "Pan-Asian Barbie," created by Mattel as part of its global push to pursue markets in Asia (Lim, 2009), features oversized eyes and a one-size-fits-all identity that hardly represents Asian women (Rossini, 2009; to judge for yourself, go to http://theillusionists.org/?p=385). On the domestic front, Mattel has launched a new line of Black dolls featuring more "authentic facial characteristics" than the previous Black Barbies (Mattel Inc., 2009). There's much to doubt in whether they are breaking the beauty barrier. According to critics, the dolls' most distinctive features – their lengthy locks and hairstyling sets that involve girls in curling and straightening their doll's hair – send the disturbing message that there is something wrong with Black women's natural hair ("Mattel introduces," 2009).

Barbie perpetuates an impossible standard of beauty and establishes the bodies of women who don't fit the white mould as deviant. In her acclaimed film *Girl Like Me* (2005), African American filmmaker Kiri Davis explores the effects of the white beauty myth on Black children's doll play. When just sixteen, Davis became interested in a famous study of colour preferences among Black children conducted in the 1940s by psychologists and civil rights activists Kenneth and Mamie Clark. In her documentary, she repeats the Clark study by asking African American children to choose between one of two dolls – a light- and a dark-skinned doll. The film interweaves clips of the children, who mostly select light dolls, with interviews of Davis's friends, who talk about the impact of white beauty standards on Black women. (Watch at http://www.youtube.com/watch?v=PAOZhuRb_Q8&feature=watch_response.) As disheartening as the results of Davis's experiment are, they raise a key question. What does it mean when girls prefer to play with dolls that do not look like them? The Clarks believed that Black children's white-doll preference indicated their self-esteem had suffered major damage in a society divided by race. However, the young women featured in

Davis's film assert that while racist beauty images and white dolls hurt their hair ego and skin image, these did not cast a shadow over their whole self or instill absolute feelings of unattractiveness. The fact that they speak passionately and knowledgeably indicates that they have not wholly internalized dominant values about Blackness.

In recent years, a new line of multiracial contenders, the Bratz dolls, has threatened to bump Barbie from first place as reigning beauty icon (Talbot, 2006). Since their debut in 2001, the "Girls with a Passion for Fashion" have grabbed an estimated 40 per cent share of the global fashion-doll market and overthrown Barbie as the best-seller in Great Britain by claiming close to 50 per cent of the market share there (Hiscott, 2004). According to analysts, the success of Bratz dolls in the battle for girls' playtimes may lie in their appeal to girls' desire to embody a sexy young femininity that surpasses the more physically mature version of womanliness represented by Barbie (who may be seen as motherly and even matronly by girls today; Talbot, 2006). Bratz dolls, with their almond-shaped eyes, fuller lips, varied shades, and exotic names (such as Yasmin and Nerva) might offer an ethnically indeterminate improvement for multiracial girls growing up today (Talbot, 2006). Some feminists even argue that they make racial difference visible and beautiful, "opening up a space in the popular imaginary for the normalization of multiracial bodies" (Guerrero, 2009, p. 194). For others, the potentially positive challenge that they pose to Barbie's pallid version of womanhood is belied by their anorexic bodies, heavily made-up faces, sexy wardrobes, and upper-class lifestyles, which still place undue importance on being rich and thin (Linn, 2009).

Growing up before Bratz dolls, many of the women in this study played with Barbie and, of those, almost all played with white Barbie. Some showed no interest in feminine-coded toys, rejecting the version of gender that Barbie offered. But for many, including Sylvie, Barbie emerged as a key tool in the toolbox of femininity, a prominent player who brought them closer to idealized femininity and shaped their understanding of how to embody that ideal. Some, like Eva, developed a conflicted relationship with the ideal she represented when others' taunts and their own awareness of difference pierced the fantasy of the kind of girl they imagined they could be.

Sylvie: I had a little rabbit fur collar that I used as Barbie's mink stole. I would wrap Barbie's mink around my neck and think I was so beautiful.

> Eva: When someone called me "fatso" was [the] first time I realized that your body counts and that my body wasn't growing the way it was supposed to grow, like Barbie.

The stories of racialized women revealed mixed responses to ethnic Barbie's body. For some, Black or Asian Barbie provided positive self-recognition and countered messages that only white women could be beautiful. However, when they saw that the supposedly ethnic doll resembled white Barbie's body more than their own, many inferred that the ethnic version must be an inferior copy of the real deal. Like Ruby, few saw ethnic Barbie as a model to which they could aspire. Because whiteness was naturalized everywhere in their lives (even in the design of ethnic Barbie), their models of beauty became white. In a context where dark skin is perceived as unpretty, some storytellers, such as Tamara, refused to play with ethnic dolls. Although many researchers would interpret this sort of rejection of "ethnic" dolls as a sign of negative racial self-concept, few of the women actually wanted to be white (though many wanted to be lighter). In describing how they appreciated looking ethnic at other moments in our exchange, they implied that rejecting ethnic Barbie was guided less by a desire to escape racial difference than to evade negative meanings imposed on that difference. Their experiences echo those of Ann DuCille (1994) in her account of doll play: like DuCille, they did not want to play with dolls that reminded them of being different because they did not want to be seen as other. Instead, they wanted to be seen as aspiring to the same standard as their friends.

> Ruby: You become very aware as a child that Barbie is an adult body form. And since it is a doll, it is probably a good body form. That influenced my perception of my image. I didn't think about the adults around me. I thought more about what was being presented as ideal: Snow White, Barbie. I had Asian Barbie, but she wasn't any different from regular blond Barbie. She didn't look Asian at all: Barbie, just a different colour. So she didn't help my image. But my mom tried.

> Tamara: Getting a Black Barbie as a kid was horrible. People thought they were doing you a favour by giving you a Black doll, which in those days were ugly. They just made Barbie Black. I remember my sister and I going, "Ugh!" We wanted a Barbie doll that was white, with blond hair, brown hair, beautiful. We took it as an insult.

Rather than being passive receivers of toys' messages about gender and race, the women brought prior cultural knowledge about femininity and difference to their engagements with dolls. Since whiteness was valued over Blackness or Asian-ness everywhere in their lives, ethnic Barbie often reinforced feelings of otherness more than she challenged the white beauty standard. For some, playing with Barbie probably did cause injury to (or at least didn't help) their sense of themselves in their own skin. However doll play alone did not instill poor self-esteem or a bad body image. Rather than moralizing about Barbie's or the Bratz's badness, it might be more constructive to consider what the popular tools of race and gender play might teach children in different social contexts. Within a context that offered women limited options for doing gender and race, Barbie helped to shape the image they created of themselves in relation to femininity, beauty, and difference. Through dressing up dolls and acting out scenarios, they experimented with femininity and, in the process, learned whether or not they fit the particular idealized version offered.

Shades of Gender

For many of us, gender is a taken-for-granted part of our lives. At first glance it appears unchanging, but on closer reflection it turns out to be more fluid: people follow different paths, cross gender boundaries, and never become exclusively masculine or feminine (Connell, 2002). To capture the ambiguity of experience, research has moved away from old notions of gender as a fixed set of traits children are born with or socialized into, towards the idea of gender as a fluid construction. In the newer view, gender is not simply a way of being that children learn as a result of social norms or pressures; rather, they take an active part in creating gender through their talk, actions, and interactions with others and the surrounding world (Davies, 2003). With the shift away from seeing gender as imposed from the outside, critical researchers have also moved away from a focus on parents as influential socializing agents of children. Increasingly, they emphasize how children reproduce gender relations by bringing their cultural knowledge about gender into interactions with peers (Blaise, 2009). This has opened important new lines of inquiry into children's rich social worlds. However, it overlooks how children still obtain gender knowledge in the most personal of social realms: families.

In making the case for reconsidering gendering processes in families, I am not arguing for socialization – the idea that children are passively schooled into assigned gender roles through the top-down transmission of norms and rules from adults. Socialization overlooks an important insight from Thorne's work on gender play – that children have agency in gendering themselves. Socialization theory also naturalizes our two-gender system. By taking for granted that children are born with a sex, acquire a gender in childhood, and develop into sexual beings later in life, the model presents a particular developmental path as inevitable, normal, and natural (Blaise, 2009). Beyond reproducing the gender binary, this story doesn't easily fit most people's experiences. For example, women in this study spoke of how they experimented with gender *and* sexuality as an ongoing process starting in childhood. And they didn't think much about their sexed body or about claiming a sexual identity until they were confronted with the cultural demand to do so in puberty. Finally, because socialization assumes there is just one gender for boys and another for girls, it misses multiple patterns of femininity and masculinity that exist in society. This stands in stark contrast to the experiences of responders who described many shades of femininity and tomboyism based on their inclinations, influences, and intersecting identities.

These storytellers' gendered experiences offer a nuanced picture of how girls negotiate gender in families. I have chosen the metaphor "shades of gender" to capture the ambiguities of becoming gendered, the pleasure that many participants found in trying on femininity and masculinity, and the frustration they felt if they failed to do it right. "Shades," in denoting the shadows cast by light intercepting objects and also a colour relationship, evokes the fleeting nature of gender and conveys the centrality of image, of looking and being looked at, to participants' gendering processes. By suggesting something indistinct, the metaphor of shade highlights how gender is never certain or complete – the women spoke about it as an ongoing construction and negotiation. Like the shadows created by the play of light on objects, shades further connotes a multiplicity of experiences, the patterns of gender that women cultivated based on meanings given to their bodies. The metaphor thus captures the shifting, elusive quality of gender as it interacts with other differences, especially race and disability, to cast shades of femininity and tomboyism that the study respondents described.

Model Mothers: A First Glimpse at Womanhood

Sociologist L. Susan Williams has proposed "trying-on-gender" to refer to the experimental, less than serious, often playful ways that adolescent girls do gender as a trying-on process (2002, 2009). While she came up with trying on gender to capture one moment of gendering – the transition from girl to woman – the experimentation she describes could also apply to girls' gendering processes before puberty. The women related how as girls they played with available possibilities for identity, yet they also spoke of the more serious, unfunny, and weighty ways that they worked at becoming gendered. Instead of gender being a "one-size-fits-all process" (L.S. Williams, 2009, p. 217), they describe how they searched their surroundings for "like others" as models to imagine their gendered selves. In answer to the questions *Who am I?* and *Who do I want to be in this body and this world?* many looked to mothers and mentors for clues. Mothers, through modelling different femininities, gave participants their first glimpse of womanhood. However, women did not simply copy or passively absorb what their mothers had to teach; rather, they looked to mothers and mentors actively on their own terms for lessons about available gender, and worked with, and against, the answers mothers gave.

The process of trying on gender emerged as a common theme in these women's stories, yet not all of them developed their self-image in relation to the *same* femininity. Rather, the shades of femininity they created depended on context. Their trying-on processes were shaped by what Susan Williams has called "local gender regimes" (2002, p. 32) or what Carrie Paechter refers to as "local communities of [gender] practice" (Paechter & Clark, 2007, p. 342): the power dynamics in families, schools, and communities that reinforced particular ways of being a girl. The women drew from versions of femininity available in families and communities, and experimented with features they saw as salient to their situations. Due to the diversity of those interviewed across a range of identities, I consider the femininities of four groups only: white, Black, and South Asian women, and those living with disabilities and differences. The following, general, typology represents their self-described femininities (which is not intended to fix these in stone but to capture different ways of being a girl that storytellers found): *privileged femininity*, the version given highest value in society, and promoted in white, middle-class families; *respectable femininity*, emphasized in the families of the Afro-Caribbean Canadian responders; and *appropriate femininity*, most often described as passed on within the families of South Asian women. In a context where disability and femininity are seen as incompatible, women with physical or facial differences and disabilities related the challenges of trying on gender when they were seen as "not quite" female without "like others" to guide them. On a cautionary note, these descriptions are meant to *acknowledge*, not *essentialize*, differences. As Uma Narayan notes, putting people and cultures into "package pictures," not only perpetuates stereotypes but also discounts the fluidity and dynamism of individuals and groups as they shift and change in relationship to each other (2000, p. 1083). Instead of fitting into tightly wrapped boxes, participants describe encountering and experimenting with different shades of gender as part of an active process of bodily self-making in childhood.

Many women learned to navigate the gender system by placing themselves in the same category as the parent whom they saw as sharing their gender. As they looked to family members for answers to the gender question, the person most frequently referred to was their mother, whom they talked about twice as often as fathers or sisters, and ten times more frequently than other relatives. In their search for cultural mirrors to help make sense of themselves, 70 per cent recounted identifying with their mothers – seeing themselves in their mothers' images and using mothers as models for gendering themselves. Some such as Kate relived the pleasure, thrill, and delight of playing with grown-up clothes or pretending to shave their legs, just like their mothers. Entering a world ordered by gender, others, like Anne Marie, responded with frustration when their mothers failed to grasp the seriousness of the gender project: the cultural demand to be recognized as a girl. These accounts may give readers pause to think about gender as an ongoing activity. How are children *active* in taking on and doing gender? And in what ways is gender shaped by the requirement to fit into a two-gender system?

> Kate: I remember my mother shaving her legs and I would pretend I was shaving my legs. I remember we were going to do this special thing: I was going to try on all her earrings. I had a bit of wanting to be like my mom. It's not that I saw other options and picked my mom. She was the only one there. She was my model.

> Anne Marie: I'd get really mad because I was seen as a cute little boy. Once I pulled down my pants in front of a little girl when we went into the washroom and this girl said, "This is the girls' bathroom. Little boys aren't allowed." I remember being so mad at my mom after that. Men would say, "What a cute little fellow" and pat me on the head. If she didn't dress me in a dress, then I was perceived as a boy. I resented her for that.

A white, affluent feminine ideal emerges in women's childhood stories as the measure by which all girls were gauged. Raewyn Connell
(1987) has called the culturally dominant way of being a man *hegemonic
masculinity* – the tall, fit, take-charge breadwinning "man's man." Because femininity is subordinated to masculinity in patriarchal society,
Connell does not use the term *hegemonic* to describe dominant femininity. Instead, she calls the idealized way of being a woman *emphasized
femininity*, the male-oriented image of the well-heeled, pretty woman
who does not question sexism but seeks out male attention and de-
fers to male authority (Currie, Kelly, & Pomerantz, 2006). While people
associate high-status femininity with adult women, images of ultra-
feminine girly girls abound in popular culture – from big-eyed Bratz
to the sexy Disney heroines. One controversial example is *Toddlers and
Tiaras* (2009–), the reality TV series in which girls as young as four are
transformed via fake eyelashes and sexy clothes into glitzy beauty pageant contestants (Pozner, 2010). Super-femininity remains a standard
against which women assess their femininity for social approval. At the
same time, it is widely parodied and lampooned in our culture (think
about how people poke fun at celebrities like Jessica Simpson, or "dumb
blonds" generally). The fact that the most highly prized femininity is
both admired and mocked indicates that femininity, in whatever guise,
is considered inferior to masculinity.

While all the women measured themselves against these ideals, they
also learned to embody diverse femininities. Many researchers have
identified multiple masculinities that men take on depending on their
status (such as working-class or Black masculinity). Few have considered how women, too, might express different femininities based on
their intersecting identities. Recently, some feminists have made a case
for reviving the phrase *hegemonic femininity* to identify the idealized
version of womanhood against which other ways of being a woman are
measured (Collins, 2004; Schippers, 2007). However, since it downplays
how even the most privileged femininity is still positioned as "less
than" masculinity, I find *hegemonic* misleading. Raewyn Connell argues
for *emphasized femininity*, which she describes as an extreme form of
femininity oriented to complying with men's needs and desires. However because the participants described an ideal that was less compli-
ant, exaggerated, and male-oriented than Connell's idea of *emphasized
femininity*, I have settled on *privileged femininity* to identify the most desired femininity participants described and to consider its relationship
to the diverse femininities many adopted. Each woman emulated the

idealized form by comparing herself against it. At the same time, they all constructed other femininities by drawing on features of the privileged version, which they combined with versions promoted in families and, later, communities to create variations salient to them.

For women with whom I spoke, early attachments with caretakers represented critical relationships where they constructed ideas about gender, experimented with the trying-on process, and learned family values about preferred femininities. Through reciprocity in mother – daughter or "other mother" – daughter relationships, they tested ways of being a girl. Mothers actively influenced their embodiment of gender – or participants' incorporation of gender into their psyche and physicality. For those raised in white middle-class households, mothers encouraged an idealized image of the pretty, proper, and perfect girl. Since mothers (and daughters) attain higher self- and social esteem if daughters conform, some middle-class mothers offered direct advice about clothing, voice, and body comportment. A few responders resisted this way of being a girl, but many others, including Jill and Fredericka, adopted the privileged version as their own. Rather than being told directly that they should fit the standards, some assimilated expectations indirectly through close attunement to their mothers' exertions. Even in childhood a few began to recognize how idealized femininity, although a potent source of female power, could also be a trap. This occurred when they became conscious of the gaze that pulled them into self-scrutiny and realized how the beauty aesthetic could be frustrating and wearying to uphold.

> Lucciana: I was the typical girl. I had a pink room, canopy bed. It was important to my mother that my hair was always done in ribbons and that my curls were just so. Being so perfect and I hated it. She was born in Italy and came here when she was 5. They didn't have a lot of money. What she said to me was, "I want to give you everything I didn't have."

> Jillian: My mom was dieting and my aunt would be fat and then not fat, fat and then not fat. They were always dieting. So there was a whole culture of dieting around. I became part of that. I'd always be trying new diets.

> Fredericka: My mother was a beautiful woman and very concerned about how people saw her. I wanted so much to be like her when I grew up. At the same time, I can see now the struggles she went through with her body, the pain she took to dress herself beautifully, to make sure she had

the make-up on before she left the house. I got that from her. My mom would say, "you're strong but don't forget that you're beautiful as well." Even as a child, I had to go through people on the street remarking on how beautiful I looked. I felt embarrassed by this. I didn't want that burden.

Women's stories describe how idealized femininity functioned through desire and fear: they felt the pleasures and joys of partaking in femininity's privileges, and witnessed or experienced the pain of being perceived as other than feminine (ugly, fat, etc.). Some distanced themselves symbolically and spatially from mothers who "failed" at femininity to escape the shame of being seen as "one of them." This was especially true for those whose mothers were fat, who registered feelings of embarrassment, fear, and disgust in response to their mothers' size. A few responders suggested that aversion to their mothers' fatness was natural or expected. Yet there is nothing inherently frightening or disgusting about fat bodies: a young child might just as easily associate a caretaker's fatness with comfort and safety, as some women did. Thus, the far more likely explanation for their repulsion was internalization of the culture's abjection of fat.

> Kasha: She scared me. She was over 200 pounds and she had gone through a lot of weight gain and loss and she was jiggly and crêpey [like crêpe paper]. I'd get scared. It was different, a body that had been through childbearing, work, and too much sun. She was not attractive to a child.

Feminists have explored the implications of idealized femininity for white, able-bodied girls. Less acknowledged are cultural myths of disability and difference that influence the gendered embodiment of disabled girls. In Westernized societies, the disabled body is coded as unattractive, incapable, and inferior. But as disability theorists have shown, disability is "not so much a property of bodies as a product of cultural rules" about what human bodies should do and be (Garland-Thomson, 1997, p. 6). Standards of beauty, fitness, and normalcy create narrow notions of acceptable bodies, which affirm and validate some bodies as they impose negative meanings on others. As a result, women without disabilities occupy a privileged position on a sliding scale of beauty, femininity, and femaleness relative to those with differences who are imagined as unattractive and as less than or not quite female. According to Rosemarie Garland-Thomson (1997), the pressures of unattainable social ideals of femininity and female bodies mean that women with disabilities often feel themselves to be ambiguously both inside and outside the identity of woman.

Surrounded by non-disabled folks, most disabled storytellers had to navigate the gendered and ablest world without like others to guide them. Because much of our society perceives women with disabilities as non-gendered and non-sexual, some participants, like Joanne, were left with little sense of gender. However, as Hilde Zitzelsberger found in her research with disabled women, being "seen as unattractive or non-gendered and nonsexed was not absolute," but depended on multiple facets of a woman's body (2005, p. 395). Thus, it was possible for those who more closely approximated conventions of idealized and normal-ized bodies to view themselves as feminine *and* as disabled or different. Since visibly disabled women are often disqualified from many of the cultural scripts associated with femininity, playfully trying on gender became a way for a few responders, including Elizabeth, to refuse sex-ist ableist assumptions. Once they realized that they could not place themselves within the narrow range of available images of femininity or adult femaleness, some women with visible disabilities became wor-ried about where they would fit in.

> Joanne: I saw myself as someone with a disability – my gender was not something that I considered and was not highlighted in my growing up. I had a disability but my identity as a female – girl, adolescent, even now is pretty much non-existent or doesn't exist very much. This happened be-cause we live in a society that doesn't accept difference. Despite my own efforts to be as normal as possible to fit in, I couldn't measure up.

> Elizabeth: I was really into clothes, even in grade 2. My auntie sewed me this pink jumpsuit. When I was 8, I got my ears pierced. It was never that I didn't want to look at myself – but I didn't spend hours examining my-self either. Whenever somebody wanted to give me presents, they always knew to give me clothes.

> Amélie: There was a constant struggle inside of me, like a lot of women. But not like a lot of women, I think I am the ideal. Then I am reminded I am not. It's a big issue because it was a major obsession in my fam-ily. My mother is so non-judgmental, and suddenly she'll say "You can never be too thin or too rich." You hear that as a child and you think "Oh God! I have a serious problem." Or "Does this exclude me? Where do I fit in?"

Ideals of femininity create dilemmas for women of African descent, who contend with the standards as they grapple with misconceptions about blackness. Stereotypic portrayals of Black women as sexually lascivious, domineering, and unwomanly have prevailed in Western culture for at least four hundred years (Cole & Zucker, 2007). These images emerged during the seventeenth century, when white Europeans justifed slavery, in part by depicting white women as models of civility and purity, and Black women as primitive and promiscuous, even predatory, Jezebels. The seductive Jezebel stereotype, deployed to rationalize sexual exploitation under slavery, has remained a staple way to portray Black women until now (Collins, 2004). Alongside this sexy siren is the bad Black mother. Her most recent incarnation can be seen in the acclaimed film *Precious* (2009), the story of a dark-skinned fat girl who is raped by her father and brutalized by her mother. The film powerfully explores one young woman's creative strategies for survival, but its arguably one-dimensional depiction of a poor mother who abuses her daughter may reinforce troubling tropes about Black mothering. One need not go to the movies for stories of poor Black women mistreating their children, which make media headlines regularly. According to legal scholar Dorothy Roberts, notions of Black women as insatiable breeders that served a slave-holding society made Black women threatening to whites after emancipation (1997). Over the twentieth century, white society stepped up efforts to regulate Black women's fertility by blaming mothers for problems in Black communities. Because women are supposed to maintain society's moral order, claims about dysfunction in African American families have largely been laid at the feet of mothers (Harris-Perry, 2009).

On the flip side of the sexy siren and bad Black mother is the selfless, de-sexualized mammy – the image of the obese, dark-skinned house servant that was manufactured during slavery to provide proof that Blacks were contented, even happy, as slaves (Pilgrim, 2000; Wallace-Sanders, 2008). Old stereotypes of oversexed breeders, abusive mothers, or asexual mammies have been supplanted in the last thirty years by new portrayals of Black women as ultra-moral, upwardly mobile superwomen. Patricia Hill Collins (2004) argues that echoes of the old mammy stereotype abound in the new slimmed-down superwoman, depicted as an asexual, devoted-to-her-job career woman who projects a super-moral image. Representations of powerful Black women in the public eye such as Oprah and Michelle Obama are examples of nonsexual superwomen (Ibanga, 2009; Kantor, 2009).

This ugly history of defeminizing, even demonizing, images of Black women in popular culture is the backdrop against which Black women's stories must be read. Situated within a tradition that pathologizes Black women's sexualities and mothering capacities, they shared how Black mothers taught them to navigate controlling stereotypes by projecting an ultra-moral image of respectability. While no one singular experience emerges, most Afro-Caribbean Canadian women (including Rebecca and Rhonda) learned to aspire to an ideal that stressed modesty, purity, and acting like a lady. Many white women received similar messages about being a good girl as part of learning to embody privileged femininity. However, those relayed to African Canadian women differed in intensity and intention. Sexuality theorist Evelyn Hammonds has shown that projecting a "super moral" image is one strategy Black women have used since slavery to resist being cast in hypersexual terms (1999, p. 97), a strategy which researchers suggest mothers may pass onto daughters through a process called "armouring" (Bell & Nkomo, 1998). All Black women in this study described how their mothers attempted to arm them against exploitative imagery of Black women and threats of sexual violation by instilling in them the importance of dressing like a lady, carrying themselves in a dignified manner, and controlling their sexuality. By stressing that they cover up and carry themselves conservatively, mothers defended, buffered, and fortified their daughters against risks and charges of abuse and immorality.

Rebecca: For most of my early childhood, I hated dresses. I always wanted to wear pants. My mom used to get mad at me. She was like, "You can't be wearing jeans because jeans make you have a tendency to sit with your legs apart. If you wear skirts, you can learn how to keep your knees and your ankles together." I didn't like wearing dresses but I was a different person on the weekends. Then I could wear my dresses and that was cool. So I think she subliminally fed me that lacey side of being a girl!

Rhonda: Spreading my legs was vulgar. "You are not sitting like a lady." You keep yourself covered. My mother would have me wearing undershirts until I was in my twenties. Skirts down to my ankles and my legs had to be covered up. You are not supposed to draw attention to yourself. Your body is supposed to be covered so none of this midriff business.

Stereotypes about sexual indecency and bad mothering have haunted Black women for generations. Mothers may have responded to demonizing images with moralizing messages to gain respect for their mothering skills and protect daughters against the ever-present threat of sexual victimization. Adopting ideals of respectable femininity helped daughters learn strategies for resisting sexual violation and racial oppression. Yet it also unfairly taught them to shoulder responsibility for escaping white society's hyper-sexualizing gaze. In a racist rape culture that normalizes sexual violence and assumes Black women are always willing and wanting to have sex, mothers may have felt that to shield daughters from such threats they had little choice but to encourage super-respectability. By teaching daughters to use conservative clothing and conduct, mothers and other-mothers unwittingly endorsed old-fashioned sexism as critical to self-protection. In racist, sexist society, Black women learn that being respectable and strong is necessary armour. But some commentators have questioned the costs of armouring for Black women's mental and physical health (Beauboeuf-Lafontant, 2005), sexual well-being (Townsend, 2008), and sense of connection and community (Reid-Brinkley, 2007). Storytellers in this study considered how the push for respectability to shield young women might get in the way of body confidence and sexual self-realization, and possibly hinder their ability to be vulnerable and connect with other women.

Ada: I hated being female. I wished to become a male and it wasn't because of trans issues but because males had more privilege. I grew up in a family where I was never allowed to wear pants, chew gum, or run around (they didn't want my legs getting scratched). I would have arguments about going over to a friend's house. I was seeing male cousins doing what they wanted and thinking, "If I were a boy, I'd be able to do that." My aunt would describe it as a safety issue: less harm would come to a boy. But the explanation didn't justify the restrictions on my life.

Maya: We didn't get my first pair of pants until I was 7. My mom didn't think it was proper. We couldn't wear tights, tops that were too tight. Back then it would have been helpful to have a role model other than my mom. I think it would have changed the way that I look at myself now, what I think, and how I see things. There were things I wished I could talk to her about, and not feel scared or feel I had to watch what I said. I wish I had someone I could be myself with. But she never came and I grew up.

Women of South Asian descent likewise wrestled with narrow norms of femininity even as they faced pervasive misconceptions about difference. Stereotypic views of South Asian women are commonplace in the Western world, especially in the aftermath of September 11th, 2001. From sensationalized news stories about dowry deaths, honour killings, and other gender violence, to frightening images of veiled figures, South Asian women are framed as passive victims of oppressive cultures and families. Images of South Asian women as passive victims have persuasive power. Yet feminists have shown that sexism in South Asian communities is fuelled as much by home-grown forms of patriarchy as by widespread racism in Western institutions. According to Yasmin Jiwani (2006) and Claire Dwyer (2000), systemic racism tends to trigger a defensive posture in South Asian immigrant populations that in turn reinforces sexism. Here racially marginalized immigrant men in white-dominated nations may give new life to old gender inequalities as a way to uplift their battered status and esteem. Most South Asian women in this study described how they had to contend with restrictive gender norms from their communities over and above the standards of femininity and stereotypes of difference they faced from the larger culture.

All South Asian interviewees described how their gender identities were shaped by familial expectations of "appropriate femininities" (Dwyer, 2000, p. 481). The version of femininity most highly valued was the "good Indian girl" – modest, pure, and committed to family and community. Family members heavily influenced women's adoption of this norm by monitoring their movements, activities, and clothing during childhood and, especially, adolescence. Migration researchers have highlighted how disaporic migrant communities, in the face of hostility from outsiders, often seek to maintain their cultural integrity by assigning women the role of guardian over cultural or ethnic values (Anthias & Yuval-Davis, 1992; Kurien, 1999). Women I interviewed acknowledged the gendered expectation that they should reproduce their parents' culture. Mothers and fathers in particular enjoined daughters to assume responsibility for passing on cultural values and practices by sending the message that they should, as Navpreet put it, "stay close to home." For daughters, staying close to home meant staying close to cultural conventions of appropriate femininities. Many women explained how such femininity, by stressing purity and modesty, downplayed physical beauty. However, with the global spread of beauty culture and better access to Bollywood, Sheila suggests that South Asian ideals of fair skin, flowing hair, and curvy bodies have become standards with which many girls in the diaspora now contend.

Navpreet: I was encouraged to play close to home or inside. If I played with the neighbourhood kids, they became indoor games. I didn't play a lot of sports. Instead you were encouraged to stay close to home and help your mom. When I got older I used to hear from my parents, "You can't be out running around with everybody else. Don't be running around."

Sheila: The ideal is for Indian women to be fair. I always thought my mom was beautiful but I wished I was as fair as her. My sister is stunning. Although they had Indian features – dark eyes, dark thick hair – they were light enough to pass. If you look at Indian movies, that's what the ideal is. The women look white – they have light eyes, they have light hair that's dyed, they are fair. If you ever read *India Abroad* magazine, the first word they use to describe a woman in the marital prospects section is "fair."

Storytellers described the ways in which family members and the wider community subjected their clothing choices and leisure activities to increased scrutiny as they approached adolescence. Such vigilance was primarily concerned with ensuring girls' sexual purity and reputation. Some noted how parents associated sexy clothing with Western girls' imagined rebelliousness and active sexuality, which posed a threat to South Asian femininity. Yet participants did not solely model themselves after mothers and other adult South Asian women. As women of colour growing up in white society, their embodiment of gender was complicated by racism. Not only did the gender expressions modelled at home (the good Indian girl/woman) often conflict with dominant ones (the sexually attractive Western woman, as Handa [2003] also found), but mainstream versions were more highly valued. Like Anjula, many learned to navigate conflicting dominant and diasporic femininities by switching between them, emulating their mothers' embodiment of gender in South Asian contexts but not in white-dominated ones outside the home. As they got older, they adopted a Westernized version of privileged femininity in mainstream contexts and an Indian version of appropriate femininity in community ones. Some secretly altered their looks and learned to lie to parents as a way of confirming their place in both worlds. Others, such as Preeta, avoided this predicament by adopting the version of femininity her parents and wider community approved of.

Anjula: I thought my mom was beautiful. But at the same time I was embarrassed to take her to school. It was because she had an accent and also she didn't dress as hip, she wore shirts with flowers on them. But when my mom wore Indian clothes, she looked beautiful. I was so happy when we went to India; I thought my mom was the most beautiful woman.

Preeta: I am very Indian; I didn't have a problem when someone asked me what I am. But when my sister was young she would tell people, "I am half Italian or half Iranian," so that she would be a little more exotic, more acceptable. I have cousins who changed their names: their name would be Sharyo but they would call themselves Westernized names like Sharon to fit in. I escaped the pressure because I have always been close to home and my mom. I'd keep a lot inside so I wasn't very influenced.

Many women spoke of emulating mothers and like others who gave them their first glimpse of womanhood. Although they described pleasurable ways they experimented with gender, their stories complicate portrayals of the trying-on process by bringing into relief the unfunny, frustrating, serious side of gender play – the cultural demand that girls fit norms and standards, and the difficulties this brings. Femininity was fraught for those with ethnic, racial, or physical differences who grappled with social expectations of feminine and female bodies. Most storytellers could put aside the conventions when these became inconvenient or uncomfortable; many also expressed unease with gendered meanings imposed on visible differences, which could not always be ignored or transcended, even in play. As they tried on femininity for size, all learned to don narrow norms and glimpsed the consequences of idealized versions for their future selves.

In the Gaze of the Father: Temporary Tomboys and Imagined Ideals

The majority of women looked to mothers as models for imagining their adult selves, and in their observations caught a first glimpse of womanhood. Many also found ways to resist, blend, or cross gender roles and norms by identifying with fathers. In Western societies, girls who act in conventionally masculine ways are assigned the in-between status of tomboy, an identity that participants often experienced as a form of resistance to pressures to become a feminine girl. Many tell how a father's encouragement of their tomboy ways offered them a temporary visa into traditionally masculine worlds, and with this, access to the pleasures of boy-coded interests and play. Yet, while some embraced the label as a badge of pride, tomboy also became a consolation identity for others who failed at femininity. Despite cultural permission to be tomboys for a while, a majority came to concede to the "correct" gender as they approached adolescence when they faced increased pressures to be seen as heterosexual and female. Daughters frequently relied on fathers for temporary tomboy status, but they also watched fathers look at mothers and other women. Observing their fathers gaze at women, they imagined embodying their fathers' version of the ideal. Whether as temporary tomboys or imagined ideals, women found prescribed answers to the question *Who am I in this body and this world?* in the gender dichotomy that adults handed them, which cloaked shades of their genders under the stereotypic mantles of boy or girl.

In the North American context, the term *tomboy* refers to girls who assume the dress, manner, and activities of boys. Tomboys have been evident in fiction since the nineteenth century, but because gender norms have varied so widely, specific meanings of tomboy have differed across time and social groups (Carr, 2005). Is a tomboy a girl who rejects a feminine appearance? Someone who combines girl-coded interests with tomboy activities? How about the girl who prefers to look and act exclusively like a boy? There are few studies of how girls themselves have understood and applied the label in different times and places. Instead, much psychological and psychiatric research has framed gender variance as a disorder and focused on finding links between boyish behaviours and becoming lesbian or trans later in life (American Psychiatric Association, 2000; Hyde, Rosenberg, & Behrman, 1977). In addition to its tendency to pathologize nonconformity, this literature problematically assumes that gender predicts sexuality (if you are butch or tomboyish you must be a lesbian), even though many girls who identify as tomboys grow up to be neither lesbian nor trans (Carr, 2005). Feminist research has found that, despite attempts to pathologize gender crossing, there are good reasons for the persistence of tomboyism.

Becoming tomboys may enable girls to reject stereotypic femininity in a bid for greater social power (Reay, 2001); participate in boy-categorized activities such as science or sports (Carr, 2005; Paechter & Clark, 2007); escape from sexual harassment and innuendos that sexualize friendships between girls and boys (Renold, 2006); and express a boy or butch identity that otherwise would be stigmatized and unnamable (Halberstam, 1998). In the 1990s, Barrie Thorne (1993) speculated that due to increased acceptance of women in sport, society was witnessing the demise of the tomboy. However, recent research demonstrates that tomboys are far from extinct (Renold, 2008). Girls today use the label but adopt a more fluid idea of gender by moving between "girly" and tomboy identities, describing themselves as "sometimes" and "sort of" rather than total tomboys (Paechter & Clark, 2007).

For women of the generation I interviewed, it was frequently (though not always) a badge of honour to say they were tomboys. This was reflected in the girl movies, TV shows, and books of the time that had tomboy heroines. According to gender scholar Judith Halberstam (1998), the heyday of the tomboy film in the 1970s and 1980s featured tough girl actors such as Jodie Foster and Tatum O'Neal. Tomboy images flourished in a feminist climate where parents believed that the most effective way to challenge gender stereotyping was to bring up children differently (this was the period of *Free to Be ... You and Me*). At the same time, backlash against an increasingly visible gay rights movement brought to public consciousness backward psychological theories that saw tomboyness as the worrisome symptom of a potentially queer adult. Halberstam suggests that as a result of the explicit link made between lesbianism and tomboyism, tomboy films "faded from view" (1998, p. 188). As depictions of spunky, tomboy girl figures declined, films featuring explicitly lesbian adult characters and strong-willed straight female protagonists increased (such as *GI Jane* and Sigourney Weaver in the *Alien* movies). According to Halberstam, female audiences have responded to these new gender-variant characters because they challenge gender norms, expand possibilities for gendered embodiment, and break down discrimination that nonconforming women confront.

Representations of risk-taking female protagonists can be found in contemporary children's cartoons such as *Dora the Explorer* (2000–). The popular preschooler's show about a gutsy seven-year-old girl may offer girls today a new role model not concerned about frills and fashion; rather, Dora likes travel, problem solving, and adventure. But even that intrepid adventurer appears to be succumbing to the pressures of femininity: recently, TV network Nickelodeon and toymaker Mattel announced that Dora would grow up and undergo a fashion makeover, so instead of being equipped with tools, map, and backpack, her new accessories would include halter-tops, mini-skirts, and glittery hairbrushes (Castro & Behrendt, 2009). While Dora's success shows that physicality, curiosity, and bravery are no longer the domain of boys, her makeover indicates that femininity, because it encourages girls' orientation towards image to sell products, is big business. So while girls have room to be tomboys, they may face compounding pressure to be girly as evidenced by the avalanche of pink products marketed to them. Dora's transformation raises questions about the contradictory position of tomboys in our culture: Under what conditions is it OK to be one? When, how, and why do girls face pressure to give up their boyish looks and ways?

A majority of participants described how they experimented with a range of gendered attributes and activities. Over time, all learned to polarize these into opposing categories of male or female. Culture offered narrow classifications that reduced the diverse possibilities of their gendered being to a two-gender, two-tier system. Many, like Aurora, conveyed how they straddled norms for boy and girl bodies and worlds, but other people classifying their appearances and capacities into opposing sides obscured their gender's fluidity and ambiguity. The in-between status of tomboy enabled many women to express attributes and interests that the feminine identity didn't allow, such as athleticism, competitiveness, curiosity, and strength. But girls' designation as tomboy meant such activities now belonged to the boys' domain. According to gender scholar Michael Kimmel (2004), because masculinity is more highly valued in our society, people perceive sissy boys as failed compared to tomboys, who at least can claim some of the positive qualities associated with masculinity. While this was undeniably true for women in my study, it misses how girls, too, can be perceived as failed at gendering themselves, and how tomboy, in this context, is not a positive or empowering label. Rather than being an admired identity, tomboy became the default category for some (including Sharon) who failed to fit the conventions of feminine girl. Powerful others used the tomboy descriptor as a way of putting down (while pretending not to) girls perceived as deficient at femininity, often due to their size, colour, or disability. As Sharon's story suggests, when adults imposed a *lesser than* identity, some became the gender that others imagined them to be.

Aurora: I saw myself as a girl but I was considered a tomboy. I used to go around doing cartwheels and things that girls were not supposed to do. My mother and her friends would make comments. My father wanted to get me into gymnastics. I was a tomboy but not an extreme tomboy; I tried to keep my feminine side. I also wore the dresses.

Sharon: My mom used to refer to my sister as Pebbles and me as Bam Bam. I felt bad, "I'm not as good as my sister." My father accepted us the way we were but my mother was constantly trying to change us. She would tell me, "Go put on the dress," and I would put on pants. I remember being very resentful when my brother was born because he got the fun toys, the baggy clothing. I didn't look like a girly girl so what's the point of wearing dresses and trying to be girlish? I may as well be what I am or what they say that I am. I guess that's what I did.

Why is it that tomboys are considered cute, and grown-up butch and masculine women often feared and disliked? Most storytellers found support for resisting, blurring, and crossing gender norms in the relationships and spaces of childhood, but their cross-gender identifications were perceived by adults as temporary and partial. They encountered increased pressure to relinquish boy-coded activities as they got older to avoid renouncing femaleness and heterosexuality. All the women who received permission from fathers to cross gender boundaries described the pain and confusion they felt when such support was withdrawn. They told how, at puberty, mothers' prodding about being more feminine and fathers' emotional abandonment pushed them to forgo their tomboy ways. Despite adults' warnings and emotional retreat, several women persisted in tomboyism into adolescence to pursue athleticism or to resist mounting pressures to fit conventions of femininity and heterosexuality.

Yvonna: I was greatly influenced by my father. Thankfully mom and dad didn't have a boy. I say that because my father's European: the boys do this and the girls do that. We always did things together until I turned 13. Then suddenly dad went, "Wait a minute, you're turning into a young woman, you're not supposed to do this." That was confusing for me. I used to hang out with my father but when my body started to change he got nervous and backed off a bit. It was like being abandoned in a sense.

Melissa: My dad didn't have boys in the family so I was my dad's boy. I had the BB gun, did the fishing, played baseball, and built tree houses. This became an issue with my mother when I started to develop. "You should be more feminine, you should wear more dresses."

Daughters also watched fathers look at mothers and other women. By observing their fathers' gaze, they formed ideas about which bodies were considered desirable. For some, like Tara, identifying with mothers as the object of their father's desire gave them an internalized standard against which they evaluated the mirror's image. When they assimilated, from observing fathers, the idea that a woman's greatest assets were her beauty and desirability, they carried this belief into future interactions with young men. Others who witnessed their fathers' evaluative gaze learned just how narrow conventions of acceptable female bodies could be.

Tara: My mother is a tiny woman. I always wanted to be that because my father talked about my mother. That's where it started for me, when I started listening to him. I wanted to be a petite girl because in my head that was the acceptable image. That's what I aspired to be as I got older.

Hannah: The only person who harassed me about my body was my father, who discovered when I was seven that I needed glasses. His main thing was: whose genes were responsible for this blight? My mother and her whole family wear glasses, proof that she came from this faulty gene pool. When I had to wear glasses, I thought, "Boys don't make passes at girls who wear glasses." But I wasn't distressed by it. Then his reaction bewildered me. I had to consider that he could be right. "Maybe I am a loser or something is wrong with me." I remember feeling needy. I had to beg him to let me wear glasses, because couldn't he understand that I couldn't see?

Participants who looked for expanded possibilities for embodying gender told how fathers' support allowed them to cross the gender divide to live temporarily as tomboys. Gender, for interviewees, was neither freely chosen nor forcefully imposed but part of each woman's active process of bodily self-creation within unequal social relations. The women's narratives raise important questions about the role of men in reproducing or resisting gender binaries and body ideals. What responsibilities do fathers and men generally have in challenging scripts of conventional masculinity and femininity? How can they assist and support daughters, sons, partners, and women generally in transgressing and transcending gender and body norms, and stereotypes of difference?

Chapter Three

Invisible in Full View

There are many misconceptions about and few positive portrayals of women and men living with physical differences and disabilities. From the disabled victim or disfigured villain in popular films to stark photographs in medical textbooks, what exists outside the norm is often seen as lacking in value (Walters & Griffis, n.d.). In Canada, an estimated 14.3 per cent of people live with a disability, including 3.4 per cent of children and 17 per cent of adult women (Bélair & Statistics Canada, 2007). Despite growing dialogue about diversity, public discourse still centres on disability as something to be shunned or overcome. Although women and men confront similar confining stereotypes, there are social expectations of appearance and abilities that are specific to gender. Even as they contend with discrimination faced by women generally and by men with disabilities, women living with disabilities are subjected to the stigma of a body seen as "less than whole," "not quite human," and "other than female" (Garland-Thomson, 1997; Goffman, 1963).[1]

Myths and Models of Disability

In a culture where women are identified socially with their bodies, ideal and abject images shape looking relations and women's own self-perceptions. While those in proximity to the ideal may become the object

---

1 I am grateful to Lorna Renooy, Fran Odette, Hilde Zitzelsberger, Eliza Chandler, Kirsty Liddiard, Ani Aubin, Wendy Porch, Lindsay Fisher, Jes Sachse, and Esther Ignagni, collaborators on *Building Bridges across Disability and Difference*, *Envisioning New Meanings of Disability and Difference*, and *Project Re•Vision*, whose understanding and insights provided the theoretical foundation for this chapter.

of the gaze, women who inhabit abject bodies, according to disability theorist Rosemarie Garland-Thomson, are subjected to "the stare" (2009). Staring, for Garland-Thomson, involves our urgent compulsion to look at disaster called the "car wreck" phenomenon (p. 3); the double take we do when ordinary looks fail and we want to know more about something different; and the intense visual exchange people engage in when we can't pull our eyes away from the unfamiliar, unexpected, the strange. Because people both crave and dread the unusual and un-known, consumer culture continuously feeds our hunger for novelty even as it enforces certain notions of "normal." And since staring often defines the relationship between disabled and non-disabled people, it is a primary site through which those who embody difference face the curiosity, fear, and hostility of non-disabled others (Tregaskis, 2002).

Representations of disability, by shaping people's taken-for-granted understandings and expectations, also inform how non-disabled folks perceive and treat those who embody difference (Garland-Thomson, 2007). The representational history of disabled people can largely be characterized as one of being either put on display or hidden away. According to disability scholar Eliza Chandler (personal communication, 3 November 2012), people living with disabilities have been, and continue to be, displayed in freak shows, medical journals, and charity campaigns, and as evil or pitiable figures in novels and films. At the same time, disabled bodies have been hidden in institutions, hospitals, group homes, and generally removed from the public eye. Even today, disability continues to be interpreted in our medicalized culture as the polar opposite of health and is thought of in terms of deficiency, limi-tation, or flaw (Metzl & Poirier, 2004). Solutions to the "problem" of disability can take a number of forms, and in our technologized world, tend to entail elimination or cure. People with disabilities sometimes seek out cures and are relieved to find them, but many impairments (like Cerebral Palsy and Down's Syndrome) aren't curable, so to ori-ent to disability as always something that needs to be cured discounts the human experience of *living with* disability (Chandler & Rice, 2013). Efforts to eliminate disability through genetic screening or prenatal testing (which often result in aborting disabled fetuses) also ignore the reality that most people acquire disability, not genetically, but through living in the world. Most of us, if we live long enough, will undergo the gradually disabling process of aging, so disability should not be seen as exclusive to a small number of people but, rather, as a central part of the human condition (Garland-Thomson, 1997).

Most often, the mainstream media frames those living with disabilities within the narrow confines of two common stereotypes: the tragic, pitied victim or the spirited survivor held up as a source of inspiration. Popular films illustrate the power of these representations. In *Million Dollar Baby* (2004), a fit female boxer who becomes disabled asks her coach to end her life, as the final gift he can offer. While the film can be read as a narrative of female empowerment, it also "plays out killing as a romantic fantasy and gives emotional life to the 'better dead than disabled' mindset" (Drake, 2005, para. 35) that offers death as the radical solution to life with a disability. Depictions of disabled people as victims frequently affirm the heroism of others who come to the rescue. A recent illustration is the Oscar-winning short *Saving Face* (2011), which chronicles the work of a plastic surgeon who helps survivors of violence involving assaults with acid.

Where characters are not pitiful victims awaiting rescue, they're placed on a pedestal as spirited survivors who triumph over limitation against all odds. This "overcoming" narrative is common in disability sports. It also appears in films such as *Penelope* (2006), where a young woman who suffers the "curse" of disfigurement conceals her facial difference as a way of finding her true self. Such storylines assume that people must overcome disability to succeed and that disability is the antithesis of achievement (Chandler & Rice, 2013). Larger-than-life portrayals also give audiences little space to make sense of the nuances and contradictions of disability experience. By disallowing vulnerability, frustration, and fear, the spirited-survivor story does not grant women (or men) permission to express a full range of emotions (Rice, Renooy, & Odette, 2008). While victim and heroine portrayals are common, real-life disabled women and men are not all represented in the same way. For example, racialized and poor people with disabilities, especially those with mental health issues, are often assumed to be lazy, angry, criminal, and drug/alcohol addicted. Consider the treatment of Kimberly Rogers, a mentally disabled college student and mother-to-be who, in 2001, died by suicide in her Ontario apartment while under house arrest for welfare fraud. The depressed young woman was pushed into suicide by moralistic public opinion and punitive social policies that treated her as a criminal simply for collecting student loans while on welfare.

In a society that equates standardized concepts of attractiveness with success and anomaly with deficiency, it would seem that women with disabilities and differences are destined to lead substandard lives. This is far from true, but misconceptions persist. For instance, charities have been criticized in recent years for framing disabilities to make people look like they have no capacity to think or care for themselves and for promoting the idea that they are entirely dependent on other people's goodwill. The charity view may not tell the whole truth, but it tells a particular story for a reason – appealing to viewers' faith in medicine to raise money. While medical interventions do sustain and improve quality of life, the mistaken belief that medicine can fix any condition makes interactions challenging for people who look and function differently (e.g., strangers approach disabled people with well-intentioned advice about a new technique they saw on TV) (Keith, 1996). It also places pressure on physicians to find a cure when none exists. Seeing disability as a medical problem ignores the reality that many disabled people are in good health, and justifies the selective abortion of fetuses with genetic conditions, the murder of children with disabilities, and the idea that "fixing" so-called flaws will "fix" a person's life. Of course, people living with disabilities do, at times, experience pain, shame, and frustration and may, at times, seek out cures for what ails them, just like everyone else. Yet given the misrepresentations of disability in which we are drenched, disability scholars relocate the problem of disability from within the individual to place it squarely in the social realm.

Although there are many ways of looking at disability, in Westernized societies, the individual medical model dominates. Disability, in medical terms, includes mobility disabilities (spina bifida and spinal cord injury), sensory disabilities (blindness or deafness), chronic illness (multiple sclerosis and cancer), intellectual and mental disabilities (mental illness, learning disabilities), facial and physical differences (birthmarks and craniofacial conditions), and any variance from the "normal" body and mind. In an individual model, disability is viewed as the result of an individual's physical condition, which is considered abnormal and pathological. Conditions considered disabling are described using clinical descriptions and medical terminology and often are attributed to genetics, failure of the body, and injury, accident, or bad behaviour. Disabilities are viewed as reducing an individual's quality of life and as causing clear disadvantages. As a result, responses revolve around identifying and understanding disability, and learning to control and alter its course. Since becoming entrenched in the twentieth century, the individual medical model has remained the dominant perspective in health, rehabilitative, and educational institutions throughout North America (Kudlick, 2005).

People are so accustomed to seeing disability as situated within the person, as a problem of their body that medicine will fix, that it can be difficult to see through another lens. For example, the social model rejects this individual understanding and instead relocates disability in society. By situating disability in the social it distinguishes between "impairment" (bodily difference such as paralysis, blindness, etc.) and "disability" (disablement by and in the social world). As the Union of Persons with Impairments Against Segregation, a formative disability rights activist group in the United Kingdom, explains: "In our view, it is society which disables physically impaired people. Disability is something imposed on top of our impairments, by the way that we are unnecessarily isolated and excluded from full participation in society. Disabled people are therefore an oppressed group in our society" (UPIAS, 1976, p. 14). The model proposes that prejudice and exclusion are the ultimate factors defining who is disabled and who is not (Allan, 2010; Titchkosky, 2001, 2007). In this view, barriers in unadapted environments produce disability (people who use wheelchairs are disabled not by their bodies but by built environments, which favour stairs over ramps). Emerging in the 1970s in Europe and North America from activist efforts, the model sees disability as both a form of oppression (Oliver, 1990) and a social and cultural identity (Clare, 2009). The brilliance of the social model is found in its radical shifting of the meaning of disability from the bodies of individuals to a product of the social world and its enabling of disabled people to claim a proud cultural identity, rather than one based on shame (Chandler & Rice, 2013). To quote British disabled artist Liz Crow, the social model has "enabled a vision of ourselves free from the contraints of disability [oppression] and provided a commitment for our social change.... I don't think it's a exaggeration to say that the social model has saved lives" (1996, p. 206).

Although brilliant in its simplicity, the social model has been heavily critiqued for the ways it elides complex global relations and intimate embodied experiences of disability. For example, Helen Meekosha (2011) has challenged social-model advocates to consider how global power relations, through sanctioning dangerous working conditions, unhealthy environments, and war, disable millions worldwide. The feminist transnational approach she proposes sheds light on conditions wrought by colonialism and capitalism that cause impairment and privilege certain bodies over others, thereby causing disability discrimination. Meekosha's analysis focuses on how the oppression of disabled bodies (high unemployment, being seen as childlike and expendable) intersects with oppressions that impair bodies (unregulated global capitalism, colonial histories that have rendered some groups more vulnerable to impairment) to produce disability as a problem. For other feminist disability scholars (Garland-Thomson, 1997; Linton, 2006; Thomas, 1999; Snyder & Mitchell, 2001; Wendell, 1996, 2008), the social model focuses on oppressive social structures in ways that ignore culture and language, and embodied disability experience. From a feminist poststructuralist perspective, for example, the meaning of disability is slippery, multiple, and temporary – in other words, it can't be fixed. Many bodily differences (such as albinism or a port wine stain) are disabling as a result of prejudice and the naming of disability itself varies depending on the context (deaf people are not disabled where everyone signs). Because the meanings of body variations shift across time and place, it is difficult, if not impossible, to set clear boundaries between what counts as disabled and non-disabled (Shildrick, 2007).

From an embodiment perspective, the social model fails to recognize people's intimate experiences of pain and pleasure, limitation and capacity, and the meanings that disability might hold for them (Lutz & Bowers, 2005; Valeras, 2010). Focusing on disabling barriers sheds light on the social roots of disablement, but by removing the body from definitions of disability, the social model leads to a denial of human fragility and vulnerability. Eli Clare argues that "there are disability thinkers who can talk all day about the body as metaphor and symbol but never mention flesh and blood, bone and tendon – never even acknowledge their own bodies" (2001, p. 364). According to Christine Battersby (1998), embodiment theory is useful to understand disability experience, but it requires a disability and gender studies lens to avoid assuming all human beings inhabit their bodies in a similar way – as bounded entities and containers for selves. The containment model is inadequate since it centres on the strong, able-bodied, self-enclosed, masculine embodiment while marginalizing embodiments viewed as unpredictable and unbounded (such as pregnancy or disability). Over the past twenty years, feminist authors within disability studies have challenged these types of omissions, often through writing openly about their own embodiments, intersectional identities, and lived experiences of impairment. A feminist disability studies approach has contributed to understanding how "the body, bodily variety and normalization" are central to all types of oppression and how "reimagining the body and embodiment" is critical for equity and inclusion (K. Hall, 2011, pp. 6–7).

Body becoming and embodiment theories offer rich correctives to medical and social models. Through these lenses, the becoming of bodily selves is seen as open-ended and unpredictable, as shaped by people's psyches and biologies intersecting with their social, relational, and material worlds. Neither a purely biological nor a purely social matter, disabilities are understood as dynamic conditions that, like other categories of difference, emerge from the interplay of participants' embodied selves with the multiple environments in which they are embedded. Situating women's narratives in the context of medical stories highlights their "counter-stories" of embodied self-becoming. Telling stories about and from the disabled body allows storytellers to articulate previously excluded experiences and to author identities in self-determined ways. Participants' childhood accounts underscore how medically oriented systems powerfully coutoured their bodily self-becoming. In systems, women became "invisible in full view" when their bodies became the focus and their personhood – their feelings, intentions, and aspirations – remained overlooked and unseen. By showing how multiple interacting forces, including our ideas about disability, play a part in influencing what participants' bodies could be, their stories suggest that revisioning disability may be critical to open up possibilities for what disabled bodies can become.

Mistreatment in Medical Systems

Women with differences and disabilities describe how they were marginalized by negative messages about the disabled body interwoven throughout cultural and clinical imagery and interactions. Most had a high level of contact with medical services from early childhood through multiple hospital admissions and operations, consultations with specialists, and outpatient and rehabilitation appointments. In medically oriented systems, all encountered pejorative assessments, painful treatments, and reduced expectations for their bodies and lives. Their early life trajectories coincided with the rise of medicine's cultural authority to define normalcy and difference, and the peak of public confidence in professionals' abilities to fix disabilities (Conrad & Schneider, 1992; Frank, 2000). These systems, steeped as they were in the medical view of disability as a problem to be fixed or overcome, lacked any positive language for difference. Instead, invalidating messages were integrated into providers' education, practice, and institutions, which framed and legitimized the routine treatment and life expectations of those with differences (Rice, Zitzelsberger, et al., 2005a; Rice, Renooy, Zitzlesberger, Aubin, & Odette, 2003; Zitzelsberger, Rice, Whittington-Walsh, Odette, & Aubin, 2002). Whether they grew up in a big city or small town, during the 1960s or 1970s, women described having little or no contact with disabled adults, disability advocacy organizations, or alternative frameworks within which to view disability, and, thus, no affirming lenses through which to view difference. The deficit model of disability hindered their own and their family's capacities to take a stand against the "lesser than" treatment.

Like non-disabled women, all recall becoming conscious of their bodies through a rich tapestry of sensory experiences, especially kin-esthetically, as they actively explored the world. Early childhood was a protected time when "everything was possible." Yet many describe "hitting a brick wall" once they became aware of non-disabled adults' lowered expectations for them. Without a fuller range of possibilities for their lives, other people's more authoritative ideas overshadowed women's surfacing aptitudes and interests, to limit who they imagined they could become. In this way, Frances, despite her own emerging aspirations, became what others believed she would be. And Fatima told how, in a culture that equates disability with dependency and requires women to assume primary responsibility for caring work, becoming a mother or a partner was considered impossible.

Frances: I've always been fascinated by figure skating. My mother and I were watching it when I said, "That's what I'm going to do when I grow up." For a lot of kids with disabilities, there is a protected time in childhood when everything is possible. Then there's a point where you come to a screeching halt. I began to understand I wasn't going to do things like everybody else when people started to superimpose their notions about what I was capable of doing. A couple of years later when I was undergoing vocation assessments my mother said, "It would be good for you to be a secretary." I had decided I was going to university. Guess what I got to be? A secretary. I didn't go to university.

Fatima: From about age six, there was a lot of emphasis on me becoming a nun. Other people viewed it as a way of shutting me away. But my parents didn't view it that way; they viewed it as a goal for me. They believed that I could get an education but they didn't think I could get a job. No sexuality. Whether they were shutting it out or were hoping it would never come up, I don't know. But becoming a nun was a big thing.

As a result of interactions within health-care institutions, each internalized the view that their bodies were broken and needed to be fixed. Medical personnel and places, rather than being supportive or restorative, were often oppressive. While the repeated assessments, painful treatments, rigorous rehabilitation, and invasive interventions may have been necessary, helpful, and valuable for some women in some situations, few women or the adults around them questioned their costs or weighed their harms and benefits. Joanne experienced intensive surgery and rehabilitation due to being born with a bone condition affecting her mobility. She describes how our culture's ability norm – the upright, bipedal (two-footed), walking being – was a difficult and, in the end, impossible standard to attain. The medical drive to define the upright two-footed posture as normal, and to reject other forms of movement as infantile or animalistic, is embedded deep in the Western psyche. In part, this may be due to influential theories of evolution that distinguish the human from the non-human through the unique capacity that (most) people have to walk upright. The ability to walk on two feet may be treated as a defining aspect of being human because it's considered a distinguishing feature separating infants from children. As such, walking may be associated with achieving a certain status as a person. Whatever the impetus for the evolutionary shift from quadrupedalism (mobility using four limbs) to bipedalism, there is no reason why we couldn't imagine wheelchair mobility and other forms of movement as equally human.

> Joanne: Because of my disability my bones would break easily. So I used to scoot around lying down, propelling myself along with my legs. Also my bones would break a lot because I was bound and determined to walk. Then I had major surgery to put rods in my legs and I was outfitted with braces so I could walk. I lasted six months. I said, "This is ridiculous. It takes me an hour to walk down the hall. This walking is not worth it."

Until the mid- to late twentieth century Western governments warehoused most disabled people in institutions. A eugenic drive to control and eradicate disability propelled the forced confinement, sterilization, and abuse of institutionalized people (Snyder & Mitchell, 2006). Participants in this study grew up at the tail end of institutionalization after efforts to de-institutionalize and integrate disabled children into communities were under way. All lived at home with their families. With de-institutionalization still in process, older responders with mobility and sensory disabilities received education and rehabilitation in hospital clinics and at segregated schools designated for disabled children. Younger disabled storytellers and those with physical differences were often integrated into regular schools. In either case, the boundaries between treatment and education blurred and overlapped, and both groups faced discrimination in institutions. Whether in the hospital or at school, they describe rehabilitative environments as highly medicalized spaces where physiotherapy and physical training were integrated into their early and ongoing education and therapy. Physical training to achieve certain standards in movement was treated as more important than other possibilities for learning and growth. For those with mobility issues, the diagnostic, treatment, and rehabilitative regimes of medicine taught them that they should strive toward ablest norms in mobility.

Gina: I remember going to therapy classes [at school] and swimming in a really hot therapy pool with this steel chaise lounge in it. Having them focus more on our physical bodies rather than what we were inside. You have to strive to be normal and be as mobile and the ultimate was to get up and walk. If you didn't walk, then it was a hierarchy of disability. They made you feel like you were less than … They really emphasized the physical as opposed to the other part of your development.

Like those with mobility disabilities, women with facial or physical differences internalized the view that their bodies needed to be fixed. Amélie rationalized the considerable pain she endured through adopting the imperative for an acceptable appearance. In the absence of alternative frameworks for understanding facial difference, her parents, in listening to the experts, agreed to aggressive and experimental treatments for their daughter. Amélie had no access to imagery of people with unusual appearances and skin conditions (such as port wine stains and albinism) depicting the pains and joys of their daily lives. No one told her about the potential gains of being different or how living with a disability could equip her with knowledge not shared by those without disabilities. As a result, she, too, came to believe her face required medical remedy and to see pain as a necessary condition of being well.

Amélie: It all starts with my face being touched and pushed by medical people. That was a big issue when I was a child: people not talking to me and not feeling like I had any control over decision-making. Then learning at age three that something was wrong that needed to be changed. I was put in the room with another boy whose whole body was burnt and a little baby whose fingers were stuck together. It was clear to me that they were there because their bodies looked different and that something needed to be done to make them look like everybody else. I suffered a lot of pain because my whole face was tattooed [birthmark removed]. Behind my ear I was burned with an iron. This was all experimental. They put me in a straightjacket because my face was bloody and scabbing. I must have had to justify going through that because I thought I needed to be fixed.

Today, there remain few representations of children with disabilities that do not assume a deficiency model (Leininger, Dyches, Prater, & Heath, 2010). The media continue to exclude disabled children (Goodley & Runswick-Cole, 2011) and even award-winning children's books, to stereotype disabilities (Hughes, 2012). Since the 1990s, a vibrant disability arts movement has emerged in Europe and North America as a new genre that gives expression to disability experience and challenges exclusions in disabling society. By harnessing the power of the arts, artists reject imposed invisibility to re-imagine bodily difference (Allan, 2005; Cameron, 2007; Roman, 2009a, 2009b). Painter Riva Lehrer, for example, creates portraits of prominent disabled people in an effort to transform non-disabled people's perceptions (http://www.rivalehrer.com/). Writers such as Eli Clare (2009) also give voice to disability experience in ways that speak back to misconceptions and create community. These perspectives have crossed into the mainstream through websites such as BBC's *Ouch!*, a blog that reflects disability culture (http://www.bbc.co.uk/blogs/ouch/). Despite these exciting developments, however, disabled children remain invisible or stereotypically visible in image culture.

Invisible in Full View

Women with disabilities in this study were not just rendered invisible in medicalized settings, they were often dehumanized too, "viewed only from the prism of their disability or impairment" (Pinto, 2008, p. 123). Almost all those born with a difference described institutional interventions marked by a lack of privacy and respect, where difference or disability was the sole focus and other aspects of their identities and care were not recognized (Zitzelsberger et al., 2002). Participants reported how their bodies were looked at, touched, and photographed without warning, permission, or meaningful consent, and handled roughly in routine contact with health-care providers (Rice, Zitzelberger, et al., 2005a/b). In medical encounters, the women often found themselves stripped of privacy and dignity, which denied their inner reality and reduced their embodied being to a body with a condition.

All participants experienced "the medical gaze," the invasive scrutiny of medical and health-care practitioners, such as when they had to appear undressed in front of a group of professionals who examined them as if they were, according to Fatima, "a medical study." Doctors gave Fatima's parents little indication that clinical routines would lead to any beneficial outcomes for her. Through such practices, she and others came to be seen as case examples of biological conditions to be compared with other cases rather than as individuals with their own emergent embodied identities.

> Fatima: A lot of pain has come from the way my body was up for grabs. Being eight years old walking in my underwear in front of what seemed to be fifty doctors. I picked up that my Dad was very uncomfortable with the situation but that he would be a bad father if he left. I don't understand why it was a regular occurrence or why I was made to walk in my underwear. I don't understand why they did it when I have a disability that cannot be cured. Mostly, those situations didn't lead to things that would assist me. It was done as a medical study. I lost a lot of my self in that.

Many social commentators, beginning with the French philosopher Michel Foucault (1994), have shown how power in modern societies is often exercised through vision, visibility, and the gaze. According to Foucault (1979), in pre-modern Western societies, power was understood as a mechanism used by few individuals. It was exercised from the top down, often by a king, and it was mostly negative in function – it oppressed, prohibited, and coerced. (Those who have studied European history or watched movies or shows about European aristocracies like *The Tudors* (2007–10) or *The Borgias* (2011) will know what Foucault is talking about. Elites often exercised their power using public torture and executions – both highly visible modes of punishment intended to terrorize populations into submission.) In the past three hundred years, traditional power has gradually been replaced or supplemented by modern techniques of power. The human sciences, helping professions, and the institutions through which these operate (hospitals and schools) have played a key role in these techniques. Foucault argues that the defining feature of modern power is not overt violence, but rather our society's pervasive inclination to control people by means of visibility and surveillance. The design of hospitals and schools is not arbitrary; instead, institutions are set up so that experts will observe and monitor student or patient bodies to train and treat them. Those subjected to such surveillance internalize and attempt to live up to teachers', doctors', and, ultimately, society's ideas and values about what is desirable, preferable, and acceptable (Foucault & Gordon, 1980).

Routine practices of invasive clinical looking combined with derogatory descriptions of their bodies as "disfigured" or "abnormal" were regular occurrences for those born with differences. By opening their bodies to doctors' authority, women experienced heightened feelings of physical vulnerability under the clinical gaze. All were subjected to medical photography and many to "public stripping." These practices not only objectified them as bodies, but, by stripping them of a name and narrative, stripped them of a sense of self. Such objectification could also be sexualized. Because sexist disabling society casts the disabled body as asexual and the developing female body as too-sexual, at puberty those undergoing photography felt forcibly yet inappropriately sexualized due to contradictory meanings ascribed to puberty versus disability. Many struggled to articulate how they felt sexualized regardless of the photographers' intentions. Like the women interviewed who were subjected to sexual abuse, for those with disabilities, medical trauma undermined their ability to experience their bodies as mediums of discovery, which diminished their physical agency, or their sense that they could have control and ownership over their bodies. Frances and others came to believe that they had little right to body privacy or physical boundaries. In this context, refusing medical photography was out of the question.

> Frances: I didn't realize how being around medical people shaped me. It wasn't until I was much older that I really developed a sense of privacy about my body. Basically doctors tended to treat kids as if you were the condition rather than the person. I have no memory of being told what was happening or going to happen to me. It continues to be very medicalized and they still treat people with disabilities differently. Several times in my life I've had what's called "medical photographs" taken where they strip you stark naked to take pictures of you. Somewhere along the line there's photographs of me when I was thirteen. I look mature, stark naked. I don't think there was any concept that I would have had a right to say, "No!"

Over the past thirty years, disabled artists have challenged these medical practices. In her series *Narratives of Disease*, photographer and cancer patient Jo Spence (1988) uses her camera to disrupt the medical gaze. By taking pictures of doctors from a patient's perspective, she makes a statement about being the subject of clinical scrutiny. She writes the word "monster" on her post-mastectomy chest to convey cultural revulsion for the female cancerous body and to reference the history of Western thought in which both female and disabled bodies have been regarded as monstrous. Self-portraiture by artist Lindsay Fisher likewise makes connections between contemporary medical photography and historical images of human "curiosities." Western fascination with the unfamiliar has a long history, but intense public interest in bodily difference peaked between the mid-1800s and the mid-1900s with the rise of "freak shows" (Clare, 2009). In these exhibitions, people paid money to gawk and gape at bodies considered strange – a broad spectrum that included, in addition to those with disabilities, individuals with body size differences (the very fat or thin), unusual appearances, and gender and sex variance (intersex and trans people), as well as those perceived as racially different from the unmarked norm (often non-disabled people of colour). In "Self-study: Sex" (figure 3.1), Fisher refers to nineteenth-century scientific images of intersex people (those with atypical genitalia). Her "Self-study: Anthropology" (figure 3.2) evokes photographs from the same period that featured racialized women from the colonized world in sexually provocative poses. Under the guise of documenting difference, such images satisfied onlookers' voyeuristic desires to see the racialized or intersexed other naked. By inserting herself into the history of sexualized representations of difference, Fisher implies that the scientific colonial gaze still holds significance for people living with differences today. This is how she describes her art practice:

I chose to do these self-portraits when I was reading about the history of freak culture. At the time, I was going through reconstructive surgery to correct my facial disfigurements, and for their records, the surgeons required that I undergo similar photo documentation of my face. I remember feeling somewhat vulnerable during these sessions because they made me acutely conscious of my difference. I felt like an alien or a specimen – an abnormality that was being examined and transformed into something aesthetically appropriate. I took these photos as a way of reclaiming the experience of being a specimen.

Figure 3.1. Self-study: Sex. Artist Lindsay Fisher makes connections between contemporary medical photography and historical images of human "curiosities" in a photography series that references her own experiences under the medical gaze alongside 19th-century scientific images of intersex and racialized people. Here she highlights similarities in the treatment of intersex bodies and other bodies of difference: both have been regarded as spectacles, and specimens, of the Western scientific gaze. Photo courtesy of Lindsay Fisher.

Figure 3.2. Self-study: Anthropology. Fisher notes that although the freak show mentality gradually gave way to a medical model over the 20th century, medicine continues to put those with anomalous bodies on display as objects of curiosity, pity, and pathology. Her composition makes important connections between modern medicine's colonization of anomalous bodies and Western anthropology's colonization of Indigenous bodies through image, visibility, and the gaze. Photo courtesy of Lindsay Fisher.

The freak-show mentality gradually gave way to the medical model of disability in the 1940s and 1950s, yet in many ways medicine continues to put disabled bodies on display as objects of curiosity, pity, and pathology. Explicit voyeurism of the unusual is accepted within the world of modern medicine, where people still experience intense visual scrutiny, where their humanity and dignity is stripped away, and where they are turned into guinea pigs, test subjects, and "specimens." Reality TV shows like *My Shocking Story* (2009–) and *Medical Mysteries* (2010–) are modern-day versions of the old freak-show format designed to titillate audiences seeking entertainment in novelty but, at the same time, security in the knowledge that they are not one of "them." Artist Coco Fusco commented on these dynamics when she and Guillermo Gomez-Peña created a performance called *Couple in the Cage* that toured museums between 1992 and 1994 (Taylor, 1998). The artists were protesting celebrations of Columbus's landing in America by re-enacting the display of Indigenous people in museums and freak shows. Although they intended the piece as a satirical "reverse ethnography" where audiences would become uncomfortably conscious of their colonial gaze on the caged performers (who wore glittery costumes, sunglasses, and tennis shoes), over half of viewers believed the ruse – that the fictitious "Indians" were real. (Watch these responses at http://www.youtube.com/watch?v=gLX2Lk2tdcw.)

Today women with differences and their allies are forging alternative views of disabled sexuality and desirability. One such attempt is *Intimate Encounters*, an exhibition created by photographer Belinda Mason to challenge the cultural myth that only those who fit standardized images of attractiveness deserve to lead active and imaginative sex lives. (View her work at http://www.belindamason.com/). Amanda Lynn Hoffman's video exploration of sexuality and disability also aims to view sex as liberating and pleasurable for all people (see "(Sex)Abled Disability Uncensored," http://www.vimeo.com/6842318). San Francisco–based performance troupe Sins Invalid develops cutting-edge performances that challenge medical and cultural paradigms of able, normal, and sexy, "offering instead a vision of beauty and sexuality inclusive of all individuals and communities" (see Sins Invalid, "Our mission," http://www.sinsinvalid.org/).

Like an invasive medical gaze, rough clinical handling increased women's vulnerability and isolation while decreasing their sense of self-value. All reported clumsy lifting, insensitive touching, manipulation of body parts, aggressive poking and prodding, rough handling, questionable use of restraints, and other improper treatments in routine contact with care providers. When they endured painful and frightening interventions without consultation or support, most women felt abandoned or betrayed by the people in whose care they had been placed. This left them with the sense that they had little protection from intrusion and confirmed their emerging view that disability made them vulnerable to abuse. Recent research supports a key insight that surfaced in their stories – that invalidation through discounting, objectifying, and hurting disabled people is a serious issue in clinical settings (Hassouneh-Phillips, McNeff, Powers, & Curry, 2005). Elizabeth's narrative offers a vivid example of such mistreatment. Born in the 1960s with a facial difference that doctors knew little about, she spent long periods in hospitals away from family and community. She tells how doctors discounted her embodied knowledge in an intervention she characterizes now as assault.

> Elizabeth: Two doctors marched into my room. I was, "What are you doing?" I was immediately scared. They didn't introduce themselves. One of them had this long red tube that was like licorice. The other one told me to lie down on the back of the bed. The next thing I know, one's holding me down on the bed, and the other one's got this tube and he's trying to stick it up my nose. It was excruciatingly painful. I kept saying, "It's not going to go up." Knowing that it wouldn't. Knowing your own body. They kept trying to force it up. One even had a hand on my head, trying to hold me down. I'm sort of shaking right now, thinking about it again. But it was so painful and there was no explanation. Now as an adult I feel like it was a real assault.

Because they had less authority than doctors, less power than adults, less status than boys or children without disabilities, and less likelihood of being believed than adults, participants became especially vulnerable to abuse. Their stories give insight into prevailing norms and beliefs about what constituted acceptable treatment during this period, including the need to normalize differences with insufficient acknowledgment of the needs, comfort, or safety of the child. Fatima speaks of the pain caused when doctors' superior scientific knowledge trumped her experiential understanding of her body. Her story captures disability's inherent instability as well as our culture's inability to deal with the unpredictability and changeability of human embodiment.

> Fatima: The greatest pain I have had in my life is when the doctors told my parents I was faking not walking. The doctors didn't know what the hell was going on. From one day to the next, I stopped walking. There wasn't any reason for it. But they didn't believe me. They told my parents I was lying. My parents believed them for a while. That was very hard.

For Foucault, and for disability scholars like Claudia Malacrida (2005), careful attention to the ways that those with disabilities are treated in systems can provide information about the workings of power in society. Routine institutional practices – such as forcing girls to stand naked or semi-clothed in a room for doctors to view, subjecting them to insensitive processing and harsh handling, and disregarding their bodily knowledge – all reflect a broader understanding about who is entitled to respect and dignity, and who is considered to deserve less-than-respectful treatment. While participants recognized that some interventions prolonged their lives and improved the quality of their lives, they also questioned the authoritative power of medicine to determine what, when, why, and how treatments were done. They speak of the heavy weight of medicine's deficient model in labelling their bodies pejoratively; experimenting with treatments whose uncertain outcomes doctors did not admit; and subjecting them, without meaningful preparation or consent, to painful interventions. A positive sense of body was difficult to hold on to when such practices taught them that they were not as deserving of consideration or respect as those without disabilities.

Although institutional experiences were mostly negative, some reported positive encounters which restored their faith that institutions could sometimes be supportive places. Joanne and Elizabeth recall both injurious clinical routines as well as constructive encounters with a few experts. These helped to mitigate intrusive interventions and lessen their fear of treatments. But because affirming interactions were not typical, they could not fully undo the ongoing invalidation.

> Joanne: I had a really good doctor who was an orthopedic surgeon. He knew a lot about the disability and encouraged my parents to allow me to be independent. It was almost like they needed to hear that before they were going to let me actually have a life. But I was still subjected to the same stuff where there would be doctors coming in and I would have to show them my legs, my arms, or my scoliosis, to what degree it had developed. I was only wearing underwear and I figured that was normal.

Elizabeth: They really rolled out the red carpet for us. The nurses all knew me, and they were really friendly and caring. It was like a homecoming almost ... My earliest memories are painful things, not positive memories. I think about all the stuff that happened at the hospital – a lot of it is really dehumanizing. There was no room for any sort of dignity a lot of times ... It's not only the nature of stuff that's done but the categorization. You don't feel very good about your whole body, your whole self, because something's wrong with it.

Since the 1970s, researchers have exposed the dehumanization of people with disabilities in institutions (McLaren, 1990; Park & Radford, 1998; Priestley, 1998) and have debated whether the careless, callous, and at times cruel treatments constitute systemic, physical, or emotional abuse (Kennedy, 1996). Describing being looked at, touched, and handled in ways they did not understand or could not control, storytellers describe how they were subjected to clinical violence. The restraint, coercion, and rough handling affected their sense of self along similar lines as women who experienced early childhood sexual abuse. Like those subjected to sexual abuse, experiencing themselves as passive recipients of unwelcome intrusion undermined their sense of body/self-agency. Not only did the clinical routines erode their ability to feel that they could have control over their bodies, but such practices, supported by the medical model of disability, undermined their ability to create other meanings or find value in difference.

Responding to Misconceptions and Mistreatment

Storytellers possessed limited power and resources in childhood to challenge the devaluing of their bodies and disregard for their needs and rights. Given the subordinate status of children generally in our culture, and especially those with disabilities, it's not surprising that those with whom I spoke had few options for resisting the abuses they experienced in institutions. Yet they still found strategies to cope with the stigmatizing labels and intrusive treatment and to improvise identities. In contrast to prior studies on childhood disability that have viewed children as passive (Connors & Stalker, 2007), these stories give credence to children's capacities to negotiate identities in disabling environments. All adopted strategies for dealing with stressful encounters by downplaying differences and managing others' perceptions, by pushing away memories of painful interventions, and sometimes even by refusing the treatments. To cope with uncertain outcomes of painful practices, a common response for those interviewed was to disconnect from the site of violation: their bodies.

Elizabeth tried to escape through a fantasy of her future self and suggested that such imagining became an important method for coping with the trauma and unpredictable results of surgery. Lacking any images of her anticipated changed appearance other than stark *after* photographs from medical journals, Elizabeth seized on the idealized image of a glamorous Asian model once her surgeon told her she would have an "Oriental look" post-surgery. Asian women, in Western imagery, are often framed as exotic and sexual, and cast as cunning temptresses, war brides, and prostitutes. At the same time, disabled women are rarely represented as sexually desiring or as desirable (Gillespie-Sells, Hill, & Robbins, 1998). Other than in pornography, there are few representations of women with disabilities as sexual beings. In this context, we might interpret the surgeon's comments about Elizabeth's post-surgical "Oriental look" to mean that he believed people would perceive her as possibly exotic, but not quite normal.

> Elizabeth: My surgeon had said to me, "You will have a 70 per cent improvement." I thought, "What's that mean?" Then he said, "You'll never look normal." Which was kind of a blow because I thought that I would. Then he said to me that sometimes people have an "Oriental look." So I saw this picture of this woman in a magazine and I seized on that and I thought, "Oh will I look like this Oriental person?" Sort of glam, but always unreal. I was never present with my body or what I was going through because it was so painful and so horrible that I always wanted to be elsewhere. It was just anything to take me out.

When left alone to cope with alienating and aggressive technologies and treatments, the women often retreated into themselves. Amélie learned to respond to stares, questions, and comments by smiling. Smiling diffused people's emotional reactions; masked her own feelings of shame that their responses engendered; and established rapport despite people's discomfort. But this strategy had a cost. By placing Amélie in charge of managing the encounter, it affirmed that others' negative reactions were a problem best dealt with on her own. For many participants, their sense of aloneness was exacerbated by the fact that the only contexts where they could talk about disability were the very settings that operated out of a deficit model. Because people both inside and outside medical systems had difficulty hearing what they endured, responders came to believe that they should not speak about the trauma in their lives. To contain and stave off memories, many learned to shut down difficult emotions associated with such experiences. Elizabeth, for example, endured treatments by resolving to stay strong and by closing off her feelings from those who remained outside the experience. Amélie also learned to push down feelings, yet even today when strangers comment on her appearance, the emotions threaten to intrude and overwhelm her.

> Elizabeth: I remember being vulnerable all the time. They would wheel me down for X-rays in this dark, cold room with big machines with white lights. Scary procedures weren't explained. I don't remember anyone being there. That's where I started to feel, "I have to do this on my own." I became very closed off. I remember going to films and my sister would be emotional. I would be rigid and tough. Because there was so much pain, I thought I could never allow myself to feel any pain because it'd just open this dam that I wouldn't be able to deal with. So I kept it down.

> Amélie: The worst time is when people ask me questions about my face. I can be happy with who I am, somebody fairly balanced. But comments destroy me. Every negative thing I've heard or felt comes together at once. The pain lasts for hours. Those millions of stares throughout our lifetime put away in a deep place all come rushing back. Like a jack-in-the box that scares you to death. They pop up and they're scary. But it all has to come out and then you have to tuck it all back in for next time.

Maintaining tight control over their emotions had costs, but for some it was necessary to get through stressful situations. Because of how others treated them as passive recipients of interventions, many did not identify this strategy as a creative response to alienating treatment. Rather, they believed they had done little or nothing to resist. As children, all lacked power to refuse or challenge invalidation. Yet resistance is embedded in their stories. Many harboured secret feelings of intense anger and dislike for doctors who disrespected them as their unspoken strategy for resisting dehumanizing treatment. When they got older, they began to talk back to clinicians. Although Gina later recognized that some providers genuinely tried to help her, talking back was her way of rebelling against those who took away her dignity and personhood. Some describe how objectifying medicine led them to question the ethics of practices that, rather than helping *them*, served to increase experts' knowledge of and authority over their bodies.

> Gina: Every year I went to this [rehabilitation centre]. I had this incredibly impersonal doctor. I hated him because he made me feel less than human. When I got older I would start rebelling, make off-the-cuff comments as my way of asserting myself. He'd make a comment about my weight and I'd make a remark about his weight! It was rude but I was trying to gain a bit of myself back because I felt dehumanized. I knew deep down that they were trying to do good. But I didn't want to be a number, to be half-dressed with people prodding and poking. I'm in this situation where I'm at my most vulnerable, a thousand people around me, then he puts me down. It made me angry and I thought, "I'm not going to take this." Maybe that's what's made me as independent as I am, because I've had to.

Because mothers provided most of the care that the women required as children, mothers confronted many of the barriers and labels their children faced (Dowling & Dolan, 2001; Mutua, 2001). Mothers secured services, carried out caregiving tasks, acquired knowledge of their conditions, and worked to create spaces in which they felt protected. Through learning to respond to their children's needs, mothers came to know their children in ways others did not and often became attuned to them, even though professionals often discounted their expertise (as other studies have found; see Goodley & Tregaskis, 2006; McKeever & Miller, 2004; McLaughlin & Goodley, 2008; Rapp & Ginsburg, 2001). Responders related how systems put mothers, and to a lesser extent fathers, in the contradictory position of being responsible for their well-being without always having the authority to speak or act on their behalf. All expressed empathy for dilemmas that their parents faced in balancing experts' treatments against what they felt was in the best interests of their child. Providers sometimes made those parents who occupied subordinate social positions (such as immigrants) feel inadequate and unfit if, on behalf of their child, they refused consent.

> Fatima: I felt like a guinea pig but, because of my parents, not as often as most people do with disabilities. They had a language barrier. But they said no to some experiments. They were made to feel like bad parents. But they listened to me. They asked me what I wanted and sometimes they

would say, "No, we think that is better for you." Other times they would say, "OK, if you don't want to do this, that's what we'll do." They really respected me, which is unusual for parents of a child with a disability.

Parents were prevented from protecting their daughters by institutional practices that didn't always allow them to be present for procedures, intervene in degrading clinical routines, or accompany their children during lengthy hospital stays. At the same time, family support helped participants to maintain a sense of self despite invisibility, such as when parents facilitated their wishes and respected their opinions about treatments, and mothers did what they could to support their daughters through stressful hospital stays. Caretakers complied with experts' recommendations, but many also acted from a competing value, validating and facilitating their children's perspectives and interests in decisions. Unfortunately, current research suggests that professionals' tendencies to think they know better still leads them to ignore parents' often more intimate knowledge and nuanced understandings of their children (Goodley & Tregaskis, 2006).

The women's stories show how myths and models of disability shaped their lives. As children prior to the disability rights movements, they had little access to alternative frameworks from which to create preferred accounts of disability. While their self-agency may not have been acknowledged or accorded value, all responded and acted – separating their bodies from themselves, closing off their emotional lives, and navigating systems as best they could to keep themselves intact. As a counterpoint to the childhood trauma of medical systems, many of those interviewed have shown great bodily self-determination in their adult lives. The convergence of the women's and disability rights movements in 1980s and 1990s enabled some to put together the agendas of both in a way that spoke to them as women with disabilities and differences. Today, a few dedicate their work lives to transforming systems and advancing social inclusion for people with disabilities. As a result of their efforts, recent years have seen exciting developments in disability representation. One of the more important aspects of this is the move away from deficiency-fixated frameworks. This encourages us to view disability for what it is: a part of human diversity. Although people with disabilities have fought for legal rights to social participation, they still face exclusions. Even thirty years after global governments pledged full equality for those with disabilities, most people don't see their lives as positively affected by these policies (Quibell,

2005). This may be especially true for children, who still don't have access to non-pathologizing language or spaces to experience difference in positive ways (Connors & Stalker, 2007). The women's narratives speak to our collective need as a society to overcome discrimination based on bodily difference.

Chapter Four

The Student Body

This chapter attends to "school lessons" about size and race, by shedding light on how schooling experiences influenced the meanings women in this study gave to their physicalities, which in turn informed their sense of identity. The messages they received about race and weight from the early 1970s to the early 1990s reveal a body curriculum, the formal learning and informal exchanges that were integral to shaping participants' understanding and assessments of their own and others' bodies at home and, especially, at school (Rice, 2007). Researchers refer to this curriculum as "biopedagogy" or "body pedagogies" – the loose collection of information, instructions, and directives about how to live, what a body should be, what a good citizen is, and what to do in order to be healthy and happy (Fullagar, 2009; Harwood, 2009; Leahy, 2009). While these instructions are conveyed via formal education, they are also transmitted in families, health care, and media (Harwood 2009; Rich, 2010, 2011). This has led some scholars to argue that ours is a "totally pedagogized society" (Bernstein, 2001, pp. 365–6) that institutes "systems of control from instruction" (MacNeill & Rail, 2010, p. 179) in all aspects of social life (Evans & Rich, 2011). Instructions targeting the body do not merely transmit knowledge, but actively engage people in self-assessment and monitoring, and in so doing, affect their emotions and sense of bodily selves (Rail & Lafrance, 2009; Wright, 2009).

The concept of biopedagogy draws from French philosopher Michel Foucault's notion of biopower – the idea that governments control individuals and populations not through overt force but through imparting values and knowledge that teach people how to manage their bodies and themselves in ways that fit with state interests (1980). Schools place students' bodies under surveillance (by evaluating their fitness levels, checking their lunchboxes for "bad" foods, or imparting the values of good character or citizenship) and instruct them to monitor themselves in order to become worthy, healthy, and productive citizens. These lessons can be benign or even beneficial, but they also work to control through instruction: they define the normal body/self (thin, white, fit, and Canadian), then proceed to label those who diverge from the norm (fat, raced, and foreign) by using praise and shame alongside expert knowledge to urge conformity (Leahy, 2009). Biopedagogies hierarchically define which "bodies have status and value," using criteria like healthy/unhealthy and fit/unfit that carry moral overtones (Evans & Rich, 2011, p. 367). Since biopedagogies draw on white, able-bodied male standards of the normal, healthy body, they tend to uphold racism, sexism, and ableism as well (Azzarito, 2009; MacNeill & Rail, 2010). The ultimate objective of biopedagogy is to produce good "biocitizens," individuals who internalize instructions for managing their bodies/selves in order to optimize their health, increase their productivity, and strengthen society (Cooter, 2008; Macdonald, Wright, & Abbott, 2010; Murphy, 2009).

This chapter unpacks biopedagogies by analysing instructions that storytellers received as well as the barriers they confronted in responding to expectations regarding size and race. All tell how body standards were communicated *everywhere* at school: through furniture and uniforms, playground interactions, and, most of all, in gym classes. Many felt the consequences of such standards in physical education when teachers conducted weigh-ins and fitness tests (such as chin-up and long-jump competitions) that favoured tall over short bodies and thin over fat ones. Although today's obesity-prevention experts claim that too much food and not enough exercise cause overweight, for many women with whom I spoke the opposite was true. The imposition of weight standards through enforced exercise and dieting frequently led them to avoid activity and engage in problem eating, which contributed to their problems with weight. Lessons often related to the importance of being fit and not fat, but biopedagogies conveyed directives about race and citizenship as well. Even though most entered school *during* or *after* official multiculturalism and anti-discrimination policies were adopted in the 1970s, women of colour confronted colourism in white-dominated schools. A hidden curriculum that treated whiteness as normal and unremarkable, and bodies of colour as out-of-the-ordinary and inferior robbed them of the right to develop identities in an inclusive environment that recognized their backgrounds, capacities, and interests. Body pedagogies, by upholding a blue-eyed, skinny, Canadian-born ideal, reproduced a monocultural vision of the student body that denied racial diversity and reinforced the assimilation of fat dark bodies to thin white norms. Responders engaged in self-making despite these instructions through reworking the negative meanings into unique expressions of identity.

How Big Girls Become Fat Girls

Despite growing calls for body diversity, there are still few positive portrayals of people perceived as fat. Most media depictions characterize fat people as unattractive, unhealthy, and out of control (Le-Besco, 2004). Alongside this, many scientists and health officials have sounded the alarm about obesity as a disease epidemic (Fairburn & Brownell, 2002; Raine, 2004). Amid escalating anti-fat attitudes, weight has emerged as a major marker of social status in Western countries. The consequences of size standards are especially far-reaching for girls and women, whose bodies are heavily scrutinized as part of their experience of being female. As a result of such critical evaluation combined with negative messages about the supposed health risks of fat, millions of women have become intensely worried about weight.[1]

In North American societies, two competing ideas shape dialogue on obesity and overweight. The first claims that obesity is an epidemic, while the second holds that it's a myth (Campos, 2004; Gard & Wright, 2005). The first idea, the epidemic of obesity, dominates public discussion. Fear of an epidemic of fat people has made obesity a hot topic. Public health institutions have fuelled fear of fat by interpreting obesity as an escalating epidemic that threatens the health and fitness of nations (Ontario, 2004; World Health Organization, 2000). The World Health Organization (WHO) has even referred to the global spread of obesity as "globesity" (WHO, n.d., 2000). The idea that there is an obesity epidemic has become so taken for granted that alternative views are considered invalid. Concerns about rising rates of obesity within Canada make headlines daily. We are told that obesity rates have doubled in the last twenty years (M. Tremblay, Katzmarzyk, & Willms, 2002) and that 25 per cent of Canadian children weigh too much (Lau, 2007). Beyond problems with health, an increasing number of political and environmental problems are being blamed on fat, from global warming (Jacobson & McLay, 2006) to America's vulnerability to terrorist attacks ("Fat is," 2006). One extreme example of fat blaming can be found in remarks

---

1 Portions of this chapter section were adapted from Rice (2009b).

made by US surgeon general Richard Camona who in 2006 claimed that obesity represented a new "terror within" because disease-causing fat compromised America's ability to defend its borders. "Where will our soldiers and sailors and airmen come from?" he queried. "Where will our policemen and firemen come from if the youngsters today are on a trajectory that says they will be obese – laden with cardiovascular disease, increased cancers and a host of other diseases when they reach adulthood?" ("Fat is," 2006, para. 3).

As recently as the 1980s, there was significant debate in North America about the causes and consequences of overweight. Academics and medical experts argued whether obesity was a body type or disease type (Jutel, 2009), debated the dangers of dieting, and acknowledged that weight prejudice was harmful in the lives of fat people, especially women (Ciliska, 1990; Ernsberger, 1987). In particular, feminist theorists provided alternatives to medical claims by showing how cultural messages about female body sizes, shapes, and abilities had serious consequences for women (Millman, 1980). However, such alternative perspectives throughout the 1980s were increasingly marginalized by the notion of an obesity epidemic. Initially adopted by the US government, Canadian institutions also embraced this idea and commissioned reports that framed fatness as an epidemic of Westernized societies. Recently, many Canadian research organizations continue to frame fat in this way, most notably the Canadian Obesity Network, which promotes an understanding of health as excluding bodies that are not young, muscular, and male. Media coverage of such research has generated public discussion and galvanized politicians in ways that have further entrenched this understanding, confirming the emerging consensus that obesity *is* an epidemic.

Despite the ubiquity of these messages, there remains considerable uncertainty in obesity research about the causes, consequences, measures, and treatment of obesity (Jutel, 2006, 2009). A careful review of obesity science reveals that its core claim – that fatness is a disease caused by overeating and inactivity – is debatable. Epidemiologists now suggest that rising weights in our society may be related to people's biology combined with obesity-causing environments (Raine, 2004). Close examination of the scientific study of fat also reveals disagreement about whether weight is a good predictor of health and whether repeated weight loss attempts are harmful to health (Ernsberger & Koletsky, 1999; Miller, 1999). We simply do not know the health consequences of obesity. We know that the relationship between health and weight is a U-shaped curve, meaning that health risks increase at extreme under- and overweight (B. Ross, 2005). While high weight is associated with hypertension and heart disease, this association does not mean there is a *causal* relationship – there is no evidence that fat in itself causes these problems (Cogan & Ernsberger, 1999). To date, there are no safe, proven treatments for "excess" weight (Ernsberger & Koletsky, 1999). Common treatments such as dieting, pills, and surgery all have health risks (Bennett & Gurin, 1983). Finally, weight measures such as Body Mass Index, or BMI (weight in kilos divided by the square of height in metres), have been called into question as accurate predictors of health (Halse, 2009). While BMI was originally meant as a screening tool (to tell if someone is at risk for developing a health problem), it is now widely *misused* as a diagnostic tool (to tell if someone needs to lose weight; Ikeda, Crawford, & Woodward-Lopez, 2006; Jutel, 2006). BMI categories have been applied inappropriately to people of all ages, ethnicities, genders, and athletic abilities (Ikeda et al., 2006; Jutel, 2009). Kate Harding (2008) developed the *BMI Illustrated Categories Project* to show the body sizes of people who fit BMI categories to get us to think critically about the measures. Watch her slide show to judge whether the categories are skewed (http://kateharding.net/bmi-illustrated/).

In response to this critique, concerned scientists have developed an alternative view of obesity that shifts our attention away from stemming the epidemic of fat folk to examining an idea – obesity as a dangerous disease – that has captured our cultural imagination. This view does not dismiss the health concerns raised, but instead questions obesity researchers' assumptions and interests, and explores why our society has become so alarmed about fat. Acknowledging the health risks of extreme obesity, investigators like Michael Gard and Jan Wright (2005) question why researchers include overweight and moderately obese people (who might not experience a significant health risk) in disease statistics, which are used to claim that nations are facing a health crisis. They write about how the obesity epidemic has become a moral panic, arguing that misplaced morality and ideological assumptions underlie our war on fat. Obesity researchers disagree about whether bad habits are responsible for obesity, but in spite of this, discussions of causes and solutions invariably come back to exercise and diet. Not only does this ignore uncertainty about the actual causes of weight gain, but it blames individuals by ignoring contexts such as poverty or weight prejudice that constrain their options for eating and activity. Paul Campos (2004) believes that framing fat as a dangerous disease allows deep-seated dread of "others" (such as people living in poverty, racialized people, and women) to be disguised and expressed as fear and hatred of fat.

In this way, fear of fat masks as it reinforces class, race, and gender discrimination.

Throughout Western history, weight has been a marker of the health, fitness, and status of individuals, groups, and nations. Historians confirm that the meanings of fat have differed across time and among societies. Sometimes fat is celebrated, other times it is shunned (Schwartz, 1986). Before the Renaissance in Europe, there was some discussion of problems associated with fat, but interpretations of overweight as a symbol of weakness and waste have escalated in recent years (Stearns, 1997). In the moral climate of today, fat people are condemned for consuming too much and for being lazy – offered as evidence that Western society itself is in decline (Gard & Wright, 2005). Such stereotypes have adverse effects on children ranging from negative body image (Vander Wal, 2004) and high depression (Barker & Galambos, 2003; Eisenberg, Neumark-Sztainer, & Story, 2003) to low self-esteem and compromised physical competence (Neumark-Sztainer, Story, & Faibisch, 1998; Pesa, Syre, & Jones, 2000). Defining obesity as a behavioural disease shifts attention away from the real roots of the health problems assumed to be caused by fat (e.g., by blaming heart disease, type 2 diabetes, and other illnesses on overweight rather than looking at multiple causal factors such as stress, hidden sugars in processed foods, etc.) (Cogan & Ernsberger, 1999). Yet the obesity epidemic idea still finds support in a political context where all socially determined health problems are regarded as having an individual cause and solution, rather than being related to the individual's place within society's structures. When structural causes of obesity are ignored and doubts about its disease status disregarded, individuals get blamed (Crawford, 2004). In a society that emphasizes taking personal over collective responsibility, people facing external barriers are regarded as lacking the skill and willpower to take healthy actions.

In the past forty years, feminists have provided alternative understandings of fat that challenge medical views. By placing personal struggles in the social context, they have brought to light the injurious effects of images that teach fat women that their bodies are unacceptable and must be changed before they can be viewed as worthy people (Schoenfielder & Wieser, 1983). To analyse the body lessons learned by the women interviewed, I draw from this rich legacy. I integrate it with body becoming theory because this view transforms our understanding of fat. A body becoming approach posits that neither genetics nor health habits determine weight; instead, individuals' weights may differ depending on the way their bodies are perceived and treated in the world. When size is understood as being produced by multiple interacting elements, the idea that fatness is caused by bad genes or bad habits is disputed. Drawing on feminist insights about the way bodies come to be, I use women's body histories show how the unfit fat body is made from interactions among large bodies, cultural ideas, social practices, and physical environments that shape body sizes.

Creating Unfitness

> Sylvie: I wasn't what a girl should be. I was going to be a big kid, I wasn't necessarily going to be fat, though. It became a self-perpetuating cycle of eating to feed myself emotionally because I didn't fit. I became fat because of my circumstance. Cultural environment shaped my size.

Women with big bodies were treated as physically and socially unfit through the ongoing dialogue of their social relations. This included cultural messages, physical environments, and verbally and physically violent exchanges, which taught them that they were overweight and unacceptable. Such negative ideas were commonplace – occurring at home, on the street, and at school. When anti-fat messages repeated across situations and relationships, they had serious implications for participants' developing sense of bodily self. For most women, Aurora included, family members first taught the significance of size through body-based comparisons with sisters, cousins, and female friends (70 per cent of those with sisters were compared to them). Like families today, parents may have picked up expert advice about the significance of weight control to child health. According to Lisette Burrows (2009), biopedagogies now blame childhood overweight on bad parenting as a way of urging parental conformity to weight norms. In the current neoliberal climate a good citizen appears healthy, active, and disciplined, so parents have become more invested in activity and diet regimes to ensure their children measure up (Macdonald, Wright, & Abbott, 2010). As a result of comparisons in their families, many storytellers internalized unequal values given to differences, including 58 per cent who learned that thin was favoured over fat. Often, the harsh comments of boys and men dictated anti-fat attitudes informing women's body images. For many, the designation as fat imposed an unfit identity by highlighting their supposed incapacities and unfemininity.

Aurora: My sister is chubbier. They'd always make that distinction. I was *"la flaca"* and she was *"la gorda."* Together, we make the perfect ten. It was terrible. They're lavishing on me and disregarding her.

Catherine: My brother started to give me the nickname *Moose* or *Cow*. Those names hurt. But I wasn't aware of it and [being big] wasn't negative until people started to comment.

Recent history shows that obesity epidemic messages have emerged as dominant partly because they dovetail with earlier state-sponsored body pedagogies designed to improve the health, fitness, and competitiveness of populations. In the late 1960s, many Western governments, including Canada, initiated public education campaigns that advocated greater physical activity to prevent fatness and promote fitness in citizens (MacNeill, 1999). Responding to growing concerns about excessive consumption and the sedentary lifestyles of Canadians, Prime Minister Pierre Elliott Trudeau launched the ParticipACTION campaign in the 1970s (Rootman & Edwards, 2004). It famously compared the fitness levels of a thirty-year-old Canadian with a sixty-year-old Swede (http://www.usask.ca/archives/participaction/english/home.html). Many ParticipACTION ads (see figures 4.1 and 4.2) imagined the ideal citizen as a thin, fit, white, able-bodied male. They further raised the spectre of the unfit, feminized, underdeveloped, and Third World other, who threatened Canada's competitiveness on the global economic stage. In this way, campaign messages associated muscular

Figure 4.1. ParticipACTION 1: The true north ~~strong~~ soft and free. Photo courtesy of ParticipACTION.

FIT FAT
August, 1970

Figure 4.2. ParticipACTION 2: FitFat. Note how in this ad, fatness and fitness are envisioned as opposites. Photo courtesy of ParticipACTION.

active bodies with national strength, and unfit, fat bodies with the nation's stagnation or decline. Because children were thought to represent the future health and prosperity of the country, they were targeted as a group needing special attention.

In Canada, memorable messages for interviewees came from state-sponsored fitness programs and public service announcements (PSAs). Some suggest that ParticipACTION ads popular in the 1970s and 1980s heightened their fear of fat by instilling the belief that big bodies were bad. In one ParticipACTION PSA entitled *FitFat* (figure 4.2) that ran on Canadian television in the late 1970s, a chubby, lazy letter-*a* cartoon character was contrasted with an able, slimmed-down letter-*i* figure. By linking thinness with fitness and positioning fat opposite to fit, the popular ad conveyed that fatness and fitness could *not* coincide in the same body. A few women in this study could vaguely remember the content of these PSAs, but as Maude's story illustrates, they vividly recall the consequences of them, including their developing sense that their bodies were in some way bad or wrong:

> Maude: I remember this feeling of dread when the ["FitFat"] ad came on TV. Once my father and I were watching, I remember a man's voice saying, "This year fat's not where it's at." This made me so self-conscious because I was already feeling bad about my body.

Many responders had some awareness of body standards even as preschoolers. All became more aware of norms in height, weight, and ability when kids were grouped together by age, grade, and physical traits in the structures of school (A. James, 2000). Most women enjoyed physical education, but many described how being framed as unfit fat girls, rather than according to their potential or actual capacities, undermined their physical abilities. When teachers and students rooted assessments of fat girls' abilities in stereotypes about their size – if you are fat, you must be unfit – almost all stopped engaging in physical activity. In this way, classroom and schoolyard practices of categorizing and evaluating students by size, gender, and athletic ability adversely affected participants' sense of physicality and possibility throughout the school years.

> Iris: Once I was a fat kid, there's limitations on your abilities. You're unfit basically ... NO, I lost confidence in that. I didn't like sports or gym. Not because I couldn't actually perform the sports. It's because I didn't like being taunted.

Research has shown that gender-, race-, and weight-related harassment is a major obstacle to girls' participation in physical activity at
school (Bauer, Yang, & Austin, 2004; Larkin & Rice, 2005). For many
respondents, routines of physical education such as fitness testing and
dress codes also increased their vulnerability to judgment. For women of
all sizes, stress resulted from compulsory participation in a government-
sponsored program called the Canada Fitness Awards. Designed to
improve Canadian children's fitness levels, the lessons awarded gold,
silver, or bronze badges for chin-up, push-up, and long-jump competitions. Some, including Rose, recall gender and size biases built into the
tests, which favoured children with long legs and upper-body strength,
and tended to give unfair advantage to tall kids and boys, and to put
short kids and girls at a disadvantage. As other researchers have noted,
the internalization of emotion, especially shame and disgust, is a key
means by which children learn to follow biopedagogical instruction
(Evans, Rich, Allwood, & Davies, 2008). The shaming of those interviewed for embodying the wrong weight was not incidental. It was a
form of "emotional bullying" in which the teachers' authority to abuse
students was legitimized by the state-endorsed curriculum that "mor-
alized and normalized" how their bodies should appear (Evans et al.,
2008, p. 396). The women's stories echo what others have found – that
such pedagogies uphold sexism and ableism by relying on able-bodied
male standards to define the healthy body (Azzarito, 2009).

Isobel: My teacher commented on how I was gaining weight, when I was
about ten. He said that I had poor eating habits. When we had to run in
the gym, he said I had problems running ... It didn't feel very good. I felt
upset in front of everybody.

Rose: I hated Canada Fitness because my friend was athletically gifted
and she always got the red excellent badge. I always got the bronze. It was
horrible to test kids in front of other kids. How many chin-ups you could
do ... Women generally can't do as many because of upper body strength.
If you have long legs it is easier to do the hurdles or the long jump.

Yolanda: I hated gym class. I hated the change rooms. I didn't want them
to see my body ... I wasn't doing very well in ParticipACTION or Fitness
Canada. I didn't like running around in shorts and I wore track pants.

There is no proof that fitness programs like ParticipACTION and
the Canada Fitness Awards are effective in preventing overweight.

Studies show that fat children are less likely to be physically active and more likely to engage in problem eating but no one knows whether eating too much and exercising too little causes children to become fat, or whether already being fat increases the likelihood that children will overeat and not exercise (or if either is true) (Boutelle, Neumark-Sztainer, Story, & Resnick, 2002; Mellin, Neumark-Sztainer, Story, Ireland, & Resnick, 2002). Michael Gard and Jan Wright (2005) believe that many children growing up in the 1970s stopped physical activity as a result of the tough physical education practices introduced in Western countries as part of national fitness campaigns. The Canada Fitness Awards certainly dissuaded many women in my study from activity. Campaigns reinforced stereotypes about fat bodies, which studies confirm have harmful consequences for children's body images (Barker & Galambos, 2003; Burrows & Cooper, 2002; Burrows, Wright, & Jungersen-Smith, 2002; Davison & Birch, 2002; O'Dea & Caputi, 2001). Recently, some researchers have argued that moralizing anti-fat pedagogies, which alienated fat women in this study from their abilities, and hence produced their unfitness, can have damaging effects on social relationships as well (Evans et al., 2008). Relationships suffered when parents, teachers, and peers urged women to scrutinize their eating and exercise, and shamed them into striving for a better body. Charting the effects of body pedagogies on this earlier generation may be critically important for assessing the implications of similar "solutions" for fat kids today.

Because being physically active is associated culturally with masculinity, female athletes often have to work hard to emphasize their feminine appearance at the same time that they display their athletic skills (Krane, Choi, Baird, Aimar, & Kauer, 2004; Malcom, 2003; Oliver & Lalik, 2004b). For participants viewed as fat, this was especially difficult to navigate. When they failed to meet either the masculine athletic ideal or the feminine appearance ideal, many began to avoid physical activity to evade judgments. Those who managed to persist in athletics (like Iris) often faced disparaging assessments of their performance despite their skill. This was especially true for women in sports like horseback riding and synchronized swimming where an attractive (feminine, thin) appearance is an unspoken criterion for evaluation.

Iris: I rode and I show jumped. In my first big horse show, I remember being given a fifth place ribbon and the judge walking up to me and saying, "You should've been first. But your job was to sit there and look pretty and frankly you need to lose weight." That's when it really hit home that these things were very important.

According to interviewees, being a big girl was not the same as being a fat girl. Instead, women's bigness became fatness within environments that produced their unfitness and lead to exercise practices typically associated with fat. Fat became a problem because it emerged out of discriminatory social relations that refused to see female fitness as embodied by anything but a thin, able form. Although ParticipACTION ended in 2001, the Canadian federal government recently relaunched the campaign to stem rising levels of obesity, once again focusing on kids as a high-risk group ("$5M to bring," 2007). With a renewed focus on fatness prevention through fitness promotion, efforts to stem today's obesity epidemic may be leading a new cohort of large kids to stop engaging in physical activity, possibly contributing to their future problems with weight.

Failing at Femininity

For most participants, fat became an overriding identity during childhood – for many, it's a defining attribute they carry throughout their lives. Framed first as unfit fat kids and only secondarily as girls with other characteristics, abilities, and aspirations, many learned, like Marianne, "to collapse people's negative reactions into my size." Gina, too, describes how she was haunted by negative judgments about her physical differences, which caused her to become confused about whether "I'm unattractive because I'm overweight, because I'm disabled, or because I'm disabled and overweight." Race-, disability-, and weight-related harassment often combined in ways that made it hard for women of colour and those with disabilities to distinguish which differences were being targeted for abuse. Yet when fatness was framed as a personal flaw or moral failure at home as well as school it became an ongoing source of shame.

> Leigh: I was the only Chinese kid in class. I didn't know: "Are they picking on me because I'm Chinese or are they picking on me because I'm bigger?" More from my family I was made to feel bad about myself. People talk about overweight people being shamed into losing the weight. That's what my mom did. My siblings heard her taunts. That's what bothered me the most: they learned this from my mother.

Women's accounts illustrate how learning culturally condoned expressions of gender was a central task of childhood. While many had permission to explore a spectrum of gendered embodiments (from girly girl to tomboy), other people's anti-fat attitudes often undermined big girls' expressions of their preferred gender. Like Gayle, fat women tell how they were perceived to possess a body that "other-gendered" them as improper, odd, or *not* girls. While the in-between status of tomboy enabled storytellers to express attributes that the ideal of the feminine girl did not allow, such as being athletic, competitive, or displaying a sense of curiosity, once labelled as fat, some girls found their tomboy personae hard to maintain. When cultural meanings of boy bodies as wiry, gutsy, and strong conflicted with interpretations of fat bodies as lazy, inept, and weak, participants were excluded from tomboy activities and pursuits. Such exclusion sometimes occurred through boys' aggressive challenges to big girls' physical abilities and strength. Often, this meant that the option of being a tomboy was taken away.

Gayle: Because of my fat I was made to feel like an improper female if I showed signs of femininity. In grade 3, I liked a boy. There was nothing remotely sexual. "Look, he's your boyfriend!" That was a shock to me, having to watch your actions so that they can't be construed as you like someone ... My "fat, ugly" label stuck and I was a loser, weird Gayle.

Sylvie: I remember my "fall from grace" from being one of the boys. When I was a kid I was stronger than they were. I didn't throw like a girl, run like a girl, fight like a girl. So no one treated me like a girl. I can remember when the boys started to become stronger. They would gang up on me so I couldn't beat them up any more. So I got banished. I became the classic fat kid. I went from being a powerful kid to totally despised.

Black and other racialized women indicate that images of an attractive body spanned a broader range of sizes in their communities than in mainstream contexts. However, participants grew up during a time when people of colour constituted less than 5 per cent of the Canadian population (Statistics Canada, 2003). For this reason, most recall being one of only a few children in their schools identified as an ethno-racial minority. Coming of age before the existence of racially diverse representations in school curricula and children's popular culture, Black and other racialized women had limited access to images that reflected their appearances and identities. Subjected to racial discrimination and isolation in their neighbourhoods and schools, many had little exposure to community knowledge that could have helped them to understand and challenge racist ideals of beauty (Poran, 2002). As a result, many, including Sharon, describe how negative perceptions of their colour combined with negative perceptions of their size to disqualify them as girls. Black feminists have analysed how Black women are seen as more masculine, aggressive, and athletic within dominant cultural ideas about femininity (Hammonds, 2001). Some Afro-Caribbean Canadian women suggest that meanings of Black femaleness as more masculine may intermingle with meanings of fatness as less vital, active, and able to position them as neither boys nor girls.

> Sharon: I didn't feel like a girl, do girl things. I was not a girl, not a boy, just someone existing. Then compound that with being a Black female. You feel, "I'm nowhere." It's bad enough being a white little girl and you're fat. But when you're fat and you're Black, it's like holy fuck. That's like the lowest. The worst thing you could ever be.

Many commentators since Foucault (Foucault, Marchetti, Salomoni, & Davidson, 2003) have argued that in modern society power is exercised indirectly and works through instruction by shaping people's desires to conform to standards. Some storytellers suggest that girls' compliance with weight norms also arises through direct, often violent control of their bodies. Because it was considered a sign of failure or rebellion against standards of the petite feminine or thin tomboy girl, girls' fatness was seen as a threatening state of embodied being (Millman, 1980). Fat girls who continued to be athletic or aggressive as they grew to adolescence encountered mounting pressure to conform to a feminine appearance to ensure that they were recognized as heterosexual and female (Barden, 2001).

> Marianne: My mother had counted the cookies. When she found out I took one, she completely flipped. She happened to have a wooden spoon in her hand so she was smacking me with it and that broke so she was whacking me with her hands. Finally my dad had to come and hold her down because she lost it. Now I can say: How wrong is that? But at the time I was like "I must be like the most disgusting, obese thing in the world."

> Katerina: I'll never forget this. [A girl at school] was walking home. A bunch of boys got together and they spit over her. Her jacket was covered

in spit. To this day I can't believe they did that to her. Her mother brought the jacket and said, "Look at this. This is what they did to my daughter."

Enforcing Problem Eating

In a culture that judges a person's moral worth by their appearance, women's narratives show that fatness is a sign of physical and social unfitness. Many recounted how adults imposed demanding dieting routines to control fat children's bodies and behaviours deemed unruly, greedy, and weak. This is especially clear in narratives of those who attended schools for kids with disabilities. At Gina's school, staff assumed that fat kids could not control their own eating, so they forced them to sit at a separate, supervised "diet" table in the cafeteria. For participants with disabilities, cultural messages about disabled people as weak and dependent (Rogers & Swadener, 2001) intersected with messages about fat people as incapable, overindulgent, and lacking willpower (LeBesco, 2004). Although both kinds of differences were regarded as problems that needed fixing, the idea that disability was an inherent attribute contrasted sharply with the claim that fatness was self-induced and could be changed. Fat disabled bodies were put under the management of officials because the kids were seen as both incapacitated and wilfully out of control.

> Gina: They had this institutional attitude about kids with disabilities. They stuck kids they perceived to be too big or too fat at the cafeteria diet table. For years, myself and my friends were at this diet table. Nothing reinforces that more because then your peers are on this side of the wall, you're on that side of the wall and they're telling you that you are being segregated ... That was very damaging because it was at public school and everybody was young and peer pressure [was intense].

Most non-disabled participants did not experience such disturbing and overt institutional enforcement of weight norms through control of their eating. Yet the scrutiny and control of their bodies caused them to develop problems with eating, including dieting, bingeing, and starving. Those labelled fat failed to qualify as girls so doctors, mothers, and others encouraged and enforced dieting routines to make big girls' bodies fit a feminine size. To do this, adults sometimes characterized their concern about girls' bodies as being related to health, but most were more worried about girls' appearances as thinness was (and is) a necessary condition of femininity (McKinley, 1999b) and, increasingly, of good character and citizenship (Halse, 2009). As Sharon's story illustrates, girls were often told to lose weight for reasons related to health as well as femininity and worthiness.

> Sharon: I was eight or nine and my doctor said, "You should try and lose some weight. Don't you want to go to your high school prom?" He said that boys don't go out with fat girls. Because my mother was there when he said this, she sat there quietly. She had brought me to him to try and help me to lose weight … They put me on pills. They just made me sleep. I didn't lose weight. I liked food, too. So don't tell a kid, okay she's a little big, but she wants to eat. That was when I started to hide the food.

For most participants, the regulation of weight through forced dieting resulted in lifelong struggles with food and eating. Some developed compulsive, binge, and secretive eating in childhood. Others took up extreme dieting, anorexic, and bulimic behaviours during puberty when they faced increased pressure to look and appear desirable. For many, the process of becoming identified as fat, which negatively affected their images and eating, began before adolescence, even though puberty is the period that many feminist psychologists argue is fraught with dangers to girls' bodies and psychological health. But whether they started secretive eating in childhood or later adopted dieting and disordered eating, *all* participants perceived as fat eventually took up problem eating practices.

Contesting Negative Meanings

> Leila: If I wasn't the team captain, I was chosen last. Most of the time I was the team captain, I made sure of that. I always tried to be the captain so I wouldn't have the rejection of being last.

The women's stories reveal that they had limited power and resources to challenge the contempt, righteousness, and fear that female fatness aroused. In childhood, they had few options for changing the broader social and cultural environments. Yet they still found some creative strategies to contest stereotypes. Some focused on developing intellectually or artistically. Others used comedy to deflect the pain of negative reaction or asserted their physical abilities to reverse the cliché of the fat girl being chosen last. Exploiting cultural associations of size with aggression and masculinity, some fat women resorted to violence to challenge their low status. Boys responded to fat girls' aggression with a vengeance because girls' use of violence flaunted the power of fat female bodies and challenged the boys' own dominant status. The narratives show that women regarded as fat found creative ways to resist an unfit identity. They reveal that fat has become a major marker of difference for children growing up in the West. Size has joined sex, disability, and race as a powerful visual symbol of negative identity that positions girls and boys as deficiently different and limits their sense of possibility as they make their way in our increasingly body-centric world.

> Sylvie: I was fighting this boy, who I knew I could beat up. But he was one of the popular boys and so all the boys got in a circle. We're having a fight in the schoolyard and I started winning and the boy started to get really angry. He stopped fighting and another boy took his place. Then when the other boy got tired, another boy took his place. So all of them fought me and after a while, I got exhausted. Then they all started pounding me. So they were putting me in my place.

Over the past three decades, obesity has been reframed. Once seen as a condition that increased individuals' susceptibility to future illness, obesity now is interpreted as a disease of epidemic proportions. This designation of obesity as a dangerous disease may have costly consequences for people perceived as fat, especially girls. According to women in this study, combined gender-, race-, and weight-related harassment seriously undermines girls' body and self-images. While surveillance of children's eating and activity has increased dramatically in a post–obesity-epidemic world, school-based biopedagogies of weight measures, fitness tests, and team selection reinforced body hierarchies for this cohort at school. From the participants' perspectives, these practices do little to promote fitness in children. Instead, by framing them as unfit, anti-fat instruction may actually produce fat children's presumed lack of physical ability and skill. And adults' fear of fat (or perhaps of being labelled as bad parents, teachers, or health providers), which fuels the imposition of dieting routines, may result in big girls' development of problem eating, including bingeing, bulimia, and anorexia. Ironically, women's experiences indicate that anti-fat pedagogies may produce the very behaviours and bodies that they are attempting to prevent!

These days, the causes and cures of obesity are said to be found either in the individual realm of biology or the social realm of the environment (Lawrence, 2004). Frameworks that root the causes of obesity in individuals typically propose interventions designed to alter people's eating and exercise in order to reduce their weight. Yet for those identified as "too big" in this study, the imposition of eating and exercise routines in families and schools did not lead to weight loss. Their bodies' failure to conform to imposed norms instead taught fear of fat, shame about their fatness/unfitness, and, ultimately, the futility of adults' health advice. In shifting the blame for fat from unhealthy individuals to unhealthy environments, social frameworks emphasize changing the broader conditions that cause fat (Brownell & Horgen, 2004; Lawrence, 2004). Yet women's stories reveal how size is produced at the intersection of biology and culture, where the unfit fat body is made from interactions among large bodies, cultural values, social practices, and physical environments that shape body sizes.

Broadening the focus beyond the personal to the social realm is an important step in identifying social factors associated with fat. However, characterizing obesity as a disease of society does little to change the negative cultural perception of fat because it retains the idea that body size always determines health as well as the idea that fat is always bad. This raises critical questions about the need for more emancipatory physical and health education policies and programs: What would a fat-, girl-, and disability-friendly physical education curriculum look like? If students were truly engaged and informed, how would they define their priorities for health and physical education?

Fitting In without Standing Out: Race as Difference

Children of colour growing up in Canada learn from an early age that they are considered different from the white mainstream, and that race matters to people's treatment of them. In the 1970s and 1980s, an overwhelming 80 per cent of participants of colour encountered racism and colourism at school. While they possessed diverse histories and backgrounds, virtually all had in common the experience of racialization: being made to feel different and subject to racism due to characteristics like hair, hue, ethnicity, and culture (Canadian Research Institute for the Advancement of Women [CRIAW], 2002). Most formed their ideas about race through stereotypic questions that racialized their bodies (Do you wash your hair?) and selves (Where are you from?), as well as through harassment and violence that treated their differences as inferior. People once believed that racial groupings were based on physical features, but most now agree that race is socially created – an idea whose power comes from the salience *we* give it. Just how reliable is appearance as a way of assigning race? Anyone who believes it's easy to group people based on physical traits might try sorting them into races in an online exercise developed by Jean Cheng and Innbo Shim (Adelman, Cheng, & Shim, 2003: http://www.pbs.org/race/002_SortingPeople/002_01-sort.htm). Often people are surprised to find that it is more difficult than they thought.

In the accounts of women with whom I spoke, race was often learned at school. Students were divided into body-based racial categories that sent mixed messages which encouraged acceptance yet enforced conformity to those with the more "normal" bodies and "better" ways of being (the white ones). Participants of colour learned to alter their physical features, presentation, and demeanour to make themselves into what sociologist Randolph Hohle has called "idealized" citizens (2009, p. 285). According to Hohle, in the 1960s, civil rights activists taught members of Black communities to "deracialize the visible body" or present themselves as "clean, healthy, strong, and fit rather than dirty, sick, weak, and fat" as a means of countering racism (p. 300). This suggests that one way members of racialized communities might resist racism and claim rights is through learning to embody cultural ideals of good citizens by changing their dress, speech, and self-presentation. Participants felt pressure at school to modify their appearance to reduce racial stereotyping and increase their sense of belonging. While physical features were clues to racial identity (as one of the main ways our visual culture assigns race), accepted racial identifiers were insufficient to capture the labels imposed on storytellers. For example, 20 per cent of white women told how they came to see themselves as "other than white" because they possessed traits such as accents or "ethnic" hair that made them feel like outsiders relative to their unambiguously white peers.

The New Racism

According to social scientists, racism can take many forms, including (a) overt racism, such as the belief in a biological hierarchy of races or use of violence to control people; (b) structural racism that is built into all aspects of society, like laws that discriminate against some groups (apartheid in South Africa) or policies that protect the advantages of others (better services going to white neighbourhoods); and (c) subtle, covert, or polite racism such as treating people differently based on their race while pretending not to (CRIAW, 2002). The cruder forms of racism have not disappeared. Yet since the civil rights era of the 1960s, individuals and institutions have increasingly practised covert racism to retain privileges of being white without appearing racist. Race scholars have coined the term *colour-blind racism* (Gallagher, 2003) to identify this new kind of discrimination. I prefer the phrase *the new racism* because *colour blind* implies there is something wrong with being visually impaired. It also obscures the extent to which colourism is deeply entangled with the new racism (in that the lightness or darkness of a person's skin affects their treatment in society).

The new racism acts as if race no longer matters, often by ignoring or denying the ways race still affects people's life chances (Frankenberg, 2001). Recent studies show that drastic income disparities continue to exist between racialized and non-racialized Canadians: racialized women make 53 cents for every dollar white men make (Block, 2010), and Aboriginal people 30 per cent less than everyone else (Wilson & Macdonald, 2010). The new racism erases the role of race in income inequality by blaming disparities on people's cultural values, their individual shortcomings, or their inability to integrate instead of the unfair conditions they routinely confront. Sometimes the new racism is not conscious or intentional, but it still perpetuates inequality since whites in positions of authority (employers, teachers) may make decisions based on unexamined stereotypes, fear, and ignorance (Lewis, 2003). The concept is useful because it explains how inequality persists even though racism appears to be less accepted in our society.

When people think of racism, they tend to think in terms of the harms inflicted on racialized people without considering the benefits afforded to whites. In North American society, being white is viewed as the norm. Often, people don't recognize whiteness as a race or acknowledge white privilege – the power relations between whites and non-whites that automatically reward whites with unearned advantages (MacIntosh, 1989). Taken-for-granted privileges range from enjoying more varied and positive media representations (Maher, Herbst, Childs, & Finn, 2008; "White authority," 2010) to learning white, European history in school (Canadian Race Relations Foundation, 2000) to occupying positions of power out of proportion with the percentage of whites in the population. Since colonization, a pervasive colour symbolism has linked whiteness with valued traits like beauty, purity, and spirituality (Dyer, 1997), and darkness with devalued ones such as carnality, uncleanliness, and evil. Not only is the English language replete with terms (such as *black heart*, *Indian giver*, and *yellow peril*) that carry racist value judgments, but stereotypes are widespread throughout cultural images as well (Moore, 1976/2006). Media studies show that darker-skinned people are still portrayed as more sexual, subservient, and menacing than lighter-skinned ones (Kretsedemas, 2010; S.D. Ross & Lester, 2011). Race scholar Monika Hogan argues that whiteness derives its power by "projecting the associations that our culture finds threatening, such as emotionalism, vulnerability, mortality, and physicality, onto racialized identity positions" (2006, p. 357). This dynamic explains how our culture casts traits that challenge ideals of the masterful, invulnerable self onto those deemed different.

Schools are charged with teaching children the values and norms of society and, as such, are spaces where young people form life-shaping identities and where governments exert influence over their lives. Schools are "spaces of possibility" with potential to undo inequalities by bringing together children from different backgrounds and levelling the field. At the same time, they are also sites of "racial fault lines" (Staiger, 2006, p. 7) where social inequalities get reproduced, often through instruction. In the 1970s, multiculturalism gained wider acceptance in some Western nations as a means to recognize and celebrate diversity. Under Prime Minister Pierre Trudeau, Canada proclaimed multiculturalism as official policy in 1971 (Jansen, 2005). In 1988, the *Canadian Multiculturalism Act* was passed into law, which legally mandated all levels of government to ensure equal opportunities for everyone (ibid.). Since then, Canada's multiculturalism has come under fire. Critics argue that although it has promoted diversity, multicultural policy has not tackled racial inequality, because it assumes equality instead of addressing systemic discrimination in institutions like schools (C.E. James & Wood, 2005). Ironically, multiculturalism may erase race by presuming that once schools recognize cultural differences in the student body, teachers and learners no longer need to worry about racism. Critics contend that relegating the study of racialized groups to a small segment of the curriculum or to specific events during the school year maintains some people's outsider status while keeping white European experiences and perspectives in place as the most relevant and noteworthy (Dion, 2005). Thus, rather than ending discrimination, multicultural policy "often works to implicitly endorse white privilege by denying the structural racism to which people of colour are widely subjected" (Staiger, 2006, p. 4).

Despite mandated multiculturalism, schools often reproduce racism and colonial relations through curriculum content (telling history from the vantage point of white Europeans), regulations that erase difference (forbidding Muslim girls to wear head scarves to school), neglecting certain groups and centring others (structuring the school year according to the Christian calendar or reading novels written mostly by white men), and streaming students into academic and non-academic programs (Dion, Johnston, & Rice, 2010; C.E. James & Wood, 2005). The ideal of multiculturalism is captured in an image from a 1970s school textbook (figure 4.3) – although different clothing, skin colours, religious ceremonies, and ways of life are captured in the montage, missing

Fig. 1-16: *There are many cultures to be found in Canada; all contribute to personality formation.*

Figure 4.3. Many cultures in Canada: In textbooks from the 1970s and 1980s, images and information celebrating multiculturalism ignored the histories and legacies of colonialism and racism that helped to create the nation of Canada. From *Health, Science and You* by Elizabeth Chant Robertson. (All efforts were made to reach the rights-holder to this image.)

are the violent histories and legacies of colonialism and contributions of racialized people in building Canada. For example, many Canadian students still do not learn about the 10,000-year history of Aboriginal people on this land or about Canada's history of slavery (CRIAW, 2002). Listen to Jacqueline who talks about what she did, and didn't learn, about history at school:

> Jacqueline: We weren't there. So we did it for ourselves, orally as a group. Let's say we were learning about the War of 1812. We would say "Why are we learning that?" That's when I found out about Black History Month. We would go find out about Harriet Tubman, about things Black people had contributed. That's how we got involved.

Partipants in this study illustrate how the heady optimism of multiculturalism masked an ugly underbelly of racism that surfaced in school structures and content. Their accounts show how, since its inception, official multiculturalism often worked together with unofficial racism to racialize students and reproduce inequalities at school. Multiculturalism, from this vantage point, might be seen as a biopedagogy that instructs students to embrace tolerance, equality, and peace as pillars of Canadian identity by erasing the history and reality of colonialism and racial oppression in this country.

In what ways do participants' stories challenge popular understandings of Canadian identity as based on a celebration of diversity and official multiculturalism? How was race stressed but, paradoxically, erased at school? What do their stories teach about how kids learn, and might unlearn, racism?

Shades of Difference

As the women I talked to attest, racial identity formation is a process that begins at home and continues at school. At home, their parents played a pivotal role in shaping their awareness of, and appreciation for, their racial history and heritage. Like the existing research on children's racial identity development in families (D. Hughes, 2003; Lalonde, Jones, & Stroink, 2008; Ward, 1996), participants described how parents prepared them for the racism they would encounter by incorporating pride and resistance into parenting lessons. Studies conducted with African American families show that such buffering works to boost racialized children's self-esteem (Neblett, White, Ford, Philip,

Nguyên, & Seller, 2008) and to help them build up resilience in the face of racism (D.L. Brown, 2008; Thomas, Speight, & Witherspoon, 2010). Many interviewees, including Sharon, indicate that the communication of "race-related resistance strategies" was critical to their cultivation of a confident identity (Ward, 1996, p. 86). Yet race lessons could also have a demoralizing effect depending on the tone and content of the messages – for example, if parents' fatalism taught children to give up the struggle or if their harsh reaction instructed kids to shoulder all responsibility for racism. While some conversations could be tricky, ignoring race did not solve the problem of how to navigate racism either. Marianne, who was adopted by a white family, explains why her family's erasure of difference actually highlighted her outsider status. So striking was the family's stress on her sameness that she began to see herself as "anti-different," that is, different in some way no one would name or explain. Teaching about race/racism was a delicate balance of communicating the significance of race and preparing children for the realities of racism without making them feel that obstacles were insurmountable or had to be overcome on their own.

Sharon: My dad was great. He would say, "You're Black, you're female, you gotta work twice as hard." We got that lecture at the age of three. You're as good as anyone else. You can be anything you want to be. Going into school I already had that lesson. But I don't think we were ready for the abuse in terms of people being blatant.

Charlene: My mother used to say to me, "You have to be better than white people because they're not going to give you a chance unless you're better." It's been hard for me to get past the "I'm responsible for the whole Black race" syndrome. I'll give you an example: when I go to the corner store I need to get a bag for what I buy because without it people will think I stole. That was drilled into my head. So I always wanted to prove that not every Black person is like that.

Marianne: Anti-difference. That was basically the cry throughout my childhood – how much I wasn't different and how much I was like everybody else. It was "You have brown eyes like I have brown eyes." Or "You have a pink tongue like I have a pink tongue." The emphasis was on my not differentness, which always made me feel like I was an "anti" something. They had brainwashed me so well that even I couldn't see that the colour of my skin was different. I just knew something was different.

This generally positive and protective process of learning about race and racism was put to the test before participants started school. Although a majority acquired skills in countering racism and cultivating a positive racial identity in their families, it was also at home that they first encountered shadism or colourism – the privileges afforded to lighter-skinned people and discrimination against those with a darker hue that some experts suggest may influence individuals' life chances as much as race itself (Burton, Bonilla-Silva, Ray, Buckelew, & Freeman, 2010; Russell, Wilson, & Hall, 1992). Family members introduced colourist values, which were rooted in a colour-ranking system that had its origins in European colonialism.

Colourism became a key divide-and-conquer strategy that European colonizers deployed to enforce their domination and keep oppressed peoples divided (Glenn, 2009). Through the spread of European value systems and power structures from the 1700s onwards, dark skin, kinky hair, and wide noses became linked with incivility, irrationality, and ugliness, and straight hair, light skin, and narrow noses with civility, intelligence, and beauty. Shadism gradually took root globally as colonized people came to value light skin tones and Anglo features under a European system of rule (Hunter, 2007). In North America today, shadism works in concert with racism by privileging whiteness, and by treating racialized people according to a sliding scale of personhood based on the lightness or darkness of their skin. Colourism is so deeply entrenched in our social fabric that light-skinned people of colour (Black, Asian, and South Asian) have higher incomes, receive preferential treatment at school, get hired and promoted at higher rates and, in the case of women, they are more likely to become celebrities. Light-skinned women also tend to be imprisoned at lower rates than their darker-skinned counterparts (Harrison & Thomas, 2009; V.M. Keith & Herring, 1991; Viglione, Hannon, & DeFina, 2011). Though colourism also affects men, because we live in a society that values women based on their proximity to white beauty, it has marked consequences in women's lives, influencing their school success, incomes, self-image, and partnership chances and choices (M.E. Hill, 2002; Hunter, 1998, 2002, 2005; M.S. Thompson & Keith, 2001).

African, Asian, and South Asian participants described various ways that parents passed on a preference for lighter skin. Many learned this lesson via media and school, but as JeffriAnne Wilder and Colleen Cain (2011) found, families first exposed them to such values. Because mothers do most of the child rearing and serve as a primary source of daughters' identity construction, they played an important role in handing down notions about colour to daughters. As Nicole suggests, fathers and brothers played a part too. The physical prejudice did not stop at skin tone but extended to other features such as hair texture and the size and shape of their noses and lips as well. Some participants, like Maya and Preeta, tell how shadism, once learned, influenced their self-perceptions, relationships with peers, and even partnership choices later in life.

> Nicole: My older brother got his friends calling me "juicy lips" just because I have full lips. That hurt. I had a huge problem with the way I looked, growing up. I think it came from my father; he used to tell me I had an ugly smile. I don't know if it was a joke but his words cut like a knife. For a long time I used to have a hand over my mouth when I smiled because he told me that my smile was ugly. So you begin to believe it.

> Maya: My mom used to tell us, "Marry a white man," because she and her family are a lot lighter than me. The only reason I'm dark is because my dad is dark. I knew she preferred lighter-skinned people because she treated them better. She talked to and about them differently. Say I brought a friend or boyfriend home, the lighter they were, the better they were. If they were too dark, she'd say "They look shifty." Shifty? Sometimes they were nicer than the ones she saw before.

> Preeta: We have a family friend who is a lot darker. Me, my sister, my cousin, and her would play together. I remember a Judy Blume book, *Otherwise Known as Sheila the Great*. In one part, the characters play a game. You pass around a sheet of paper with questions, "What we like about you. What should be changed." We decided to play that game and the comments we wrote were not nice. The darker girl got Black. I got hairy. Someone else got fat. That was a big mistake because it hurts when you are taught at a young age that it is not good to be fatter or darker.

Many people are unaware of light-skin preference because a white beauty aesthetic is so widespread. In North American media, we are bombarded with images of light-skinned bodies. Even African American celebrities tend to be light-skinned with long hair and Anglo-coded attributes or have their differences airbrushed out of the picture. A few years ago blogger Courtney Young juxtaposed a candid photograph of Beyoncé with a stylized L'Oréal ad of her, to show that the latter photo may have been edited to make her skin lighter and her nose narrower (http://msmagazine.com/blog/blog/2010/03/28/what-can-we-do-about-colorism/). In another example, *Elle Magazine* featured a cover image of the bodacious, darker-hued actress Gabby Sidibe (Oscar nominee and star of the film *Precious*), whose skin in the splashy shot appeared to be several shades lighter than her normal colour (http://www.dailymail.co.uk/news/article-1312928/Did-Elle-magazine-lighten-skin-Precious-star-Gabourey-Sidibe-cover-photoshoot.html). Shadism draws on historical values left over from colonial times and is also fuelled by the global spread of Western-made media images that infiltrate cultures all over the world. Only a few months after the offending photo of Gabby was published, Indian actress Aishwarya Rai Bachchan threatened to sue *Elle Magazine* when a "white-washed" image of her, too, appeared on its cover (http://jezebel.com/5718169/did-elle-lighten-aishwarya-rai-bachchans-skin-on-indian-cover). Toronto filmmaker Nayani Thiyagarajah, working with young women of African, Caribbean, and South Asian descent, made a documentary to spark dialogue about shadism (http://vimeo.com/16210769). Women's stories in this film highlight what colourism researcher Margaret Hunter (2007) also stresses: shadism is difficult to fight because ideal images of lightness and abject images of darkness are everywhere, and the rewards and punishments are real.

Families of a majority of participants taught them to favour light over dark skin. Parents and relatives often reinforced the colour status quo, but they sometimes played a pivotal role in contesting colourist attitudes. This was true for Rosetta and Jacqueline, who learned to challenge shadism through studying colonialism and through supportive caregiver relationships. Like Nicole, those women who, as children, felt constrained to accept the unfair ranking system that adults or siblings endorsed did not always buy into the colour hierarchy when they got older. Instead some set out to *not* treat others the way they had been treated. Even in childhood, the women were not passive screens on which others projected colourist values, but active beings who often questioned imposed meanings and searched for more loving ways of looking.

Jacqueline: My mom she was very loving. Negative: my aunt. She had a complex about colour, hair. She used to tell me, "Don't go out with Black guys." When she babysat us, she would get the white kids on the street and comb their hair while we were sitting there watching her. I felt very hurt because she would treat the white and mixed girls better. My mom and sisters talked about it later. We distanced from her because of that.

Rosetta: My dad and I talked a lot about skin colour. Talking to my mom, I learned that they had a class system based on colour. If you were Black you married someone lighter to move up. I learned that I was whiter than her, and she's darker than her mother.

Nicole: Thinking back on it now, I would never do that to my child. Because I have a niece who's chocolate brown and has her hair natural. I tell her that she's beautiful, so even if somebody else says something, she knows that her aunt thinks she's beautiful. Because at least if you just have that one person who means enough to you. It's good enough.

Afro-Caribbean, South Asian, and Asian Canadian women encountered colourism at home, and caregivers played a pivotal part in passing on prejudice. Their stories reveal the existence of a "skin colour paradox" (Wilder & Cain, 2011, p. 597) wherein family members promoted positive racial identities and provided members with a safe haven from racism, while simultaneously perpetuating shadism. This paradox might be understood as a type of racial biopedagogy adopted by families and communities since colonial times to teach members how to resist racist stereotypes of the "dirty and unkempt self" by modifying themselves to fit in and find success in white society (Hohle, 2009, p. 299). But families were only one site of learning about racism and colourism. Many women stressed how school structures and peer cultures taught troubling lessons about race and shade that echoed and amplified messages from home.

School Daze: Racism and Colourism at School

Schools are often described as microcosms of society and spaces of possibility since they reflect and respond to inequalities in the outside world. Though many educators have looked at racism in schools, few have focused on shadism. For the racialized women interviewed here, colourist attitudes passed down in families pervaded their schools as well. Most Canadian boards of education had adopted a multicultural vision of racial equality by the time the women attended school. Multiculturalism policies made schools more welcoming for minorities, but as researchers have noted, they did not succeed in undoing discrimination, since white-driven structures still pushed kids of colour outside the mainstream student body (C.E. James & Wood, 2005; Kelly, 1997). In spite of mandated multiculturalism and anti-racism, the majority of racialized women confronted a colour hierarchy in hallways and classrooms. Race became a salient aspect of their identities when peers targeted physical features according to a racial geography of the body. For many, colourism and racism were impossible to disentangle, since the most overt and pervasive form of racism they encountered was based on perceptions of their physical features.

Although little research has been done in Canada, studies conducted in the United States have found that colourism plays a significant role in student success. For example, lighter-skinned African American students on average complete more years of schooling than darker-skinned ones (M. Hughes & Hertel, 1990; V.M. Keith & Herring, 1991) and darker-skinned Mexican American students have lower educational attainment than their lighter-skinned counterparts (Murguia & Telles, 1996). According to Margaret Hunter (2007), teachers' colour biases influence learners' success: if educators expect light-skinned students to be smarter or better behaved than their darker-skinned classmates, students tend to rise or fall to meet those expectations. One Canadian study has found that teachers' racist low expectations were a major factor in racialized students not doing well at school (Canadian Race Relations Foundation, 2000). Other studies reveal that students see lighter-skinned peers as more attractive and intelligent (Craig 2002), and that the lightness or darkness of a student affects their engagement with and inclusion in school activities (such as fashion shows and ballet; Atencio & Wright, 2009; Oliver & Lalik, 2004a). There are many ways that skin-colour prejudice might operate in schools, but as Margaret Hunter has put it, "the bottom line is that the lighter kids benefit and the darker kids pay the price" (2007, p. 244).

Storytellers described shadism in encounters with whites as early as preschool. A sizeable number, Salima included, developed consciousness of colour through interactions in neighbourhoods. More than any other characteristic, peers attributed race on the basis of appearance; and more than any other bodily attribute, hue was the basis for approval. Implicitly and explicitly racist ideas from adult culture influenced their white peers' emerging understandings of race. A common misapprehension was that dark skin was dirty. Historian Anne McClintock (1995) has argued that the association of darker skin with dirtiness has its roots in the nineteenth-century British Empire. At the time, upper-class Victorians aspired to maintain their social position at home and their racial superiority abroad by linking whiteness with cleanliness and civilization against working-class and racially polluting others whom the privileged classes viewed as dark, dirty, and uncivilized. White children (often unknowingly) employed such racist associations in interactions with kids of colour. Questions and comments laden with stereotypes exposed white children's fearful fascination with the darker hues of their non-white classmates. When colour became women's most salient feature, they experienced "physical stereotyping" – the reduction of their embodied being to a few simplified, exaggerated traits.

> Salima: When I was five, some people moved in next door. Their kid was indoors so he was looking at me through the mesh of the window. He said "Hi, sweet lips." Because he was looking at me through mesh he didn't realize what colour I was. When he did realize, he was terrible to me. He was racist and there was one point when it got to him throwing rocks at me and my brother when we were riding by on our bikes.

> Nicole: When I went to school I found out about how I looked, I wasn't allowed to go to a few friends' homes because Black people were dirty. I remember once my friend invited me over. At the door she said "I'm going to ask my parents. Let them know you're here." I was standing at the doorway when I heard somebody say we could play outside because outside is outside, "But don't you dare bring her in my house!" She came back crying and told me she couldn't have me over.

> Charlene: I remember the first day of school somebody asked me, so innocently, "Do you wash your hair?" It comes with the idea that there is uncleanliness with skin colour, because it's dark, maybe it's dirt.

For most racialized women, harassment got worse as they got older. Verbal taunts reinforced racial divides by normalizing whiteness while drawing attention to and marginalizing non-whiteness. Because the English language offers many pejorative figures of speech for non-whites and virtually none for whites, women could not rebut their harassers effectively. Rose and Rebecca report that white kids rooted racial slurs not in their attributes but in stereotypical notions of racialized bodies. White children thus did not discover racial difference by comparing themselves with children of colour. Rather, white peers picked up on and projected visual stereotypes about African, South Asian, and Asian bodies onto minority children. Comments heightened the colour consciousness of every woman interviewed. But realizing that harassment was based on a visual stereotype, rather than a view of their body that they could recognize, helped some to preserve their prior positive sense of body.

Sheila: There are so many words you can use for non-white people, but when it comes to WASP there is not that much you can say … Because there is nothing wrong with being white. But there is something wrong with being non-white. So there was no defence.

Rose: Asian women were seen as unattractive because of physical stereo-types, which are so not true. Slanted eyes. There are people of European descent who have slanted eyes. So it's not all Asian women and they don't all have slanted eyes. Also a flat nose, people would make fun of me for my flat nose. But not all Asians have flat noses either.

Rebecca: This kid said to me, "You're lips are really big." I thought to my-self "Actually, no they're not." Being perceptive enough to realize he must be thinking "Oh all Black people have thick lips." He wanted to see that so that's what he was going to see, when my lips were smaller than his. Later on, when I thought about the incident I wondered how he knew those ste-reotypes. Because I only became aware of those features once kids started making fun of me. It was interesting that this kid was aware of features that are unique or stereotypical to people of different races.

Textbook images reinforced these stereotypes. Some African Cana-dian interviewees recall seeing anthropological images of bare-breasted "native" women in social studies textbooks from the 1970s and 1980s (see figure 4.4). Since colonial times, Western anthropologists have por-trayed Indigenous women as primitive, passive, and exotic others, and nowhere has this depiction been more evident than on the pages of the *National Geographic*. For much of the twentieth century, the magazine was known as the only mainstream venue where people (especially adolescent boys), under the guise of spreading cultural knowledge, could see topless women (C. Williams, 2002). Images of bare-breasted women were permitted due to racist and sexist double standards that barred white women from exposing their breasts while stripping In-digenous women of the privilege of concealing clothing (O'Grady, 1992/2003). Magazines like the *National Geographic* often depicted racialized women as sexualized others for whom white standards of decency did not apply. Participants who saw this type of imagery in

ACTIVITY 7

1. These pictures show some of the activities that Wagga, Oona and their families do each day.
(a) What important things do the men do?
(b) What important things do the women do?
(c) What do the children do to help?

Morning

Evening

Afternoon

13

Figure 4.4. Social studies textbook picture from the 1970s: Textbooks from the 1970s and 1980s drew on the conventions of Western anthropological images to depict bare-breasted "native" African women as sexualized others for whom white and Western standards of modesty and respectability did not apply.

their textbooks tried to assuage their fear by reassuring themselves that the pictures were authentic. When they compared the abject images of bare-breasted Black women with idealized representations of lingerie-clad white models that they also saw as children, this strategy didn't work. Even at young ages, they knew there was something exploitative about the imagery. Contrasting the abject images that were supposed to represent them with white ideals, which they learned that they should emulate, exposed them to symbolic racism.

> Nicole: Growing up as a little girl with this Black body I felt scared seeing African women being portrayed as bare breasted in textbooks. I tried to appease my fear by saying to myself, "Oh that's how they dress there." But there was something exploitative about the imagery and different from images of white women I saw. I would see catalogues of white women in their bras. Then I would see images of Black women and I would think to myself, "Oh no. I look like the women in the film and not in the catalogue. What am I going to do?" Because I can see what's considered acceptable.

Skin tone became problematic because respondents grew up in a world where lightness is linked with beauty. This association is apparent even in the meaning of the word *fair*: while it is often taken to mean being light-complexioned and light-haired, fair also signifies something of beauty or great value. Skin colour, figuring strongly in women's body images, caused those seen as darker to develop greater body dissatisfaction than those who were lighter, a finding supported by other researchers (Hunter, 2005; Sahay & Piran, 1997; Telzer & Garcia, 2009). Even at young ages, some became acutely aware of boys' preferences and felt conflicted about whether to reject racist ideals or aspire to them to gain boys' attention and approval. Hunter (2005, p. 38) has called this body hierarchy a "beauty queue" to capture how multiple traits (weight, colour, hair texture) work together to determine a woman's desirability or beauty quotient in the dating market. Like what Hunter found in talking with African American women (2005), most women with whom I spoke admitted wanting to have lighter skin, longer hair, or whiter-looking features at some point in their lives due to the pain of being denigrated for being darker. Intertwined with the high value placed on white beauty was envy that many felt for girls who appeared to possess the desired traits.

> Nicole: I had full lips and the broad nose, and even though I was fair skinned, I was still Black. So that was reflected in the comments I got. One

person said to me, "You're pretty for a Black girl." Do I say thank you? Do I kick them? What do I do? That was such a profound statement. It gives me the sense that generally we are not pretty.

Vera: There was a blond, blue-eyed, pretty girl in our group. All the boys found her attractive. I wasn't blond or blue eyed so they didn't pay any mind to me. At the same time I knew that they talked about women on TV so I cut a picture of a woman out of a magazine. I was going to give it to them as a present. I don't know whether I was thinking that they would associate the picture with me but I remember carrying the picture all day and then at the last minute thinking, "This is stupid." I threw it away.

A majority of white women did not see themselves as possessing a racial identity, because in our society whiteness is not racialized – that is, not turned into a significant identity or source of inequality. Researchers have argued that such silence is not accidental. Rather, with the rise of new forms of racism characterized by denying racial inequalities and having difficulties discussing race, white kids growing up in the post–civil rights period have been taught to maintain their privilege through silence and avoidance (Kenny, 2000). Although most white women had little to say about race, 20 per cent reported feeling that they were "not white enough." Their stories reveal that whites have a fluid understanding of racial identity, where people can gain or lose their claim to being white based on their attitudes, accents, or physical attributes. Hope and Eva realized that even though they weren't seen as having a racial identity, they didn't fit white norms either, and as a result, came to perceive themselves as "other than white." Since almost all equated looking white with looking attractive, their experiences show how our standards of beauty, through conflating attractiveness with whiteness, are racist.

Hope: I'm a white Jamaican. When I came I had an accent. That set me apart. I also have really thick hair compared to these white girls at school. I remember thinking that I would've given anything for their stringy blond hair and sensitive white skin, which seemed to be the way a girl should look. When I spoke, kids would ask, "Why aren't you Black?" That made me wonder, "Why am I not Black?" "Why am I not one or the other?"

Eva: The first time I realized anything my sister said, "your nose" and laughed at me. Then I realized, oh my God, there is something wrong with my nose. It became the symbol of my ethnicity. It reflected Balkanism and that felt like a total loss of neighbourhood. Everyone had small noses, freckles, blond hair, and it was hard looking the way I looked.

Jill: I was short and squat with dark, curly hair and Jewish looking. They were all tall, blond, and skinny. I spent untold hours and money trying to straighten my hair. I wanted to look like them and there was no way I ever could. So it was definitely a feeling of looking different and really striving to be like everybody else.

Colourist attitudes undermined interviewees' sense of belonging because such stereotyping erected a boundary that included those seen as normal and ordinary, and excluded anyone perceived not to fit (S. Hall, 2002). The deep estrangement felt under the gaze of whites caused a few women, like Charlene, to want to look or pass as white in order to fit in. Extreme de-racialization of the body was thus a strategy that she and others envisioned for debunking stereotypes and claiming rights. For this small minority, colourism created shame and the desire to pass. However, rather than passing, greater numbers described dealing with loss – of belonging, community, and possibility – when others saw them first as a race and only secondarily as children with other interests and aspirations. In response, some, like Anita, searched for acceptance from the dominant culture, while others, such as Erum, looked to racialized groups as a way of contesting marginalization.

Charlene: I used to look at the mirror and think, "What's going on here? Why am I so dark?" I wished to be white, actually: to close my eyes and when I opened them I'd be white.

Anita: I remember telling people that I had a tan and that my tan never faded … I've had hard times accepting who I am. I feel that I never really belonged.

Erum: My friends were mostly white. I was a friend but I wasn't a friend, because they wouldn't really include me. So I became part of the brown crew. They were the first people who accepted me.

A majority of racialized woman describe race as a status shaping identity. For 25 per cent, however, race did not play a defining role in their experiences at school. Rather than overriding other identities, race, for them, was one facet of the self among many. The experiences of these women differed dramatically from most racialized interviewees who worked to fit into white-dominated schools. They have more in common with youth in today's metropolitan schools who have expanded opportunities to negotiate and challenge imposed identities in racially diverse environments (Staiger, 2006; Veninga, 2009). In these spaces, youth may fit into groups whose racial background is different from their own by dressing, styling their hair, dancing, and talking like students from their chosen racial groups. When women I spoke to reflected on what enabled them to cross boundaries in these ways, many related it to living in multiracial communities and attending racially diverse schools. Some came together with like-minded friends to create "third spaces" (Bhabha, 1994, p. 1) – peer cultures where they crossed borders and combined racial, religious, and class differences to create hybrid identities and cultures. Virtually all who attended multiracial schools experienced racial stereotyping by the time they finished middle school. Yet their capacity to form or access hybrid spaces enabled them to create countercultures of difference at school.

> Jacqueline: I have to think about why I didn't notice race. You know why? It was multicultural. Everybody got along. It was a mixture of the Caribbean. So it seemed that everybody, even those that were white, were Black. Whiteness wasn't the centre. These three white guys used to fool the teachers because the teachers thought they were from the Caribbean because they talked Black. They didn't look it. They walked it, dressed it, their girlfriends were Black. Even the white girls were like that.

> Amy: It didn't occur to me that I was different when I was younger, that I wasn't Caucasian. I just was. There was so many first-generation kids that everyone was in the same boat. So I didn't feel different and I think even if I did, it would not have been negative. I was very fortunate.

People tend to see appearance as superficial, as having little to do with racism. However, mounting evidence indicates that looks may influence individuals' social status as much as their sex, ability, and racial categorizations do. Almost all participants of colour confronted stereotypes about racialized bodies as out-of-the-ordinary and inferior in schools. Because they had little access to alternative frameworks with which to challenge meanings attached to differences, they were especially susceptible to incorporating these into their body and self-images. Colour continues to be a factor shaping people's school success and life chances and some scholars suggest that this may be worsening (Bonilla-Silva, 2002; Jones, 2000). Since the civil rights era, changes in attitudes and laws have resulted in more interracial couples and multiracial children. As current racial classifications disintegrate and growing numbers of people identify as multiracial, discrimination based on colour is likely to rise. Western societies may be more racially fluid, but because people are less willing to deal with racism overt racism is going underground (Bonilla-Silva & Dietrich, 2009). In this context, colour and culture are performing the role once played by race, where racialized people experience hidden discrimination based not necessarily on race itself, but on the lightness or darkness of their skin and on other signs of difference such as clothing, religion, and accent.

Most liberal-democratic societies have banned gender and race discrimination. At the same time, states have adopted body pedagogies that shift responsibilities for well-being and belonging from institutions onto individuals (Macdonald, Wright, & Abbott, 2010). To save governments from having to fund costly interventions, people learn that they can and must become good biocitizens – citizens who manage their bodies to meet social norms and maximize health and happiness (Rose & Novas, 2005). The push to produce good bio-citizens may, in some ways, represent the continuation of late-nineteenth and early-twentieth-century eugenics thinking that attempted to control people's fertility based on their physical characteristics, race, and heritage (Halse, 2009). Liberal governments today do not intervene directly in people's reproductive lives; instead, they exert influence over populations indirectly by instructing them to work on having the right character, values, conduct, and physicality to prove their virtue and worthiness. Through these processes, governments both exercise control over people's bodies and provide a means by which people can present themselves as good citizens. Urging conformity to imposed standards deflects people's attention from the social-justice issues that continue to afflict communities and nations (Halse, 2009). Treating bodies as indicators of morality and value also deepens injustice, since it buys unearned privileges for some while creating unfair liabilities for others. This discussion raises important ethical questions about body standards at the beginning of the twenty-first century.

Chapter Five

Puberty as Sexual Spectacle

Hasina: When you are young, your parents don't look at you like you are a girl, you're just their kid. Once you hit puberty, you are now a girl. So you have these restrictions.

Hannah: Developing. That was the first time I noticed that there was a division between my body and self. There's this weird thing that you experience as a woman where having cycles forces you into an intimate awareness of your body. At the same time, there's a culture objectifying it and it creates a weird relationship to negotiate this inside/outside thing.

When is one a girl? When is one a woman? What roles do biology and society play in the transition from girlhood to womanhood? Contrary to conventional wisdom, what makes a girl a woman is not puberty, or the development of sex characteristics like genitals and breasts – girls become women through the social reading of their pubertal bodies as womanly. What makes this process fraught is not the raging hormones said to trigger emotional and physical turmoil. Nor is it girls' too-early development, alleged to amplify their sexual danger. Instead, sexual maturation is psychologically and socially difficult because the meanings given to the body processes that make a girl a woman are ambiguous, exposing, and mostly negative. This simple insight may have great utility in explaining many of the stresses and struggles experienced by girls coming of age in the contemporary Western world.

In contemporary Westernized cultures, social and scientific constructions cast puberty as a precarious period that poses particular challenges for girls. Over the past forty years, experts have contributed to creating a climate of concern surrounding female sexual maturation by associating a litany of physical and mental health problems with developing bodies of girls. Problems said to be on the rise for those passing through puberty range from depression and body dissatisfaction to premature sexual activity and teen pregnancy (Brody, 1997; Brooks-Gunn, 1984). In the past decade, growing fears about girls' too-early maturation have seized the scientific and cultural imagination. From a burgeoning body of research debating the disease status of early or "precocious" puberty to a barrage of media reports decrying girls' premature sexual maturation, public and professional discourse increasingly has focused on *early* development as a serious problem to be prevented or overcome (Mazzarella, 2008; Pinto, 2007; Posner, 2006). A dominant narrative has emerged that places the burden and blame for puberty's difficulties and dangers on the bodies of developing girls.

Puberty is a central drama in the social process of becoming a woman. But the stories women tell diverge in critical ways from the dominant view. By focusing on our culture's puberty narrative for girls, this chapter raises critical questions about conventional wisdom that regards physical maturation as a purely biological matter. Puberty can be grasped instead as a social process of sexing the body and self, where girls grapple with cultural meanings ascribed to the physical changes en route to creating new identities as young women. But what is the dominant cultural story of puberty and how does it influence women's personal stories? In what ways do their accounts conform to, contradict, challenge, and talk back to the dominant view? What other stories of puberty do they tell? Many women describe embodied experiences shaped not by biology or psychology alone, but more often by mixed and mostly negative meanings that have framed and fused with the physical changes.

Through analysing the story of puberty told by research reports and newspaper articles, I uncover how official accounts frame puberty in ways that do *not* serve girls' interests or support them in the transition to womanhood. Rather than illuminating their experiences and perspectives, scientific and popular stories participate in "making the child woman" by sexualizing girls' development while disciplining their becoming sexualities. Contrasting excerpts from women's puberty narratives with the dominant story illustrates how cultural meanings powerfully shape girls' physical experiences of their changing bodies. Their stories show how the culture's coupling of puberty with sex and sexuality, rather than the physical maturation process itself, may create the "conditions of possibility" (Gremillion, 2003, p. xv) for many of the psychosocial problems associated with puberty in girls. Drawing on feminist poststructuralist and new materialist theories, this chapter develops an alternative story of puberty that privileges neither the biological nor the social, but shows how the body becomes through its physiology and other forces acting on it.

Plotting Puberty

In Western society, puberty is understood as a biological process of sexual maturation that marks the shift from childhood to adulthood – the physical changes a child undergoes to become an adult, sexed being capable of reproduction (Liao, Missenden, Hallam, & Conway, 2005). According to our culture's puberty narratives, bodily changes that girls go through include hormone shifts and the development of sex characteristics such as breasts, genitals, pubic and body hair, menstrual periods, and fat (Marshall & Tanner, 1969). Within a parallel development story, boys' bodies go through their own hormone changes, and experience the growth of sex characteristics including voice, genitals, muscle mass, sexual sensation, and size (Marshall & Tanner, 1970). In contrast to puberty, the broader term *adolescence* refers to the physical combined with the psychosocial growth experienced in the transition to adulthood. While adolescence is seen to encompass the manifold challenges associated with becoming an adult, people tend to regard these as having physical origins. Adults often talk about teens as being ruled by "raging hormones" and blame problems as wide ranging as depression, aggression, and risky behaviours on their hormonal mayhem. Rather than seeing such problems as emerging from the social representations or relations of adolescence, researchers and lay people often perceive these as originating in the biological changes brought on by puberty (see, for example, Buchanan, Eccles, & Becker, 1992; Faden, Ruffin, Newes-Adeyi, & Chen, 2010; Graber, Brooks-Gunn, & Warren, 2006).

Despite the primacy of this biological story, we know that social forces profoundly influence pubertal processes. For example, the age at which menstruation occurs for girls growing up in the Western world has dropped significantly in the past two hundred years. Today, the average age of menarche, or first period, is twelve. Yet in the 1830s, girls coming of age in England and North America had their first periods when they were about seventeen years old (Tanner, 1962). This means that in a span of less than two centuries, the age of onset for first menses has dropped by an astounding five years! According to British pediatrician James Tanner (1962), who first described this trend in the 1960s, the timing of menarche had dropped from about seventeen to just under thirteen (12.8) years old. Since Tanner, researchers have noted that the falling age of first menses seems to have stopped, stabilizing at around age twelve (Dann & Roberts, 1973; Adams Hillard, 2002). Although many *agree* that the average age of first periods appears to have levelled off for girls in North America over the past forty years, they *disagree* about whether the age of other signs of sexual maturity, such as breasts and pubic hair, still may be declining (Herman-Giddens, Slora, Wasserman, Bourdony, Bhapkar, Koch, & Hasemeier, 1997). Are girls developing breasts at earlier ages? If so, what are the causes and consequences? Most investigators now concur that better nutrition due to massive socio-economic changes has lowered girls' age of menarche. However, many debate whether girls are getting breasts and body hair a couple of years earlier than before, and if the falling age of puberty is a result of factors more worrying than better food such as hormonal responses to stress (Ellis & Garber, 2000), rising obesity (Kaplowitz, Slora, Wasserman, Pedlow, & Herman-Giddens, 2001), and environmental toxins (Steingraber, 2007).

Such dramatic changes in the body's timetable show that puberty cannot be explained as a biological process stripped from its broader context. Ongoing uncertainties about how to measure puberty and what the measures mean likewise reveal ways in which cultural values influence the biological story we tell about puberty (Petersen, Tobin-Richards, & Boxer, 1983). Since the 1960s, researchers have debated using markers as diverse as breast buds (thelarche) and first period (menarche) in girls; hormone and skin changes, genital, bone, and body hair development (pubarche), and growth spurts in girls and boys; and first ejaculation (oigarche), first nocturnal emission, first masturbation, and first sexual attraction in boys. Efforts to plot puberty's progression "objectively" began with the Tanner Scale, a system that relies on categorizing children's body changes according to five stages (in boys, penis size and pubic hair development; in girls, breast and pubic hair development and presence or absence of menses (Marshall & Tanner, 1969, 1970). Originally developed by Tanner and Marshall to get a clearer picture of the physical events that constitute puberty and to distinguish normal from abnormal development, this scale has a dubious history. Tanner created it based on images of the naked bodies of abandoned children who lived in a group home in England, who were photographed every three months from the start of puberty (Marshall & Tanner, 1969, 1970). (To see his visuals of the changes in girls go to http://adc.bmj.com/content/44/235/291.short and of the changes in boys go to http://adc.bmj.com/content/45/239/13.)

Viewed today, these images raise troubling ethical questions about the larger scientific project of charting pubertal development. Why the preoccupation with the sexually maturing body? What has this project, with its questionable practices, been in service of? Clearly, the medical photography that Tanner and Marshall used to develop their scale did not benefit those subjected to it. Instead, this practice can be seen as part of a long history in Western science to discover, document, and know difference, including race, disability, and, in this case, developmental sex difference. Leaving aside such ethical issues, the data Tanner generated were considered so comprehensive that his findings have become the basis for current "objective" definitions of puberty (Kaplowitz, 2006), that is, categorizing the pubertal stage by a visual examination.

More recently, experts have attempted to measure puberty *subjectively* by asking individuals (adolescents currently or adults retrospectively) to self-report on the changes. Responding to questionnaires, girls and boys or men and women rate their height, body hair, and degree of development; girls rate breast development and periods; and boys evaluate facial hair, voice changes and, depending on the scale, erections (Brooks-Gunn, Warren, Rosso, & Gargiulo, 1987; Earls, Brooks-Gunn, Raudenbush, & Sampson, n.d.). By asking research subjects to assess the type and timing of physical changes relative to peers or an imagined norm, researchers hope to better understand the psychological implications of maturing earlier or later. Yet a sexist double standard often informs these measures. Many ask boys and men to report on physical and sexual maturation, while they place greater stress on girls' and women's reproductive system development. There is a noticeable silence about girls' experience of sexual sensation or arousal as a marker of *their* maturation. Regardless of the markers and measures used, or their ethical and sexist implications, there continues to be a lack of consensus on parameters of normal and abnormal puberty. Do we define normal according to the type and timing of changes compared to a larger population? According to people's own sense of timing relative to peers? If so, compared to what peers or population?

Too Much Too Soon, Too Little Too Late

The puberty stories of women in the research group demonstrate that normal is not a fixed, but rather a highly fluid concept determined by their pace and perceptions of change relative to others. Anjula tells how even though she began to menstruate at age thirteen (the dead-on average age for women in North America), she experienced puberty early compared to her main confidante, her mom. Most wanted the power, status, and freedom associated with becoming an adult, but rejected or wrestled with being seen as different due to developing into an adult female body. Significantly, the vast majority (80%) saw their changing bodies as other than normal. This included early developers (40%) (such as Anjula) who relate how they acquired a deviant body, unfeminine because it was considered overdeveloped and too sexual. It also meant the late bloomers (38%), whose underdeveloped bodies were seen as sexually immature and not womanly enough (according to Charlene and Ruby). Even those who developed "on time" often felt dissatisfied for being merely average (as Claire describes it).

Anjula: I didn't know what a period was until I got it at age 13, because I was young. Afterwards I got upset with my mom because I didn't know about it. I asked, "Why didn't you tell me?" She said, "I got mine when I was sixteen. I didn't know you would get it that early. That's why." In terms of my shape, I started growing boobs around my period time. All the girls were so flat that I hated my boobs. I was embarrassed and uncomfortable.

Charlene: I didn't really start to notice until I was thirteen or fourteen. I was a late bloomer, later than everyone else. Other girls had their periods and I didn't; other girls had breasts and I didn't. Then of course I was waiting for my breasts to develop, still am. They say good things come in small packages but … I wasn't too impressed with how I looked.

Ruby: My body started to change but it didn't change very much! That was a big disappointment because I was wondering what was happening, expecting bigger changes. I started to menstruate when I was thirteen. Among my close friends, I was the later bloomer. When I think of that time I think about not measuring up and getting passed over because of my size and my shape. Frustration because there wasn't anything I could do about it.

Claire: I remember feeling scared. I wasn't fat or flat-chested, but I wasn't terribly pretty or busty either. I was the middle ground that gets ignored. I can remember standing in front of the mirror staring at myself then remembering images from TV and movies, and thinking, "I don't look anything like that." Feeling that I was just average.

Critical health researchers have shown how scientists frequently frame their understanding of phenomena by drawing on prior values and beliefs to craft a theoretical account plausible to their peers and the public (Gard & Wright, 2005). This suggests that the scientific story of puberty may rely as much on culturally influenced theoretical frameworks as on the data researchers generate (Mazzarella, 2008). For example, Victorian doctors first understood precocious (or early) puberty not as the early ability to procreate but as disability, as a body deviating from the norms of bodily development. In the precocious development of puberty's physical markers, they found undeniable evidence of the bodily's uncontrolled eroticism and sensuality (Peterson, 2008). Because precocious puberty showed marked deviation from a normative growth standard, they saw it as dividing the "primitive" from the "civilized" races, associated it with people of darker, warmer climates, and framed those affected as throwbacks to an earlier stage of human evolution. Their detailed descriptions of pubescent girls as "little women" with "perfectly formed," "large and prominent" breasts demonstrate their elision of categories girl and women and more ominiously, of possible male sexual desire for the female child (quoted in Peterson, para. 32).

At the turn of the twentieth century, experts first described adolescence as the tumultuous time between child and adulthood triggered by puberty (G.S. Hall, 1904). For concerned psychologists and educators such as Stanley Hall, controlling young people's sexual urges and channelling their energies into sex-appropriate pursuits became the driving force behind defining adolescence as a distinct developmental stage (Lesko, 1996). Because he saw the transition as stormy and stressful, Hall believed maturing boys and girls required sex-specific guidance to ensure their safe passage to adulthood. While redirecting boys' sexual desires into higher intellectual interests could safeguard them from mental and sexual "degeneration" (Bederman, 1996), this was not thought to be the case for girls. Because female bodies were believed to be naturally defective and highly prone to pathology, experts advised parents to discourage girls from a demanding education in favour of gentler domestic pursuits (Ehrenreich & English, 2005). In this way, families and institutions were charged with the responsibility of preserving natural sex differences by making maturing "boys more manly and girls more womanly" (G.S. Hall, 1904, "The Education of Girls," para. 8).

Beginning in the 1960s, experts again sought to identify and understand new psychosocial difficulties such as disordered eating and depression believed to be brought on by development (Brooks-Gunn, 1984; P.D. Duncan, Ritter, Dornbusch, Gross, & Carlsmith, 1985; Ge, Conger, & Elder, 1996; Silbereisen, Petersen, Albrecht, & Kracke, 1989). Though many debated whether the transition constituted a developmental crisis in general for children, most considered it to be a critical period that posed particular challenges for girls (Petersen, Tobin-Richards, & Boxer, 1983). Girls identified as especially vulnerable included those who entered puberty earlier than their peers – they were thought to experience the greatest emotional and social difficulties (Graber, Lewinsohn, Seeley, & Brooks-Gunn, 1997; Smolak, Levine, & Gralen, 1993). Experts also perceived early development to have damaging effects for girls with prior emotional or family problems (Ge et al., 1996; Graber et al., 1997). To explain why the transition was a time of heightened risk, researchers attributed puberty's problems to psychological stresses accompanying the physiological changes. Throughout the 1980s and 1990s, many held the developing body and self, not society or sexism, to be primarily responsible for setting off girls' emotional turmoil and wreaking havoc on their prior physical equality with boys.

Second-wave feminists similarly saw the passage to womanhood as a watershed period for girls. But rather than situating problems in female bodies or psyches, feminist perspectives placed greater responsibility on social expectations that silenced and straightjacketed girls (American Association of University Women, 1991; L.M. Brown & Gilligan, 1992; Orenstein, 1994). At puberty under patriarchy, when the tidal wave of cultural pressures about becoming a woman hit, girls' self-confidence plummeted as they learned to limit themselves and submit to the demands of femininity. Many women in this study describe puberty as a turning point that brought with it a loss of confidence (Jill), heightened physical vulnerability, and lowered body esteem (Fernanda and Sylie). By focusing on girls' experiences at this critical juncture, Gilligan, Brown, Orenstein, and others proposed a new story of female development that emphasized the centrality of relationships over more culturally valued attributes of autonomy and separation. These writers poignantly described how the developing bodies and selves of adolescent girls collided with cultural ideals and norms in dangerous ways that led to a crisis of confidence (Pipher, 1994), low self-esteem

(Orenstein, 1994), and eating problems (Steiner-Adair, 1990), among other issues. Their scholarship illuminated how the risks of adolescence were not the result of innate biology, inner personality, or even inevitable developmental crisis, but of the social contexts that shaped girls' lives.

Jillian: I think of myself during puberty as feeling less sure of myself. It was that time when you're getting to be sexual, and I felt very inadequate. Maybe feeling different physically came to a head. I didn't feel pretty.

Fernanda: I remember puberty as a time where I became totally reclusive: I was no longer into sports or activities and I tended to be really shy, self-conscious, insecure. The boys considered girls with small hips and big chests to be in the "good looking" category. I wasn't in that category. That's when my body- and self-image was the lowest.

Sylvie: As a child I used to be very dare-devilish until my "fall from grace." One day the older boys said to the younger boys, "We're not going to play with you if she's here." I associated that with developing, getting fatter, becoming more different.

In present-day North America, anxieties over pubertal girls' health have not abated. Experts generate voluminous research reports and educational programs designed to protect girls from the apparent psychological difficulties and sexual dangers brought on by development. Throughout research and popular media, for example, adolescent female sexuality remains a problem linked to sexually transmitted infections, sexual violence, and teen pregnancy (Fine & McClelland, 2006; Irvine, 1994). Panic surrounding young women's fertility has served to make those deemed unfit – namely, the poor and racialized – the target of moral regulation and social/statistical surveillance (Posner, 2006). At the same time, young women receive conflicting messages regarding their sexualities and bodies. From cover-girl culture to the fashion industry, sexualized images sell sexy bodies as a source of female pleasure and power. Conversely, girls learn in sex and puberty education to view sex as risky or sleazy and to see periods, breasts, and body hair as dirty or difficult changes that must be controlled or concealed. While consumer culture sexualizes girls of all races, Black girls (and boys) also confront what Ann Ferguson calls "adultification" – the attribution of adult motives to their bodies and desires. Here they are sexualized but differently – not seen as innocently but as dangerously sexual (2001).

Tracing the topography of puberty uncovers a cultural drive to define normal in order to determine what abnormal might be. It also shows how the atypical has been framed as disability, associated with the racialized, and as highly sexualized or as desexualized. Because racialized and disabled girls have not been included in formulating trajectories of puberty, any divergence on their part translates into abnormality. Girls' subjective sexual sensations are written out of definitions of normal puberty, while their bodily changes are infused with sexuality as soon as they begin budding breasts. It is critical to attend to how the cultural legacy of concern and suspicion surrounding girls' sexual expression might play into the scientific study of puberty. It is equally important to consider research that challenges the conventional view of sexual development – of the attainment of sexual dimorphism – as a natural process of bodies.

Beyond the Natural Female Body

Many people take as truth the belief that genitals, hormones, and chromosomes provide the definitive markers of sex difference: that maturation of our reproductive bodies makes us women or men. Yet whether biology can uphold this natural story of sex has been called into question by researchers working both within and outside the sciences. One example of the inadequacy of the biological, binary account is found in hormone research. Most people see hormones as the building blocks of sex. However, since all human bodies produce the chemical substances we call sex hormones, the concept of *sex-specific hormones* had to be created by scientists. According to science historian Nellie Oudshoorn (1994), at the beginning of endocrine research in the early twentieth century, "female" hormones were thought to exist only in women and "male" hormones only in men. By the 1920s, scientists found that no such separation existed: not only did each sex contain the other's hormones but estrogen and testosterone were found to be chemically similar, and testosterone to convert into estrogen in the body. Since each possessed both hormones, it was scientifically inaccurate to "classify people as fully male or female" and more accurate to discuss "overlapping sexes" (Meyerowitz, 2002, p. 28). But rather than abandon the two-sex model, scientists resolved the confusion by establishing that sex differences were a matter of quantity not presence or absence of hormones. Science scholars today argue that because scientists are not trained to recognize the ways in which they are engaged in creating facts, they cannot see the influence of their world views on research (Asberg & Birke, 2010). Looking at sex research through a historical lens, we can see how researchers unwittingly replicated cultural stereotypes in their theories even as they assumed they were revealing the truth about nature (C. Roberts, 2002).

To preserve the concept of natural sex, endocrinologists throughout the twentieth century have continued to write about hormones as male or female even though they know this terminology is imprecise (Petersen et al., 1983). By labelling each hormone as belonging only to one sex, they created a binary narrative, which according to biologist Lynda Birke (2000b) has acquired currency in the wider society because it fits so neatly with cultural stereotypes. Today, some scientists have argued for replacing the old labels with the less dualistic terms *androgenic* and *estrogenic* (see Dorn & Rotenstein, 2004). Yet because *andro* comes from the Greek meaning man and *estro* means anything that drives a person mad, few realize how this nomenclature still upholds a sex dichotomy and hierarchy! A feminist reading shows how scientific language, by emphasizing differences over similarities and by viewing one sex as superior to the other, reproduces and reifies the two-sex model (Oudshoorn, 1994). According to Oudshoorn, twentieth-century endocrinology missed opportunities to reveal sex diversity in human beings, and instead moved to "adhere to the traditional gender classification system" (p. 146).

A feminist reading of puberty science further shows how puberty is located not in bodies but in meanings given to developmental changes occurring at the end of childhood. Although sex is thought to be dormant until sex hormones switch on at puberty, feminist biologists have shown that there are no clear biological boundaries separating asexual from sexual bodies (Fausto-Sterling, 2000). Sex hormones act on bodies from conception and sex characteristics develop from infancy. Endocrinologists maintain that human beings undergo not one but two puberties: the first occurs when sex hormones are active during infancy and the second at the end of childhood (Steingraber, 2007). Some experts contend that puberty is a continuum of development that spans the first two decades of life (Dorn & Rotenstein, 2004) and that we need to rethink puberty not as a distinct transitional phase but, in feminist biologist Sandra Steingraber's words, as a "parade of hormonally driven changes" (2007, p. 16). Finally, while sexuality is thought of as dormant until puberty, many of us recognize through recollections of child sex play and through witnessing children we know that children are sexual beings. Regardless of people's lived knowledge of sexual expression prior to pubescence, puberty is viewed as the advent of sexuality for boys and girls. Thus, even though people take puberty to be the biological trigger of sexual experiences and differences, the association of puberty with sex and sexuality is largely a socially created coupling.

The Making of the "Child-Woman"

In 1997, a hallmark study changed the landscape of puberty science by sparking controversy about whether girls growing up today are maturing earlier than in prior generations. In her study of 17,077 girls visiting their doctors, Dr Marcia Herman-Giddens found herself at the centre of a media storm for finding that puberty was beginning among American girls at earlier ages than previously recorded in the literature (Herman-Giddens et al., 1997). This was particularly true for African American girls. Herman-Giddens concluded that while the downward trend had unknown causes, its implications were troubling, especially for "otherwise immature children needing to cope with bodies that are maturing earlier" (p. 511).

Experts faulted her findings on several counts. First, many argued that using the Tanner Scale to assess pubertal development biased her findings because visual inspection alone could not distinguish chest fat from breast tissue in "chubby" girls. Second, many criticized Herman-Giddens for failing to differentiate early from true "precocious puberty," which, they quarrelled, is a real disease caused by premature activation of sex hormones (Dixon & Ahmed, 2007). Doubters contended that if doctors disregarded the symptoms of precocious puberty, girls might not receive proper diagnosis and treatment, which could lead to serious health problems (Dorn & Rotenstein, 2004). Third, her study suffered from what researchers call *selection bias*; because it included girls up to age twelve only, it excluded late bloomers, which inflated the numbers of early maturers (Slyper, 2006). Despite these controversies, people mostly have embraced the Herman-Giddens findings. Conceived in a culture that regards pubertal development as incompatible with childhood, the research has helped to reframe altered puberty as a troubling trend that poses difficulties for parents and health providers, as well as potentially serious health concerns for affected girls.

Since then, the scientific study and media coverage of puberty has accelerated (Posner, 2006). Much of the research and reporting has focused on girls entering puberty early, ignoring later-maturing girls and boys maturing at any age. To date, the handful of studies on boys find that early puberty benefits or has fewer negative consequences for them than for girls (see M.L. Ahmed, Ong, & Dunger, 2009; Siegel, Yancey, Aneshensel, & Schuler, 1999; van Jaarsveld, Fidler, Simon, & Wardle, 2007; Zehr, Culbert, Sisk, & Klump, 2007). Demographic research into racial differences in age of maturation has claimed that African American girls enter puberty earlier than their white peers (Euling, Selevan, Pescovitz, & Skakkebaek, 2005; Kaplowitz et al., 2001; Nadeem & Graham, 2005) and encounter stresses as a result of becoming what one researcher called "child-women" (Talpade, 2004, 2006). Researchers tend to treat white girls as the unmarked norm against which others are compared, especially Black girls, whose maturation has been subjected to the greatest scrutiny of all (Butts & Seifer, 2010). Although girls with neurodevelopmental disabilities such as cerebral palsy have been found to enter puberty earlier than other children (Siddiqi, Van Dyke, Donahoue, & McBrien, 1999), they don't typically enter into this discussion of timing norms.

In addition to timing trends, studies into the causes and consequences of early puberty have mushroomed. Researchers debate whether the drop in age of development is the result of changes in girls' nutrition and body weight, increased exposure to estrogen-like chemicals in the environment (such as hormones in milk), or their susceptibility to ultra-sexy body images in popular culture. What is more worrying for many researchers than possible *causes* are the potential *consequences* of early puberty in girls, which are thought to include a multiplicity of mental and physical health problems. At the same time, potential trends and possible causes and consequences of shifts in boys' biological timetables have largely been ignored.

Causes and Contributors of Early Puberty

As a result of demographic research, many researchers have declared the falling age of puberty as "the new norm" that is neither normal nor good (Steingraber, 2007, p. 21). To explain the downward drop, scientists have debated possible causes and contributors that can be grouped into five categories: weight and nutrition; stress and adversity; environmental exposure; media; and hormones and genetics (table 5.1, p. 172, shows numbers of studies on various causes of early puberty published up to 2009.) Of all the factors seen to cause or contribute to premature puberty, the most commonly identified one, by far, is fat (Kaplowitz et al., 2001; Lee, Appugliese, Kaciroti, Corwyn, Bradley, & Lumeng, 2007). Until recently, most puberty scientists positively framed the

Table 5.1. Causes/correlates of early puberty

Weight and nutrition	
Overweight	33 references
Over nutrition	27 references
Physical inactivity	9 references
Low birth weight followed by rapid weight gain / Prenatal nutritional environment	13 references
Stress and adversity	
Stress in childhood / Parents' stress / Family conflict / instability / Bad parenting	19 references
Father absence	12 references
Child sexual abuse	3 references
Low SES	3 references
Evolution	11 references
Environmental exposure	
Endocrine disrupting chemicals	17 references
Media	
Excessive TV or computer / Sexual images of kids	4 references
Genetics and hormonal	
Genetic	21 references
Non-white ethnicity	12 references
Disability – CP, seizure disorders, head injury, intellectual disability	1 reference

relationship between higher caloric intake and lower age of puberty as improved nutrition. In the wake of growing worries about rising obesity, overweight has been negatively reframed as a contributor to early puberty via overeating and inactivity. While some researchers have found an association between higher weight and lower puberty (S.E. Anderson, Dallal, & Must, 2003; Davison, Susman, & Birch, 2003; Wang, 2002), to date no studies demonstrate direct causality between fat and early maturation (or fat and overeating, as chapter 4 discusses). This leads me to wonder about how the dramatic reversal in experts' framing of a falling age of puberty onset might reflect the fact that menses can be hidden from view while breasts and body fat cannot.

Another commonly identified contributor to early puberty is stress. Stresses and adversities associated with puberty's falling age span family conflict and breakdown (Bogaert, 2005; Ellis & Garber, 2000; Graber, Brooks-Gunn, & Warren, 1995), bad mothering and not having a father (Ellis, 2004; Moffitt, Caspi, Belsky, & Silva, 1992; Tither & Ellis, 2008), childhood sexual abuse (Romans, Martin, Gendall, & Herbison, 2003; Siddiqi et al., 1999), and being poor (Downing & Bellis, 2009; Gluckman & Hanson, 2006). Although research in this area appears to shift blame for altered puberty from individuals to broader social conditions, it tends to naturalize early puberty as evolution's response to stressful circumstances. For example, one often-quoted, controversial theory draws on evolutionary biology to explain premature puberty as a "reproductive strategy" that developed early in human evolution (Belsky, Steinberg, & Draper, 1991, p. 647). According to this position, girls growing up in adverse, resource-scarce environments with uncertain futures increase their chance of reproductive success by accelerating physical maturation and beginning reproduction at an early age (Ellis, 2004; Gluckman & Hanson, 2006). While it is plausible that stress might trigger puberty, the "reproductive strategy" theory relies on questionable assumptions that have unwelcome consequences for girls and women. In assuming that evolution determines age of reproduction, the theory ignores how social forces such as sexism and classism shape women's reproductive choices in much more immediate ways. By naturalizing the relationship of adverse experiences to reproductive decision making, it downplays our collective responsibility to create conditions that advance women's reproductive rights.

A third theory posits that altered puberty may result from exposure to environmental pollutants called *endocrine disruptors* (Hotchkiss, Rider, Blystone, Wilson, Hartig, Ankley, Foster, Gray, & Gray, 2008). These hormonally active agents are found in many consumer products as well as in pesticides, packaging, and building materials. According to this explanation, early puberty is a hormonally triggered event rooted in exposures to environmental toxins that have adverse effects on puberty timing (Golub et al., 2008). Support for the theory is found, among other places, in studies of children exposed to suspected endocrine disruptors. Such studies document breast development in those accidentally given estrogen-containing substances (Aksglaede, Juul, Leffers, Skakkebaek, & Andersson, 2006), or acne and pubic hair growth in those inadvertently exposed to testosterone products (Kunz, Klein, Clemons, Gottschalk, & Jones, 2004). This is why some researchers, notably Sandra Steingraber (2007, p. 59), see early puberty as an "ecological disorder." The environmental-exposure hypothesis raises vitally important questions about the link between puberty-inducing chemicals and reproductive cancers. However, some experts, in an effort to bring attention to the significance of their work, have placed undue emphasis on the role of toxins in triggering too-womanly bodies, which directs attention towards the spectacle of girls' sexualities and away from the greater cause for concern: cancer risk.

In a fourth theory of causation, some experts speculate that sexualized media content may induce pubertal onset. Although such an association hasn't been tested empirically, the sexy-imagery theory is cited repeatedly. While the critique of hyper-sexual images is important, reiterating this hypothesis in the face of little evidence may reveal more about adults' fear of girls' sexual awakening than anything about early puberty itself.

Many puberty scientists now argue that environmental and genetic factors may activate premature puberty by switching on pubertal hormones (Dorn & Rotenstein, 2004; Yun, Bazar, & Lee, 2004). In addition to stimulating physical development, pubertal hormones are thought to reorganize brain circuitry in ways that lead to cognitive changes and create psychological distress (Grumbach & Styne, 2003). Some scientists hypothesize that the limbic centres of the brain (thought to be associated with a person's lowered sensitivity to risk) mature earlier than frontal lobes, which are thought to be responsible for self-regulation (Faden et al., 2010). As a result, earlier puberty poses increased risks for bad behaviour because limbic changes occur before a young person has fully developed frontal lobes associated with impulse control capacity. While this theory offers one plausible explanation for problems such as drug use, unprotected sex, and truancy, it relies on debatable claims that exclude other possible reasons for such behaviours. In a context where adults and peers often respond to girls' changing bodies in ways that produce trauma and erode self-esteem, it seems more plausible to deduce that early-maturing girls might adopt high-risk and self-harming behaviours to protest their newly difficult and dangerous situation.

In stark contrast to the dominant story that naturalizes early puberty's causes as solely biologically based, participants in this research frequently identified other people's perceptions and actions as a main source of stress about their developing bodies, whether early, on time, or late. Women suggest that when they entered puberty they looked at other girls to compare the pace of their own physical development. But comparisons with friends did not alone fuel their anxiety and worry. Instead, they relate twice as many moments when their bodies became objects of appraising looks. Thus, gendered looking relations learned in early childhood (as previous chapters make evident) became well established during puberty. Aside from boys and men's apparaisal, participants felt the evaluative gaze of multiple outsiders – parents, teachers, parents, and more popular peers. Their changing bodies were increasingly subject not only to looks and stares, but to harsh and harassing comments.

> Rosetta: I remember how scared I was about the transition from being a girl to a woman. I had to deal with people commenting, "Rosetta's really starting to bloom," and me thinking "I'm still a kid." When I developed my mom was always, "Be good. Be nice. Be the girl I want you to be. Step out of line and I won't speak to you." Stepping out of line meant dating the wrong guy. She had things about boys. Someone once told me that people expect people with disabilities to be asexual. So she would be, "You shatter the image of my beautiful little asexual daughter." You're only a little angel without those types of feelings.

> Moira: From a very young age, I was athletic. That was probably the best time around my body: feeling good when I played sports. But when I started puberty, my dad would comment, "Your hips are getting bigger." When I saw other girls being teased I never wanted to be like that. I remember getting messages that women should be big on top and small on bottom. My brothers and father bought into that whole-heartedly and would make comments about a woman with big breasts and small hips being very beautiful. In grade 8, the boys started to comment on how tight our jeans and sweaters were. We never commented on their size! We were a lot more accepting of the boys than they were of us. We were critical with each other about make-up, clothes, hair. I was one of the worst ones because I was raised to be very watchful and critical about people. Pretty and popular, but in a negative way.

Whose Problem Is It, Anyway?

What is more worrying for many researchers than possible *causes* are the *consequences* of early puberty in girls. These are thought to include a multiplicity of mental and physical health concerns: high-risk and anti-social behaviours such as smoking, drugs, and crime; psychological issues ranging from depression to eating disorders; risky sexual practices leading to STIs, pregnancies, and higher rates of sexual victimization; adult obesity; and reproductive cancers. (Table 5.2, p. 176, summarizes

Table 5.2. Early puberty consequences?

Anti-social behaviour	
Aggression / delinquency / conduct disorder / truancy / crime / Older and deviant peers / gangs	19 references
Substance misuse – Drugs, alcohol, cigarettes	22 references
Psychological problems	
Psychological problems generally	32 references
Anxiety / distress / depression	27 references
Low self-esteem / negative body image / eating disorders / increased suicide attempts	32 references
Poor school performance / lower academic education	9 references
Sexualization, sexual health issues, sexual violence	
Early sexual activity / intercourse / sexual promiscuity / sexual risk taking / short relationships / early pregnancy / increased STIs/ unprotected sex	24 references
Sexualization / harassment / peer victimization / sexual abuse, rape, unwanted sexual advances	15 references
Child woman / instant adult / adults at 12 / Little women	12 references
Weight problems	
Overweight / obesity / physical inactivity / unhealthy nutrition	25 references
Diabetes / high blood pressure / cardiovascular disease	10 references
Physical health problems	
Reproductive / breast cancer	14 references
Shortness / incomplete brain re-sculpting / underdeveloped learning	7 references

studies published up to 2009 on the consequences of early puberty.) Despite the certainty with which experts make these claims, evidence remains uncertain and any conclusions about early puberty's negative consequences are controversial. In her review of this literature, Rachel Blumstein Posner (2006) finds that psychosocial problems linked with earlier maturation appear to be transient – such problems tend not to endure over the long term. She also notes that although early development is assumed to predict sexual activity, few studies have shown a link between earlier pubertal timing and sexual risk taking or teen pregnancy.

In my reading of this literature, I found that scientists often make claims about the negative psychological consequences of altered puberty even where the evidence does not support their conclusions. Ellis (2004), for example, argues that falling puberty leads to "a variety of negative health and psychosocial outcomes" (p. 920), even though his review focuses on *causes* not *consequences* of early maturation. In another study that investigates whether pubertal timing is affected by girls' weight status, Davison et al. (2003) claim that overweight girls are at risk of "negative outcomes associated with early puberty," including delinquency, reproductive cancer, and adult obesity (p. 820). Again, these outcomes are assumed rather than shown or supported by evidence. M.L. Ahmed et al. (2009) assert that the link between childhood obesity and early puberty has "major public health implications" (p. 237) without adequately establishing what these might be. In yet another study that found no drop in puberty age among Danish children, researchers concluded it was "crucial to monitor the pubertal development closely in Denmark in the coming decades" due to "the advent of the ongoing obesity epidemic in Denmark" (Juul, Teilmann, Scheike, Hertel, Holm, Laursen, Main, & Skakkebaek, 2006, p. 253). Besides offering scant evidence for a Danish obesity epidemic, the authors make speculative claims about the adverse consequences of another trend, falling puberty, which has not yet occurred in that country. In a particularly egregious example of early-puberty panic that has no basis in evidence, Talpade (2006) claims that African American girls experience early puberty at higher rates than other girls, which causes "a number of psychological and behavioural problems" as well as "health problems such as childhood obesity and diabetes" (p. 91). She then goes on to claim that

> past studies have revealed positive body image perceptions among AA [African American] girls. However, it is a compelling finding that there were no differences between the girls as a function of early sexual maturation. If the child-women are not aware or do not adapt their behavior to their changing bodies, the possibility of problems such as statutory rape, sexual activity and teenage pregnancies emerge with other psychosocial challenges. (p. 100)

As is evident in these examples, researchers draw upon body- and behaviour-blaming discourses that hold girls responsible for the exploitative acts of others. Schreck, Burek, Stewart, & Miller (2007) invoke this discourse when they contend that even girls' victimization results from their "offensive or annoying" behaviour due to the distress of early puberty, which causes others to respond in retaliating ways (p. 397).

Here the pubertal body – not social readings or others' reactions – is positioned as primarily responsible for altering girls' social interactions in ways that promote victimization and produce problem behaviour. In a similar instance, Lanza and Collins (2002) argue that higher rates of substance misuse among early-maturing girls result from the disparity between their psychological and physical maturation: "Although physically developed, they [early maturers] may still be psychologically immature, lacking the cognitive skills to resist social pressures from peers" (p. 80). These explanations draw on the widely touted "mismatch theory," which contends that psychosocial problems associated with early puberty emerge from the dissonance between girls' physical and psychological development. As Downing and Bellis (2009) put it, because early maturers' "social maturity lags behind physical maturity by a greater period than any other time in history," they are ill equipped to deal with "sexual and other exploratory urges" (p. 446). While the mismatch theory does not fully fault girls for early puberty's bad outcomes – these arise instead from the clash between their bodies and psyches or bodies and society – it does identify their changing bodies as one of the main culprits.

Many social scientists call for close management of pubertal bodies to lower the risks associated with maturing too soon. Ellis (2004) concludes that further research into early puberty will help in "controlling the pubertal transition" (p. 950). Although he does not say how the transition should be managed, given his gloomy predictions about early maturation's adverse effects, readers might reasonably take this statement to mean delaying development as long as possible. In a similar vein, researchers often recommend changing children's eating and exercise to prevent the weight gain linked with early puberty. Johnson, Gerstein, Evans, and Woodward-Lopez (2006) advocate healthy eating as a primary way of preventing early puberty to break the "generational cycle of obesity" (p. 100). Obesity, in this view, is seen as causing early puberty and early puberty as contributing to obesity. The model typically holds girls or their parents responsible for the over-consumption and sedentary lifestyles that are assumed to trigger weight gain and early puberty, which results in adult obesity. Others posit that early developers' own psychological shortcomings combined with adults' failure to send cautionary messages may leave them ill-equipped to manage boys' or their own sexual drives and desires. For instance, Talpade (2006, p. 91) in the passage I quoted earlier calls on "child-women" to "adapt their behavior to their changing bodies" to prevent rape and teenage pregnancy. By advocating individual change, proposed solutions download responsibility for early puberty's problems onto girls' developing bodies.

In casting those who mature sooner as "child-women" (Talpade, 2006, p. 91), "adults at twelve" (Bellis, Downing, & Ashton, 2006, p. 910), and "little women" (R. Nelson, 2007, p. 25), researchers conflate early puberty with too-early sexuality and a too-womanly body, and see it as a sign of improper womanhood. Even the scientific language of *precocious puberty* carries sexualized meanings: though "precocious" *denotes* the disease of very early development, it also *connotes* girls' sexual forwardness. In employing such language, experts assume that puberty sexualizes girls and that early puberty accelerates and intensifies that sexualization. Rather than the experts holding the culture accountable for imposing adult sexuality onto their pubescent bodies, girls themselves are made to shoulder the blame.

The conflation of puberty with sexuality ripples throughout media stories as well. For example, one journalist worriedly wrote that girls should be "reading fairy-tales, not fending off wolves." Another described early puberty dramatically as "the making of an eight year old woman" (Belkin, 2000). In many newspaper articles, reporters exacerbate parents' anxiety about their daughters' psychosocial adjustment, noting that as daughters develop breasts, they become targets of sexual violence. Even in the progressive press, anxieties about girls' too-developed bodies are given free rein. For example, in an otherwise well-balanced article examining the impact of chemicals on early puberty among African American girls, biologist Sandra Shane (2008), the white mother of an adopted Black daughter, makes troubling statements like "my own daughter, who is now almost ten, remains delightfully flat-chested" (p. 29). Why delightful? Does this imply that ten year olds with developed breasts are displeasing or objectionable? In another news story, Eisner (2001) reports that parents are disturbed by their daughters' early puberty because they regard pubertal development as incompatible with childhood and think early puberty causes sexual abuse (which begs the question: why do causes and solutions inevitably rest on girls' bodies rather than on the social forces that fuel harassment?). In a *Time* magazine article, Lemonick (2000) also regards girls' sexuality as problematic, and is nostalgic for the "good old days," which is clear in the article's tone. For instance, he concludes his article with this passage:

Angelica Andrews also has her parents watching out for her. Recently, the teenager experienced her first French kiss – but her family knew all about

Figure 5.1. Early puberty: Why girls are growing up faster: This *Time* magazine cover captures cultural anxieties about girls' sexualities and the taken-for-granted sexualization of developing female bodies in our society.

it, and the boy was immediately instructed not to call again until she was sixteen, or maybe eighteen. It's unfortunate that such vigilance has become necessary for the families of many twelve- and thirteen-year-olds, whereas a generation ago, most parents could relax until a girl was sixteen. But as Angelica puts it, "Welcome to the twenty-first century."

This analysis suggests that hegemonic messages in media and academia cast girls' bodies and behaviours as primarily responsible for early puberty and many of its adverse effects. While untimely maturation is regarded as a problem due to its harmful health outcomes, the culture's greater preoccupation with girls' compared to boys' pubertal timing betrays its deeper anxieties over girls' sexual coming out. Even where the discourse shifts blame for the negative consequences of early puberty from girls' bodies to the cultural forces that sexualize them (as we shall see in chapter 6), this critique remains inadequate, since it leaves little room for girls to be healthfully and positively sexual. Analysing the early-puberty discourse is important because it surfaces underlying social processes that sexualize girls at puberty while disciplining their becoming sexualities.

Puberty as Sexual Spectacle

According to women in this study, early puberty alone did not cause their too-early sexual development. Rather, cultural perceptions of pubertal female bodies as charged with adult sexuality contributed to their sexualization regardless of their own desires, understandings, or experiences at puberty. The imposition of adult sexuality occurred when others responded as if they were sexually mature women simply because they showed outward signs of physical development. In a culture that celebrates girls' sex appeal but laments their sexual expression, others looked on interviewees' maturing bodies with many conflicting emotions. When adults focused their misgivings and suspicions on women's apparent sexual awakening, this prevented some from exploring sexuality at their own pace (such as Eva and Navpreet), and pushed others into becoming sexual in the ways that people already imagined them to be (like Anita and Harriet). The cultural meanings embedded in responses to their changing bodies, *not* the changes themselves, generated much of the distress they felt. Their stories suggest that girls' changing bodies may be less culpable in the bad psychosexual outcomes linked with early puberty than people's fraught reactions to the changes. According to early maturers, the sexualizing and moralizing climate created the "conditions of possibility" for many of the psychosexual difficulties they faced.

> Navpreet: First you are child then suddenly you are a growing woman: you become a danger to yourself and a danger to others. There is the extreme worry of pregnancy. In Indian culture, the greater concern is the appearance of anything improper. As soon as you start to become a woman, people gossip about you, parents worry about your reputation.

> Eva: Until puberty I was fairly healthy in terms of sexuality, exploring my body and other people's bodies. But when I got into puberty, I felt very lost as to how I would do anything.

> Anita: The peer pressure was unbelievable, at times. Fitting in, I did a lot of rebellious things too. I smoked. I was always out. I drank a lot. I was having sex before I should have been having sex.

> Harriet: I got the message that my period was related to sexuality, and that you're not allowed to express yourself sexually. I thought it meant that I was a little overeager to be sexual. I was what would be labelled "promiscuous" in adolescence: I slept with a lot of guys. Sometimes I wonder if I was acting out in response to the messages I was given.

According to cultural critic Sharon Mazzarella, anxieties about early puberty reflect adult fears of girls' bodies that "transgress culturally prescribed dictates of childhood innocence," causing adults to "confront girls' sexuality at an earlier age than they are comfortable with" (2008, pp. 22–3). At puberty in sexist society, girls face many sexual problems ranging from unwanted pregnancy and STIs to rape and a bad reputation. Given these risks, adult worries about their too-early maturation make sense. Yet in assuming that puberty pushes them into sexuality and womanhood, this worry misses the mark by fixating on girls' development rather than the culture that casts their changing bodies as too sexual and by focusing on their sexualities over the inequities that adversely affect their health. If we really wanted to safeguard young women's emotional and social well-being, wouldn't we invest our energies in uncovering premature puberty's causes and advocating girls' sexuality rights instead of fixing a frightened or fascinated stare on their maturing bodies? If health were the main motive, wouldn't researchers turn more attention to boys' biological timetables, a topic that has sparked little concern? If puberty were not so entangled with sexuality in our cultural imagination, would people be so alarmed about early puberty in girls? In a context where developing female bodies are both highly sexualized and highly regulated, when do young women get to feel in control of their bodies and sexualities? What do girls at puberty need from adults, schools, and society at large in order to transform their experiences of the transition?

Feminists argue that the agenda underlying recent research into early puberty is to suppress girls' sexuality and delay their development in order to control their sexual activity and fertility (Posner, 2006; Tolman, 2002). Silence about boys' timetables may reflect the prevailing assumption that boys' sexual expression invigorates their virility and makes their manliness. As Posner notes, this point is well supported by the fact that early-maturing boys generally do not suffer the same self-esteem drop as their female counterparts do; rather than being scrutinized or harassed, they tend to be admired and emulated. In our pill-popping culture, which looks to chemical solutions for complex problems, it is troubling that some pediatricians and endocrinologists now promote development-delaying hormones in order to stave off the sexual pressures and psychosocial problems that early-maturing girls may face (Carroll, 2010; Hirsch, Gillis, Strich, Chertin, Farkas, Lindenberg, Gelber, & Spitz, 2005; Ibáñez, Ong, Valls, Marcos, Dunger, & de Zegher, 2006; University of Iowa Hospitals and Clinics, 2006). In assuming that girls' changing bodies push them into sexual maturity, researchers ignore how their own assumptions contribute to sexualizing girls. This may have particularly negative consequences for girls of African descent. In failing to uncouple puberty from sexuality, experts may inadvertently reinforce cultural stereotypes about racialized girls as oversexed in comparison to white girls, who tend to be seen, in this discourse, to embody the mythical norm.

For racialized storytellers and those with bodily differences, the sexualization that accompanied their physical maturation was especially fraught. Before puberty most had discovered they were seen as different. When their bodies began to change, however, misconceptions of body differences intermingled with the distorted gaze on their developing bodies to amplify their sense of being flawed. Along with this intensified gaze came a powerful injunction: that sexual expression was taboo.

Marcia: I was pretty early. When I was about age ten a family friend made halter-tops for my sister and me. We were so excited we couldn't wait until we wore them. When I put mine on, my dad said "Where are you going with that on? You need to put a top on." I realized that had I been smaller-chested, he would not have thought anything of it. But because I was larger he saw me as potentially being sexualized.

Gayle: Even before I started to develop I felt like an improper female. For me, it wasn't breasts but it was fat, fat, fat. I felt like an "improper female" if I showed any sign of femininity. Other kids thought I was fat and weird. Having thrown in your face acceptable images of female sexuality. Finding you do like boys but they don't like you.

Elizabeth: My girlfriends were developing before I was. So I was anxious to start wearing a bra. But I didn't want to stand out in any way. It seemed so incongruous that I was starting to develop but that I wasn't considered a woman in any way because I wasn't looked at as dating material.

To date, only one group of researchers has sought to understand the emotional impact of early puberty by asking early-maturing women to talk about their experiences. Liao et al. (2005) found that the women they interviewed were uncomfortable with their early maturation due to the cultural belief that femininity is equivalent to sexual availability, which contributed to their harassment. The participants regarded themselves as different and deviant as a result of their untimely maturation. They were uncomfortable with early puberty because it blurred the lines between childhood and adulthood and one woman reported being traumatized by the idea that sexual abuse caused her early puberty. (She was told this was the cause, even though she was not an abuse victim.) The experiences of early-maturing women in my research resonate with those of Liao's responders. According to those who had endured sexual abuse, abuse did *not* result in early puberty. Instead, they noted that sexualization at puberty was both unlike child sexual abuse and more of the same: similar in that it represented another oppressive imposition of adult sexuality onto them, and different in that it made them vulnerable to new kinds of exploitation. Whether women entered puberty with or without prior abuse experiences, the forced sexualization that accompanied puberty's changes accelerated and intensified their sexual vulnerability. The cultural positioning of the pubertal female body as sexual and violable permitted and even sanctioned others' oppressive treatment.

Ada: I was sexually abused. One of the last incidents was when he said after assaulting me, "You're so beautiful, it's a pity you don't have any breasts." As part of becoming and being seen as a woman, I realized that having the body that everybody said I should have made me vulnerable in a new way. I began to think that's why the abuse was happening, because I was considered pretty. I went from thinking it happened because I was weak to it happened because I was pretty and weak. I still have no idea what "feeling comfortable in one's own skin" feels like.

Salima: A lot of what I have experienced growing up has been based on the way I look – my size and my colour. I was also sexually abused. The abuse affected my relationship with my body sexually because I saw sex as power, especially when I entered puberty. The way I presented myself would get me attention, and attention gave me power, confidence, and the feeling of control, even though later on I realized how limiting that was. After I developed, I felt this double-edged tension surrounding being thin and sexy: it gave me power but also unwanted attention.

Juxtaposing the dominant story alongside embodied accounts raises questions about girls currently going through puberty. Are their hormones really fast-forwarding their biological timetables? If so, should we be worried? To what extent are parents and professionals more concerned with controlling girls' sexualities than advancing their sexual health and rights? If processes of puberty fluctuate, then what is "normal female development"? Mounting evidence showing that environmental contexts shape girls' pubertal processes calls into question the idea that there must be a single normal path to becoming a woman – or a natural way to be one. Unpacking the dominant story of puberty allows us to see how social forces contour girls' becoming. Although our culture denies it, girls' bodies are not suddenly sexed at puberty, nor do their sexualities awaken abruptly at the end of childhood. Instead, a cultural interpretation of puberty as synonymous with sex and sexuality interweaves with the physical processes to shape women's experiences and perceptions. The participants' stories uncover how puberty is not the discrete phase of maturation that marks the closing of childhood. Rather outsiders' frequent and forceful responses to the bodily changes inculcated in participants cultural notions of what it means to look and feel like a woman.

Chapter Six

A Body That Looks, and Feels, Like a Woman

In North American society, puberty is understood primarily as a biological process in which a child's body undergoes physical changes to become an adult woman or man capable of reproduction. Yet, as we saw in chapter 5, the experience is profoundly social and cultural. As their bodies undergo the physical changes of pubescence – developing breasts and body fat, growing body hair, and getting their periods – girls are viewed as moving from the androgynous body of childhood to a body culturally coded as womanly. Many look forward to the expanded possibilities they associate with becoming women but girls also encounter contradictory meanings given to their physical development and differences. These include interpretations of menstrual blood as powerful yet polluting, of fat as unfeminine and out of control, and of breasts as sexy and life giving but also hyper-visible sources of vulnerability. For the first time, many face confounding meanings ascribed to their "becoming women" bodies. In response to the culture's worried reaction, they learn to manage the changes in order to close the gap between their developing differences and society's pervasive body standards.

Contemporary feminist theory sees the sexed body as neither socially constructed nor biologically determined; rather, it becomes through interconnections with psyches and the surrounding world. While the women in my research, what were the joys and traumas of becoming women? How did they transition with the bodies they were handed and the meanings given? What did developing mean for those who experienced a good fit between biology and culture? For those who faced the impossibility of fitting? While they went through the physical processes of puberty, all learned to modify the changes in an attempt to fit the cultural image of a properly sexed form. In this way, they actively intervened in puberty, managing their periods, containing their breasts, controlling their weight, and removing their body hair to embody an image of an acceptable woman. Becoming a woman was not automatic or absolute; instead, each woman described it as a social and relational process that pivoted on how her changing body felt and was seen.

The participants' puberty stories reveal the multiple ways that girls' physical processes are regarded and regulated in society. The braided feelings of excitement and anxiety, surprise and shock, awe and dread that underpin women's puberty narratives suggest that North American culture still views developing womanly bodies as abject. As they moved towards adulthood, many explained how boys got rewarded for maturing bodies deemed capable and powerful, while girls lost status for changes coded as messy and scary. The worry and distress they described not only reflected the contradictory qualities ascribed to becoming womanly bodies. These emotions also arose from the requirement that they cope and come to terms with the changes as part of accepting their newly ambiguous status as sexually different. The painful process of having to acclimatize to and embody a newly devalued identity was their "predicament of puberty." This chapter builds on the analysis of puberty offered in chapter 5 to explore how the women I interviewed dealt with imposed sexual difference to "qualify" as women. Reflecting on participants' experiences allows women (and men) to see how we are made – how many forces contour and constrain our "becoming" – and how we can intervene to change compulsory scripts.

Puberty Blues

In North America education about puberty mostly focuses on "plumbing," or physiology. Feminists are concerned about the scientific style of puberty education because it masks hidden ideologies at work under the language's apparent objectivity. Commercial instructional materials illustrate this point. Since the 1920s, manufacturers of menstrual and puberty-related products have developed educational materials designed to promote brand loyalty among consumers. Well-known booklets such as *Growing Up and Liking It* (1940–74; Personal Products Company, makers of Modess pads) and *Very Personally Yours* (1948–61; Kimberly Clark, makers of Kotex) were once marketed to mothers and daughters to introduce product lines and teach scientific facts about menstruating bodies. (To view examples, go to http://www.mum.org/

GULIcov.htm.) In recent years these have been supplemented or replaced by interactive websites, first-period starter kits, and school-based puberty education programs. Viewing the classroom as an incubator for future consumers, manufacturers have distributed teachers' manuals and student guides covering a range of topics about developing bodies. However, despite stylistic changes over time, most classroom materials stress the biology of puberty and present products as solutions for puberty's hygiene problems (which include blood, body odour, and acne).

Instructional materials do more than present facts or push products. They also reinforce certain ideas about female and male bodies and sexualities. To identify these, consider school resources such as Tambrands' *The Inside Story* (1990; see below) or older films like *Molly Grows Up* (1953; http://www.archive.org/details/MollyGro1953) and *As Boys Grow* (1957; http://www.archive.org/details/AsBoysGr1957). Reflect on key messages that these resources send, including the following Tambrands' *Teacher's Guide*:

> **Teaching about Menstruation and Feminine Protection Products:** Menstruation is regarded as a significant event in almost all societies, and the onset of menstruation is commonly considered the moment a girl becomes a woman. Yet many girls, especially those who mature early, are not prepared for their first periods. They often lack correct information, and may be confused and scared by the appearance of the menstrual flow. Your presentation of menstruation as a normal, natural process – part of being a healthy adult woman – can do a lot to ease anxieties and correct misconceptions that are common among preteen girls. In fact, it's a good idea to spend a few minutes discussing specific old wives tales and myths about menstruation, many of which persist today. By leading students in a discussion of what one can do (shower, wash hair, exercise) and can't do (virtually nothing!) while menstruating, you can help them separate fact from superstition. Changing resources have been provided to help you teach about menarche and the menstrual cycle.
>
> **Teaching about the Changes of Puberty in Boys:** Voice change, hair growth, growth of genitals – like girls, boys also need information on the changes they experience during puberty. Unlike girls, most boys in grades five and six are relatively underdeveloped, so they generally need reassurance that this is normal and they'll soon catch up. Other topics you may want to discuss with your male students include erections and involuntary erections, ejaculations, and nocturnal emissions. In addition, boys

need to know how to care for their changing bodies. Changing resources will help you provide boys with this information and reassure them that they are developing normally into unique, individual adult men. (Tambrands Canada, 1993)

Even though they were produced in different gendered contexts, materials like the *Tambrands* 1993 guide and the 1950s instructional films share a similar underlying message: in both cases, menstruation is seen as the most significant pubertal event for girls, while erections, ejaculations, and wet dreams are the events for boys. By reassuring girls that menstruation is normal and boys that wet dreams are to be expected, such messages effectively erase girls' sexual sensations. The scientific model emphasized here also views reproductive maturation as the central purpose of puberty rather than just as one of its outcomes (Diorio & Munro, 2003). Defining puberty as reproductive maturity naturalizes heterosexuality by marginalizing non-heterosexual and non-reproductive sexualities (where anything outside of penis/vaginal intercourse is not real sex), and erases sexed body parts (like the clitoris) that are not directly connected to reproduction.

The erasure of girls' non-reproductive sexed body parts and sexual pleasure is evident in contemporary instructional drawings of boys' and girls' bodies, which habitually name and explain the functions of the penis and testes but *not* the clitoris. For example, compare how girls' and boys' genitalia are depicted in Proctor and Gamble's *Always Changing* (2009), a puberty education program endorsed by non-profit organizations in Canada and the United States. (To review the guide, go to http://www.phecanada.ca.) Many programs, like this one, stress a "science-based" reproductive model that makes little reference to external female genitalia such as the labia, vulva, or clitoris so that girls can't match the pictures and descriptions with what they see or feel. Male pubertal bodies are presented as visible and known whereas female ones are more mysterious, difficult, and invisible (Driscoll, 2002; Erchull, Chrisler, Gorman, & Johnston-Robledo, 2002). This second point is apparent in the 2010–11 student booklet of the *Always Changing* program, which defeats its aim to demystify female bodies by discussing external parts of girls' genitals without identifying the clitoris. By insisting on heterosexual reproduction as the primary purpose of puberty, programs such as this one silence other possible meanings and experiences of pubescent bodies and sexualities (Diorio & Munro, 2003). (Although Proctor and Gamble, sponsors of *Always Changing*, describes the program as a school-based health education resource, the corporation declined permission to reprint the program's anatomical drawings here. In my view, any company that exempts its instructional material from critical analysis should *not* be permitted to describe its resources as "educational." See figures 6.1 and 6.2 for a reasonable likeness of the *Always Changing* program.) If we were designing educational materials from a gender diversity and sexuality rights perspective, what changes might we make?

Science-based puberty education does little for prepubescent girls who are far more interested in learning about girls' embodied experiences of puberty such as what it feels and looks like to have a period (Erchull et al., 2002). The puberty stories of women in this study further reveal how the disembodied scientific approach of puberty education

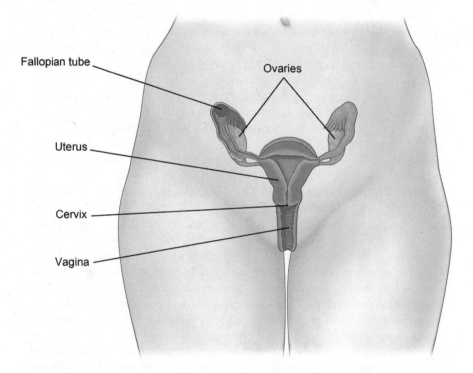

Figure 6.1. Sexuality and U: Female reproductive system. A facsimile of the female reproductive system widely used in health curricula across Canada.

neither adequately demystified the changes nor guided them through important events such as their first period. Despite prior puberty education, many could not figure out what was happening with their bodies and neither the anatomical drawings nor the written instructions assisted them in managing the mechanics very well. Instead, period pedagogy typically contributed to their discomfort, anxiety, and fear, because women couldn't match the disembodied descriptions with their felt and lived bodies. Lessons from the official curriculum contrasted sharply with those from other sources, according to some

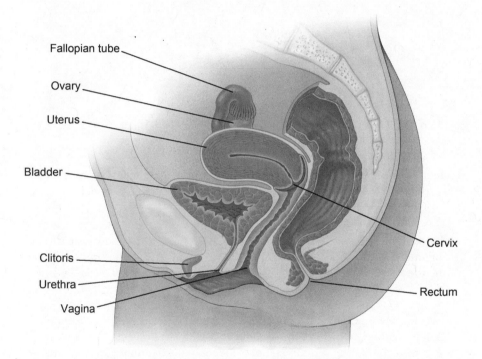

Figure 6.2. Sexuality and U: Female reproductive system with clitoris: Some government ministries, boards of education, and health education organizations now provide illustrations that clearly label the clitoris. However, even these curricula tend to give educators two versions of the female reproductive system: one without and one with the clitoris labelled. This allows conservative school boards and teachers to avoid talking about female sexuality and pleasure while enabling progressive ones to do so.

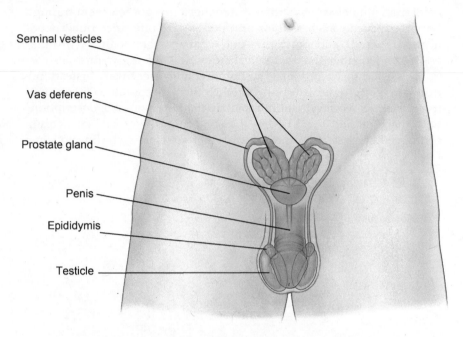

Figure 6.3. Sexuality and U: Male reproductive system. A facsimile of the male reproductive system typically used in health curricula across Canada.

storytellers, such as Yolanda and Ruby, who picked up useful information and meaningful insights about the joys and fears of menarche from the affectionately remembered book *Are You There God? It's Me, Margaret* by Judy Blume (1986).

> Venita: My first period: such a horrible night! My years of sex education didn't sink in. You don't think about that stuff when it hits you. I was, "What is this? Why is it this colour?" I went to the bathroom and I found pads. So I was turning the thing over, figuring out how I was supposed to apply it. Because they never taught us how we were supposed to use it.

> Corey: At home I was given a book, *Doctors Talk to Nine to Twelve Year Olds*. At school, our health class was on plumbing. So there was no concept of how people develop differently or what it feels like. There were just anonymous diagrams. When I had my period my mother was at work.

I phoned her up convinced I was dying. She called the local drugstore and they delivered pads and a belt. I don't remember receiving instructions. How I figured it off the box, I don't know. None of it made sense.

Ruby: If I was going to name a popular culture element that played a role in my experience: Judy Blume. That book prepped us in the fact that every girl wasn't buying pads with belts. We used to read parts of it out loud.

Yolanda: We had our sex-ed class, the really uncomfortable one with the boys and the girls, taught by a male teacher who didn't feel comfortable teaching it. By then I had read *Are You There God? It's Me, Margaret* by Judy Blume. I remember reading it, "Oh, that's what my period's going to look like." I felt prepared. It told me what the colour would look like because they talk about blood coming out and you think, bright red. It's not. And the wet feeling, I knew what to expect. When Margaret in the book gets it, she's so excited, so I was excited when I got it. It was good.

Over the past fifty years, North American puberty education has emphasized the biology of girls' reproductive processes and boys' pleasures and role in reproduction. In this model, boys' gratification is taught as integral to procreation while girls' sexual pleasure is seen as immaterial to their reproductive maturation. One might argue that male sexual gratification *is* fundamental to reproduction, but such a position fails to consider how this may be true only in the context of sexual inequality. We could just as easily imagine a world where male sexual desire and satisfaction were viewed as superfluous and female pleasure as critical to successful conception. In her award-winning novel *The Maerlande Chronicles* (1992), science fiction writer Elizabeth Vonarburg imagines a future world where a nuclear war has left badlands, mutations, and a mysterious plague, which kills some girls and almost all boys. To maximize fertility, a pacifist religion has evolved that instructs the few men who make it to adulthood to offer sexual services to fertile women. Trained from puberty as travelling sperm donors, the men learn that their sexual satisfaction is of little importance relative to the greater social goal of pleasing and helping their female partners achieve pregnancy. Rather than presenting matriarchy as superior to patriarchy, Vonarburg questions any society where the rights and pleasures of one sex are subordinated to those of another.

The erasure of girls' external genitals from puberty education should not be surprising given that even medical texts contain misconceptions about the clitoris. In the 1970s and 1980s, it took feminist researchers working in women's health centres to discover that the clitoris is not a small organ but an entire organ system (Federation of Feminist Women's Health Centers, 1981). They found that it's a mass of nerve endings (6000 to 7000), more than any other organ in the male or female body. Recently, urologist Dr Helen O'Connell confirmed this finding ("The clitoris needs," 2005). Lack of knowledge about female bodies contributes to denial of female sexual pleasure, but giving girls explicit information is risky business. In 2005, a grocery chain pulled *Seventeen Magazine* from 2500 stores because of an article on female sexual anatomy (Howze, 2005). The article, called "Vagina 101," showed a drawing of girls' genitalia that clearly labels the clitoris. (Go to http:// feministing.com/2005/10/17/vaginas_are_so_last_year/ to see what caused the fuss.) Due to its themes of menarche and sexuality, disgruntled adults have even attempted to remove Judy Blume's sensitive coming-of-age novels from library shelves, making them among the most challenged books in US schools (http://www.ala.org/ala/issue sadvocacy/banned/frequentlychallenged/challengedauthors/index. cfm). It is troubling that our culture uses one biological story of puberty to suppress other narratives, including ones that might offer students a better understanding of menarche, sexual diversity, and desire. Despite claims to the contrary, it's evident that cultural values are heavily implicated in our stories about biological sex.

Developing Identity through Sexual Development

Of all the challenges associated with growing up, the physical process of puberty is often identified as one of the most difficult for girls. But is puberty inevitably difficult? If the changes are challenging, what makes them more so for girls? Despite the cultural importance they place on puberty as the passage to adulthood, puberty researchers have tended not to examine how girls experience their changed bodies. What research exists concerns either the *status of puberty*, meaning the measurement of the physical stages, or the *timing of puberty* and its causes and consequences for girls. Since researchers generally use quantitative, rather than qualitative, methods, girls' voices are not well represented. Experts thus know a lot about pubescent bodies but less about the meanings and emotions that puberty evokes (K.A. Martin, 1996). Feminists more than others have emphasized girls' perspectives, with most focusing on menarche (Kissling, 2006; Janet Lee, 2008, 2009), and only a handful on changes such as breasts or weight gain (Janet Lee, 1997; Summers-Effler, 2004). This means that, on the whole, girls' bodily changes are more fully documented than the meanings given to their maturing bodies or how these might shape their sense of self.

One influential contemporary theory developed to explain how cultural messages inform girls' self-images at puberty is objectification theory (Fredrickson & Roberts, 1997). Building on the work of de Beauvoir and others, theorists argue that maturing girls' most pressing image problems emerge from being initiated into a culture of objectification that regards women as bodies for the use and pleasure of others. This dynamic is evident throughout the life stories of women in this research – in family relations, medical and school systems, and, most visibly, at puberty. Closely related to the problem of objectification is sexualization, the rapid rise of sexualized images and products aimed at girls (such as thong underwear and push-up bras) that has become a major concern (American Psychological Association, 2007; Orenstein, 2011). While sexy images appear to empower girls by presenting them as actively desiring, such imagery may also be read as a new, more insidious form of objectification that repackages the sexy body as a primary source of female identity and value (Gill, 2008, 2009). Psychologists contend that one serious consequence of objectification is self-objectification (see chapter 2). That is, girls turn the gaze on themselves and treat their bodies as objects to be evaluated for their attractiveness (Calogero, Tantleff-Dunn, & Thompson, 2011). Studies show that self-objectification is gendered, with girls self-objectifying more than boys (Knauss, Paxton, & Alsaker, 2008; Slater & Tiggemann, 2010), and is implicated in girls' body shame and dissatisfaction (McKinley, 1998, 1999a), eating disorders and depression (Durkin & Paxton, 2002), and diminished physical competencies (Fredrickson & Harrison, 2005).

Objectification research builds on decades of feminist thought on how sexual objectification can damage girls' body esteem. However, it has been critiqued for ignoring female agency (Lerum & Dworkin, 2009), denying girl sexuality (Egan & Hawkes, 2007), and overlooking complex cultural meanings given to physical differences. From a media studies perspective, theorists miss key questions about viewers' active interpretation of images (Coleman, 2008). For example, are all girls affected by idealized images in the same way? Do images sometimes satisfy their needs and desires? Critics also note that objectification can carry different meanings depending on a woman's context, history, and relationship with observers; for example, whether she is gazed at by a lover or a stranger, or at home versus on the street (M.S. Hill, 2010). Because it ignores the salience of such dynamics, the theory cannot explain why women willingly make themselves into objects of desire or under what conditions this might enhance their sexuality or sense of self. Instead, by seeing them only as victims of the "fashion-beauty complex" (Bartky, 1990, p. 39), the theory overlooks two decades of feminist debate on female agency in response to an oppressive beauty system. Researchers therefore miss rich feminist insight about the contradictions of embodiment – how women, those in this account included, experience their bodies as objects "looked at and acted upon" (Young, 1990, p. 150) *and* as vehicles of their own intentions and actions.

Sexy images are troubling since they reproduce inequality. Yet critique of such imagery may be problematic insofar as it fails to challenge societal fears about girls' sexuality. Feminists have noted that concerns about protecting children's innocence from corrupting popular culture have surfaced periodically over the past century and that current debates about the media must be understood in this light (Egan & Hawkes, 2007). While worried scholars today recognize that children are sexual beings, they rarely clarify what constitutes non-exploitative sexuality for girls (Egan & Hawkes, 2008). Instead, by seeing girls' sexual expression as an effect of sexy images, commentators downplay their sexual agency, ignoring vital questions such as: is dressing sexy or engaging in sex play always sexualization? What is a healthy, safe expression of sexuality in girlhood? The problem of sexual agency is further complicated by what I call *sexual sexism* – the contradictory belief system that values girls primarily for their sex appeal yet sees their moral worth as rooted in their sexual purity. In a context rife with such double-edged messages, critiquing sexy images without questioning the twin imperative of sexual purity may deny girls *any* sexuality (Vanwesenbeeck, 2009). This debate indicates there is urgent need for feminist conversation that puts the girls' voices at the centre and takes their sexual rights as a starting point. What are possible avenues for protecting girls from the harms of imposed sexualization while still promoting their sexual rights and selves?

Finally, objectification/sexualization theory overlooks the complex dynamics of body differences in social relations. There are many forms of objectification such as the treatment of disabled bodies as sources of entertainment or of women's bodies as vessels of reproduction. Through focusing on sexual objectification only, researchers miss the multiple gazes girls may be subjected to when their bodies begin to change.

They thus miss *abjection*, the rejection of bodies, or aspects of bodies, that threaten cultural norms about how human bodies should look and behave. According to feminist scholars, properties seen as unique to female bodies such as menstrual blood, fat, and breasts become associated with the abject in a patriarchal social order. This explains why sexual development may trigger girls' body problems. "Overburdened, submerged," as de Beauvoir once put it, by the negative meanings imposed on her becoming woman body, a girl going through puberty "becomes a stranger to herself because she is a stranger to the rest of the world" (1974, p. 369). According to women's narratives, conceptions of developing female bodies as dirty or deficient substantially contributed to the worry and fear they felt when they became visible as sexed bodies. Their discomfort came not from sexualizing looks alone, but from other gazes that cast their developing, and often already-different bodies as inadequate, excessive, a source of shame, and other.

Although sexualization theory focuses too narrowly on sexual looks and images, and fails to attend to bodily agency and diversity, it can help to explain the process by which girls come to invest energy in appearance in response to an evaluative gaze. The women's narratives don't reveal any simple cause–effect relation between media images and self-objectification. Rather, they underscore how both the frequency and intensity of looks escalated at puberty (discussed in chapter 5). Both males and females scrutinized participants' changing bodies. In our sexist and heterosexist society, however, boys and men were handed greater authority to evaluate the changes according to an external standard of sexiness and womanliness. Women's changing bodies were subject not only to appraising looks and stares, but to harsh commentary. As a result, all wanted to create a body that was safe from critical looks and judgments.

> Tara: Puberty was hard to accept because we were all asexual beings. Then suddenly, the dynamic changed. Your male friends aren't friends anymore. They're looking at you a lot differently. I wasn't ready for it.

> Marcia: I remember learning that it was acceptable for boys and girls to like each other but not acceptable for boys to like boys and girls to like girls. That struck me as strange because girls were constantly being starred at and judged, so why wouldn't girls stare at or judge girls? It didn't make sense to me. If I was seeing girls out there judged on how attractive they were, then it makes sense that everyone would look at them.

Storytellers indicate that the predicament they faced at puberty was *not* a developmental crisis brought on by biology. They instead confronted an identity crisis precipitated by cultural messages that defined their developing bodies as different and deviant. Feminists have explored how *sexual identity* – girls' understandings of their sexual desires and practices – is an important part of the transition from girl to woman (Tolman, 2002). Yet none have examined how *sexed identity* – girls' interpretations of their physical changes – is similarly central to becoming women. Participants' stories show how sex, rather than being a biological fact of birth, was an identity embodied during puberty. Entering puberty, women for the first time faced the cultural consequences of a womanly body and most had no advance warning about the ways that the culture imagines that body as other. As they encountered cultural perceptions of their pubertal female bodies, none knew how to contend with the mixed meanings. This was their predicament of puberty.

Most moved through adolescence with a deep sense of difference. This feeling emerged when they grasped how their changing bodies diverged from a culturally normal body (the androgynous body of childhood) *and* failed to fit an acceptable female form (shaped by media ideals and medical norms). All wanted to taste the increased status and social power they associated with becoming an adult. At the same time, they had to contend with a growing gap between their changing bodies and our culture's idealized images. For many, this widening rift was difficult, if not impossible, to close. Thus they also faced a "paradox of puberty" – the increased disparity between their actual and idealized bodies – when others began to scrutinize their physical development and differences. All navigated the looks, stares, and comments through managing the bodily changes and amending differences as best they could in an attempt to create a socially acceptable image. Some, like Amélie, tried to affirm their becoming woman identity through aspiring to desirability, while others such as Preeta resisted being seen as a woman by suppressing or denying bodily signs of sexual otherness.

> Amélie: Because of my facial difference, I was vulnerable as a child. After I developed, I was still different looking because I was less shapely, younger looking. I had other reasons to be comfortable about my body though. Clothes can make you feel good if society reacts positively. I was very well dressed. I got the messages about my birthmark but I started to see that my body was fine. Sensual and sexual were compensation. That

came from looking different because I permitted myself to explore things other people couldn't explore. So I think of that as a big gift.

Preeta: I resisted puberty. I knew how people looked at bodies. If I was to develop a chest or get hippy, I didn't want them to see me differently. I wanted them to see me as a guy, because no one looks at or comments on a guy's body but guys comment on girls' bodies. I didn't want them rating or judging me. I still sometimes deny that I am a woman. It's resistance. I don't want to be seen as a woman.

Attending to the embodied voices of women in this study shifts focus from analysing the effects of imagery to illuminating how girls come to experience and know their bodies through looks and images.

Qualifying as a Woman

Despite second-wave feminist attempts to transform girls' experiences of puberty, storytellers expressed how coming of age in a female body provoked feelings of shame, anxiety, and disgust. Many received at least some positive puberty education in a post–Judy Blume world, yet almost all described developing, to varying degrees, negative feelings about the changes that undermined how they felt about themselves. Puberty scholar Karin Martin (1996) makes the important point that while many feminists have tried to figure out why girls' self-esteem drops during adolescence, few look closely at puberty or first experiences of sex. She argues that the self-esteem disparity that emerges can be explained, in part, by divergent meanings attached to male and female sexualities, which teach girls to "associate sexuality with danger, shame, and dirt, and boys to associate it with masculinity and adulthood" (p. 20). Martin rightly draws attention to meanings associated with female sexuality that erode girls' sense of themselves. However, by focusing solely on sexuality, she misses how our culture's reading of sexed bodies also plays a prominent role in girls' growing uncertainty and dissatisfaction.

In addressing the failure of feminist research to consider the effects of pubescent sexuality on girls' self-making, Martin's scholarship has made an important contribution to feminist puberty studies. Although this field has been referred to as *tween studies* (Mitchell & Reid-Walsh, 2005), I favour *puberty studies* because it brings the focus back to lived bodies and cultural practices that shape girls' pubescent experiences.

Puberty emerges in participants' accounts as more pivotal than other bodily events because it marks the period when bodies socially become sexed.

In our culture, the maturing female body is associated with the abject. For Julia Kristeva (as we saw in chapter 1), the abject applies not only to what threatens cultural norms of human bodies and identities, but also that which crosses borders and confuses. Puberty emerges as a site of abjection since it forces the adolescent into an unstable body and in-between identity category. To grasp the extent to which the pubertal body is linked with the abject, consider how its transformations – its sudden growth of lumps, bumps, and hairs – are imagined as frightening in our cultural zeitgiest. Think, too, about how this might be magnified for girls, whose bodily processes are already viewed as alarming. It is hardly coincidental that horror films such as *The Exorcist* (1973) and *Carrie* (1976) focus on girls at the threshold of puberty. While we can dismiss *Carrie* as a wacky film about a girl with telekinetic powers awakened by menstruation, we can also read it a story about a young woman whose newly acquired powers to create and destroy are not yet socially harnessed, and thus as a tale about patriarchal fear of female bodies (Creed, 1993). "Plug it up," Carrie's classmates chant as they pelt her with pads and tampons. Could this be the horror of the abject female body that bleeds, that must be kept under wraps lest it overwhelm the social order?

Contrary to the conventional story, not all women in this study distinguished becoming a woman as the moment when they experienced first menses. Many began to see themselves as women when their bodies changed in more visible ways and they were sexed by perceptions of their breasts and weight. Although most wanted the status and freedom they associated with adulthood, many rejected or wrestled with being seen as different due to developing an adult female body. A majority (80%) saw their breasts as too big or too small, but rarely quite right. Almost all (95%) viewed their weight as exceeding or lagging behind an imagined norm. A vast majority (85%) recalled mixed or negative experiences of menarche. Body dissatisfaction emerged or increased dramatically between ages nine and sixteen, when they encountered negative attributions of sex differences along with mounting pressures to appear as desirable. Most felt they had to qualify as women and hoped for cultural acceptance.

In what follows, I weave together women's stories with cultural narratives about the developing female body. Most anticipated the changes yet also described how outsiders' intensified gaze fuelled their fears about impending womanhood: heightening the risks and pleasures of becoming, or not becoming, breasted; the worries about weight gain; the secrecy and messiness of menstruation; the racism, ableism, and fat phobia they faced even at nine or ten; and the conflicting emotions that discovering, knowing, and creating themselves as women provoked. While being cast as other was a universal experience, participants, too, confronted a sliding scale of beauty where some were judged to be more desirable than others. Within this hierarchy, all struggled to find and create themselves, negotiating the demand to accommodate to a devalued identity while trying to qualify as acceptable and desirable according to cultural benchmarks.

Censored Bodies and Stolen Sexualities: Becoming Breasted

In our society, women are barraged with images of breasts. Size matters in a sexist commodity culture where big breasts are associated with sexual desirability and pleasure, and signal that a woman may be sexually available or even for sale. Small breasts, in contrast, are frequently framed as deficiencies and operate as a sign of a woman's status as tomboy or worse, feminist and lesbian. Breasts are closely associated with women's sexual identity, yet they can be de-sexualized due to their links with mothering and breastfeeding. Philosopher Iris Marion Young (1990, p. 190) argues that breasts are seen as scandalous in sexist society since they "disrupt the border between motherhood and sexuality." Breasts unsettle the nurturing and pleasuring roles ascribed to women. Because breastfeeding involves sharing bodily fluids, breasts blur the boundaries between self and other, violating the culturally-erected borders of the bounded, closed off self. Breasts may be markers of sexuality and womanhood, but paradoxically they seldom are seen as belonging to women themselves. Rather, they tend to be regarded as the property of men and infants (Janet Lee, 1997). Though the large, spherical, and firm breast is idealized, most breasts, whether fleshy or flat, are viewed as abject. Given conflicting representations of breasts as sexual and maternal, as belonging to others yet possessed by the self, and as potentially idealized but mostly inadequate, it is not surprising that many girls experience developing breasts in confusing and contradictory ways.

Feminists have long argued that first menses is the most dramatic marker of the transition into womanhood (Janet Lee, 1997) but because breast development occurs an average of two years before menarche (Alsaker, 1995), breast growth may be the first visible symbol of sexing for girls. Women I interviewed equated puberty with breast buds, and referred to breast development as much as periods and twice as much as weight gain in their puberty stories. Growing up in a breast-conscious culture, most became acutely aware of budding breasts and of the meanings surrounding size that informed their experiences of becoming large or small breasted. Many longed for breasts because they coveted the adult status associated with a womanly body; most remembered, too, the negative implications of breasts as signifiers of difference in a society that devalues women. Breasts for some were a source of pride and pleasure. At the same time, most learned that it wasn't permissible for girls to view their developing breasts as desirable because only boys and men had the authority to make that call. In a culture that covets girls' sexiness while requiring their sexual purity, participants were instructed that they should contain and manage their breasts to project a respectable image. Regulation of breasts frequently led to body censorship since close scrutiny alienated those interviewed from sensual feelings accessed through their breasts. Sexualizing looks further affected their sexualities when imposed sexualization left women with little possibility for genuine engagement with their breasts as sources of their own pleasure. This was true for those who developed earlier or bigger breasts – they were not only seen as different from their male peers but as too developed in relation to girls as well. It was equally the case for those who developed later or smaller breasts, who were regarded as different from boys and lesser than other girls. In relating stories of becoming breasted, women emphasized three themes: breasts as signs of womanliness, sexual attractiveness, and otherness; breasts as targets of sexual desire and scrutiny; and containment of alienated breasts through bras, clothes, and curtailment of movement.

TOO-MUCH OR NOT-ENOUGH WOMEN?

For interviewees, becoming breasted meant they were now regarded as women. But simply by developing earlier or larger breasts than their peers, 39 per cent tell how their breasts violated our culture's body standards. These included the societal norm of the male body and the scientific norm of healthy puberty. Because female bodies are imagined as other in relation to the male body, which is taken as the standard for the human body in our society, developing a woman's body meant that suddenly participants were seen as different. Some, like Hasina, equated normal with the pre-sexed, boyish body of childhood. In a cultural context that classifies the prepubescent boy body as standard and the female sexed body as different and deficient, the women articulated how developing breasts meant acquiescence to an inferior body. Storytellers not only described their developing breasts as diverging from an androgynous norm; those who began puberty before their peers explain how their bodies deviated from another standard: the medical norm of healthy puberty. By comparing themselves to peers, many formed an inner picture of the preferred pace of puberty. This was difficult for late developers who saw their "too little, too late" bodies as not womanly enough. It was possibly more stressful for early developers, whose "too much too soon" bodies violated the imagined norm of puberty.

Hasina: Growing up was getting away from what I was used to. It was easier to be treated equally as a youngster than it is as a female. All of a sudden I was different and that bothered me. I just wanted to be normal.

Ada: As a kid, I was called a boy. But by age twelve, I wasn't seen as strong or competent enough to be male so I was far from having privileges of masculinity. Also, I wasn't seen as having the right girl's body. So I didn't have the privileges associated with a developed female body either.

Hope: I reached puberty young. I started to menstruate and developed little breasts. I was ashamed because I thought it was much more feminine to be flat as a board. The pretty, affluent, popular girls were still, it seemed to me, small and slow developing. It's that whole image of being other than the norm. I developed very young and the normal girls developed later.

Like other early developers, Hope saw her breasts as too developed compared with those of the affluent girls who had more "normal" bodies. This is not surprising in a culture that interprets development as the advent of girls' sexuality, and associates breast size with sexual conduct and class. The assumption that early-developing girls are more sexually knowledgeable may have special meaning for working-class girls. Our culture encodes the bodies of working-class women as out of control and excessively sexual compared to middle-class women's bodies, which are seen as more respectable and restrained (Skeggs, 2002). In a context where class and conduct are read off of a woman's body, developing breasts may mark a girl as vulgar, brazen, and not respectable (Janet Lee, 1997). Stereotypic associations of size with sexuality and social class are rife throughout popular culture. One example is the film *Pretty Woman* (1990), starring Julia Roberts. The main character, Vivian, a vivacious and busty prostitute, transforms herself into a demure, classy princess with the aid of a wealthy customer. Because Roberts herself was considered too svelte to play a street prostitute, a bustier body double was used in the sexier scenes while her own body was used for the classier shots (Loprete, 1992). This example shows how associating big breasts with sexual impropriety might frame working-class girls' breasts as potentially pathological and unduly sexual compared with middle-class girls, who are assumed to have a healthier, more controlled developmental pace (regardless of their breast size).

In media culture, big breasts tend to be seen as objects of men's sexual desire. Most male-oriented porn is characterized by cookie-cutter casting where the prototypical sex symbol is the woman with manicured or removed pubic hair, blond locks, and big breasts. And we know that the curvy siren in cinema, from Mae West to Angelina Jolie, is an enduring ideal. It is hardly coincidental that successful small-breasted icons, such as Katherine Hepburn and Cate Blanchett, have become famous for playing virgins, tomboys, and other desexed female characters. There are a few exceptions to these conventions. One rebellious representation is found in the film *The Itty Bitty Titty Committee* (2007). Its flat-chested heroine, Anna, is a just-out-of-high-school lesbian who works as a receptionist in a plastic surgeon's office. Though she harbours some of the same insecurities as implant-seeking clientele for not being big-busted, she subversively tells clients that they are beautiful despite what the beauty establishment wants them to believe. The film plays with stereotypes about lesbians as flat-chested amazons while sending the message that young women can find and accept themselves for who they are. The taken-for-grantedness of heterosexuality and of the male gaze – men's assumed right to determine a woman's desirability – is challenged by diversely endowed actresses who see themselves as sexual objects and as subjects in relationships with other women.

Over the last thirty years, sexualized images of breasts have increased dramatically. This may be due, in part, to the "pornification" of popular culture – the blurring of boundaries between porn and pop culture that has wallpapered media with sexual imagery. Feminists have debated fiercely whether the migration of sexualized images from the margins to the mainstream has promoted sex-positive attitudes and brought diverse desires out of the closet, or has contributed to the sexualization of girls and the creation of a new porn-star ideal (Gill, 2009). While this debate rages on, most writers agree that pop culture's flirt with porn has not been about advancing women's sexuality rights. Rather than challenging stereotypes, media producers have exploited conventions once confined to porn – big-breasted, ready-for-sex bodies – to seduce consumers. And instead of representing sexual diversity, these portrayals tend to promote traditional heterosexual relations where guys are dominant, girls are submissive, and sex is for sale (Levy, 2006). Typifying the trend is the genre of men's so-called lifestyle magazines. While genre standards like *Maxim*, *Zoo*, and *Details* differ in demographic, they share an obsession with big breasts. Britain's *Zoo Weekly* made headlines when it announced the "Zoo Boob Job Competition," which awarded one winner a $10,000 breast enhancement for his girlfriend based on photos of her cleavage ("Win a boob-job," 2005; Welch, 2007). Even at Lakehead University in Ontario, *Maxim* stirred up controversy when it refused to cancel a campus search for the "Thunder Bay Boob Idol" despite student protest (Ende, 2004).

Our culture has a breast fetish. Interviewees tell how breasts bestowed status on girls. Yet those who developed earlier or bigger breasts were in a precarious position: looks that conferred desirability could just as easily other them, by reducing their embodied being to an oversexed body (Janet Lee, 1997). Since in our culture only bad girls look or act sexual (Tolman, 2002), participants recalled struggling with the risks of a bad reputation if they developed earlier or became bigger breasted. Sometimes they saw their development positively as symbolic of femininity and desirability. More often, they navigated negative associations of big breasts with being a slut. When a variety of others began to scrutinize their changing bodies, early developers felt caught in a complex web of looks that drew discomforting attention to their breasts, and made their bodies more noticeable than those of boys or other girls. Janet Lee (1997) and Erika Summers-Effler (2004) have found that early-developing girls experience breasts as shaming and embarassing because they feel humiliated by the looks and stares. Early-maturing and large-breasted women I interviewed found the scrutiny intrusive and felt uncomfortable with their greater visibility.

Marcia: I looked forward to developing into a woman, secretly thinking when I saw these melons on my chest, they were beautiful. But I knew they meant something else, outside of that space.

Elena: When they were growing they were perfect sized. That's when I enjoyed it. Then they would not stop growing. Men would look right at your chest. When I would go swimming, someone would grab me under the water. Anything I wore was sexy. My mother would say, "Don't wear that top." But there was nothing I could do: with big breasts you can't *not* be sexy. I used to imagine that guys would think, "I can't bring this girl home to my mother," because of my breasts. It made me feel terrible.

As if stares weren't enough to contend with, many dealt with unwelcome comments as well. As with looks, these were gendered: mothers, sisters, and female friends tended to give moralistic advice telling girls how to manage their breasts, while fathers, brothers, and other guys directed the more sexually appraising or demeaning remarks at them. Women and girls did the dirty work of teaching them how to cope with and control their breasts' movement. At the same time, some recognized that such regulation served a protective purpose: in sexist looksist society, this advice was intended to shield them from being stereotyped as too sexy. Without guidance or gear to manage their newly developing differences, participants felt defenceless in the face of harassment. Despite efforts to minimize their breasts' size and movement, early developers dealt with unwanted sexualization, which they vividly described as mortifying, belittling, and frightening. In a context where breasts are viewed as signs of sexuality but not as belonging to women themselves, breasts turned the early-developer's body into a sexual spectacle. Breasts announced her new status as sexually developed and womanly. When read as a beacon of sexuality, developing breasts gave outsiders permission to disregard the feelings and desires of the girl in the body. This left Rosetta feeling like a little girl trapped in a woman's body, an identity bind that early developers in particular confront (Summers-Effler, 2004). The imposition of sexuality undermined possibilities for early developers' authentic engagement with their breasts because it robbed them of the right to explore, experience, and know their sexual bodies on their own terms and in their own ways.

Fredericka: I was put in a place of being ashamed of my body. Cutting myself off and trying not to make it a part of me. I faced constant ridicule because my breasts started developing earlier than my peers'. I remember intercepting a note in grade 4 that had a drawing of me showing my breasts spilling out of my overalls. I was very embarrassed. After that I've had the worst relationship with my breasts. I started slouching and my posture became awful. I tried to hide behind big sweaters. The whole thing took a minute to play itself out but it's still clear as day in my head.

Claudia: By age fifteen, I was a very grown-up-looking girl. I experienced absolutely relentless, non-stop, horrific street harassment. It got to the point that I wanted to have a reduction because I was so sick of men screaming about my breasts. I always thought the street reaction had a class aspect. I kept thinking, "These men think I'm trashy and stupid. If I didn't look like this, they wouldn't dream of approaching me."

Rosetta: I felt clumsy and scared, I was this little girl but I started getting breasts thinking, "Something's not right. I have to wear bras, but can I play with dolls?" I had to deal with having a woman's body with a little kid's mind. Not even verbalized in my head, just having these emotions.

It is significant that 36 per cent of the women expressed feeling uneasy about how their underdeveloped breasts and slower pubertal pace were read as signs of sexual immaturity, making them less likely to be seen as womanly than their big girlfriends. Developing later helped to protect them from being viewed as oversexed or labelled a slut. At the same time, late bloomers risked ridicule due to the perception that they didn't measure up. Outsiders disproportionately viewed Asian participants as late bloomers compared to their white, middle-class counterparts, who were often seen to embody the norm. This suggests that the medical definition of healthy puberty, which tends to coincide with the developmental pace of white, middle-class girls, reinforces white bodies as normal.

Rhonda: I didn't feel as attractive. My breasts weren't developing as quickly. I felt really odd, like I wasn't part of the attractive girls.

Vera: Puberty was horrible mostly. I didn't feel that my body changed at all! I did not feel like a woman at all. I always felt differently because of my breasts. I remember reading something about Asian women's "adolescent bodies." I felt resentful because I thought it was true in a way. We have these bodies that seem to be on the way to developing but they have stopped. Yes, we are at the preadolescent body stage and that's it.

Along with disappointment and frustration, every late developer expressed anxiety about how her underdeveloped body was seen as childlike, sexually immature, and not womanly enough. Many wondered whether they could ever qualify as women without the visual symbols of sexing. Imagining that large-breasted women were not only more desirable but, further, more desiring, Vera implies that in Western symbolic systems, large breasts translate into heightened libido. Because they were unable to differentiate their bodies adequately from the bodies of children or male counterparts, storytellers' attempts to qualify as women were interpreted as inadequate and destabilizing by visually communicating that sexual differences may not be so clear cut after all.

Gelorah: My friends would call me the "hormoneless girl." No boys would look at me as being a girl – they would see me as being a kid. So when people see me as a kid, nothing was going to happen.

Jane: Would I ever become beautiful and have breasts that were big enough for men to be interested in? Or would I stay a brain? My friends' bodies started to become visible. They were coming into women's bodies. I didn't see my body as qualifying as a woman's body. I had a real sense of being left behind. It was true in terms of my currency with guys. When girls grew big they became valuable. It wasn't going to happen for me.

Vera: Breasts symbolize sex, sexuality, and being beautiful. Sometimes I think I can't be fully beautiful, sexual or sensuous either because I don't have big breasts. If I don't have large breasts like models or women in porno, I am not experiencing sex as great as it could be. Maybe if you have larger breasts, you are more sensitive or if you have bigger veins, you get the whole experience. Then I think that's stupid. Sometimes I am happy and sometimes I'm not. The majority of the time I am happier but it's an issue. It always has been an issue and it probably always will be.

While the cultural coding of breasts as "sexy" means that becoming breasted results in being sexualized, this was not the case for women with disabilities. When they entered puberty, those with disabilities discovered how people disregarded their sexualities due to the misconception that they would be unfit mothers and partners. Since breasts are highly sexualized but disabilities are de-sexualized in society, the bodies of early developers with disabilities were sometimes seen as inappropriate and unseemly. North American, medically oriented society has a long and dishonourable tradition of sterilizing women with disabilities as a way to eliminate so-called defectives. Although forced sterilization is now illegal, suppression of disabled girls' sexual maturation still continues. Some women, including Fatima, described how medical interventions that blocked their fertility and sexual sensations ensured that they would neither look nor feel like a woman.

> Frances: Often girls with spina bifida go into puberty early. So at age nine, I got breasts very quickly and dramatically. Then I got my period. I felt very mature, very odd, not part of my peer group. That's one of my first memories of being aware there was something extraordinarily different about me. I don't remember boys. But girls were extremely fascinated by my breasts. Kids starting calling me "lady." They saw breasts, a mature look, so they thought I was old. My father was embarrassed by my maturity. I was not allowed to dress in any way that was even remotely provocative.

> Fatima: I was put on Depo Provera, a drug that chemically takes away your desire to be sexual. They told me it was because I have epilepsy and it would control my seizures. My body changed but I don't remember a lot about sexuality or becoming a woman because of the Depo. I accepted that I would not have a sexuality. If I was wearing a shirt with the top button unbuttoned or if I had a low-cut top, my mother would say: "Your teachers must hate this." The message was: you have a disability, you shouldn't be sexual.

Fatima's experience of being medically denied her sexuality may not be unique. The hormonal and surgical suppression of disabled girls' pubertal processes was recently brought to light in the United States with the case of Ashley X, the severely disabled six-year-old girl subjected to high-dose estrogen, complete hysterectomy, and mastectomy to remove all signs of womanhood (Hall, 2011; Kittay, 2011). Parents and doctors defended the decision to arrest Ashley's sexual development by arguing it would ease her transfer, prevent the discomfort of big breasts and messiness of a monthly period, and shield her from sexual abuse (Gunther & Diekema, 2006; Liao, Savulescu, & Sheehan, 2007). Yet their assertions that "a full-grown and fertile woman endowed with the mind of a baby" was "grotesque" (Dvorsky quoted in Liao, Savulescu, & Sheehan, 2007, p. 19) unmask a deeper phobia – people's discomfort with the perceived developmental disjuncture between Ashley's body and mind. This dovetails with the popular view of people with disabilities as unfinished adults, as unable to complete the stages necessary to reach mature adulthood. Disability theorist Alison Kafer (2013) argues that in aligning Ashley's body and mind, the "Ashley Treatment" aimed to prevent a too-big, too-sexual, too-fertile infantile woman from coming into being, thus protecting the larger society from having to deal with a womanliness deemed as pathological. Although one of the main justifications for enforced asexualization is that pubescent girls with disabilities might be more vulnerable to abuse, neither drugs nor regulation of their sexualities and sexed bodies is likely to prevent or even reduce this possibility. As feminist philosopher and mother of a severely disabled child, Eva Kittay writes of Ashley X, "If one is perverse enough to sexually abuse such a girl, might he or she even be attracted by the strange history of a child whose parents removed her breast buds? ... Only careful supervision and respect for these girls and women can offer the needed protection" (p. 623).

TAMING THE ABJECT BREAST

Throughout Western history, women have used a variety of devices to restrain, support, and enhance their breasts. The modern brassiere was originally developed in the early twentieth century to replace the corset, and has become the standard method for shaping a woman's breasts (Farrell-Beck & Gau, 2002). Today, the manufacture and sale of bras is a multi-billion-dollar industry, with the global lingerie market exceeding $29 billion annually (Warburton, 2011). The so-called training bra, introduced in the 1950s to prevent pubescent boobs from sagging, has become a rite of passage for girls in North America (Brumberg, 1997). The bra is still charged with contradictory meanings: symbolic of a woman's coming of age and as an icon of femininity, it's also a symbol of repression in sexist society. The bra became politicized in 1968 when reporters created the myth of the bra-burning feminist following protests at a Miss America pageant. Although reporters only imagined that demonstrators set their undergarments on fire, people still believe that feminists burned their bras. (For photos of the protest, go to: http://uic.edu/orgs/cwluherstory/jofreeman/photos/MissAm1969.html.)

Women in this study learned to confine their breasts by wearing bras, dressing in concealing clothes, and adopting specific postures to protect themselves from unwanted attention. Most began to wear bras to protect themselves from moral judgments and sexual violation, and many adopted the gear to present themselves as feminine and womanly. A majority straddled positive and negative motivations as they felt the varied gazes of others. Mothers, sisters, and female friends often coached participants on how to manage breast development, and sometimes issued vague warnings about the consequences of their failure to do so. Regulation intended to teach participants how to present an acceptable image and safeguard their sexual reputation. But for most, it contributed to shame about becoming breasted. Fernanda and others tell how wearing a bra often opened their bodies to being touched by those whom it was not permissible to touch back. People sometimes argue that bras can prevent health problems such as back pain. However, there is no medical evidence to support this or the opposite claim that bras cause cancer (Love, 2005; Ray, 2010). It was the spectacle created by unrestrained breasts, rather than the supposed aesthetic or health benefits of bras, that lead women in this study to adopt the gear needed to contain them.

Jillian: My friend said, "I have to tell you three things: you should wear a bra, you should wear deodorant, and you're not very nice to your dad." It was so humiliating.

Yolanda: One of the popular girls came up to me in class to tell me that it was about time I got a bra. I brushed her off. But I was secretly embarrassed, ashamed almost. I walked around hiding myself because I didn't want everybody to see what she saw. Sure enough, as soon as I could I asked my mother if I could get a bra.

Fernanda: I was one of the girls who started wearing bras earlier. The boys would come up trying to unsnap it. They would make fun of the different sizes and threaten to fondle us.

In public spaces, interviewees often experienced their breasts as hyper-visible and as breaking unspoken rules about the respectable body. Besides confining their breasts with bras, many covered themselves with oversized clothing or tried to hide their physical changes by slouching. Despite such efforts, breasts rendered them available and their visibility made them targets for harassment. Many tried to alter and curb their physical activities to appear less noticeable and pass through space without comment. Early maturers explained how they began to curtail their activities and restrict their range of movements as a strategy for stopping boys' looks and stares. Like Sylvie, these women longed for their former flat-chested bodies because the hyper-visibility of large breasts meant that they no longer could run freely. More than in any other space, early developers felt vulnerable in gym classes. Here breasts impaired their movement not because large breasts decreased mobility, but because girls feared exposure to appraising others. As Fredericka describes it, control of breast movement became essential to preserving one's physical abilities since sexualizing stares and jeers drew attention away from women's physical capacities and onto their developing breasts.

> Sylvie: I didn't have breasts you could run around in. When your breasts are small they aren't moving up and down, and that to me was liberation.

> Fredericka: I started becoming secretive about my body, hiding it. Being ashamed it was changing. In organized sport, I didn't want to go through the embarrassment of running around in front of people other than my family, who accepted me for the way I looked. I didn't want to have my breasts thumping all over the place. That's what I saw in my head. I wouldn't be fast or strong enough. People would see me differently.

According to Iris Marion Young, breasts are valued in male-dominated society only when they are modelled on male desire and according to a male norm. The "best breasts" are those that achieve a "high, hard, pointy look that phallic culture posits as the norm" (1990, p. 195). In an image system where the desired breast is hard and high, some women indicate that their jiggling, swaying, and thumping breasts threatened notions of fit bodies. Boys made girls conscious of their "too-big" breasts, while coaches, gym teachers, and other adults conveyed that breasts in motion compromised girls' abilities. Many responders came to associate unruly breasts with the abject body. Learning that physical activity was conditional on their control of breast movement, many confined their breasts as a condition of physical freedom. It is commonly assumed that a bigger breast size naturally decreases a woman's mobility. But is this really the case? Does having big breasts compromise women's athletic abilities? Some women imply that large breasts inhibited their movement not due to the size or density of their breasts alone but because bouncing breasts breached ideas of athletic bodies.

> Elena: When I got heavier breasted I couldn't go out for track because the teacher said, "There's no way that you would be able to do it." Because of my breasts. I thought "How can that be?" But then I thought "She's right."

Marcia: I grew breasts quickly compared to my peers and I was scared. Because I was fairly large breasted, I got messages from boys that I was provocative. At a young age trying to cover them up and being conscious of them. I loved running but I hated it because it was embarrassing, my breasts wouldn't rest when I ran. It was hard to find a bra to run in.

According to participants, girls need positive sexuality education *before* they become breasted because of the negative ways their breasts are appropriated in sexist visual society. Sexuality education is required to help them understand what is happening not just physically, but socially and culturally. Some concerned educators, health providers, and parents maintain that we should focus our energies on stopping girls' compulsory sexualization rather than pushing for empowering sex education. However, the women I spoke to indicate that such a strategy will do little to preserve girls' body confidence or promote their sexuality rights. Despite coming of age before the proliferation of sexy images, the cohort of women I interviewed experienced unwanted sexualization of their breasted bodies. Their stories indicate that even if we managed to shift the emphasis away from sexiness as a source of female value, girls' sexed bodies and sexual sensations would still be censored by enforced sexualization without matching effort made to advance their sexual self-knowledge and rights. This raises important questions about sex education today. What does sex education teach girls about their developing breasts? Does it give them the knowledge they need to make sense of their sexual bodies and desires? Or give young men what they need to enter into more mutual sexual exchanges and relationships?

SEX EDUCATION OR MISEDUCATION?

In North American society, girls and boys learn about sexuality from media and at school. While evidence of sexuality is everywhere, official knowledge of sex is managed through the curriculum. Throughout the 1990s, conservatives in the United States advocated for the elimination of sex education, believing that silence about sex would lead to decreased sexual activity. According to sociologist Janice Irvine (2002), the right has since replaced their call for suppression of sex instruction with a new tactic: sex education for abstinence only, a model that favours married heterosexuality and frowns on other sexualities. In the past twenty years, pro-abstinence, anti-gay messages have entered

Canadian classrooms through right-wing organizations, and some school boards in Alberta, Ontario, and British Columbia have enacted abstinence-only programs as well. At the same time, because provincial and federal governments in our country mandate comprehensive sexuality education, a majority of Canadian schools still emphasize "plumbing and prevention" or the biology of sexuality. While the scientific model favoured in Canada is a vast improvement on the moralizing one promoted in the United States, like puberty education explored earlier, its masked ideologies reproduce sexual inequalities.

Feminist writers such as Michelle Fine (2006; McClelland & Fine, 2008), Marnina Gonick (2006), and Deborah Britzman (1997) have identified three major messages about female and queer sexualities in schools and sex education today: (a) promotion of discourses of female sexual risk and responsibility, where girls learn to defend themselves against disease, pregnancy, sexual violence, and being used, and learn to take responsibility for the negative outcomes of their sexualities; (b) suppression of female desire, where sexual danger is highlighted and any mention of female sexual entitlement is followed by warnings about the high costs and harmful consequences of being sexual; and (c) the privileging of heterosexuality and conventional gender-sex categories, where students learn not to question the naturalness of heterosexuality or our sex/gender norms. Fine argues that educating girls about the risks of sexual exploration is important, but it becomes problematic when danger is the main message and desire drops out of the discussion. The pressure to look or act sexy has intensified in pornified culture, but female desire merits nary a whisper in sex education. Mostly, the message given to girls is still prescriptive – good girls don't – but in the wake of increased sexualization, it's been repackaged as responsibility – smart girls won't. Unlike young men whose desire is taught as biology (boys have wet dreams and nocturnal emissions) most young women do not have access to knowledge about their sexual pleasure. This not only contributes to the denial of girls' desires but naturalizes boys' role as active agents of desire and gives them their greater power to control sexual relations with girls.

Dominant ideas about sexuality in schools also marginalize queer girls, and contribute to exclusions ranging from censorship in the classroom to hostility in the hallways. Beyond overt censorship, school boards have failed to provide an inclusive curriculum, since most sex education materials see heterosexuality as natural and conventional gender/sex categories as normal. Even the Ontario Curriculum

Guidelines view grade 2 students' ability to distinguish gender differences as an important learning goal. Recent attempts to revise this
curriculum to be more respectful of gender variance and sexual minorities have failed in the face of conservative backlash (find out more
at facebook.com/youthneedfacts and ophea.net). In addition, schools
have failed to protect queer students from harassment. In one recent
Canadian study, 68 per cent of trans students, 55 per cent of female
sexual minority students, and 42 per cent of male sexual minority students reported being verbally harassed about their perceived gender or
sexual orientation, and almost two-thirds of queer students felt unsafe
at school (C. Taylor & Peter, 2011).

This discussion highlights the importance of creating a positive and
empowering sex education curriculum that acknowledges girls' sexed
body parts and pleasures, and supports girls in creating their own materials on sexuality. *The Little Black Book for Girlz* (2006), a guide to sexuality written by and for young women, is a great example of this strategy
(http://www.ststephenshouse.com/littleblackbook/lbb_1.shtml). Another is the Coalition for Positive Sexuality, an organization formed by
youth to provide positive sexuality information through booklets, a
website, and campaigns such as "Girl Germs" (see figure 6.4) designed
to empower girls to take control of their sexualities (http://www.posi
tive.org). Empowering sex education could create safer spaces for girls
to discuss their range of sexual experiences – from the painful to the
pleasurable and powerful. In these conversations, they could stop hiding their desires, start defining their values, and talk about their status as virgins, curious, or experienced. They could connect with their
body's capacities for pleasure, learn about masturbation and bodily
sensations, and create their own discourses of desire. Unfortunately,
we are a long way from making views like those advocated by the Coalition for Positive Sexuality and *Little Black Book for Girlz* a reality for
most young women.

Virtually no one I spoke to received sex education that helped her
come to terms with her developing breasts or sexual sensations. Instead, becoming breasted involved a loss of power associated with being sexualized. While breasts endowed some with desirability, most
described how this was unpredictable since the male gaze alone determined their allure. As a result, a majority formed ambivalent views
about their breasts. Feminists have raised concerns about the proliferation of sexy images of girls in merchandising and media due to
the harmful messages it sends about female identity and value. The

La educación sexual debe ser más que biología o historias de horror sobre las E.T.S. (Enfermedades Transmitidas Sexualmente). Sex education should be more than biology and STD horror stories. Yeah, we need to learn about menstrual cycles and how you get pregnant, but girls need practical information, too. Ciertamente necesitamos información sobre la menstruación y como quedar embarazada, pero necesitamos información práctica. La educación sexual no es simplemente "dicir que no." "Just say no" isn't sex education. Lots of teens have sex. Muchos jóvenes tienen sexo. The more we know about sex, the better our choices. Mientras más sepamos del sexo, mejores decisiones tomamos. We need to know what kind of birth control is safest for teens. We need to know how es más el seguro para las jóvenes. Necesitamos saber cual método anticonceptivo es más el seguro para las jóvenes. Necesitamos saber que tipo de latex nos protege contra las E.T.S. y el VIH.

Vagina
Clítoris (clit)
Orgasm / Orgasmo
Masturbation / Masturbación
Safe sex / sexo seguro

vulva

latex can protect us from STDs and HIV. We need sex ed to include respect for gay, lesbian, bi, and Necesitamos que la educación sexual incluya el respeto a la homosexualidad, lesbianismo, bi-sexualidad y straight sexualities. Teachers, parents, and doctors should talk to us openly about sex. We can teach heterosexualidad. Maestros, padres y doctores deben hablar abiertamente sobre el sexo. Nos podemos auto-educar ourselves by reading books and sharing info with our friends. We can even do some research on leyendo libros y compartiendo información con nuestras amistades. Podemos hacer hasta nuestras propias ourselves. Hey, guys do it. Why not girls? Exploring our bodies is fun and educational. investigaciones. Háganlo jovencitas ¿porqué no? Explorando nuestros cuerpos es educativo y divertido. La Masturbation is safe sex—it can't hurt you. Anyone can do it, and lots of girls do. Remember—the clit is masturbación es sexo seguro. No te dolerá. Cualquiera puede hacerlo, muchas lo hacen. Recuerdecé que el clítoris it! Girls need to know how our bodies work and feel, so we can take care of ourselves. es el punto. Las jóvenes necesitan conocer cómo sus cuerpos sienten y cómo funcionan, para así podernos cuidar.

For more info: Para más información:
Coalition for Positive Sexuality (773) 604-1654 3712 N. Broadway PMB#191, Chicago, IL 60613 www.positive.org e-mail: cps@positive.org

Figure 6.4. Coalition for Positive Sexuality: This positive sex education resource aims to empower through acknowledging girls' sexed body parts and pleasures.

case against sexualization is important because it draws attention to the precariousness of desirability as a source of self-esteem and social power. However, denunciation of sexy images may be counterproductive, since in the absence of any positive messages about sexuality, such censure may contribute to the further stigmatization of girls' sexual expression. In a context where young women are encouraged to appear desirable without knowing their desires, this is especially likely without a corresponding effort aimed at advancing their sexual subjectivity and rights. In fact, conservatives have used the case against sexualization to argue that girls who dress and act sexy are mentally disturbed, morally reprehensible, and responsible for their own rape. In sexist consumer culture, sexualization censors girls' sexual sensations and alienates them from their breasted bodies by rejecting their right to determine their own sexual identities and lives. Feminists must find a way to respond to this appropriation without inadvertently silencing girls' rights to freely explore and express their desires.

Regulating the Menstruating Body

Over the last one hundred years, methods for managing menstruation have become big business, with menstrual markets today topping $13 billion globally ("Feminine hygiene products," 2008). Manufacturers have capitalized on myths of menstruation as dirty and shameful by selling sanitary products as scientifically superior ways to cope with the messiness of monthly periods (Kissling, 2006). Sending messages of secrecy and shame, they have contributed to a "culture of concealment" (Houppert, 1999, p. 13). While our culture's methods of keeping menstruation under wraps have shifted dramatically over the past century, our beliefs about menstrual blood, depressingly, have not. Many people assume attitudes have transformed, if not on account of commercialism, then because of feminism. However, the stories of my participants show that despite some inroads, they did not witness a radical shift in menstrual consciousness at puberty. Coming of age in the 1970s, 1980s, and early 1990s, these women represent a cohort confronted with contradictory meanings attached to monthly bleeding: the older responses of shame and concealment that have prevailed for a century versus the newer values of pride and celebration advanced by feminism. While acknowledging the ways that commercialism and feminism have influenced popular attitudes, women's accounts interwoven with cultural barometers such as menstrual ads, teen magazines, and medical treatments reveal how myths of menstruation as unsightly, unhealthy, and in need of sanitizing still have pervasive power.

UNDER WRAPS: CONCEALING THE BLEEDING BODY

Prior to the twentieth century, Western women practised a variety of methods for managing their menstrual blood, including undershirts, pads, and sponges. They started menstruating later than contemporary women due to deficiencies in nutrition; they stopped for long periods because they married earlier, had more children, and breastfed longer; and they ended earlier because of sickness and early death (Brumberg, 1997). Menstruation throughout the nineteenth century mystified medical men. Some Victorian physicians saw menstruation as a sign of a woman's subordination, reminding her about her lowly status as wife and mother (Napheys, 1889). Others viewed it as the marker of a girl's transition to womanhood that signalled her capacity to conceive, a capacity that, Victorian sensibilities dictated, needed to be protected (Chavasse, 1878). According to historian Joan Jacobs Brumberg (1997), first menses became a significant transitional event only after improvements in middle-class girls' daily nutrition lowered their average age of menarche from seventeen to twelve. As a result of this revised timetable, Victorians recast the new life course – the extended period between first menses and marriage – as a precarious time for girls. Adults began to monitor girls' menstruating bodies to guarantee that they would remain sexually pure before marriage.

Because the culture now interpreted menstruation as evidence of female sexuality, its arrival and departure had to be kept under wraps. In 1921, Kotex marketed the first successful disposable pad by explaining, as in the ad shown here (figure 6.5), that during the First World War nurses used bandages as an effective sanitary absorbent. By framing menstruation as a problem of hygiene rather than sexuality, marketers sanitized puberty, transforming the maturational event into a commercial transaction, and heightening girls' consciousness about the need to manage appearance to hide any evidence of staining or soiling (Brumberg, 1997; Kissling, 2006). To successfully sell products in a culture that concealed menstruation, they used medical authority, silent purchase, and mail order (Houppert, 1999). Even with medical endorsement, pads sold well only after women could buy them without speaking to a clerk, such as by using a silent purchase coupon or by putting money into a container beside the product. Mail-order companies also provided a discreet way for women to buy menstrual products without embarrassment.

You dispose of it

easily without embarrassment

Why 8 in 10 better class women have adopted this new way in personal hygiene — supplants old-time "sanitary" makeshifts . . . *what it is*

By ELLEN J. BUCKLAND, *Graduate Nurse*

THERE is one problem every woman knows — discarding the usual sanitary pad. This new way overcomes it.

It offers, too, charm, immaculacy and *peace of mind* impossible under old conditions.

As a nurse, I recommend it to you for better health's sake. As a woman for the comfort it provides.

What it is

It is called KOTEX. Nurses in war time France first discovered it. Now 8 in 10 women in the better walks of life use it. The bad habit of makeshift methods is rapidly being ended.

60% of many ills common to women, according to numerous authorities, are due to improper, old methods. That's why doctors so strongly urge KOTEX.

What it does

KOTEX is a newly discovered material. Made of Cellucotton, it is far more absorbent than ordinary cotton. *It absorbs 16 times its own weight in moisture*

It is hygienically treated. Hence does not invite dangerous germ life to increase and multiply — the cause of many ailments.

No trouble disposing of

It is as easily disposed of as a piece of tissue — simply discard it. No embarrassment, no difficulty

Women who seek daintiness, peace of mind, exquisiteness and safety under all circumstances, use it. Once you do, no other method will ever satisfy. And millions will tell you this.

Easy to get KOTEX

All drug and department stores have KOTEX in plain packages. Get it without embarrassment simply by saying "Kotex." 12 snowy white, immaculate folds in the medium package.

I would like to send you a new booklet for women on this subject, written by a doctor. Just write for it. And if you have never tried KOTEX, I will be glad to send you a sample, free.

Write today for booklet or sample to

ELLEN J. BUCKLAND, G. N.
Cellucotton Laboratories
166 W. Jackson Blvd., Chicago, Ill.

KOTEX

Figure 6.5. Kotex, You dispose of it: Kotex marketed the first disposable pad successfully in 1921 by framing menstruation as a problem of hygiene rather than sexuality.

Historians of the family argue that children coming of age in the 1930s were the first generation who, rather than aiming to become their parents, tried to surpass their elders. Marketers capitalized on this shift by conveying to mothers that daughters, as members of a distinctively modern generation according to one Kotex ad, "reject old fashioned sanitary makeshifts" and "want something else."[1] Or as another Modess ad coaxes, "Come On, Mother – Be a Sport," since the daughter of today "will not tolerate the traditions and drudgeries which held her mother in bondage." Tampax was the first company to mass-market tampons successfully (Houppert, 1999). Describing a new day for womanhood, their ad boasts: "Thousands of women have already tried Tampax and would no sooner go back to the old-fashioned napkin than they would go to the methods in use fifteen years ago." Because tampons were worn on the inside, religious leaders objected to them on the grounds that women would find them erotic or girls would lose their virginity. Mothers also worried about rupturing their daughters' hymens. Using code words and medical references, tampon ads reassured women that tampon use would not endanger a girl's virginity.

Like today's campaigns, early ads celebrated active women and hyped freedom and cleanliness. Many featured affluent white women and used language that associated tampon use with education, mobility, and liberalism. This aimed to entice immigrant and working-class girls to buy tampons as markers of class mobility and modern womanhood (Brumberg, 1997). Advertisers often tried to make sales by convincing women that products would free them from the bondage of female bodies and preserve their femininity against the taint of menstruation (Kissling, 2006). At the same time, they masked their Western prejudices about menstrual blood by displacing these onto so-called primitive cultures. For example, myths of menstruation as dirty, unhealthy, and a sign of inferiority are Western in origin, yet the author of *Magic and Medicine in Menstruation* (Schering Corporation, 1934), a drug company booklet produced for doctors and patients, attributes these misconceptions to other cultures, especially Indigenous ones (To read, go to http://www.mum.org/scher1.htm).

Contrary to the questionable claims made in this resource, Cree/Metis scholar Kim Anderson (2000) has shown how the menstrual rituals

---

1   Unless otherwise noted in a citation, all historical advertisements discussed in this chapter were can be seen at the Ad*Access On-Line Project, Duke University, at http://library.duke.edu/digitalcollections/adaccess/.

of many Indigenous cultures did not denigrate menstruating women but rather honoured them. A current example of the Western tendency to misattribute menstrual myths to "backward" cultures can be found in *Always Changing*, which tells students that "many countries around the world" have menstrual taboos "handed down from generation to generation" (Always & Tampax, 2008, p. 28). By attributing rules like "I can't do any exercise" (p. 28) to other cultures and peoples, this resource disregards complex meanings given to menstruation across cultures, dismisses women's rich knowledge derived from embodied experiences, and fails to recognize how science itself perpetuates menstrual taboos. For example, in the 1950s medically endorsed instructional film *Molly Grows Up* (1953), a school nurse clearly recommends that menstruating girls refrain from square dancing!

Since the 1960s, ads have assumed girls' autonomy but also stimulated angst, playing to concerns about their cleanliness, sexual purity, and self-confidence. In one 1992 Kotex ad, the text suggests that concealment is critical because "if he found out, you'd change schools." In another 1990 image, Tampax reassures girls that they will still be virgins if they use tampons. A third 2005 Always ad equates young women's self-confidence with protection from shameful menstrual stains. Although advertising today is more open, marketers continue to present monthly periods as a hygiene problem. The threat of leakage is a recurring theme – one Tampax ad featuring a female diver facing a possible shark attack with the caption "A Leak Can Attract Unwanted Attention." (This can be found at http://www.mum.org/GULIcov.htm.) While Kotex laudably created the first campaign to depict menstrual blood in red, ads still alleviate concerns about leakage by containing the blood in a perfectly round, impermeable sphere. Some feminists have praised Kotex's most recent commercials "So Obnoxious" and "Reality Check" for exposing the fakeness of menstrual ads and for poking fun at silly codes used (like blue liquid for blood or flowers for femininity; view at http://www.youtube.com/watch?v=tUnFfInfpdg). Yet these, too, can be critiqued for promoting cynicism rather than changing attitudes.

Beliefs about menstrual blood as unclean prevail in Western culture, but they have not gone unchallenged. Since the 1970s, feminists working to unmask menstrual myths have contributed to a vibrant counterculture and positive discussions about menses. Judy Blume's novels are one example, but there are many others ranging from Judy Chicago's art installation *Menstruation Bathroom* (http://womanhouse.refugia.net/)

to Gloria Steinem's hilarious essay *If Men Could Menstruate* (1978/2004). Some researchers suggest that interventions may have had a favourable effect on girls' menarche experiences, especially the white, middle-class girls who have been the focus of most studies. While women in earlier research reported mostly negative memories (Janet Lee, 1994), girls today recount more positive and less shame-filled first periods (Fingerson, 2005; Janet Lee, 2009), though some studies contradict this finding (A. Burrows & Johnson, 2005). Coming of age in the late 1970s and afterwards, this cohort of participants began menstruating amid changing cultural meanings. Confronted by conflicting views of menstruation as positive yet polluting, a sign of maturity and inferiority, and something celebrated but secretive, many experienced menarche as a contradictory event. While 40 per cent reported negative and 45 per cent mixed experiences, 15 per cent related primarily positive ones. In relating stories, they emphasized four themes: concealment of monthly bleeding; sexual and reproductive maturation with its dangers and pleasures; shame as a result of soiling and staining; and supportive communities and special rituals to guide their rite of passage.

Women's menarche experiences varied widely depending on community norms, age of first menses, prior preparedness, and supportiveness of mothers and friends. Older participants who began bleeding with little preparation or limited support, including Sharon and Zoë, emphasized negative aspects such as humiliation and shame. Some younger informants reported negative experiences, but many others, such as Anne Marie and Hannah, related how more favourable meanings and supportive friends and family contributed to mixed or positive feelings, such as embarrassment intermingled with excitement and pride. Due to the imperative for concealment using "sanitary products," almost everyone internalized beliefs about menstruation as a hygiene problem and menstrual blood as unclean and smelly. Thus, whether menarche was joyful or painful, the majority told stories about the necessity of concealing their periods and about the fear they felt if their secrets were revealed. Many described concealment practices that included refraining from talking openly about bleeding (such as inventing code words); concealing evidence from boys and men; and keeping pads and tampons hidden (in lockers and purses).

Sharon: I was eleven when I got my period. I didn't know what to do because my mother didn't talk to us about being a woman. When I told her, she sent my sister and me to buy pads. When we got home, she freaks out 'cause we bought tampons. I had to go back to the store. I'm humiliated and I feel like shit, right? Every time I think about it, I feel yucky.

Zoë: I got my period before my friends. I didn't know what it was. My older sister came to talk to me because my mom didn't want to deal with it. She said "You got your period, you are a woman now." Me thinking "I am not even eleven yet. How can I be a woman?" Her bringing the sanitary napkin belt and showing me how to do it. Me thinking this was the worst thing that could ever happen, so uncomfortable, so self-conscious.

Hannah: I got my period the day I went to a friend's house for lunch. She didn't have pads or tampons so she had to call around to our friends to see if anyone could bring any to school. By the time I got back our whole class knew and people were patting me on the back. I felt embarrassed but at the same time a sense of pride about it. It wasn't treated as the feminine ritual that it should have been because it was accompanied by embarrassment and the whole dirty and shock feeling. But there was this kind of subtle, childish sense of ritual that I'd become part of some club.

Anne Marie: All my friends had it so I was waiting for it, wanting it to come. It came at a New Year's Eve party and everyone made a big deal about it: this was my entrance, I was now part of the world. I was embarrassed but excited because we had to go find some protection for me.

Concealment featured prominently in these women's accounts, and surfaces as a defining feature of menstruation in research conducted with North American girls today (Janet Lee, 2009) and middle-class women across cultures (Uskul, 2004). Sexist taboos frame bleeding not simply as a bodily function but as a defect that must be masked for women to participate in society (Merskin, 1999). While secrecy enables women to manage the negative meanings, it leaves them to grapple on their own with gender politics surrounding bleeding. Challenging the culture of concealment exposes the sexual politics framing menstruation. Speaking openly also increases women's understanding of menstrual events occurring throughout their lives, which promotes their health (S.C. Cooper & Koch, 2007). Greater frankness about menstruation may be vital for enhancing girls' sexual agency because it nurtures their knowledge of, and confidence in, their bodies and sexualities (Teitelman, 2004).

Concealment goes hand in hand with commercialization. Companies want women to adopt disposable products to cloak their bleeding because this generates profits. Although 70 per cent of women in North America and parts of Europe use tampons, usage falls to the single digits in Japan and Mexico, and is not even measurable in much of the world (E. Nelson & Jordan, 2000). To market tampons, Procter and Gamble has tried pyramid techniques where female sales agents teach young women how to use tampons in "bonding sessions" that resemble Tupperware parties (E. Nelson & Jordan, 2000). In Africa, the company initiated the "Protecting Futures" campaign, which aims to supply African girls with menstrual pads to prevent them from skipping school during their period (Deutsch, 2007). According to campaign creators, they also developed the program to build loyalty to the brand. Yet it's questionable whether such efforts can keep girls in school. A recent study conducted by Emily Oster and Rebecca Thornton (2011) found that giving Nepalese girls menstrual cups did not increase their school attendance. (Menstrual cups are reusable bell-shaped silicone devices worn inside the vagina to collect blood.) Many girls adopted the cup but told researchers that they skipped school because of factors unrelated to menstruation. We know there are health effects from tampon use. The increase in Toxic Shock Syndrome (TSS) was related to Procter and Gamble's Rely, a super-absorbent rayon tampon introduced in 1978 (Centers for Disease Control and Prevention, 1997). Procter and Gamble pulled Rely from the market in 1980 after thirty-eight women died of TSS. Since then, TSS has not disappeared. The Centers for Disease Control (Foege, 2006) have recorded roughly 70 to 100 cases per year. There are alternatives to commercial products, such as reusable pads and menstrual cups, but many women have limited knowledge about them.

BLEEDING AS SEXUALIZING AND SHAMING

What accounts for the imperative to hide women's bleeding? Since our culture sees menarche as the trigger point of female sexuality and fertility, girls starting their periods are often viewed with concern as sexually vulnerable or with suspicion as promiscuous (Janet Lee, 2009). These reactions may be rooted in social anxieties about the maturing female body that develops the capacity to reproduce without cultural authority to do so. Concealment of menstruation may reflect adult attempts to regulate girls' sexualities that threaten to spill out of control. Although most participants looked forward to becoming women, some explained how first menses was fraught with sexual overtones because it was framed as the advent of sexuality and reproductivity. Many who recalled shaming, restrictive, or punishing responses were of Afro-Caribbean and South Asian Canadian descent. They described getting confusing and threatening messages from home and school that linked menarche with sexual dangers such as pregnancy and rape. While such patterns featured in the accounts of many racialized women, Black women disproportionately received vague warnings and moralizing messages about their virginity and fertility. This is consistent with research conducted with low-income African American women who reported receiving limited information from mothers and only when they started their periods (S.C. Cooper & Koch, 2007). The extreme negative reaction of some mothers in this study, such as Maya's, may have been rooted in Black mothers' unspoken drive to uphold a super-respectable image in order to defend daughters against stereotypes of sexual deviance and hyper-sexuality and reproductivity.

Ada: Menstruation was a problem. I felt vulnerable in a different way. Due to the protection issue, my family secluded me more; they monitored my movements and phone calls because they were so paranoid about me talking to boys. It almost gave me a reason to rebel, because the control factor seemed so much more overt, stronger, more suppressing. If I were to talk to a boy I'd get pregnant. It felt that bad.

Jacqueline: When I first had my period my mother told me, "You can't let any boys touch you when you are on your period." So I thought that if I allowed a boy to touch me I would be doing something wrong because she didn't go into detail. I had to ask her questions because I didn't know what to do. She didn't say much and I was afraid to ask much because I didn't want her to think anything bad. I felt really awkward.

Maya: The worst years of my life were from eight to thirteen. I got my period when I was nine after a back operation to correct my scoliosis. I hid it from my mom for two months because I didn't know what it was. I thought I was dying so I asked "What is this?" First, she said it was because I had an operation. I was a smart kid and that didn't sound right to me! "No, that can't be it." Then she lost it and said I must be messing with boys. I thought "that's not right because I know I'm not doin' nothin'." So I asked my sister. Then after that, I never asked my mother anything ever again. When she blamed me, I felt disgusted, like I had done something wrong even though I hadn't done anything wrong. I felt ashamed, especially since none of my friends got it until two years later.

Like many Black women, South Asian women in this study received confusing and moralizing messages about menarche. They told of parents who began to look at and relate to them as sexually maturing young women and to impose restrictions as a way of ensuring their sexual safety and purity. Although it's probable that at least some South Asian participants came from one of approximately half of the world's cultures and regions (including in South India) that celebrate menarche with rituals and ceremonies (Uskul, 2004), none with whom I spoke experienced such formal recognition of first menses. As feminist researcher Anita Handa (2003) found in her research with South Asian girls growing up in Canada, the women I interviewed were caught between contradictory requirements for sexuality and gender: one set imposed by their families and communities and the other, by the dominant/Anglo-white culture. Like the South Asian Canadian girls in Handa's study, participants here walked the "tightrope of culture" (2003) because, in communities under threat, women were made responsible for upholding collective norms, including values of sexual purity. Due to changes in nutrition brought on by migration, many South Asian women began bleeding at younger ages than their immigrant mothers. In some cases, caught off guard, even shocked mothers, who could not make sense of their daughters' earlier menarche, misattributed the blood to the loss of virginity. Their stories raise questions about what mothers may have been thinking and feeling, including the meanings they made of their daughters' earlier menarche and the worries they may have had about protecting daughters from community judgments.

Tamara: My period was awful. My poor mother was in a new country but mentally at home. If it wasn't for her friend there it would have been a more horrible experience because my mom was going to slap me across the face and ask me what boy I had been with. She thought I had lost my virginity, that's why I was bleeding. Then her friend said, "What are you doing? The child is having her period." We never talked about it again.

Hasina: When I got my period, I knew what happened but I didn't want to believe it because I didn't want it to happen. I couldn't tell my mom so I told her I had to get some pads. She freaked because she was sixteen when she got it and I was thirteen. For her it was a shock. Then she started getting rude. "How come?" I actually feel bad for her when I think about it because it was so different for her. I remember thinking if I act more boyish, if I don't think of certain things, my period wouldn't happen. I was so upset.

Menstruation signifies the onset of women's reproductive abilities; yet for many, it arouses shame and disgust. Why? Feminists starting with de Beauvoir (1974) have argued that staining is shaming because it marks the female body as other to the male norm. Historically, philosophers and physicians such as Aristotle, Galen, and Hippocrates interpreted menstrual blood as a sign of women's inferiority and toxicity just as de Beauvoir argues: for example, Hippocrates thought it was caused by fermentation in the blood because women lacked the supposed male ability to dissipate impurity through sweat; Galen believed menses was the residue of undigested blood in food because women lacked the male ability to digest properly; and Aristotle saw menstruation as excess blood not incorporated into a fetus (Angier, 1999). According to researcher Janet Lee, notions of bodies as toxic reflect "bodily power relations" in society, which cast certain groups (including women, fat people, and the poor) as more contaminating and threatening (2009, p. 616). In her analysis of television and film references to periods, cultural studies scholar Elizabeth Kissling found a recurring theme of menarche as a powerful reminder that girls, no matter what they say or do, "are still female and Other" (2002, p. 8). Internalization of negative meanings was apparent in the stories of many women in this study, Gayle and Rosetta included, who told about the shame and trauma they associated with bleeding. Use of the term *trauma* by some conveyed the extreme distress and emotional shock they felt and how they experienced their first period almost as a physical injury.

Rosetta: I started my period when I was eleven. A counsellor at school pulled me in and said, "You have your period." I remember crying and asking God to take it away. I hated the pad game. They had to show me how to use those belts with a pad. Then my mom bought me mini pads thinking I was just a kid but I needed full size. I felt clumsy, awkward, stupid, dirty.

Gayle: It's supposed to be a wonderful time of a girl's life, really! "Oh, you're becoming a woman!" I can't relate to that. I can put it into these terms now but back then there was a sense of dread, not quite dread but in the back of your mind, the great unknown, something to be feared, anxiety. I did not want to menstruate. Watching the other girls, I don't know if anyone was proud. But for me, it was a fearful, traumatic thing.

Letters to the editors of *YM*, *TeenVogue*, and *Seventeen* indicate that girls today continue to internalize messages about the "stain" of menstruation. In *Twist Magazine*'s "True tales of mortifying moments," one teen writes that "Tampons and pads fell on my head!" and another exclaims: "Tim McGraw saw my period!" Staining is only one example of loss of bodily control. Snotty noses, sweat on clothing, and farting in front of boys are other examples of liquids, smells, and sounds of the leaky body that threaten to betray girls' imperfect femaleness and humanness. Perhaps we reject these bodily processes because we associate them with the uncontrollable, and because they remind us of our vulnerability. Feelings of humiliation, disgust, and fear of the leaky body abound in the period stories that women told me. Many internalized derogatory cultural beliefs about menstrual blood and felt at fault in not being able to control leakages.

Yolanda: Leaking! I was so embarrassed. I remember seeing that there was a big red stain on the back of my pants, going "How long has that been there?" I was dirty. My period was such a new concept that I didn't know how much I had to do. That coupled with where do you keep the pads when you're in junior high? Do you put them in your bag? In your locker? That was a big deal because we didn't always have access to our lockers. So a big leak would happen and I thought everybody knew.

Rhonda: There were times when I had really heavy flows and there used to be a lot of leakage. So people would notice a stain on the back of my pants. They would go "Hey blood!" That was horrible.

MENSTRUAL SUPPORT VERSUS SUPPRESSION

While many storytellers vividly described the shame they felt and the negative or mixed responses they received, some remembered their first period as positive and shared stories of pride and pleasure at its onset. Among women with positive memories, supportive mothers and friends, and acceptance and celebration, emerged as key. This suggests that women's specific social contexts and relationships filtered cultural ideologies about menstruation. Research has shown that mothers are girls' primary source of learning about menstruation, but that until recently, many mothers felt neither comfortable nor competent in teaching daughters about their periods (Costos, Ackerman, & Paradis, 2002; Janet Lee & Sasser-Coen, 1996). For women in this study, how mothers approached daughters had a powerful impact on their first period experiences. Those with the best memories, such as Fredericka, described preparation in the form of special talks and shared rituals to mark the event initiated by emotionally supportive mothers or sometimes other caregivers. This finding is supported by Janet Lee's (2008) research conducted with young women going through menarche at the end of the millennium, which found that mothers played a critical role in helping daughters negotiate concealment. Many of these mothers – who grew up with feminism and amid increased openness about bodies – supported daughters by providing a buffer against misogynistic cultural messages. For some participants, like Eva, their mothers' lack of emotional engagement suggested that a supportive maternal response may have become a cultural expectation, especially for middle-class girls brought up with period-positive pro-feminist messages. In her research with teens, Anne Teitelman (2004) has found that a supportive scenario may be more common in affluent families where mothers have the time and resources to prepare daughters for their periods.

> Fredericka: My mom was the first one I told. She made me completely comfortable. We'd also had so many talks about what happens that it was actually boring. But after that, I didn't tell my dad. My mom did that and not with me around. So it was secret in a way. It was kind of joyful and nervous, nerve-racking and a little bit scary.

> Eva: I was normal in terms of my period, everybody else had gotten theirs that year and I wasn't waiting for mine. It was fine, but because my sisters went through it first, nobody dealt with me. My period was a big deal to me, but it was not a big deal to anyone else so I thought it was overrated.

Many of those with positive memories identified supportive peers, especially female friends and older sisters, as an important source of menstrual information and affirmation. Like Laura Fingerson (2005), who describes the ways girls forge friendships at this time, some women in this research, including Jillian and Jane, described their periods as a time for connection and solidarity with other girls. The teens Fingerson interviewed drew on knowledge and experiences of their menstruating bodies "as a way of building a sense of their femininity and connecting to other girls and women" (2005, p. 106). Even those like Sophia, who had negative memories of monthly bleeding, highlight how young women can form a community of support through their shared experiences to protect each other from the humiliation of leakages. These narratives underscore the ways that a culture of camaraderie has emerged as a counterpoint to the culture of concealment, especially as a result of girls coming together to create new meanings and make change. Some women who had thoroughly negative first-period experiences also expressed that they wanted to teach future generations different lessons than they had been taught. In their roles as mothers, teachers, older sisters, and mentors, many had already become proactive, supportive, and engaged communicators.

> Jane: Getting my period was a really happy story. I was really worried that I wouldn't get it. So when I got it I was on the phone with a friend and I was like "I just got my period!" We were cheering and jumping up and down and I felt so womanly. Still I adore my period. I love my period!

> Jillian: My best friends had already started their periods and I was waiting for mine. Then one day there was blood everywhere. I remember being happy because my friends had it. We had this joke that began when one of my friends had started her period and said, "I couldn't find a spot of white on my underpants today." That was our code way of saying that we had our period. So we were walking to our first dance and when I went to meet them I said, "I couldn't find a spot of white on my underpants today."

> Sophia: One time I walked to the front of the class and when I was coming back someone pointed out a bloodstain on my dress. Oh! All the girls helped me get it out. It was embarrassing because the guys saw it. But it was nice that the girls banded together and went to the nurse's office to get out the stain. Girls giving support! Another female in need here!

The participants' period stories show evidence of changing practices through a supportive female culture. This does not mean that derogatory understandings have disappeared. In fact, the culture of concealment may be giving way to a culture of menstrual suppression through cycle-stopping birth control pills. In 2003, the pharmaceutical company Barr Laboratories released Seasonale, a birth control pill designed to suppress menstruation (Loshny, 2005). Health Canada approved Seasonale in 2007 (Magnan, 2007), and a second-generation version,

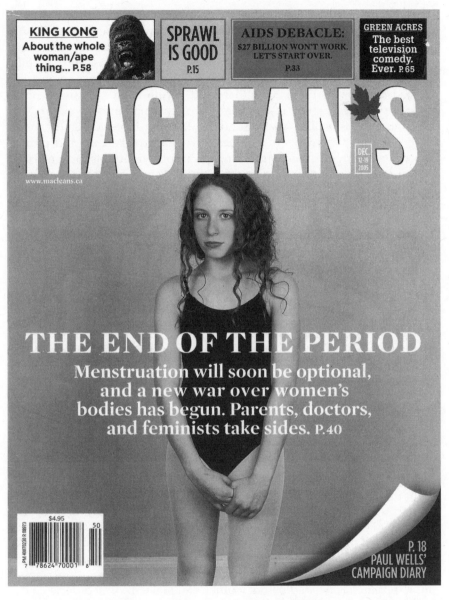

Figure 6.6. The end of period: Despite the push from feminism to create positive imagery for girls and women, the culture of secrecy and shame surrounding menstruation may be giving way to a culture of menstrual suppression through cycle-stopping birth control pills.

Seasonique, in 2011 ("Seasonique™," 2011). These birth control pills are taken for eighty-four days with a placebo or lower-dose pills taken for seven days, which limits menstruation to four periods a year. The drug giant Wyeth also launched Lybrel in 2007, the only FDA-approved pill taken 365 days a year, without placebos so that it suppresses a woman's period entirely (Kaplan, 2007). Barr and Wyeth have capitalized on a theory posited by some researchers that menstruation is an evolutionary anomaly, as well as a hassle and health hazard for women (Loshny, 2005). Popular women's magazines have since picked up and publicized the case against menstruation. Few publish rebuttals to menstrual suppression, including evidence for the link between contraceptives and breast cancer, blood clots, and bone loss (Hitchcock & Prior, 2004). The controversy has also received considerable attention in the news press, including a *Maclean's Magazine* cover story (George, 2005) that declared "The End of the Period" (see figure 6.6).

Framing menstruation as unhealthy medicalizes women's bodily functions by defining them as diseased and prescribing questionable treatment. While medical sexism isn't new, what is new, according to researcher Helen Loshny (2005), is renewed medicalization of menstruation. The menstrual suppression pill is marketed to prevent a range of conditions from menstrual discomfort to cancer. But feminists argue that there are good reasons for women to menstruate aside from childbearing. For instance, menstruation affords a break from high hormone levels – such a break may be important for breasts and bones, particularly among adolescents who are at a crucial time in their development (Hitchcock & Prior, 2004). The Society for Menstrual Cycle Research (2003), a scholarly organization, has identified three major problems with marketing menstrual suppression pills: (a) safety issues, since there is not enough evidence to conclude that cycle-stopping pills are safe (Hitchcock & Prior, 2003); (b) cultural attitudes that the marketers manipulate, because these are better predictors of women's use of menstrual suppression than women's medical symptoms (Hoyt & Andrist, 2003); and (c) media bias, since advocates of suppression and its benefits are afforded more space than opponents and risks (Johnston-Robledo & Barnack, 2003). The Society concludes that while menstrual suppression may be a good option for those with severe menstrual problems, more research is needed before women can make informed decisions.

Despite feminism and the positive memories some women recalled, the prevalence of shame points to the continued circulation of menses' negative meanings. This is especially true for racialized women who confronted clashing values and moralizing messages as they experienced menarche in the period before the new millennium. Since then, more girls and women have found strategies to shield themselves from disparaging messages and to challenge norms of secrecy within girl culture and mother–daughter relationships. However, it's questionable whether such responses have transformed societal values. Girls and women still learn to talk about menstruation in derogatory ways and continue to confront the cultural obligation to keep it under wraps (Kissling, 2006). A strong message that female bodies are unacceptable encourages and enforces body-altering practices at puberty such as containing breasts and masking menstrual blood (T.A. Roberts, 2004). Some feminists argue that young women's more positive responses to menarche may reflect the rise of girl power, a new version of active, dynamic, and empowered femininity (Janet Lee, 2009). However, the image of the empowered young woman that menstrual marketers have helped to create may serve less as a sign of bodily freedom than as a clever decoy by downplaying girls' negative experiences and deflecting attention from the ongoing construction of menstruation as polluting and pathological. Evidence presented here, such as menstrual ads, the banning of menstruation-themed books, and the renewed medicalization of menstruation via cycle-stopping pills, indicates that attitudes may not have changed very much. Over the past thirty years, feminists have challenged mainstream messages about female sexed bodies and sexualities. Today, young feminists and queer activists continue to mount this challenge. Yet because of powerful corporate and conservative interests, sex equality remains elusive.

Chapter Seven

In the Mirror of Beauty Culture

The History of Beauty Culture

For most of us, mirrors are the oldest and most ubiquitous image-making technology in our day-to-day lives.[1] When reflecting surfaces became a staple of stores and homes in the late nineteenth century, images of their bodies for the first time became accessible to women and girls (Brumberg, 1997). Before the Victorian period only the wealthy could afford mirrors. In the sixteenth century, for example, a small glass mirror framed in precious metals and jewels cost the equivalent of a luxury car in today's currency (Melchior-Bonnet, 2001). Technological advancements in the nineteenth century saw massive increases in mirror production and installation in public and private spaces. The new department stores, such as Eaton's in Canada and Macy's in the United States, used reflecting surfaces to inundate interiors with light (O'Brien & Szeman, 2004). Retailers hoped this would incite consumer desire. At the same time, mirrors became permanent fixtures of middle-class homes, especially in bathrooms and bedrooms, as well as portable accessories for many girls and women. We know that a woman gazing at herself in the mirror is a common theme in art, advertising, and popular culture. While being looked at has been coded as feminine throughout Western history, a majority of Western women began to subject their bodies to greater scrutiny only with the introduction of affordable image technologies. From its status as precious item to commonplace object, the mirror has come to occupy an important place in our imaginations. Amplifying our awareness of our bodies as images, mirrors

---

1 Portions of this chapter were adapted from Rice (2009a).

and other image technologies have made sight, not touch, a primary sense through which we experience our physical selves (Rice, 2003).

Within contemporary image culture, appearance is portrayed as paramount to women. Yet in the nineteenth and prior centuries, beauty was believed to derive from inner qualities such as character, morality, and spirituality. A moral aesthetic governing beauty associated make-up with "painted ladies," a Victorian euphemism for prostitutes (Peiss, 1999, p. 30). Women who paid too much attention to image ran the risk of being perceived as shallow and vain and, more alarmingly, sexually impure. To overcome these associations and orient female buyers toward the consumption of cosmetics, advertisers invited them to see beautification as an acceptable moral lapse, an innocent sin. Marketers heightened women's image consciousness by reminding them of other people's critical scrutiny. For example, one ad warns women "Strangers' eyes, keen and critical – can you meet them proudly, confidently, without fear?"[2] Another claims "Your husband's eyes, more searching than your mirror." Positioned as objects of an outsider's gaze, female viewers of commercial culture were, for the first time, invited to see themselves as recipients of evaluative looks.

Historically, skin became women's first body project as they learned the power of complexion to advance or undermine their social inclusion. From ancient times, pallor was associated with high social status; women at work outdoors tanned and aged faster, whereas high-status women were not obliged to work in the fields, but stayed indoors and were pale skinned. To be fair (in the sense of skin and hair colour) was to be fair (in the sense of beauty) – and beauty of person was strongly associated with beauty of soul. During the seventeenth, eighteenth, and, especially, the nineteenth centuries, this superiority of white over dark was scientifically proclaimed, as white Europeans needed a convincing justification for slavery and colonization. As a result, women of every hue attempted to improve their social standing through skin whitening, the most popular cosmetic of the nineteenth century (Brumberg, 1997). In period advertisements, skin whiteners for white women promised to enhance their complexion, while products for Black women pledged to remove their dark skin. For instance, one "face bleach" ad claims to "turn the skin of a black or brown person four or five shades lighter,

---

2 Unless otherwise noted in a citation, all historical advertisements discussed in this chapter came from the Ad*Access On-Line Project, Duke University, at http://library. duke.edu/digitalcollections/adaccess/.

and a mulatto person perfectly white" (St Louis Palladium, 1901, as cited in Rooks, 1996). According to beauty scholar Noliwe Rooks (1996), these ads persuaded African American women to buy products by presenting dark skin as an ugly imperfection and by suggesting that skin lightening would promote women's class mobility and social acceptance in colourist, white supremacist society.

Surprisingly, ordinary women were industry innovators. Canadian working-class farm girl Elizabeth Arden, poor Jewish immigrant Helena Rubinstein, and African American domestic servant and daughter of slaves Madame C.J. Walker became successful entrepreneurs (Peiss, 1999). Feminist historian Kathy Peiss (1999) suggests that these socially marginalized women built their businesses by attracting other women to act as sales agents, and by using stories of their own struggles to attract customers. Early entrepreneurs brought to advertising the idea that women could improve their situation through personal transformation. Madame C.J. Walker, who is credited with popularizing the "hot comb" for straightening hair, sold such products as Black women's "passport to prosperity" (Rooks, 1996, p. 65). She saw Black women's beauty in a political light – as a vindication of Black womanhood demeaned by slavery and as a pathway to prosperity and respectability denied by white society (Peiss, 1999; Rooks, 1996). Many feminist and critical race scholars have debated whether Madame Walker preyed on African American women's feelings of inferiority or promoted pro-Black beauty through dignifying their beauty practices (Byrd & Tharps, 2001; Russell, Wilson, & Hall, 1992). In her advertisements, personal letters, and public talks, Walker did not seek to mimic white ideals. Instead, beauty was a way to challenge stereotypes of Black women as unfeminine and unattractive and in so doing, raise Black women's self-confidence and contribute to their collective advancement.

By the 1920s, the beauty business had mushroomed into a mass market taken over by male manufacturers (Peiss, 1999). Possessing more capital to supply retailers and to advertise products than the early female entrepreneurs who had innovated pyramid-style marketing, new manufacturing firms soon dominated markets (Peiss, 1999). Male owners authorized their involvement in women's appearance work by representing themselves as "experts" in the "science of beauty." Drawing from the social permissiveness of the period, advertisers connected women's cosmetic use with greater individuality, mobility, and modernity. The caption of one ad exclaims "The Lovely Rebel Who Fought for Youth and Won!" and a second reads "Be as MODERN as you like – for you can still be lovely." While marketers sold make-up as a means for women to assert autonomy and resist outmoded gender expectations, by the end of the 1930s messages increasingly equated beauty with a woman's "true femininity." For example, in one ad entitled "Beauty Lost – Beauty Regained," readers are told how a "lovely lady who goes to pieces" recovers her mental health by "regaining her lost youth." Beauty ads now encouraged women's investment in appearance in the name of their emotional well-being and psychological health. When image became intertwined with a woman's identity, personality, and psychology in this way, modifying the body became, for many, a principal method of caring for the self. In this way, a woman's appearance came to be read as a prime measure of her self-esteem, feminine essence, and mental health.

Throughout the 1930s, marketers encouraged middle-class mothers to invest energy in their own and their daughters' appearances in the name of physical and emotional health (Brumberg, 1997). During the Second World War, beauty became a means for women to support the war effort, with copy announcing that "beauty is a duty," that "fit" bodies increased women's productivity, while "lovely" faces enhanced troop morale. In one Canadian ad, women are told that time-saving beauty routines would allow them to "work for victory and stay lovely." It was not until the 1950s that cosmetics companies first targeted teenage girls, who had started to hold part-time jobs and had their own disposable income, with ads designed to appeal to their sense of generational distinctiveness and romantic desires. With copy encouraging readers to get "The 'natural' look men look for," ads for Seventeen Cosmetics spoke to girls' romantic desires to fit with prevailing heterosexual scripts by reinforcing their wish to attract admiring male eyes.

In today's media, explicit reference to an evaluative other is no longer necessary. Take a look at the cover of a recent *Cosmopolitan, Vogue,* or other fashion magazine. Who is the woman on the cover looking at? Who does she imagine looking at her? The cover image operates not only as an object of vision for male, but also for female audiences. As viewers, we might imagine ourselves to be a male or female spectator looking at the model with envy or desire. Alternatively, we might imagine ourselves to be the beautiful, sexy model looking back with confidence, desire, or the conviction of our own desirability at the male and female spectators who are looking at us. In either case, through this complex relay of looks, the model becomes an object of desire for imagined spectators who want her or want to be like her.

Today's Body Projects

Messages in today's magazines echo the efforts of women in my study to close the gap between their body differences and desirable ideals. Fashion magazines deliver the beauty business's messages to female consumers; their primary purpose is to enlist readers into image enhancement through continuous consumption. Copy encourages women to partake in perpetual body improvement. Rather than advocating one ideal, magazines try to democratize beauty by convincing readers that they can achieve their "best bodies." (If you doubt this, pay attention to the number of times magazines use headlines such as "Get your best hair," "clothes," or "look.") This message ostensibly enables girls' and women's expression of individuality and celebration of difference. Yet it also portrays body modification as critical to self-expression and pulls diverse audiences into preoccupation with body improvement. TV shows like *America's Next Top Model* likewise instruct girls and young women that they can bridge the gap between their bodily differences and images of desirability by re-visioning their differences as desirable. Such shows frequently reinforce the idea that the greatest power a young woman can wield is her sexual sway over men and they invariably present makeovers as the ticket to success. Despite purporting to represent diversity, they thus still promote a narrow notion of beauty and encourage body modification through consumption to achieve the desirable look.

Beauty pageants in which contestants are women with disabilities are yet another example of the idea of re-visioning differences as desirable, again within narrow confines. *Miss Ability* is a reality TV beauty contest from the Netherlands that started in 2006; contestants have to display a "handicap visible to the eye" (Eye2Eye Media, as cited in Sherwin, 2006). The winner of the first pageant, crowned by the Dutch prime minister, was a young woman named Roos who wears a cervical collar due to an acquired disability affecting her neck. The cervical collar is the only indication that she has any physical disability or difference and that she's not an average model. Roos manages her disability by using the cervical collar sometimes and lying prone sometimes, yet images often depict her as very desirable and sexual. While it can't be ignored that she is disabled, the nature of her disability is socially acceptable – no dribbling, sudden movements, speech impairments, or any deviance from social protocols that make people uncomfortable. Thus, the winner is someone the non-disabled population can relate to in fundamental ways. She can look "normal," albeit for very brief periods; she is seen as sexually desirable; and she meets the expectations of what is feminine. Even in a forum where it's supposedly celebrated, disability must remain invisible (Rice, Renooy, & Odette, 2008). Due to the show's high ratings in the Netherlands, broadcasters have snapped up the rights to remake Miss Ability in Britain, France, Germany, and the United States (Sherwin, 2006). In 2008, the BBC launched *Britain's Missing Top Model*, a series in which eight women with various disabilities participate in a competition, with the winner appearing in *Marie Claire* (Stanley, 2009).

As a result of cultural messages about difference and desirability, many women relate to their bodies as self-making projects (Beausoleil, 1994). They also come to see different body sites – skin, weight, hair, and breasts – as personal problems. For example, 90 per cent of those in this study saw themselves as over- or underweight, 80 per cent believed their breasts were too big or too small, over 50 per cent that they were unattractive, 31 per cent that their skin was too dark, and 27 per cent that their hair texture or colour was wrong. Body dissatisfaction increased dramatically between ages nine and sixteen, when everyone confronted a growing gap between their changing and idealized bodies. Coming of age in a consumerist, image-oriented society, they dealt with the disparity between differences and ideals of desirability by imagining, as Frances put it, their "best possible" body. Many (like Kasha and Leigh) came to perceive their bodies as images through everyday objects, including mirrors and clothing, which taught them to gauge their features relative to restrictive standards. When they fantasized about embodying ideals, they were not splitting themselves off from their actual bodies. Rather than detaching from their physical selves, they were trying to separate from the ways these were marked as other. All navigated puberty by envisioning or adopting diverse practices – from hair relaxing and eating disorders to cosmetic surgery – to remake their differences desirable.

Leigh: I don't have a [double eyelid] crease. Doesn't matter how much make-up the sales staff put there, it is not going to matter! I am not going to have a crease.

Frances: I never had an image of me that wasn't in the chair. But I would create images of me looking different in the sense that I would be prettier, slimmer, more popular. The most attractive image I could imagine becoming: my best possible image of myself ... I would pore over fashion magazines, make sure that I was really stylish, wear make-up that was just so. But then feel that I was covering up something that everybody was still going to see. It was always going to haunt me.

Kasha: Strange, but when you put on leggings, you feel that the model's body is going to come with them. I'll put on a pair of pants and think of the magazine image and when I see my butt I'll think, "People will laugh."

There is a noticeable groundswell in feminist writing about beauty, both critical and celebratory. While feminist commentary on beauty has mushroomed since the 1970s, many writers continue to wrestle with the same old debate: Are beauty practices manifestations of sexist, racist, and market oppression of women? Or do they afford women opportunities for self-expression, empowerment, and pleasure? Some critics contend that patriarchal and commercial interests push women into painful beauty work to satisfy our culturally created desires and assuage fears of difference (Clarke & Griffin, 2007; Dow, 2003; Gill, 2007a/b; Jeffreys, 2005; Stuart & Donaghue, 2011; Weber, 2007). Others argue that women are not cultural dupes but active agents who strategically alter their appearance in their best interests (Bae, 2011; K. Davis, 1995; Gimlin, 2002; Holliday & Sanchez Taylor, 2006; Scott, 2005). Women's actual beauty practices don't fit neatly into either frame of this debate. Responders' more ambiguous perspectives suggest that beauty culture both oppresses and gratifies those participating in it, signalling a surrender to ideals, resistance to abjection, and often both responses at once. Reading their stories alongside feminist commentary (Adrian, 2003; Bae, 2011; Felski, 2006), I argue for a more nuanced, context-sensitive, intersectional understanding of the role that beauty plays in women's lives. Few, if any, storytellers failed to recognize how an uptake of ideals worked to reproduce the beauty status quo, but they also identified multiple reasons for undertaking appearance-enhancing body practices, ranging from pleasure, convenience, and economic advantage to self-esteem and well-being. The embrace of beauty among those who embodied difference additionally served important political ends – pushing against the boundaries of the body beautiful. By negotiating between their embodied differences and beauty standards, many searched for an image that conveyed their intersectional identities (such as being of mixed race), and all struggled with the contradictory ethical implications of practices that hurt and oppressed even as they gratified and sometimes empowered.

The Weight Project: Getting the Body "Right" by Treating It Wrong

In Westernized cultures, people value thinness as vital to the body beautiful. The thin female body is associated with sexiness, self-discipline, and success. Fat, as chapter 4 discusses, is seen as unattractive, unhealthy, and lacking in body- and self-control. Today's magazines criticize women's bodies whatever their weight. Headlines such as "Battle of the Bones" and "Stars' Worst and Best Beach Bodies" regularly invite readers' criticism of famous bodies and encourage comparison based on looks and size. Coming of age in our size-obsessed culture, 66 per cent of the women in this study came to feel their "too-big" bodies violated size standards and 24 per cent that their "too-thin" ones failed to fit weight norms. The voices in their heads echoed messages from mainstream media: that no size is acceptable or safe.

In 2006, the Spanish government banned too-thin models from fashion shows in Madrid in response to public fears that ultra-thinness glamorized anorexic bodies and galvanized young women to adopt anorexic practices (Yeoman, Asome, & Keeley, 2006). While many praised the Spanish government's proactive response, this move raises questions about solutions to restrictive standards that involve increased surveillance of women's bodies. What is the effect of regulating individuals' weights rather than changing our concepts of beauty or the looking relations that position women as objects of our gaze? To what degree does this move unintentionally contribute to the problem by intensifying surveillance of women's bodies and enforcing weight norms that make no size feel acceptable or safe? Participants who internalized the message that regardless of weight, every body is vulnerable to assessment and amenable to alteration had this to say:

> Hasina: People started to call me skinny in high school. I had trouble gaining weight. In gym class when we were yelling out how much we weighed, people would speculate "I don't know why she's so thin."

> Christian: At puberty, I started to say to myself, "You've got to accept the harsh reality, you're the fat girl." I became ashamed of my body, didn't like to be seen in public, didn't like to be looked at. I'd put myself on diets, fail, hate myself for failing. Thought my body was so ugly.

Historically and cross-culturally, thinness has been interpreted as both a sign of morality and purity (e.g., fasting saints in the Middle Ages) and a signifier of disease and death (HIV/AIDS and tuberculosis). Fatness, too, has been read as a marker of wealth or waste, depending on the period and person bearing the trait. The West's framing of fat as undesirable and diseased suggests that fatness has become abject. Moreover, such othering is not gender-neutral since female bodies tend to have a higher percentage of adipose tissue than male ones. Fat, as a defining feature of female bodies, may be rendered abject because it reminds people of our connections with the maternal body, and thus of our finite lives and inevitable death. On pro-anorexia and pro-bulimia websites, young women utterly reject the fat body and imbue idealized svelteness with values of purity, perfection, and power. These sites mimic messages about the ideal and the abject body in mainstream media, including rejected *before* and idealized *after* pictures of those who undertake extreme weight loss. While such sites send deeply problematic messages, girls also use them to create alternative accounts of disordered eating. They correctly frame eating disorders as logical outcomes of living in a culture that privileges fit, flawless bodies while punishing those deemed unfit.

Although only about 3 per cent of young women in North America have eating disorders according to medical criteria (Woodside, Garfinkel, Lin, Goering, Kaplan, Goldbloom, & Kennedy, 2001), 40 per cent perceive themselves as too fat (Boyce, King, & Roche, 2008), and 50 per cent admit to extreme weight control including fasting and vomiting (Neumark-Sztainer, Story, Hannan, Perry, & Irving, 2002). The high prevalence of problem eating notwithstanding, eating disorders are interpreted as mental *illness* (American Psychiatric Association, 2000). However, feminist critics have long noted that an eating disorder, like all diagnoses, is a social construct (Rabinor, 2004). The term *disorder* incorrectly establishes a clear dichotomy between mental illness and wellness; yet given the pressure for women to control their appetites, it is often difficult to distinguish normal from pathological eating (Cohen, 2004; Rice & Langdon, 1991). According to the criteria for bulimia, for instance, a person who binges and purges between one and seven times a month is *not* bulimic. But does the eighth purge really make a difference? The criteria for anorexia stipulate that a woman must lose three consecutive periods and fall below a minimum normal weight to be considered anorexic. But what about food-restricting women who continue to menstruate or remain "overweight"? Unfortunately, many experts debate these criteria, but few consider the concept of a *continuum* of eating problems.

Beyond specific concerns with eating-disorder diagnoses, there are many problems with psychiatric labelling more generally – not only do labels stigmatize people, they also tend to be applied to the least powerful groups in society (Caplan & Cosgrove, 2004). Young women's emotional struggles tend to be pathologized more than young men's, so that there are fewer diagnoses to capture the downsides of masculinity (like excessive risk taking and incapacity to express emotion) than of femininity (depression and eating problems). Examples of psychiatric labels that have been proposed – such as dressing disorder and compulsive shopping disorder (Caplan & Cosgrove, 2004) – expose how power relations between men and women often arbitrate what is considered stereotypical behaviour and what is labelled a psychiatric condition. Many feminist therapists have been critical of psychiatric treatment for eating disorders, which positions women as pathological for adopting socially induced behaviours (Fallon, Katzman, & Wooley, 1994; Rice, 1996). In her ethnographic research, Helene Gremillion (2003) has found that treatment programs tend to substitute one set of disciplinary practices that regulate women's bodies for another – disempowering female patients by replacing culturally condoned food and weight control with medically condoned surveillance of their eating and weight. Hospitalization can save lives, yet statistics belie the effectiveness of interventions: re-hospitalization of young women with eating problems is common (Health Canada, 2002), creating a revolving-door experience which suggests that treatment often does not work.

In the past forty years, feminists have provided alternative understandings of eating issues that challenge medical accounts. Concerns of activists and clinicians mounted throughout the 1980s when the increased prevalence of eating problems led many to focus attention on the profound consequences of the slender ideal for girls and young women (Orbach, 1979; Székely, 1988). Leading theorists and therapists at the time emphasized the role of context in body-related struggles, and approached problem eating as a way of disconnecting from the body as a site of sexual and sexist violation (Fallon, Katzman, & Wooley, 1994). Expanding on this tradition, feminists throughout the 1990s moved beyond gender alone to consider how race, class, and other axes of power and difference contoured diverse women's body issues (B.W. Thompson, 1994). Since then, those influenced by poststructuralism have argued that language's importance in shaping reality is unrecognized by those working from social frames (Malson & Burns, 2009). Through analysing medical discourses, they uncover how our ways of talking about eating problems may limit possible understandings of causes and solutions. Constructivist theorists and therapists do not see eating struggles as expressions of innate pathology or cultural conformity but as negotiations of identity: ways that people in constraining circumstances attempt to embody socially desired identities through their food- and body-related practices.

Cultural theorist Susan Bordo (1993) argues that far from being a superficial fashion trend, the fit feminine body straddles contradictory pressures for women to appear as girly and sexy yet independent and self-contained – an androgynous ideal "purged" of womanly presence and power. Coming of age in toxic image environments, 35 per cent of women in my study took up problem eating, including 40 per cent of white participants and 30 per cent of racialized ones. With only four telling how they sought out or received help from medically oriented eating-disorder services, their narratives point to problem eating as a widespread cultural syndrome rather than a narrowly defined medical one. In keeping with how Bordo has decoded the slender body, some informants felt themselves attracted to the boyish body ideal for the aura of autonomy and escape from womanhood it seemed to offer. Through problem eating, they sought to erase signs of maturing femaleness and, in so doing, escape multiple gazes and gendered pressures everywhere. Others, including Gayle and Sylvie, described how they began demanding dieting and disordered eating as a way of amending the abject fat form. Rather than rejecting a womanly body, thinness for them signified conformity to an acceptable size. When those perceived as too fat were positioned as "other than female," many adopted problem eating to escape being labelled as deviant. Whether they started secretive eating in childhood or adopted disordered eating to amend size differences, *all* participants identified as fat took up problem eating.

> Fredericka: There was too much to being a woman. I got caught up in what people expected of you as a woman. So I separated myself from being a woman. One of the main things during my eating disorder was to get rid of any body shape that had to do with me being feminine. I didn't want that attention from men. I didn't want comments from my friends.

> Gayle: At least I felt normal enough and desirable enough [when bulimic] that I could actually contemplate a sexual relationship. I could actually let go of protecting myself and enter into a relationship.

> Sylvie: The times I have felt love are times my body has been the most socially acceptable [through starving and purging]. It makes me profoundly

sad that the only ways of accessing those feelings are through having a conventional body.

Most of us mistakenly believe that eating problems are the exclusive property of privileged white girls. While research has only contradictory evidence to offer about the demographics of eating disorders, weight restriction became a way of life for a majority of women I interviewed – Black, Asian, South Asian, and white. Racialized participants told how ultra-thinness was viewed more critically in their communities, where images of attractive bodies spanned a broader range of sizes. But most grew up during a time when communities of colour constituted a small portion of the Canadian population, and thus many had little access to an alternative aesthetic that called into question white weight standards. With stereotypic portrayals of starving African bodies circulating in Western media throughout the 1970s (such as in children's charity commercials), slenderness also became abject for Black women I interviewed who bore the trait. According to postcolonial scholars, Western images have mythologized Africans since the colonial period as innocent yet savage, human and animal, as dark presence and ghostly absence (Kaspin, 2002). By portraying emaciated Africans as blameless victims of starvation or brutal embodiments of civil war, Western photography has reduced a complex continent of cultures and peoples to a few simple stereotypes. In an attempt to scare Western girls out of self-starvation, only a few years ago one eating disorder campaign unwittingly drew on these injurious associations (see figure 7.1) to render the emaciated African form, faded and ghostlike, as an abject sign of strife and famine.

Growing up in this racially charged image environment, Rhonda and Maya describe how they got caught between racist stereotypes of starving African bodies in mainstream media and sexist pressures to conform to conflicting feminine size ideals from both the dominant culture (thinness) and their communities (roundness). Pictures of starving African bodies even shocked one white participant, Francine, *out* of anorexia by othering the ultrathin body that she had previously idealized. The meaning given to a woman's size depended on her race, which suggests that the emaciated brown body operates as an implicit other against which the thin white beauty ideal gets defined.

Rhonda: In the Caribbean community you are supposed to be bigger. So I have always been harassed for being skinny ... This image stuck in my

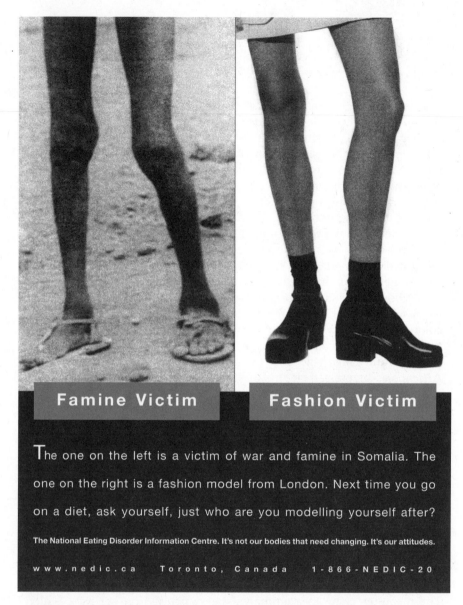

Famine Victim   **Fashion Victim**

The one on the left is a victim of war and famine in Somalia. The one on the right is a fashion model from London. Next time you go on a diet, ask yourself, just who are you modelling yourself after?

The National Eating Disorder Information Centre. It's not our bodies that need changing. It's our attitudes.

w w w . n e d i c . c a   T o r o n t o ,   C a n a d a   1 - 8 6 6 - N E D I C - 2 0

Figure 7.1. Famine victim/Fashion victim: This eating disorders campaign draws on negative associations in the North American mindset of the emaciated African body with famine, strife, and civil war in an attempt to scare Western girls out of ultra-thinness and self-starvation. Photo courtesy of the National Eating Disorder Information Centre.

mind because this girl said I look like one of those starving children with the big stomachs in the World Vision commercial. That was the most hurtful thing that anybody has ever said to me. I thought, "I should be bigger and more normal because I look like those poster kids."

Maya: Even if they saw a white person as skinny as me there is a little difference because I'm supposed to have a body, breasts, and butt. But if a white girl is as skinny as me, that's OK. She can still pass. Because I'm Black, I should have the breasts and butt and if I don't, well then there's something wrong with me even though she might look the same as me.

Francine: There was a newspaper article with a really skinny Biafran girl starving in Africa. My cousin showed me and she said, "You know, you're skinnier than that." I went, "Oh my God. Really? She's a skeleton." I wanted to be normal, I knew I wanted to be normal.

Marcia: I was heavier than most girls because I was muscular. So I went on these crazy diets, where I'd only eat yogurt. I consumed so much that the bacteria started to affect my stomach. So I ended up in the hospital with "anxiety attacks." But I was just trying to make myself look the way I was supposed to look in society.

No professional identified any woman of colour in this study as having an eating problem. Instead, because clinical data in the 1970s and 1980s mostly came from white experts working with upper-middle-class white patients (Hesse-Biber, Leavy, Quinn, & Zoino, 2006), professionals interpreted the struggles of racialized storytellers as something other than problem eating. Failure to recognize eating disorders in racialized women, as in Marcia's case, may be rooted in a deeper reluctance to recognize the complex role of culture in shaping embodiment (Bordo, 2009; Nasser & Malson, 2009). Susan Bordo (2009) cites a study conducted in Fiji by anthropologist Anne Becker as an example of that influence. She notes how before the introduction of Western television in 1995 Fiji had no reported eating disorders. Just a few years after Western broadcasting arrived, Becker found that 11 per cent of girls reported vomiting to control weight and 69 per cent had tried dieting (Becker, Burwell, Gilman, Herzog, & Hamburg, 2002). For Bordo (2009, p. 54), "the incredible spread of these problems to extraordinarily diverse groups ... over a strikingly short period of time, and co-incident with the mass globalization of media imagery, strongly suggests that culture is the 'smoking gun' that is killing people." Few feminists would deny that Western culture is implicated in the global spread of eating disorders. Yet some, such as Mervat Nasser and Helen Malson (2009), caution against imposing Western or white mainstream meanings onto non-white and non-Western women's experiences. They argue that this denies cultural complexities and local specificities in the body practices of diverse women, such as how problem eating might signal an adoption of Western ideals (like Marcia's attempts to starve away her muscularity) and rejection of racial othering (her possible refusal to be cast as an overly muscular Black girl). By showing how the meanings of body sizes and eating practices vary across and within Westernized contexts, this exploration reveals important differences in experiences but leaves many questions unanswered. If eating disorders are not longer a "white girl" or "Western" problem, what challenges confront us in trying to explain them? How do we make meaning of problem eating without imposing Western or white meanings on non-Western and non-white women's experiences?

The Skin Project: No Fairness in Fairness

As a result of Western colonization and widespread racism and sexism, many cultures associate light skin with beauty, which fuels and is fuelled by a profitable business in skin-whitening products. While some feminists suggest that skin whitening is a practice relegated to our racist past (Peiss, 1999), Amina Mire (2005) calls the rapidly growing global trade in skin-lightening products the globalization of white Western beauty ideals. (If you doubt Mire's claim, do an Internet search for "skin lightening." It will yield over two million hits.) In the West, many cosmetics companies market skin lightening to aging white women by associating light skin with youth and beauty. The aging process in ads is frequently framed as a pathological condition that can be mitigated through measures such as bleaching out age spots. Globally, companies also sell skin-whitening products to women of colour, often covertly via the Internet to avoid public scrutiny or state regulation of their products (Mire, 2005). This is partially because many products contain unsafe chemicals such as hydroquinone and mercury, which inhibit the skin's melanin formation and are toxic. The dangers of mercury poisoning from skin lighteners – neurological, kidney, and psychological damage – are well known. However, the hazards of hydroquinone, which has been shown to be disfiguring in high doses and to cause cancer in laboratory studies, are less well documented. Press reports suggest that while governments have banned the most dangerous lighteners, in many countries these are smuggled into domestic markets (Barnett & Smith, 2005; Van Marsh, 2007).

In Africa and other regions of the global south, skin whitening is traditionally associated with white colonial oppression, when waves of European conquerors instituted economic, political, and cultural hierarchies based on language and skin colour. Because women who practise skin lightening were and are harshly judged as suffering from an inferiority complex due to colonization, many engage in the practice secretly (Mire, 2005). Companies rely on covert advertising to mitigate women's secret shame about their perceived deficiencies, as well as their need to conceal such practices in order to avoid condemnation. Selling covertly also prevents public scrutiny of injurious stereotypes used in advertising campaigns. In some campaigns, explicitly racist ads associate dark skin with "diseases" and "deformities" such as "hyperpigmentation," "melasma," and other "pigmentation pathologies." In contrast, they typically associate light skin with youth, beauty, and empowerment. In its Internet ads, L'Oréal, a leading marketer of skin whiteners, such as Bi-White and White Perfect, references the inferiority of dark skin and the superiority of light complexions. Bi-White features an Asian woman unzipping her darker skin (www.youtube.com/watch?v=l0zsVIA3x6Y). Directed mainly to Asian consumers, the ad uses medical language to suggest that Asian bodies produce too much melanin, which Bi-White will block. As Mire (2005) writes, darkness in this ad is associated with dirtiness, ugliness, and disease. Lightness is seen as healthy and beautiful.

There is a growing trend for many Western-owned cosmetics corporations to rely less on covert Internet marketing and more on splashy TV and print campaigns to reach customers in Asia (Timmons, 2007). Since 1978, Hindustan Lever Limited, a subsidiary of the Western corporation Unilever, has sold its skin-whitening products to millions of women around the world (Melwani, 2007). Fair & Lovely, one of Hindustan Lever's best-known beauty brands, is marketed in over thirty-eight countries and currently monopolizes a majority share of the skin-lightening market in India (Leistikow, 2003). An industry spokesperson recently stated that fairness creams are half of the skin-care market in India and that 60 to 65 per cent of Indian women use these products on a daily basis (Timmons, 2007). Ads for Fair & Lovely frequently feature depressed young women with few prospects who gain brighter futures by attaining their dream job or desired boyfriend after becoming fairer

(Hossain, 2008). Other commercials show shy young women who take charge of their lives and transform themselves into modern, independent beauties. Appealing to women's dual aspirations for desirability and economic equality, ads feature tag lines such as "Fair & Lovely: The power of beauty" and "Fair & Lovely: For complete fairness" (see ads at http://www.youtube.com/watch?v=KIUQ5hbRHXk&NR=1). The accounts of Nicole and other racialized women in this study echo these ads' sensibilities in that all learned, often from both the dominant culture and their own communities, that lighter skin was associated with beauty, virtue, and economic opportunity.

> Nicole: Black women have a hierarchy of beauty because of colonialism. The Europeans brought in the ideal of beauty, and the ideal person looks the closest to white without being white. There's a caste system in the Caribbean, and the lighter you are the more opportunities you have.

> Salima: Being in the West Indian community I was more attractive, and with people who weren't West Indian I was more acceptable because I wasn't as dark. So I had an easier time from all groups because I am supposedly that ideal.

> Zoë: All my life white people have said "I lie in the sun so I can look like you. You have the perfect skin colour." So it is a real privilege to have this skin colour because it is not too dark. I can't imagine if I was a lot darker that people would be saying "Your skin is such a beautiful colour."

Globally, women are fed a persuasive beauty myth: that fairness is glamorous and that lighter skin is the ticket to getting ahead in life. Of course, cosmetics companies deny that the promise of fairness has anything to do with colonial and gender relations or with the idealization of white looks (Melwani, 2007; Timmons, 2007). To complicate things, Western psychiatrists frame skin whitening and other risky body-modification practices as signs of mental illness, unconnected to colonial or other oppressive histories. While feminists have debated whether beauty practices are tools of oppression or opportunity, individuals' experiences suggest that appearance alteration reflects both positions – that skin lightening signifies women's capitulation to oppressive ideals and opposition to abjection (Rice, 2009c). Skin modification may represent one of the few options for racialized women who get caught between the colonizing effects of white supremacy and competing desires for feminine beauty and social acceptance. In the narratives of those interviewed, women aspired to light (rather than white) ideals to straddle conflicting demands: to affirm their ethnic looks and escape being seen as other. Many spoke of avoiding sunlight, wearing light concealer, and using skin lightening in an effort to create a desirable image that enabled them to evade demeaning racist and sexist comments while not erasing their difference.

Marcia: I saw neither beach nor bathing suit in high school! I was already Black and with people who weren't Black.

Farah: The desire for fairer skin was the feeling of wanting to belong ... It has taken the best part of these twenty-one years to feel comfortable, accept myself that I don't have fair skin.

Preeta: We have a family friend who is a lot darker than we are. She bought Fair & Lovely and when everyone found out, they used to say "Oh, she uses Fair & Lovely." The fact that we talked about it is mean. The fact that she feels she has to use it is terrible.

Any exploration of skin lightening among racialized women raises important questions about the skin-altering practices of white women, especially those who tan. Many white women are well aware of the cultural associations of dark skin with devalued status. Yet in a cultural context where race is read off multiple body sites (skin colour, facial features, hair texture, etc.), tanned skin may be viewed as a temporary, detachable adornment rather than an essential feature that signifies someone's racial status (S. Ahmed, 1998). Ironically, white women often see skin darkening as a beauty project. After the First World War, tanning became a statement about high social status; a tan proclaimed the leisure to lie out in the sun and the money to go to tropical beaches in midwinter. White women who tan can thus connect their bronzed skin to health, wealth, and attractiveness, secure in the knowledge that they still are seen as white and regardless of the health implications (increased risk of skin cancers, premature skin aging). Why is there a greater emphasis on white women's attainment of a sun-kissed glow while racialized women feel pressured to aspire to the glow of fairness? Is the obsession with fairness simply a bad case of a "colonial hangover," or is it an example of a Western cultural imperialism that uses global media to spread white beauty ideals?

The Hair Project: In Search of Social Acceptance

Within a racial hierarchy of beauty, Black women encounter complex messages about hair due to associations of long, flowing hair with social mobility and femininity (Byrd & Tharps, 2001). An estimated 80 per cent of African American women in the United States straighten their hair (Swee, Klontz, & Lambert, 2000). In 1993, the World Rio Corporation marketed a hair-straightening product on its late-night infomercials that targeted these women. In the Rio ads, good hair was equated with straightened hair and bad hair with untamed curls. Ads used the now familiar format of abject *before* and ideal *after* shots featuring women who had been given a complete makeover. As Noliwe Rooks notes (1996), models in the *before* shots were without make-up, jewellery, or accessories (p. 123). They looked unhappy and their hair was wild, unstyled, and unkempt, almost made to look primitive. The *after* shots featured women who had complete beauty makeovers. While the manufacturer claimed Rio had low levels of acid, it actually contained harsh chemicals. Many who used it experienced hair loss, burns, blisters, and sores on their scalps. Of 340,000 people who purchased the product, over 3000 filed complaints, the largest number ever received in the United States for a cosmetic product (Swee, Klontz, & Lambert, 2000). In infomercials, women were repeatedly told that Rio would deliver them from the "bondage" of chemically treated hair (Rooks, 1996, p. 121). Rio sold itself as a product that would enhance Black women's self-worth, freedom, and social mobility. It thus sent a message designed to resonate with female consumers: that they could escape sexist and racist oppression through relaxing their hair.

Many Black interviewees explained how they used hair relaxers, not because they desired whiteness, but because they wanted to avoid othering and enhance their sense of self.

Ada: In high school, people would say, "What are you?" I realized if I blow-dry my hair to get it straight I might not identify as anything separate. The less I try to visually look like some stereotypes from the media or their beliefs, the less I am singled out.

Maya: I had bad hair. My younger sister, she had good hair: thinner, more manageable. When my mother started relaxing my hair, it became easier. They always said the longer it was, the better.

Those who think that stigmatization of natural hair is a thing of the past might consider this: in October 2007, *Glamour* magazine developed a presentation called "The dos and don'ts of corporate fashion" that showed an African American woman sporting an Afro with a caption reading "Say no to the 'fro" (Dorning, 2007). The presenter told a women's luncheon at a Wall Street law firm that Black female attorneys should avoid wearing "political" hairstyles like dreadlocks or Afros, because these styles were seen as unattractive and unprofessional. Members of the audience were justifiably upset with the replay of negative stereotypes about "natural" hair as overly political, unfeminine, and unprofessional. Not only do these attitudes have an impact on Black women's beauty perceptions, but as Nicole and Sharon tell it, they also are linked to blocked educational and economic opportunities. Like the racialized women in my research (see chapter 4), many African Canadian girls report witnessing or experiencing racial harassment in schools arising from perceptions of their hue and hair. Some school boards in the United States have suspended African American students for wearing cornrows, dreadlocks, and other hairstyles seen as making an overly strong political or cultural statement (Rooks, 2001). Black women have even been fired from jobs in major corporations for styling their hair in dreadlocks and braids. Virtually all Black women I interviewed worried that if they wore their hair naturally, they would not succeed in their career or romantic aspirations. Seen in this light, it would be a mistake to interpret hair straightening simply as another example of women's internalization of sexism and racism. Instead, their accounts suggest that managed hair could carry social benefits, including boosting status, control, and success. And because of the ways in which unstraightened hair may be seen as connoting an oppositional identity, offending styles are also banished in public spaces, thus undermining women's rights to represent themselves in preferred ways (Rooks, 2001).

Nicole: My mom almost lost her mind when I cut my hair. She thought that I wouldn't make it because a girl with nappy hair wouldn't get a job. You are not going to see somebody in the [financial district] in a suit and dreads. I told her "I have two degrees! The way that I wear my hair has no bearing on the job I can do." Cutting my hair was my statement.

Sharon: There's a lot of anger because if I go on interviews, people have a pre-made assumption about Black women and therefore about me. When

I put in a bid for a job, it is all paper. So it isn't until the interview that they meet me. So you go into a room of ten people and they're all white. Then in walks little Blackie in her braids. You can see the shock on their faces.

Rhonda: An Afro is not seen as beautiful. Maybe now it's a little bit more accepted because of Lauryn Hill and Erykah Badu. But for the most part, it's still not. It disturbs me because there are so many young girls out there. They're seeing people telling them that they are not beautiful because of their skin colour – they're not beautiful because they have natural hair.

Along with the presence of long-flowing hair on a woman's head, the absence of body hair is a critical but unmentionable characteristic of the acceptable female body. Few North American women removed their underarm or leg hair before the twentieth century; with the rise of beauty culture and body-baring fashions, hair removal became commonplace by the end of the Second World War (Hope, 1982). Like cosmetics, hair removal initially was considered immoral because skimpily clothed chorus girls practised it (Hope, 1982). To convince respectable middle-class consumers to buy depilatory products, marketers framed any hair not on a woman's head as unsightly and ugly. By the 1920s, ads linked female hairlessness with femininity, whiteness, and beauty as one Neet Hair Removing Cream caption implies, "His quick eye saw the soft white beauty of her underarm" (see figure 7.2). At the same time, physicians began to label as pathological "excess" hair on parts of the female body (like the face) typically associated with hair growth in men (Herzig, 2000).

Any sorting of the normal from the pathological has proven to be difficult: there remains no agreed-on measure of normal amounts of hair in women and no clear markers to distinguish male from female hair growth. Men are thought to be naturally hairier, though patterns of hair growth overlap since women have the same number of hair follicles as men and, like men, produce testosterone (Ferrante, 1988). There may be even more variation within than between the sexes because hair growth differs based on age, climate, lifestyle, and genes (Ferrante, 1988). The number of hairy women who have an endocrine problem is unknown, with rates ranging from 1 (Ferrante, 1988) to 80 per cent (Azziz, Carmina, & Sawaya, 2000). (The higher percentages should be treated with caution since they may reflect renewed medical attempts to pathologize female body-hair.) Whether or not an underlying medical condition is present, any fuzz deemed excessive is labelled "hirsutism," which is

Figure 7.2. Hair removal: Early ads tried to convince respectable middle-class consumers to buy depilatory products by linking hairlessness in women with femininity, whiteness, and beauty, and women's body hair with dirtiness, ugliness, and disease.

related to the Latin *horrēre* meaning rough, shaggy, and to bristle with fear ("Hirsute," n.d.). This history suggests that in Western society, female body hair has been imagined as repellent, and the unaltered womanly body as frightening and feral.

From the pages of fashion magazines to illustrations in biology textbooks, the image of the hairless woman has emerged as a pervasive norm (Schick, Rima, & Calabrese, 2011). Today, those sprouting body hair may invite ridicule, as Julia Roberts found out when she made headlines for neglecting to shave her armpits before a red carpet event (Turner, 1999). Mo'Nique's display against depilation also incited furious fan reaction when she flaunted her unshaven legs at the Golden Globes (McCann, 2010). Although unshaven men are considered acceptable and their body hair removal optional, studies show that in Anglo-Western countries between 80 and 100 per cent of women spend an average of 30 minutes per week removing unwanted face or body hair (Basow, 1991; Tiggemann & Hodgson, 2008; "Veet® survey," 2011). A strong cultural connection exists between hair and sex – the absence of body hair is interpreted as a sign of femaleness, whereas its presence signifies maleness (Herzig, 2000; Toerien & Wilkinson, 2003). Despite feminist challenges to sexual dualism, Western thinking still understands femaleness and maleness as opposites that do not overlap. In this context, the vast majority of women, for whom hairlessness is not a natural state, must remove their hair or have their sex called into question. A lucrative market in hair removal products has resulted, with global sales in shaving gear topping US$25.7 billion in 2010 ("World shaving products," 2010) and US sales for depilatory products at $1.8 billion (Mintel, 2008). So ubiquitous is the puberty rite of shaving that Nair launched Nair Pretty, a depilatory aimed at "first-time hair removers," that is, girls ten to fifteen years old (Newman, 2007). Ads running in *Seventeen* asserted that being stubble-free was a path to self-liberation. "I am a citizen of the world," reads the copy. "I am pretty. I am determined. I am not going to settle for sandpaper skin."

A majority of women in this study committed at puberty to a lifetime of hair removal, which became a routine part of the hidden work of having an acceptable female body. The hairless norm is so ubiquitous that although pubic hair is an important marker of puberty, its discovery was horrifying and embarrassing for 25 per cent (like Hannah), who had no prior knowledge that growing hair "down there" was typical. Many began removing leg and underarm hair to feel more attractive and a majority also told how they conformed as a way of shielding themselves from people's disapproval and their own discomfort. Studies show that young women's worries about harsh judgments are not unfounded: women with body hair are rated as less attractive, smart, and hygienic, and as more masculine and aggressive than those without it (Basow & Braman, 1998). From puberty onwards, peers, parents, and others regulated participants' visible body-hair growth by introducing and encouraging hair removal. Their intimate experiences reveal broader symbolic meanings attached to hair: anomaly, undesirability, and blurring of boundaries between the sexes. For some such as Erum, facial hair was particularly frightening because it was read as a sign of maleness, visually undermining her sex, and eliciting the scary feeling that she was not really a woman. Even though 40 per cent of all women naturally grow facial hair (Bindel, 2010), being hirsute was emotionally and socially damaging for those in this study, fuelling depression, body consciousness, and fear of relationships.

> Hannah: The first time I remember being shocked by my body was when I developed pubic hairs. Suddenly one day, I looked down at myself, thinking, "where I pee from looks different." There was something wrong, something came out that wasn't supposed to. I was quite horrified.

> Erum: I remember looking in the mirror thinking "Oh my God! Why are these hairs hanging out of my face? What if my friends see it and think I am so strange?" … I never thought of myself as woman. I thought of myself as a girl struggling. I didn't feel normal. I would think, "What if I really am a boy? What if I have internal male genitalia? I look like a woman on the outside but I have hair on my face. So what does that mean?" … I think if they told me I was not female I would have had a breakdown.

Studies of racial differences in body hair are contradictory (Azziz et al., 2000; Yildiz, Bolour, et al., 2010). Some researchers suggest that Black, South Asian, and "Mediterranean" women are hairier than northern European women and others claim that whites are the hairiest and Asian women the least hirsute of all (Toerien & Wilkinson, 2003). A majority of South Asian women identified body hair as a problem trait, far more than any other group I interviewed. Most assumed they were naturally hairier. But their accounts point to sexual dualism and racist stereotyping as the more likely roots of their hair worries. Historically, racialized women from the colonized world have been imagined as more masculine, deviant, and diseased than white northern

European women. In the wake of Darwin's theories of evolution, scientists began to see body hair as a measure of racial difference and to classify amounts and thicknesses of hair according to a racial hierarchy (Herzig, 2000). Both scientists and the lay public exhibited great interest in racialized bearded women because they were seen to represent the missing link between animals and humans. As we saw in chapter 1, in this context Julia Pastrana became a freak show performer due to her facial hair. Associations between race and hair haunt the stories of South Asian Canadian women today who tell how their body hair conjured up ideas about racialized women as hairier, more masculine, and hyper-sexual within white-dominated culture.

> Erum: Good [Indian] girls don't have hair on their faces. I heard people making comments about the "bearded lady." It got to the point that even teachers would comment on it. One said, "You have a lot of hair on your face. Why don't you get electrolysis done? Do you have hair on your breasts as well?" Even the doctor said: "It is common for Indian girls to have hair on their face." I know lots of Indian girls who don't have hair on their faces. Italian women are hairy too. So it's not true. It's a stereotyped generalization.

The 1970s feminist movement brought an acceptance of body hair, but the push for hairlessness has rebounded to become a thriving industry today. Consumer capitalism combined with the growing availability of free pornography and demand for body-baring fashions have influenced which women today depilate and how often. The cohort I interviewed came of age before the popularity of pubic hair removal. Over the last several years, the Brazilian wax, which leaves behind a strip of hair above the pubic bone or takes all hair away, has gone from being a risqué novelty to a basic grooming practice. To give an indication of how popular pubic hair waxing has become, one researcher searching for the term "Brazilian wax" on the Internet in 2001 yielded 133 hits (Labre, 2002); when I searched for the same phrase in 2011, I got close to 5 million. Surveys have found that 85 to 95 per cent of Western women polled have tried removing hair from their groin area (Tiggemann & Hodgson, 2008); and 50 per cent regularly practise pubic hair removal (Riddell, Varto, & Hodgson, 2010). Many shave or wax because they see their hair as ugly and unclean. The association of female body hair with the abject is highly evident in women's descriptions of their preshorn bodies as disgusting and gross.

The Breast Project: Amending the Abject

Despite headlines to the contrary, cosmetic surgery rates in North America remain greatly skewed by gender: in 2010, over 91 per cent of cosmetic procedures were performed on women by mostly male doctors who made up 91 per cent of surgeons (American Society of Plastic Surgeons, 2011). According to the American Society for Aesthetic Plastic Surgery (2011), demand for plastic surgery increased by 9 per cent in 2010 and by a whopping 155 per cent since statistical collection began in 1997. Breast augmentations topped the list (318,123) beating out breast reductions (138,152), which placed fifth in popularity. It's difficult to get an accurate read on how many Canadian women seek breast surgery because the government does not keep track of procedures ("Cosmetic surgery," 2008). However, it is estimated that between 100,000 and 200,000 Canadian women have implants. According to the Canadian Institute for Health Information, in 2006 over 5000 women got breast-reduction surgery in a Canadian health facility (Edwards, 2008). Little reliable data are available on the race of those undergoing reductions and augmentations, but statistics indicate that 30 per cent of all North American procedures in 2010 were performed on non-whites, who make up a growing percentage of recipients (American Society of Plastic Surgeons, 2011). The American Society of Plastic Surgeons (2011) reports that reductions are popular among African American women, while Asian American women most commonly request augmentations. These statistics do not reflect actual numbers, however, since the rise of medical tourism means more people seek out cheap surgeries in places like India, Costa Rica, and Thailand (K.P. Morgan, 1991/2009; see, for example, http://www.worldmedicalandsurgical.com). As surgery goes global, augmentation has become the second most sought-after procedure, with reductions coming in at sixth worldwide (International Society of Aesthetic Plastic Surgery, 2010).

Techniques used in cosmetic surgery were originally developed to treat the facial burns and soft tissue wounds of male soldiers returning from the First World War (Haiken, 1997). Over the twentieth century, doctors gradually drew a distinction between plastic surgery, aimed at restoring the body's normal appearance or functioning, and cosmetic surgery, intended to enhance features already deemed normal (Heyes & Jones, 2009). Early augmentations involved injections of infection-causing paraffin wax or body fat directly into the breast (Haiken, 1997). Solid silicone sacs filled with salt water or silicone gel were not introduced until the 1960s. By 1991, controversy about the possible effects of silicone implants lead to a fourteen-year moratorium on their general use. Almost two decades after fears that leaking implants could cause connective tissue disease (like rheumatoid arthritis), North American governments approved a new generation of "safer" implants for the market (CanWest News Service, 2006; for more information go to: http://www.hc-sc.gc.ca/hl-vs/iyh-vsv/med/implants-eng.php).In the wake of this reversal, promotional pitches have escalated. Although direct-to-consumer advertising of medical drugs and devices is illegal in Canada, implant-promoting messages still trickle across our image-permeable border. For example, ads for Natrelle Breast Enhancement Collection in *Elle* magazine (December 2007) liken implants to jeans and jewellery, framing augmentation as a fashion accessory rather than major surgery with serious risks. (View this ad at http://www.coloribus.com/adsarchive/prints/natrelle-breast-implants-shoes-10538005/.) On Facebook, Natrelle has started to give away free "Breast Augmentation Kits" so that women considering implants can try different sizes at home. Earlier ads that used images of flowers, the word *blossom*, and a just-out-of-puberty model suggest that the campaign is designed to appeal to an adolescent audience. (Current ads feature a video of a mother-daughter duo talking about the daughter's quest for implants; view the video at http://www.natrelle.com/pre_consultation_kit.aspx.) Other examples of implant-plugging messages include boob-job contests, such as the one a Calgary radio station recently announced ("Calgary radio station," 2011).

In makeover culture, cosmetic surgery is no longer reserved for celebrities or the super rich. Popular media and surgeons alike now promote procedures as viable solutions to ordinary image problems. Reality TV shows like Fox's *The Swan* and ABC's *Extreme Makeover* create appetites for nips and tucks in audiences seduced by the fantasy that changing bodies will transform lives (Markey & Markey, 2010). Proliferating images of medical makeovers do not in themselves enlist viewers to go under the knife (Nabi, 2009). Instead, they put surgical options on what I call viewers' "horizon of possibility" – inviting them to imagine seeking out the scalpel to ease their image distress. For-profit medicine boosts surgical sales in similar ways. Physicians have long framed surgical breast reduction as a necessary treatment for macromastia (big breasts), an apparent disorder causing physical pain and emotional problems in affected women (Daane & Rockwell, 1999; Mello, Domingos, & Miyazaki, 2010). Recently, the American

Society of Plastic Surgeons has also classified small breasts as a disease: micromastia (Ehrenreich, 2001). Despite efforts to establish clear lines between elective and restorative surgery, labelling small breasts as a disease indicates that the boundaries between profit-driven medicine and the beauty industry have blurred as medicine transitions into big business (Sullivan, 2001). In Canada, the medicalization of large breasts gives women access to needed surgery through our publicly funded health system (Naugler, 2009). Yet medicalizing size may serve to deflect attention away from broader forces onto breasts themselves as the sole source of women's distress. Evidence indicates that this reframing is working: according to the American Academy of Cosmetic Surgery (2009), the number of people who approve of cosmetic surgery has climbed steadily over the last decade.

Immersed as we are in a media sea of successful transformations, it is troubling that we don't have easy access to information about surgery's downside: the health consequences of augmentations and reductions. In my role as a researcher, I have spoken with women who were satisfied with their surgeries and had no regrets. However, as a counsellor, I have worked with those who bitterly regretted their decision. Some felt lied to, misled, kept in the dark about the procedures' negative consequences, and angry about the long-term costs to their bodies and lives. Beyond the pain, infection, and scarring associated with any surgery, complications from reductions and implants include partial or full loss of sexual sensation in the nipple, inability or restricted ability to breastfeed, and necrosis or death of nipple tissue (R. Reardon & Grogan, 2011). Of women receiving implants, most will have complications requiring additional surgery or implant removal (Tweed, 2003) because of rupture, deflation, and leakage that occurs in three-quarters of recipients (S.L. Brown, Middleton, Berg, Soo, & Pennello, 2000). There is no medical consensus on how long implants last, although reputable surgeons acknowledge that *all* women with implants will require replacement at some future date (Singer, 2008). Anywhere from 25 to 100 percent of those with implants deal with capsular contracture, where scar tissue forms around the implant, causing implanted breasts to become hard, painful, or lopsided (Tweed, 2003). There may also be a link between silicone-gel implants and autoimmune diseases such as fibromyalgia (S.L. Brown, Pennello, Berg, Soo, & Middleton, 2001).

For the eight participants in my study who contemplated surgery, othering was implicated in their decision making. Like Debra Gimlin (2006) found in her research on women considering surgery, they described getting reductions and implants as a way to escape abjection more than to embody an ideal – that is, as a means of alleviating unwanted negative feelings and alienation associated with being seen as an other. Many experienced physical and psychological problems associated with too large or too small breasts, which they connected to discomfort caused by looks, stares, and criticisms more than to the size or weight of their breasts alone. These women describe cosmetic surgery as a way of averting hurtful looks and harassing comments – a way to resist sexual and racial sidelining. At the same time, all were aware that to get Canada's publicly funded health insurance to cover the procedures they had to make the case that size constituted a serious medical, and not merely social, problem. Their accounts challenge the usual ways that feminists think about cosmetic surgery by offering reasons for why women pursue surgical solutions without relying on the "beauty myth" as the main argument. Instead, as Holliday and Sanchez Taylor (2006) contend, surgery seekers in this study described how they exercised choice within a given set of constraints and engaged in a project of self-making.

> Marcia: I got messages that I was provocative. I remember doing trampoline. A group of guys, who I thought were waiting for their turn, came to watch me. That hurt. Later, I had a breast reduction. I didn't want to buy into some patriarchal, racist notion of what my breasts were supposed to look like. But I felt so restricted.

> Maya: [Before my implants] I felt so uncomfortable hiding my breasts. I used to take off my bra, get under the covers, make sure it was dark so you couldn't see. I wouldn't let him touch the smaller one. If he did touch it, then he'd be "How come one's smaller?"

Today, responses to surgery remain moralistic. Many women find they have to justify their decision making against charges of vanity, like those quoted in Kathy Davis's study who told how they treated their surgery as a "slightly shameful secret" for this very reason (1995, p. 7). On the flip side, attitudes towards elective surgery have become more permissive in our neoliberal society, which frames appearance alteration as a pathway to emotional stability and social success (Bordo, 1999b). It is troubling that cosmetic surgery is now advocated as the only reasonable solution to girls' and women's body dissatisfaction resulting from harassment. One article in Toronto's *Globe and Mail* (MacDonald, 2001) went so far as to present surgery as the *only* viable response for adolescent girls dealing with racism and sexism at school. By promoting surgical answers to verbal abuse, the article ignored possible systemic solutions, such as passing and enforcing anti-harassment policies (Larkin & Rice, 2005). In a context where the body is tied to a person's morality and body modification is seen as a self-improvement strategy, there is a danger that what was once a difficult choice for some might become compulsory for many. Since a sizable minority of women now pursue surgery to enhance self-image or to ease emotional turmoil and, at times, physical pain, surgery's spread may increasingly create a conundrum for a majority of women since it contributes to a hierarchy of bodies and a narrowing of norms.

The Real Woman Project: When Real Creates More Than One Ideal

Over the past few years the phrase *real woman* has popped up in popular media. The film *Real Women Have Curves* and the Dove Campaign for Real Beauty are only two instances of this trend. In Dove's campaign, ads featuring women of different ages, sizes, and races have been a welcome relief for consumers. As an adviser to the Real Beauty campaign in Canada, I've heard from many applauding Dove's efforts to broaden images of beauty. (I discuss the contradictions of trying to make change through consumer capitalism in the concluding chapter.) While the representation of diverse-looking women *is* positive, the widening colloquial use of the phrase *real woman* implies that there are two groups of us: real and artificial. Celebrating some women for being curvaceous, natural looking, or unadorned implicitly puts down others for being less authentic. Ultimately, this strategy still divides us, encourages scrutiny of our looks, compels us to prove our femaleness when it's called into question, and reinforces yet another standard to uphold. Notions of the natural gave some participants, like Aurora, a sense of pride in their womanly body. These ideas created anxieties for others, such as Gelorah, when they didn't feel they fit the image of what they imagined a real woman to be.

> Aurora: My internal image of me as a woman is that I have the functions: having kids, breastfeeding. So I felt good when my period started, because it makes you feel like a woman. I wanted to feel like a woman. I felt good about developing breasts because breasts made me feel like a woman.

> Gelorah: When I started puberty, I felt like an ugly duckling, asexual. When you look like a kid, no one is going to recognize your age. As a

result you don't feel like a woman. Because my mind and body didn't fit, I had to wait. Eventually I passed through puberty and became reasonably happy with my body.

Although people assume that whatever we call natural must be innate, the image of the natural woman is socially created. In many ways, this norm operates as a cultural myth that keeps power relations and social differences between men and women in place. Unlike the active, sexually aggressive, and unexpressive "real man," the natural woman is imagined as soft, sensitive to the feelings of others, and concerned about nurturing the well-being of her family and community. The unnatural woman is everything the natural woman is not. Tough, ambitious, sexually assertive, and lacking in nurturing abilities, she possesses many qualities that our culture stereotypically ascribes to feminists and to lesbians (and to men). Although it should be acceptable for women to embody a range of identities, those who step outside expected roles are often considered deviant. In this way, the so-called real woman becomes another standard against which all of us are judged.

One example of this norm's power to regulate women's choices and actions can be found in 1970s news reports on the emerging women's movement. Many reporters tried to discredit feminism by creating a new stereotype of the monster feminist – the shrill, hairy, braless, man-hating, intentionally unattractive woman whose main goals were to push lesbianism, promote divorce, and wreck the nuclear family (Douglas, 1994). Conservatives and traditionalists accused feminists of being deviant because some didn't shave their legs or wear bras. Such caricatures have not disappeared from popular culture, as right-wing commentators' rabid framing of feminists as ugly, "militant feminazis" shows ("Repeating 'feminazi' comment," 2006). These attacks indicate that possessing female genitalia is clearly insufficient to qualify one as a woman, but that qualifying hinges on an individual's ability to comply with culturally created norms of femininity and female bodies. Just like the ideal woman, the natural woman does not exist. And like the beauty ideal, it has a controlling effect by pressuring all of us to comply in order to avoid being labelled as ugly and unwomanly.

Ethno-racial minority women in this study confronted the pull of beauty standards that valued light skin. Many faced, as well, the contradictory push to conform to images of how a real Black, South Asian, or Asian woman should look. Like the natural woman, images of real Black or Asian women were difficult to uphold. Researcher Amina Mama has argued that since the 1970s identity politics, linked to physical charac-teristics such as hair, dress, and colour, have created greater space to value Blackness as a positive attribute. On the downside, identity move-ments have generated "stereotypical prescriptions of what an authentic African or black person should look like" (Mama, 1995, p. 136). Similar to the women quoted in Mama's research, African Canadian women in my study described wearing their hair natural as a way of making a positive statement with a trait historically associated with the nega-tive. Embracing an alternative hair aesthetic was empowering for many, yet some were troubled by the message that there was only one way to look and be authentically Black. Those who straightened their hair were often told that they were trying to be white or weren't Black enough; however, they described hair processing as an attempt to be seen as at-tractive more than to pass as white. Facing conflicting pressures to ap-pear racially real versus aspire to a beauty ideal, many felt constrained to fit one stereotypic image of a Black, Asian, or South Asian woman. A number told how people often used names like *coconut*, *Oreo*, and *banana* to criticize their failure to live up to certain "authentic" images. Despite the contention that there was only one way to be real, Navpreet and others resisted this imposition by developing an alternative under-standing of race as an improvisational way of embodying an identity.

Nicole: I would get more attention with my long hair and light eyes. Now nobody looks at me. But cutting my hair off gave me freedom. When you have your hair straightened you are burning it so someone can say you're cute. It hurts, it's annoying, and it's a lot of money. So I said to myself, "Why am I putting myself through this agony for other people? Forget it."

Rhonda: Women who process their hair can be looked down on by women who go natural. It's part of Black pride to be proud of your kinky hair. But sometimes that doesn't respect diversity. There might be different reasons other than [that] you don't want to associate with your Blackness. You can process your hair and still be pro-Black.

Sophia: Black women tend to have more ample figures whereas I don't. One of my girlfriends said "You're not really Black! You don't have the Black butt!" Even though it was a joke, I felt funny. Black women have a range of colours, shapes, and sizes, like white women, like Chinese women. It seems that even our culture tries to pigeonhole you. You must look like this or be like that or else you're not Black.

Navpreet: I don't think there's one authentic way of being anything. You have to engage in it [your racial identity]. Thinking about it and trying out different things and seeing where you feel the most comfortable.

In general, women use cultural meanings given to bodies to shape their bodily self-images, and take up body projects ranging from dieting and disordered eating to skin lightening and surgery. They explain how, rather than encouraging one ideal, beauty culture attempts to democratize beauty by re-visioning differences as desirable, albeit within a narrow range of options. Even images of "real" women, which many propose as a counter to ideals, still have created moralizing and normalizing standards for women to uphold. Reading individuals' accounts against the culture of beauty leads me to conclude that women do not modify their bodies because they are dupes of sexist or racist media culture. Rather, they respond by seeking a "best possible" body and self. Viewed through the prism of their experiences, I've come to see the pursuit of beauty as individuals' attempts to navigate an image system in which bodies have become critical markers of identity and value. Admittedly, women's solutions to the hegemonic image system have come at a high cost, intensifying and diversifying our body projects and problems into the twenty-first century.

Conclusion: Out of the Shadows

This book tells the story of becoming woman in image culture. I have explored the ways that the first generation coming of age against an onslaught of images have responded to the messages they received and constructed a sense of body and self through and against the images handed to them. I now turn to survey opportunities and barriers for making change individually, socially, and symbolically, through culture.

Changing Our Bodies or Our Situations?·

Feminists since the 1970s have advocated consciousness raising as a key strategy for challenging beauty codes that inhibit women's freedom and confidence. During the second wave, many argued that developing a critical consciousness would give women the ability to resist oppressive beauty standards and reduce their body distress (Orbach, 1979; Wolf, 1992). As a response to second-wave discussion about the female body as a site of oppression, third wavers have highlighted the satisfaction that many women find in body alteration, and have stressed the ways that, through media savvy, playful objectification, and self-reflexive body enhancement, bodies can become a source of possibility and pleasure (Holliday & Sanchez Taylor, 2006; Mitchell, Rundle, & Karaian, 2001). Today, feminist psychological perspectives continue to propose individual solutions to image issues – urging women to critique beauty codes and cultivate stronger self-esteem to build immunity to the pressures. At the same time, choice has become the byword of our neoliberal world that assumes inequality has ended and women's body projects are a result of free choice (Stuart & Donaghue, 2011).

Despite its celebration of female autonomy, the free-choice argument ignores the limits that sexist commercial society places on women's agency, including ideologies of beauty that reward those who comply while punishing those who fail to do so. This has led some feminists to argue that a key challenge facing feminism is to complicate discussions of agency (Braun, 2009; McNay, 2010; Stuart & Donaghue, 2011) so that we better understand how available images might expand or limit our choices and actions. For other writers, the challenge is to rethink the concept of beauty itself (Felski, 2006; Frueh, 2001) so that we can create a non-oppressive aesthetics that would enable each of us to reclaim beauty in our lives.

Embodied Agency and Resistance

In psychology, agency is typically defined as people's ability to make choices and to act on them (Eriksen & Goering, 2011), and tends to be understood as an individual personality trait. In social and political thought, agency is seen less as an attribute than as a social process shaped by time and circumstance. As such, agency emerges from the past (the habitual ways of acting that people learn), future (alternative possibilities that they can imagine), and present (their judgment based on the demands and uncertainties in the moment) as well as the contexts in which they act (Emirbayer & Mische, 1998). Building on these ideas, feminist theorists define agency as people's responses and actions that show varying degrees of conformity and inventiveness, which they carefully distinguish from power, or the constraints and opportunities that shape those actions. In this view, even conformist body practices like aesthetic surgery require agency since they involve "attention and effort" (Emirbayer & Mische, 1998, p. 973) and can have political and critical ends. For many authors, agency is also inherently embodied since "self-understanding and action is [sic] achieved through the body" (Campbell, Meynell, & Sherwin, 2009, p. 8). This definition usefully enables us to recognize the authoritative influence of culture while identifying the ways that ordinary women adopt, adapt, and challenge body standards within (and against) the forces that constrain them.

Becoming Women has brought to light the experiences of women situated between the end of the second and beginning of the third waves of North American feminism as well as those who grew up with little access to second- and third-wave ideas or organizing. The cohort I interviewed benefited from feminist efforts, but they were also barraged with hegemonic messages from visual culture. Racially diverse responders and those with bodily differences faced body-related inequalities and felt types of body distress that more privileged participants did not encounter. Since creative strategies and tools for intervening in representations (e.g., do-it-yourself media making, blogging) were not yet being elaborated by the third wave, interviewees tended to express resistance in the everyday contexts of their lives. As Sylvie and Anita attest, their covert, indirect, and unspoken responses resulted from their lack of status as girls and young women with multiply marginalized identities, which limited their capacity to openly or collectively challenge imposed norms or injurious acts. They thus struggled to express the ways that negative meanings of differences overlapped and intersected to inform others' perceptions and their own responses. (Intersectionality theory was only being developed at the time of the interviews.) For example, Isobel had difficulty explaining how lying about being a virgin counted as resistance. Yet in a context where others linked her status as a virgin to her status as undesirable and where she couldn't name the colourism and sizism she experienced, lying allowed her to mask feelings of shame about her bodily differences, and to focus attention on the pride she felt for her racial identity. Thus, the stories participants told and the forms of agency they found reflect ways of understanding and responding to reality available – at the time of both the experiences and the interviews.

> Isobel: I didn't belong because I was Black and fat. When my friends talked about sex, I would lie, "Yeah, me too." I got active in Black struggles. I had a great excuse for not going out on Saturday night.

> Sylvie: There was this dramatic moment from my adolescence where guys threw snowballs at me but I refused to move. I was crying, so they knew it hurt. But I wouldn't leave. It was almost an act of resistance, a way of saying, "You're not going to defeat me. You're going to hurt me, but I'm going to still stand here." It was passivity, but it was also resistance.

> Anita: I tried to fit in so much when I was a teenager. I later realized that I am unconventional and searched out people like that to be around me. I now think I'm unique in my look. I want to find my niche somewhere to learn about life from interesting people – diverse, open-minded.

Women reported two overarching types of actions in response to body standards: *changing their bodies*, which often reproduced the beauty status quo, and sometimes led to harmful body image problems and risky body-alteration practices; and/or *changing their situations*, which often involved challenging ideals and improving bodily self-images. Virtually all negotiated both strategies: they tried changing certain aspects of their bodies to fit their situations and altering their relationships and environments to find acceptance and belonging. They made decisions about body modification that reflected, in addition to their histories, values, and circumstances, the possibilities for embodiment offered in the moment. In supportive contexts, many found value and acceptance for their unique embodiments, cultivated their own body aesthetics, and learned to redirect their energy to create life circumstances where self and social value were based on things other than appearance. They also noted that changing their environments was especially challenging during specific times, such as adolescence, where they had limited capacity to alter the all-important contexts of school or home (Rice, 2009c). Significantly, a woman's capacity to alter her environment emerged in each narrative as key to her greater control and ownership of image.

At different times in diverse bodies and spaces, participants vacillated between following and flouting the expectation that they embody an acceptable standard, or if they failed to fit norms, between embracing or rejecting the demand that they give up on femininity and desirability. None were passive recipients of the images they were offered, but all made decisions and acted in negotiating with, adopting, adapting, subverting, and resisting representations. Neither society nor psychology, or personal will power or effort, determined their choices. Rather, participants' agency emerged from their personal and social histories, and from what was possible in the social moment and imagination. Despite facing varying degrees of marginalization, they found opportunities to resist through everyday acts – of opposition, withstanding, and endurance. These included: engaging in passive resistance (Frances); using lies and humour to deflect from othering (Fatima); forging connections with supportive others and severing relationships with the critical or competitive (Tara); and other strategies depending on what was possible. Resistance often remained covert and individualized, but strategies enabled storytellers to make alternative meanings and, sometimes, talk back to misperceptions.

Frances: I was twenty-nine before I finally talked back to my twit of a doctor. When I was a teenager, I did passive resistance. I had an indwelling catheter [tube used to drain urine from the bladder] that emptied into a bag. This doctor told me that it would drain better if I put the bag lower on my leg. He didn't know that at my high school girls were not allowed to wear pants. So I would do what he said before I saw him. When I left the clinic, I would go back to hiding it.

Fatima: At church, women would say "You poor thing! Pray to God to get better!" I would nod and look away. They would end up talking to my mother, ask what happened, what hardships my mother had to go through. My sister and I, overhearing this, would laugh, thinking it was funny. I was considered a burden and a cross, my mother's cross. That became a joke in our family. Leaving for school, I would say, "Your cross is going to school now." I would laugh like it wasn't negative to me.

Tara: Having a friend helped a lot. A good friend, not a dieting friend. Not the kind of friend who would go, "You lost another ten pounds!" No, but a friend who helped me.

The pleasures of embodiment were often overshadowed by negative experiences, but expressions of desire and delight, of connection and satisfaction, were interwoven throughout participants' accounts. Recently, social psychologists have begun to identify characteristics unique to a positive image, including: appreciation for the physical features and abilities of one's body; acceptance and love from self and others, including for attributes that don't fit idealized images; care and respect via healthy behaviours; and filtering of cultural messages in a "body-protective manner" by internalizing the positive and rejecting negative information (Iannantuono & Tylka, 2012; Wood-Barcalow, Tylka, & Augustus-Horvath, 2010, p. 112). Storytellers describe how constructing a positive image was a fluid process that was provisionally achieved within intimate relationships and supportive contexts, and that shifted as their bodies and/or circumstances changed. As is clear from Sophia and Marianne's stories, positive sexual experiences enabled them to become more connected with and aware of their physical needs and desires. Greater experiential knowledge of their sexualities contributed to increased body confidence and comfort, which translated into a more positive image. Through connecting with and coming to know their bodies, storytellers identify how being embodied female, while at times a source of pain and shame, could be a site of immense pleasure and pride.

Sophia: I feel worst and best about my body during sex. Where I've felt the most pain has been around sex, so it is where I feel the most pleasure.

Being in a positive relationship, feeling trusted and protected, is healing. I never felt this way before. I was never able to fall asleep with other partners. But I can fall asleep in my current boyfriend's arms. I don't feel ashamed to let him see what I look like. He totally accepts me.

Marianne: When I came out, I was the largest I had ever been – and my lover revelled in it. Even though I was large, I started moving in my body the way I had when I was younger, when I felt I could do anything physically. I started walking around like I owned everything.

The Divided Legacy of Feminism

Researchers exploring links between a feminist consciousness and a positive image have found that feminism provides tools for resisting oppressive cultural messages, thereby giving women a buffer against body dissatisfaction (Murnen & Smolak, 2009; Peterson, Grippo, & Tantleff-Dunn, 2008; Peterson, Tantleff-Dunn, & Bedwell, 2006). This was true for many women who rebuffed idealized images and stereotypes of differences by mining possibilities for sexuality and womanhood that second- and third-wave feminism and related social-justice movements offered. Most used any openings available, including intellectual training (Joanne), creative expression (Elizabeth), athletic abilities, volunteerism, and political organizing (Sharon), as pathways for becoming women. Feminism taught them not only to be more critical about conceptions of female bodies, but also to question conventional femininity and to develop positive self-definitions based on attributes such as intelligence, athleticism, and creativity. They thus accepted or revised the differences dealt them based on the possibilities they saw for identity and womanhood.

Elizabeth: I would never look normal, therefore I could never find somebody who could love me. I set out in my own way to develop: I was going to be an artist, I was going to travel. Be my own woman.

Joanne: Getting involved with feminism and disability rights made me realize that we live in a society that doesn't accept difference. Because I didn't measure up to what other women were or were portrayed to be, I had to focus on another part of my life: school and the mind.

Sharon: I, myself, and other women of colour, we developed a group around body image issues. Because at that time I was very active and would ask questions like "we don't see ourselves anywhere. We're every-where, but in media, magazines, we don't see ourselves."

Some studies show that feminist ideas help "protect against extreme dissatisfaction with the body" (Murnen & Smolak, 2009, p. 193) but that a critical consciousness enables women to challenge cultural val-ues more than transcend their shame or discontent (Liimakka, 2008; 2011; Rubin, Nemeroff, & Russo, 2004). However, feminist psychologi-cal perspectives that urge women to resist misrepresentations through strengthening their sense of self may also reproduce the mind/body split because they teach women to "change the way their mind per-ceives their body" (Liimakka, 2011, p. 818). Reinforcing the mind/body split is problematic because it privileges the mind over the body, which devalues the physical realm (the body, nature) and perpetuates sexist oppression in contexts where women have been historically associated with the body. For some, second- and third-wave feminism did help to alleviate their image anxieties and create alternative options for em-bodiment. Yet as Leigh suggests, a critical consciousness sometimes re-sulted in the "splitting" of their subjectivities, enabling them to decode ideals and imagine other possibilities while leaving untouched their culturally induced discontent. This created a double bind for those who felt caught between conflicting requirements for being a feminine (attractive, desirable) versus feminist (autonomous, self-determining) woman.

> Leigh: My teacher exposed me to feminism. After that, I rebelled against femininity: I stopped caring about how I looked or worrying about getting dates. But I also know there is another part that says, "If only I lose weight my life would be happier." Since then, I have dealt with tensions between what society expects a woman to look like and what I want for me.

Despite feminism's strides in recent history, women continue to be subject to high levels of scrutiny and pressures to adhere to notions of idealized femininity and beauty. As bodies become even more impor-tant markers of personhood and social success, tensions surrounding beauty practices have intensified. Pleasure, choice, health, and self-care increasingly justify beauty regimes, ignoring the expense, time, and pain they involve and hiding the degree to which nonconformity has serious consequences. With its emphasis on self-responsibility, neolib-eralism has made it difficult to name the problem of beauty – requiring women to attribute their practices to personal choice alone and not to a social reality that constrains their actions (Stuart & Donaghue, 2011). Rather than teaching women that they should be smarter or stronger, feminism might better serve women's equity projects by proposing interventions that recognize the inextricability of the physical and social in embodiment. Embodiment and body becoming theory, which acknowledge the entwined roles of culture, psyche, and physicality in shaping bodily experience, offer promising avenues for intervening in image-related issues. From an embodiment perspective, individuals are embodied beings who act in and through their physical connection with the world. Rather than advocating greater control over bodies, embodied approaches that acknowledge and enhance individuals' interconnections with the physical (such as by exploring and taking pleasure in their bodily sensations and capacities) would increase their body appreciation and satisfaction. Beginning from the premise that our cultural and material worlds shape embodiment, a body becoming perspective would also consider how to alter environments in ways that expand possibilities for bodies and support people in developing capacities unique to their physical diversities. Concretely, this might mean changing school policies to stop body-based harassment and redesigning built environments to maximize the abilities of the broadest range of bodies (such as designing bicycles and exercise equipment for fat and physically disabled people).

Their stories told in a time of massive feminist change, participants suggest that resistance to physical ideals and norms can't rely on individually focused strategies, but that equity-minded people from all walks of life must target the intimate relationships, institutions, and material and cultural structures that enforce body standards. Beyond individuals' improvisational efforts to affirm their bodies and talk back to dominant views, another critical way that the women have changed their situations is through changing family relations and the broader institutional and image environments.

Changing Our Family Relations

Since mothers are given greater responsibility for child rearing in our society, they play a major part in shaping girls' body and self-images. Many researchers have highlighted mothers' responsibilities in instilling a negative image but few have shed light on how mothers positively support daughters or how fathers influence girls' image formation. Mothers and other female mentors who had the most profound influence affirmed girls' appearances and differences, yet at the same time told the truth about their own issues and struggles. Their insights resonate with those of researcher Gail Marchessault (2000): that mothers who demonstrate a politicized understanding of colour, disability, and weight bias, who openly discuss body politics, and who encourage body appreciation most successfully enable daughters to resist cultural pressures and preserve body acceptance. For those interviewed, mothers supported daughters, and, in turn, some daughters also brought new values into the home space that opened up possibilities for mothers' and daughters' mutual empowerment.

> Renée: My mother's weight was an issue most of her life. She would say "Don't worry" because she didn't want to impose what she had gone through on us. She wanted us to be positive about our looks. I remember being called fat and thinking it to a certain extent about myself. What made me deal with it positively was maybe the way my mother dealt with it. If she had been critical or controlling then that combined with kids calling fat might have made me take action, develop an eating disorder.

> Jacqueline: My mom and I talked about hair and skin. It made me more aware of my history and accept who I am. My mom's father is mulatto so my mom is light. But my dad's dark and this is how I came out. So what? I accept it. You take it in and deal with it. I was able to be mature about it because my mother wasn't like that. My mom was very loving, positive.

> Sheila: She's more comfortable with my body and I am comfortable with her body. Having three daughters, her confidence has unbelievably changed since she was young. My mom has become empowered because all of us live at home. Having her daughters always around, my mother is not isolated with my dad. She has taught us to be assertive, self-confident, and educated.

According to participants, what mothers do influences girls' body images, but what mothers *say* is also critical. Mothers who owned their struggles, stresses, and biases while affirming daughters' looks and abilities went a long way to help their daughters build body confidence. Such affirmation was not easy: it sometimes involved mothers' courageous re-evaluation of their attitudes and values and going against the cultural grain by putting forward principles of fairness and equity in defence of their daughters. Those fathers who refused to participate in gendered looking relations also positively influenced girls' developing images. This did not mean that making comments about daughters' bodies was always wrong; as long as the women interviewed weren't being evaluated or held to a certain standard of ability or attractiveness, compliments were, in general, welcomed. Women's early memories of close connections between mother and daughter, and of their mothers' refusals to devalue difference, represent hidden knowledge in mother–daughter relationships. These may provide a key for mothers and daughters to break – and break free of – the mirror's cultural authority.

Changing Our Institutions

Since the nineteenth century in the Western world, institutions have gained authority over ordinary people's lives by using labels, tests, and ranking systems to create and impose standards of "normal." While the women interviewed were subjected to criteria of normality in all aspects of their lives, it was in medical and educational settings that norms were applied to their bodies – they were judged on weight and size, how well they performed certain physical skills, the time they took to go through puberty, and so on. All spoke about the ways they learned to measure themselves against expert criteria and cultural standards, and to experience failure if they didn't measure up. Most assessed themselves against criteria for being a successful student and citizen or for having a good body, and described how fears of failure and threats of exclusion motivated them to strive for the norm.

Failing to live up to our society's criteria for being "adequate" can have profound effects, as the stories throughout this book confirm. For the women with whom I talked, these included body dissatisfaction, eating problems, self harm, substance misuse, anxiety, despair, and alienation as well as isolation, disembodiment, physical and sexual dis-enablement, and the loss of community and the sense of possibility. Rather than enforcing shame-inducing norms, health policies might better serve girls and women (and boys and men) by shifting focus from changing people's bodies to altering aspects of social worlds that impede their options for embodiment. As a response to participants' dilemmas as well as those of children today, a few years ago equity educator Vanessa Russell and I (2002) proposed a "body equity" approach to health policy in schools (and elsewhere) that advocated acceptance of diverse bodies, greater options for enjoyable activities, and better access to good food choices. Beyond adopting policies for stopping stigma, we argued that educators, health providers and policymakers who took a "body equity approach" would critically question the meanings and values regarding bodies, health, beauty, and fitness that they reproduce in their professional roles. This approach would also involve re-examining medical language used to talk about differences, and developing less pejorative terms that capture people's embodied experiences (i.e., using phrases such as "unusual appearance" or "anomalous body" instead of derogatory terms like disfigurement or deformity). I continue to believe that an equity approach that incorporates lookism, ablism, and weightism into school and health care policies and practices is a good start. But I now think our strategy is limited because it does little to challenge our binary thinking about bodies, such as our default association of thinness and able-bodiedness with fitness and attractiveness or of fatness and disability with unfitness and ill health.

Poststructuralism teaches us that when we create binaries of norms and differences where one term is privileged over the other – thin/fat, fit/unfit, ability/ disability, healthy/unhealthy – we invite "better than" and "lesser than" judgments that inevitably cause harm. For instance, at the Canadian Obesity Network's recent summit on weight bias, experts declared that "society must fight obesity, not obese people" ("1st Canadian Summit," 2011, para. 1). While this message commendably attempts to destigmatize the obese, it imposes a certain negative reality on fat bodies by once again fixing them as unhealthy and unfit. Obesity-prevention biopedagogies with their moralizing undertones create a dichotomy of either/or (you're either fat and unfit or thin and fit), which precludes the possibility of exploring or learning about the in-between and otherwise. Instead, fatness remains a powerful signifier of body otherness by conflating size with health.

Rather than advising people to adopt imposed norms, how do we create the conditions that will enable them to imagine other possibilities for their bodies? How might we make space for more ethical responses to physical differences? A health-promotion/equity approach informed by feminist poststructuralist and new materialist ethics would move away from current cultural practices of *enforcing* norms toward more creative endeavours of exploring physical abilities and possibilities unique to different bodies. Unlike biomedical frameworks that predict and prescribe what bodies will and should be, a body-becoming approach would ask how physical, psychical, environmental, and cultural forces might expand or limit possibilities for what bodies could become. How a body-becoming pedagogy might guide our responses to bodily differences is an open question, but at the very least it would invite us to think in dynamic, interactional, and systemic ways about differences and the effects of meanings we give to them. It would also ask us to question mechanistic models and moralistic biopedagogies, to let go of normative notions about able bodies, and consider how our ways of knowing bodies might influence what they can be. It would ask us to consider critically how much physical agency we lose by imposing expectations on bodies and how much creativity and beauty we miss in attempting to regulate bodily diversity. Finally, it would posit that we have to perceive differently if we want bodies to become differently.

Critical to this project is changing our image environments.

Changing Our Image Environments

Making Change from Within: The Dove Campaign

Feminists since the second wave have worked to transform media by challenging stereotypic images and creating more inclusive representations. The Dove Campaign for Real Beauty is one highly visible example of this strategy that has involved well-known feminist writers and clinicians like Susie Orbach from England, Ann Kearney-Cooke from the United States, and Lucrecia Ramirez from Argentina. In my role as a Dove adviser I learned that a majority of media makers working on the campaign were women from the same generation as those whose experiences are illuminated in this book. Many endorsed a popular version of feminism. Most were educated, and middle or upper-middle class (though not necessarily white) women. By viewing the Dove campaign from the perspectives of those I interviewed, I have come to think about it as one striking illustration of how our generation has attempted to resolve the beauty myth for itself.

I became involved in the Dove campaign in 2003 as an academic and clinical consultant providing research data on body image issues, giving expert feedback on media materials developed by Dove, and, later, doing media interviews on the campaign itself. Although I initially hesitated to lend my name due to ethical challenges that I anticipated might arise in working with the Dove's multinational owner Unilever, after careful consideration I decided to take this risk because I really liked the smart, passionate women who approached me about the campaign; because I ensured that I retained the right to speak freely about the campaign during and after my involvement; and because I wanted to understand first-hand how advertising industries actually work and to see what was possible, and not possible, from inside the belly of the beast. In the end, what tipped the decision for me was this: in the hundreds of talks on image culture that I've given over the years, audiences have repeatedly said, "We have to get to the advertisers." My engagement with Dove was a response to this challenge – an experiment in what happens when feminists attempt to transform commercial media. Money was not a motivating factor; I already enjoyed a busy career and saw the honorarium paid as a bonus for my intellectual work. But, if I were being completely honest, I must admit that I was swayed by the prestige and boost to my profile.

In a neoliberal climate that promotes unfettered free markets and pushes for government cuts to social welfare and cultural spending, big companies may be the only entities that have the resources needed to bring people together to talk about social problems such as the effect of beauty industries on women's body esteem and social power. What I got from the Self Esteem Fund Advisory Committee meetings that Dove hosted in New York and London was an opportunity to meet some of the most accomplished people in my field and to work with some of most creative artists in advertising from around in world. This was exciting and intellectually, politically, and creatively stimulating. What I brought to the campaign was an awareness of women's split subjectivities: the understanding that while marketers typically capitalize on women's worries by preying on our distresses and desires to embody the ideal, they could also sell to our contrary yearning and longing to be accepted for who we are. This was my main message to Dove. I believe that it was heard by supportive marketing managers as well as by the corporate naysayers ultimately in charge of the brand and of other products like Slim-Fast or Axe deodorant that the company also peddled using stereotypically sexist and sizist ads.

The Dove campaign ads featuring women of different ages, sizes, shapes, and races have been a breath of fresh air for consumers. I have heard from countless women who applaud Dove's efforts to broaden images of beauty. The campaign has served as a much needed starting point for change by teaching critical media consumption and encouraging women to discuss issues of beauty, challenge standards, and support one another. It has also celebrated women's creativity through sponsoring "Beyond Compare," a photo exhibition of female photographers' interpretations of beauty that featured stunningly distinctive subjects. Finally, it sparked important conversations between women and young girls, through a public service announcement about girls' body-image issues and through a self-esteem fund. From my perspective as a participant, I observed how the artists, advertisers, and advisers involved in creating these elements appeared to approach the campaign as an opportunity to resolve some of the contradictions our cohort faces, namely, between the push to live up to narrow standards propagated by consumerism versus the pull to embrace values of body acceptance advocated by feminism. Using expanded definitions of beauty to sell products, they crafted the conciliatory message that it was possible for women to come to terms with their bodies while at the same time aspiring to improve them.

While the use of diverse-looking models and messages of body acceptance *was* positive, there are serious limitations to social change funded by a for-profit company (Johnston & Taylor, 2008). I knew that in addition to Slim-Fast, Unilever made a deodorant called Axe marketed to men through what has been dubbed the world's most sexist advertising for recycling the tired idea that women are promiscuous playthings who will do anything, and betray everything, for sex. (A few of the more insulting ads include women getting their butts tattooed or switching sides in an election for men who wear Axe.) Somehow, I could accept such garden-variety sexism, probably because it is the air that we breathe in this culture. But it wasn't until I discovered that Unilever's subsiduary in Asia, Hindustan Unilever, sold Fair & Lovely, one of the world's most popular skin-bleaching creams that I began to feel more deeply politically compromised and ethically torn. Building a relationship with Dove implicated me as a privileged white woman in sending the message that non-white and non-Western women should aspire to whiteness to achieve beauty, economic opportunity, and equality.

I came to see that there are real problems with the "real beauty" images. First, as other feminist critics have noted, the campaign sends contradictory messages, promoting self-acceptance while encouraging women's consumption in order to feel good about themselves (Johnston & Taylor, 2008). As well, although the Dove campaign includes women with diverse bodies related to age, size, skin colour, breast size, and minor variations in appearance, it excludes those whose bodies deviate significantly from cultural norms (Heiss, 2011). Significantly, the few times I brought up the possibility of including women with disabilities and differences in ads, I was met with silence. And when another advisory committee member asked about taking on the sexual politics of valuing women based on beauty, corporate insiders quickly redirected the conversation. In many ads, the large models look toned, without a dimple, ripple, or ounce of cellulite on their bodies. In fact, one account executive told me that many fantastic women who showed up for castings were rejected because their skin was not deemed firm or smooth enough. The pro-aging ads show women with grey hair and a few wrinkles but from the neck down their bodies appear firm and whole – no marked up flesh or missing parts. Their bodies are invariably hairless and none are visibly disabled. Given that all women have body hair and most will experience disability at some point in their lives (Bélair & Statistics Canada, 2007), the absence of such differences is noticeable. This omission may reflect our cultural preferences for the able body and reinforce our deeper belief that disability falls outside definitions of beauty – if not outside the realm of the real or natural (Heiss, 2011).

None of this is meant to critique the individuals involved or undercut their efforts to push the envelope. Instead, these realizations, though painful, gave me greater awareness of what racialized women and women with disabilities are up against: powerful global forces that endorse a whitewashed ideal of beauty and narrow notions of body diversity. They also taught me how consumer capitalism exploits people's vulnerabilities and adopts hypocritical messages in order to make money. I learned that despite a rhetoric of social responsibility, corporations are, at best, amoral. When Dove folks reminded the advisory board when we started to get political "to remember that this is a business," I learned how the bottom line is *always* the bottom line. Companies will not fund causes when these conflict with the more primary aim: profit. And finally, by getting up close and personal, I learned how capitalism could not solve the problem of beauty for women. Had I known this at the beginning, I probably would have turned down Dove's offer. In some ways, I am glad I didn't know, because my experience taught me first-hand to see engagement with commercial media as only one starting point, to recognize the difficulties of making lasting change from within the money-making machine, and to search out other possibilities for challenge and transformation.

Making Change from the Margins: Reclaiming Beauty and Revisioning Difference

Feminists have critiqued the Dove campaign for not acknowledging the existence of a beauty hierarchy among women and for failing to represent a broader range of bodies (Heiss, 2011; Johnston & Taylor, 2008). While the campaign was intended to appeal to the part of each of us that wants to love ourselves, it excluded many women because they were seen as residing outside of the ordinary. But who are these missing women? And where do they find affirming representations?

On the margins, in countercultures, and in arts communities one can find clues about how to see difference differently. Feminists artists and activists, for example, have created representations that disrupt dominant ways of portraying difference and that dare to depict the abject. One example is "fat drag," live performances that poke fun at cultural stereotypes about fat, such as the performance troupes Pretty Porky and Pissed Off (http://www.allysonmitchell.com/action/ppod.cfm) and Fat Femme Mafia (http://blip.tv/random-videos-from-a-queer-in-toronto/fat-femme-mafia-in-trinity-bellwoods-park-243843). Another is 'Da Kink in My Hair, a play that has captured critical attention for exploring Black women's diverse embodiments and relationships to beauty (http://treyanthonystudios.com/index.html). The work of photographer Holly Norris and model Jes Sachse offers another illustration; they created American Able as a spoof of American Apparel ads to reveal how women with disabilities are made invisible in mass media (see figures 8.1, 8.2). A final example in this vein is the art activism of the Guerilla Girls, who don gorilla masks as they deliver facts and funny visuals to expose the ugly underbelly of visual culture: the sexism and racism that are rampant in art and film (at http://www.guerrillagirls.com/).

With the development of social media like Facebook and blogs, activists and ordinary people have taken media making into their own hands. As a result, body pride movements have sprung up across the web. Some popular sites include The Body Positive (http://www.thebodypositive.org/), Adios Barbie (http://www.adiosbarbie.com/), and Charlotte Cooper's The Obesity Timebomb (http://obesitytimebomb.blogspot.ca/). Image issues are discussed on feminist sites such as Shameless, a blog and magazine for girls and trans youth (http://www.shamelessmag.com/); About-Face, a site that turns the gaze on our toxic media environment (http://www.about-face.org/); The Crunk Feminist Collective, an online space for Hip Hop Generation feminists to talk back to representations of Black women (http://crunkfeministcollective.wordpress.com/); and Jezebel (http://jezebel.com/), which offers political commentary on celebrity, sex, and fashion. The increased affordability and accessibility of image technology

Meet Jes.

American Able®

Figure 8.1. American Able 1: Meet Jes. Photographer Holly Norris and artist Jes Sachse created the "American Able" campaign through re-enacting American Apparel advertisements featuring young, thin, and semi-naked women. Their images draw our attention to the absence of women with visible physical disabilities in commercial culture. Photo courtesy of Holly Norris.

has put digital media-making tools in the hands of ordinary people. This has led to filmmaking projects like Project Re•Vision, which turns the gaze on societal views of difference. In Re•Vision's intensive workshops, women who embody difference have opportunities to learn the fundamentals of filmmaking so they can speak back to dominant representations about their bodies and lives. By daring viewers to look at their bodies and think about how it feels to look like them, filmmakers Jes Sachse and Lindsay Fisher challenge audiences to acknowledge

Little black dress.

American Able®

Figure 8.2. American Able 2: Little Black Dress. Photographer Holly Norris with models Jes Sashse and Dana Levine for the American Able campaign. Photo courtesy of Holly Norris.

our responses to their differences and, ultimately, our relationship to our own. (See their films at http://www.envisioningnewmean ings.ca/?page_id=40 and http://www.envisioningnewmeanings.ca/ ?page_id=28.)

Like nuanced imagery of people who embody disability, images of agentic, aesthetically interesting women who are fat remain on the fringes. From fat-activist Elana Dykewomon's "naked lady pool parties" (which she proposes to deal with fear of bodily and other differences [2002, p. 457]) to Julie Wyman's experimental film *Bouyant* (2004) which explores the unique properties of fat, many artists and activists who have attempted to resignify fat have often done so by portraying fat women as active and able in water. Examples of attempts to revision fat as agile and strong are found in the film *Weightless* (2010), about a group of fat women divers, and performances of the fat synchronized-swimming troupe, the *Padded Lilies*. While one could argue that these images and narratives re-essentialize old stereotypic associations of fat with fluidity, nature, and femininity (and I think they often do), they can also be read as attempts to valorize the unique properties of fat flesh – its fluidity, buoyancy, and weightlessness in water – and thus to revision fatness as potentially capable and mobile in its own ways and on its own terms. Importantly, each of these interventions into the representational field is distinctly material and experiential in its approach. Compared to activisms that focus on persuading people to act/think differently, these focus on embodying and materializing change among individuals/groups to challenge social scripts about body, ability, and normality.

Like representations of difference, debates about beauty have a long history. What makes someone beautiful and who gets to define beauty are questions that have occupied thinkers for over two thousand years (Holliday & Sanchez Taylor, 2006). Beginning with Plato, Greek philosophers saw boys and men as embodying the ideal human form, which they associated with love, truth, symmetry, and virtue (Koggel, 2004). Because the female body required enhancement to come close to the male standard, philosophers more often thought that deception and guile rather than truth or goodness were behind the scenes if a woman appeared to be beautiful (Holliday & Sanchez Taylor, 2006). As this book shows, concepts of beauty increasingly carry weight in our image-driven world. In a context where beauty is currency for women, it is not difficult to understand why feminists have cast a critical eye on the concept (Koggel, 2004). Theorists have tended to focus not on questions of what beauty is but rather on who is in charge of its standards and how these have been used against women. Writers have rarely considered whether women can escape beauty standards entirely, and if so, what we might forfeit in the process. Yet some feminists now argue that insofar as accepted theories fail to account for how beauty is fraught with "complication and conflict," they must be judged as inadequate (Colebrook, 2006, p. 141). A few have even proposed that we rethink beauty.

Contemporary art and beauty scholars contend that we cannot eliminate concepts of beauty entirely because judgments about what is beautiful seem to be universally present in societies and because there is no such thing as a "natural" or asocial body to which we can escape. For Linda Scott (2005), criticisms of ideals that rely on claims regarding the value of the "natural" body are illogical since all humans engage in grooming practices. Ruth Holliday and Jacqueline Sanchez Taylor (2006) support her point in arguing that setting up women who have cosmetic surgery as victims or collaborators in misogyny creates another hierarchy between women (those who are natural and fake), which supports the false idea that "natural" beauty exists and is more legitimate than artificial beautification. Rebecca Popenoe (2004) agrees, drawing from her research on fattening practices among women in Niger, Africa, which reveals that in every social context, "the 'natural' body is never enough" – the body must always be made to conform to society (p. 7). Some feminists working in the area of environmental aesthetics suggest that recuperating beauty may serve an important political end – environmental protection (Lintott, 2010). Others propose that reclaiming beauty may be an imperative for those groups of women historically decreed to be unbeautiful (Bae, 2011; Hobson, 2005).

Doing away with the idea of beauty may not even be desirable. Some writers wonder what we would lose without it – without the visual and tactile, the gesture, smell, and sound, or any sensory pleasure in our lives (Colebrook, 2006; Felski, 2006). To change our limiting, image-driven dominant conception of beauty, they argue for creating a feminist aesthetics – an inclusive theory of feminist beauty and sensory pleasure. Art historian Joanna Frueh does this by envisioning beauty as an embodied "soul-and-mind-inseparable-from-body" experience based in sexual desire and love, a feeling that is attitudinal and process-oriented rather than aspirational or predefined (2001, p. 33). In order to reframe beauty in a way that avoids shame-induced body surveillance or punishment, refuses to be reduced to the visual, and includes anyone who seeks it, she develops the concept of "monster/beauty." She defines monster/beauty as a condition emerging "from intimacy with one's aesthetic/erotic capacity rather than as the hopeless pursuit of perfect appearance … a sensuous presence, image, or situation in which the aesthetic and the erotic are inseparable" (p. 11). For Frueh, women who embody monster/beauty do not reject body management but see education and cultivation of their embodied selves (whether weight training, eating chocolate, or reading a good book) as integral to building capacity for self-celebratory beauty, bodily confidence, and sensory pleasure. Rebecca Coleman and Mónica Moreno Figueroa (2010) are also interested in beauty in a temporal sense, arguing that its past and future orientation (i.e., longing for the body we once had or hope to have in the future) needs to give way to a present orientation in order to make it less cruel and harmful. In their view, beauty could function in women's lives not as something to aspire to but as an embodied feeling of aliveness or vitality recognized as it is happening in the present. Such theories are promising because they offer ways of rethinking beauty so that we might begin to reclaim self-love and sensory pleasure in our lives.

I see the interventions of the feminist, anti-oppressive artists, filmmakers, and performers discussed here as "body-becoming pedagogies"—as interventions that create alternatives to conventional biopedagogies whose instrumental, outcomes-oriented methods and moralizing overtones enforce physical conformity over diversity and creativity. Rather than being instrumental and outcomes driven, a body-becoming pedagogy is presence and process oriented, interested in body-affirming images and spaces, and in expanding possibilities for bodily becoming. In this way, a body-becoming approach aims to refocus energies on improvising the properties and potentialities of all bodies. How can we translate the body abilities and aesthetics captured in these theories, experiences, and artistic interventions into actual pedagogies that expand options for becoming? Once translated, how can such pedagogies be experimented with in schools, hospitals, and other sites of physical-activity learning? What conditions would enable people to imagine and improvise these and other possibilities for their bodies? By posing such questions, I hope to make a case for pedagogies that expand openings for physical experimentation, creativity, sensory pleasure, and beauty and hence, for remaking the once-abject into embodied, even celebrated, identities.

These are only a few examples that exist for altering our image landscape and ideas that might help us to expand possibilities for bodies. For misrepresented groups, cultural interventions offer a critical avenue through which to take apart stereotypes and transform imageries. Feminists have shown how limitations of resources, space, and opportunity, rather than lack of creativity or courage, have constrained us from imagining new possibilities for representations and embodied experiences. Ideal and abject images shaped the subjectivities of women whose stories animate this book in different ways depending on their diverse embodiments. Yet all described how they searched for a self by mediating differences with improvisational body and self making as a constant and dynamic process. The transition to womanhood is where their stories end, yet the search for visibility and personhood doesn't stop in adolescence. Entering adulthood, the women whose body histories are told here navigate the culture's body regimes through charting diverse routes for being and becoming differently. It remains for us to give careful thought to this generation's fault lines and failures, its insights and successes, as well as its radical visions as we chart our pathways forward.

Appendix A: Participant Profiles

Participant pseudonym	Age	Self-described racial/ethnic background	Country of birth	First language	Disability, physical difference, or chronic illness	Sexual identity
Ada	27	Trinidadian, Black, Chinese	Trinidad	English		Bisexual
Amélie	31	Franco-Ontarian	Canada	French, English as a second language (ESL)	Facial difference, asthma	Heterosexual
Amy	21	French Canadian, Greek, Chinese	Canada	English		Heterosexual
Andrea	37	Canadian	Canada	English	Depression, chronic fatigue syndrome, Fibromyalgia (acquired as an adult)	Heterosexual
Anita	30	Trinidadian, South Asian, Hungarian	West Indies	English, Hungarian		Uncertain
Anjula	21	South Asian, Hindu	Canada	Hindu, English		Heterosexual
Anne Marie	24	French Canadian	Canada	English		Uncertain
Aurora	26	Ecuadorian	Ecuador	Spanish, ESL	Scoliosis in early adolescence	Heterosexual
Catherine	37	White Protestant	Canada	English		Heterosexual

Education	Class background	Current income (limited under $30,000)	Self-identified size	Self-described puberty experience
University, art school	Upper middle class	Immigrant, mother, family benefits	Has identified as too thin since childhood	Early developer, felt overdeveloped, too big in adolescence
University	Middle class	Limited, arts	Mostly average, fine, thin as a child, underweight in adolescence	Later developer, felt underweight, too small and young looking
University, vocational studies	Immigrant, middle class	Limited, cook	Fluctuates, thin in childhood, worried about weight since adolescence (age 16)	Late bloomer, experienced her breasts as too small, felt fine about being an average shape
College	Working class	Disability benefits, dental assistant	Fluctuates, identified as too thin in childhood, overweight in adulthood	On-time puberty but developed large breasts, felt "too sexy" and "too visible"
College	Immigrant, working to middle class	Limited, arts, phone sex worker	Average, fine	Early developer, experienced her breasts as too big, early period
University	Immigrant, middle class	Student	Worried about weight since early adolescence (grades 5 and 6)	Early developer in relation to her mother, shocked by her period, felt too fat, hairy
University	Working class	Limited, arts	Fluctuates, too thin in childhood, worried about overweight since late adolescence	Late developer, too small breasts and underdeveloped body, developed feelings of being too big through adolescence, was scheduled for a breast reduction at time of interview
College	Immigrant, working class	Student	Has identified as too thin since childhood	Late developer, felt "not enough," breasts too small, and too skinny throughout adolescence
College	Working to middle class	Middle, teacher	History of fat identity from late childhood (age 8 or 9)	Early developer, felt breasts and body size too big

(*Continued*)

Participant pseudonym	Age	Self-described racial/ethnic background	Country of birth	First language	Disability, physical difference, or chronic illness	Sexual identity
Charlene	39	Black Canadian, Bermudan	Canada	English	Chronic pain in adulthood	History of defining as lesbian, now heterosexual
Christian	21	White Canadian	Canada	English		Bisexual
Claire	34	European-descent Canadian	Canada	English		Heterosexual
Claudia	35	Canadian, Irish, Catholic	Canada	English		Heterosexual
Corey	39	Canadian, Caucasian	Canada	English	Severe allergies as a child	Heterosexual
Cynthia	28	Irish Protestant	Canada	English	Childhood onset diabetes	Heterosexual
Elena	30	Italian	Canada	English		Heterosexual, some lesbian experience
Elizabeth	36	Canadian of Dutch-Belgian background	Canada	English	Facial difference	Heterosexual
Erum	22	South Asian, African, Middle Eastern, Muslim	Canada	English	Polycystic ovarian syndrome	Heterosexual

Education	Class background	Current income (limited under $30,000)	Self-identified size	Self-described puberty experience
Some university	Immigrant, middle class	Middle, office worker	Fluctuates, identified as too thin in childhood, worried about weight in adulthood	Late bloomer, felt too small, underdeveloped
University	Poor, welfare	Student	Fluctuates, identified as overweight in adolescence (grades 6 and 7)	On time but felt overdeveloped, too big in adolescence, felt vulnerable to the sexualized gaze of others
University, art college	Middle class	Limited, photographer	Fluctuates, identified as overweight since adolescence (age 14 or 15)	On time, the middle ground that gets ignored
University	Middle class	Middle, consultant	Fluctuates, thin as a child, worried about weight since adolescence	Early developer, felt overdeveloped, too big in adolescence, "too big" breasts were constant source of unwanted attention
University	Working to middle class	Middle, mother	Identified as fat since late childhood (age 10)	Early developer, experienced breasts and body size as too big
College	Middle class	Student, health care worker	Fluctuates, worried about weight since childhood (grade 1)	Puberty was a non-event, late developer, felt she had small breasts and body
College	Working class	Middle, mother	Fluctuates, worried about weight in adolescence and adulthood	On-time puberty but developed very large breasts, felt "too sexy" and "too visible" and wanted a breast reduction
University	Immigrant, working class	Middle, community worker	Average, fine, thin as a child	Late bloomer, breasts too small, felt underdeveloped
University	Immigrant, working class	Student	Fluctuates, identified as overweight in adolescence (grades 7 and 8)	Early developer, felt overdeveloped, too big, fat, and hairy in adolescence

(Continued)

Participant pseudonym	Age	Self-described racial/ethnic background	Country of birth	First language	Disability, physical difference, or chronic illness	Sexual identity
Eva	31	English, Scottish, Serbian	Canada	English		Heterosexual
Evelyn	33	Chinese, Canadian	Canada	English	Infertility	Heterosexual
Farah	42	South Asian, Muslim	Pakistan	English, Urdu		Heterosexual
Fatima	34	Portuguese	Canada	English, Portuguese	Cerebral palsy	Heterosexual
Fernanda	24	Italian	Canada	English, Italian		Heterosexual
Frances	45	WASP	Canada	English	Spina bifida	Heterosexual
Francine	34	French Canadian, Anglo, white	Canada	English		Heterosexual
Fredericka	27	Canadian	Canada	English		Heterosexual
Gayle	26	Welsh, English, Scottish, Metis	Canada	English		Uncertain
Gelorah	38	Iranian, Persian	Iran	Farsi, ESL		Heterosexual

Education	Class background	Current income (limited under $30,000)	Self-identified size	Self-described puberty experience
University	Middle class	Middle, counsellor	Felt fat from grade 6, worried about weight since adolescence	On time, felt too fat, and had "too small" breasts, felt underdeveloped and overweight in adolescence
University	Immigrant, working to upper-middle class	Middle, physiotherapist	Average, fine, identified as thin in late childhood, adolescence	Late bloomer, too small, felt underdeveloped
University	Upper middle class	Immigrant, middle, community worker, translator	Worried about weight since early adulthood	On time, felt self-conscious and exposed in a womanly body, too hairy
College	Immigrant, working to upper middle class	Middle, mother, community worker	Average, worried about weight in adulthood	Late developer, development delayed due to being given Depo Provera drug, which delayed and suppressed her sexual sensations/desires
University, college	Working class	Middle, journalism	Identified as overweight since adolescence (grades 6, 7, 8)	Early developer, felt overdeveloped, too big in adolescence, but also felt her breasts were too small
Some college	Working to middle class	Working class, secretary	Identified as overweight since early adolescence	Early developer, too big breasts
University	Middle class	Middle, business, advertising	Fluctuates, worried about weight in adolescence (from age 16 or 17)	Late bloomer, too small, felt underdeveloped
University	Upper middle class	Middle, trainer	Fluctuates, worried about weight since adolescence (grade 5)	Early developer, felt overdeveloped, too big in adolescence
University	Middle class	Student	Identified as fat since childhood (grade 2 or 3)	Early developer, breasts, body felt too big, felt like an "improper female"
University	Upper middle class	Immigrant, limited, trained as a doctor	Worried about being too thin in childhood, overweight in adolescence and adulthood	Late developer, felt too skinny, breasts too small, belly too big from age 12, looked too much like a child

(Continued)

Participant pseudonym	Age	Self-described racial/ethnic background	Country of birth	First language	Disability, physical difference, or chronic illness	Sexual identity
Gina	36	Estonian	Canada	English	Cerebral palsy	Heterosexual
Hannah	29	Palestinian, Lebanese	Canada	English		Heterosexual
Harriet	34	WASP	Canada	English	Chronic illness, adulthood	Bisexual
Hasina	26	South Asian, Pakistani, Muslim	Canada	English		Heterosexual
Hope	35	White Jamaican, Canadian	Jamaica	English		Heterosexual
Hyla	31	Russian, Jewish, (Samarkand)	USSR	Hebrew, ESL		Heterosexual
Iris	32	English	Canada	English	Auto-immune deficiency (thyroid), late childhood	Heterosexual
Isobel	31	African, Brazilian, Celtic	Brazil	English	Schizophrenia diagnosis in adolescence	Lesbian
Jacqueline	27	West Indian, Jamaican	Jamaica	English	Heart murmur	Heterosexual
Jane	25	WASP	Canada	English	Severe asthma as child, chronic illness from adolescence	Lesbian

Education	Class background	Current income (limited under $30,000)	Self-identified size	Self-described puberty experience
High school	Working class	Working class, office worker	Identified as overweight since childhood (grade 2)	Early developer, felt overdeveloped, too big in adolescence
University	Upper middle class	Limited, journalist	Fluctuates, worried about weight since adolescence (age 14)	On time in relation to peers, but felt too big and wanted to delay development
University	Upper middle class	Middle, activist, mother	Fluctuates, identified as too thin in childhood, worried about weight from age 15 or 16	Late bloomer, too small, felt underdeveloped
University	Immigrant, working class	Social worker	Fluctuates, too thin in childhood and fat in adolescence	Late developer, felt too skinny, accused of being anorexic even though she was not
College	Immigrant, working class	Limited income, child care worker	Fluctuates, worried about weight since adolescence (age 14)	Early developer, felt overdeveloped, too big in adolescence
College	Immigrant, middle class	Immigrant, mother, family benefits	Identified as fat since childhood (grades 3, 4, and 5)	Very late developer, felt fat prior to puberty, breasts felt too small, felt too hairy
University	Middle class	Limited, academic	Fluctuates, identified as fat in late childhood (age 7 or 8)	Late developer
University	Immigrant, working class	Disability benefits, arts	Fluctuates, identified as fat since age 10	Early developer, too big breasts, too big body, experienced breasts and body as too big, uncomfortable periods
Some university	Immigrant, working class	Limited, mother	Fluctuates, identifies as overweight in adulthood	Early developer, felt overdeveloped, too big in adolescence
University	Upper middle class	Student, law school	Identified as too thin since adolescence	Late bloomer, felt underdeveloped, breasts too small, vulnerable in a womanly body

(Continued)

Participant pseudonym	Age	Self-described racial/ethnic background	Country of birth	First language	Disability, physical difference, or chronic illness	Sexual identity
Jillian	39	Jewish, Eastern European background, white, North American	Canada	English		Lesbian
Joanne	35	Irish/French	Canada	English	Mobility disability from birth	Other than heterosexual
Kasha	24	Ukrainian	Canada	English		Heterosexual
Kate	20	Canadian Scottish, English, Irish	Canada	English	Mobility disability from birth	Heterosexual
Katerina	32	German, Austrian	Canada	English	Psychiatric diagnosis in adulthood	Heterosexual
Leigh	24	Chinese, Trinidadian (2nd generation), Canadian (1st generation)	Trinidad	English		Heterosexual
Leila	34	Scottish	Canada	English	Spinal problems from birth	Heterosexual
Lisa	21	English Canadian	England	English		Bisexual
Lucciana	20	Italian Catholic Canadian	Canada	English		Heterosexual

Education	Class background	Current income (limited under $30,000)	Self-identified size	Self-described puberty experience
University	Middle class	Middle, mother, student, activist	Identified as fat in childhood and adolescence (grade 2)	On time, but felt unattractive, too big, unacceptably different
University	Upper middle class	Middle, activist, community worker	Fluctuates, worried about weight since adolescence (age 16 or 17)	Late bloomer, too small, felt underdeveloped, no one noticed the difference
College	Immigrant, working class	Limited, costume designer	Fluctuates, worried about weight since age 11	Late bloomer, experienced breasts as too small, hair style and length were issues
University	Middle class	Student	Fluctuates, worried about weight since adolescence (grade 6)	On time but felt too small and a bit chubby
University	Immigrant, working class	Limited, bank clerk	Average	On time in relation to peers
University	Immigrant, working class	Middle, urban planner	Fluctuates, identified as fat in childhood and adolescence (grades 1 and 2)	Early developer, breasts and body size too big
Community college	Working class	Limited, office worker	Identified as overweight since late childhood (grades 4, 5, and 6)	On time, average but felt too fat
University	Middle class	Limited, office worker, student	Fluctuates, worried about weight in adolescence (grades 10 and 11)	On time, but felt too tall, awkward, underdeveloped and unacceptably different
University	Working to middle class	Student	Fluctuates, identified as thin in childhood, worried about weight since grade 4	Late developer in relation to peers, felt flat-chested but too fat and curvy, and wanted to delay development

(*Continued*)

Participant pseudonym	Age	Self-described racial/ethnic background	Country of birth	First language	Disability, physical difference, or chronic illness	Sexual identity
Lucy	37	Chinese	Hong Kong	Chinese, ESL		Heterosexual
Mabel	24	Canadian	Canada	English, French	Facial difference	Heterosexual
Marcia	37	Co-racial: African Canadian, First Nations, Scottish	Canada	English		Heterosexual
Marianne	33	Cultural: European, Ethnic: African American	Canada	English		Lesbian
Maude	27	White Canadian	Canada	English	Blind from adolescence	Heterosexual
Maya	22	Jamaican Canadian	Canada	English	Scoliosis from childhood	Heterosexual
Melissa	43	English, French Canadian	Canada	English	Foot and spinal problems from childhood, psychiatric history from adolescence	Heterosexual
Moira	30	French Canadian, Irish	Canada	English		Heterosexual
Muni	22	African, Zeruru, Zimbabwean	Zimbabwe	English		Heterosexual

Education	Class background	Current income (limited under $30,000)	Self-identified size	Self-described puberty experience
University	Immigrant, middle class	Limited, admin. assistant	Identified as too thin since early adulthood	Late bloomer, too small, felt underdeveloped
University	Middle class	Middle, media	Fluctuates, worried about weight since adolescence (from grade 9)	Late developer, used starvation to delay development
University	Immigrant, working class	Middle, community worker	Worried about weight since adolescence	Early developer, felt overdeveloped, breasts and body too big in adolescence
University	Middle class	Limited, public relations	Identified as overweight since late childhood (age 9 or 10)	Early developer, felt overdeveloped, too big in adolescence
College	Working class	Limited, massage therapist	Fluctuates, identified as fat in childhood (grade 2)	Late developer, but felt too big in adolescence
College	Immigrant, working class	Mother, family benefits	Identified as too thin in childhood and fat in adulthood	Early period, but felt like a late bloomer, because of being skinny, having small breasts, and breasts different sizes
High school	Middle class	Middle, human resources	Fluctuates, worried about weight since late childhood (age 6 or 7)	Early developer, felt overdeveloped, too big in adolescence
University	Middle class	Limited, military	Fluctuates, worried about weight since adolescence (grades 7 and 8)	On time but developed bigger hips and small breasts, felt pear- instead of hourglass-shaped
High school	Middle class	Immigrant, limited, student	Average, worried about weight since adolescence (grades 6 and 7)	Late bloomer, but felt that breasts, body size, and especially hips were too big

(*Continued*)

Participant pseudonym	Age	Self-described racial/ethnic background	Country of birth	First language	Disability, physical difference, or chronic illness	Sexual identity
Navpreet	27	Punjabi, Sikh	Canada	Punjabi		Heterosexual
Nicole	25	Jamaican	Jamaica	Patois, English		Heterosexual
Patricia	32	Aboriginal	Canada	English	Vitilago from early adolescence	Heterosexual
Preeta	29	South Asian, Hindu	Canada	English		Heterosexual
Rebecca	24	Trinidadian	Canada	English		Heterosexual
Renée	23	French Canadian	Canada	French, ESL		Heterosexual
Rhonda	32	West Indian Canadian	Canada	English	Fibroids	Heterosexual
Rochelle	34	White Newfoundlander	Canada	English		Heterosexual
Rosalind	44	Scottish, Polish	England	English	Fibromyalgia	Heterosexual

Education	Class background	Current income (limited under $30,000)	Self-identified size	Self-described puberty experience
University	Immigrant, working class	Student, law school	Identified as fat in childhood and adolescence (grades 3, 4, and 5)	Early developer, felt overdeveloped, too big in adolescence
University	Immigrant, working to middle class	Middle, teacher	Worried about weight since late childhood, adolescence (grade 3 or 4)	On time but developed bigger hips and legs and small breasts, felt too muscular, not womanly or curvy enough
University	Poor, welfare, working class	Student, community worker	Fine, "Marilyn Monroe" figure	Early developer, felt overdeveloped at young age, but puberty also experienced as "normal and natural"
University	Upper middle class	Middle, marketing	Worried about weight since adolescence (age 15 or 16)	Late bloomer, too small, felt underdeveloped, resisted puberty and becoming a woman
University	Immigrant, middle class	Limited, actress, data entry	Average, fine	On time but felt too big, bulky, and overweight in adolescence
University	Middle class	Student	Fluctuates, worried about fat since age 12 or 13	On time, felt too big and hairy in adolescence
University	Working class	Limited, community worker	Identified as too thin in childhood and adolescence	Late developer in relation to peers, felt flat chested, too skinny, not curvy enough
High school	Working class	Limited, unemployed	Fluctuates, worried about weight since adolescence (age 15 or 16)	Early developer, felt overdeveloped, too big in adolescence
College	Immigrant, working class	Limited, mother, data entry, disability benefits	Fluctuates, identified as fat since late childhood, early adolescence	On time but developed large breasts and felt too fat

(*Continued*)

Participant pseudonym	Age	Self-described racial/ethnic background	Country of birth	First language	Disability, physical difference, or chronic illness	Sexual identity
Rose	24	Korean-born, Canadian raised	Korea	English		Heterosexual
Rosetta	33	African, Guyanese	Guyana	English	Blind from birth	Heterosexual
Ruby	25	Trinidadian, Chinese, Canadian	Canada	English		Heterosexual
Salima	30	South Asian, Indian	England	English		Heterosexual
Sharon	31	West Indian	England	English		Heterosexual
Sheila	22	South Asian Canadian, Hindu	Canada	English	Low estrogen secretion	Other than heterosexual
Shirley	31	Caribbean, Jamaican	Jamaica	English		Heterosexual
Sophia	26	Black Canadian of Trinidadian heritage	Canada	English		Heterosexual
Sylvie	38	Italian/Scottish	Canada	English		Lesbian

Education	Class background	Current income (limited under $30,000)	Self-identified size	Self-described puberty experience
University	Immigrant, working class	Limited, bank clerk	Fluctuates, identified as thin in childhood and as overweight since adolescence (age 15)	Late bloomer, experienced breasts as too small, body as having no curves, felt underdeveloped, like a boy
University	Immigrant, working class	Middle, mother, office worker	Fluctuates, thin in childhood, worried about weight since late adolescence	Early developer, felt overdeveloped, too big in adolescence
University	Immigrant, working to middle class	Limited	Average, fine, identified as thin in childhood	Late bloomer, too small, tiny, no curves, felt underdeveloped
College	Immigrant, working class	Working class, day care worker	Fluctuates, identified as fat in early adolescence (grades 6, 7, and 8)	Early developer, breasts and body size too big
University	Immigrant, working to middle class	Middle, policy analyst	Identified as overweight since childhood (age 7 or 8)	Early developer, felt overdeveloped, too big in adolescence
University	Upper middle class	Student	Identified as fat in childhood and adolescence (grade 4)	Early developer, felt overdeveloped, too big in adolescence, too chesty and hairy
College	Middle class	Immigrant, limited, administrator	Fluctuates, worried about weight since adolescence	Late bloomer, average body size but felt too big from early adolescence
University	Immigrant, middle class	Limited, marketing researcher	Worried about weight since early adolescence (age 12)	Early developer, felt overdeveloped, too big in adolescence
University	Working class	Middle, manager	Identified as fat since late childhood (grade 4)	Early developer, felt overdeveloped, too big and hairy in adolescence

(*Continued*)

Participant pseudonym	Age	Self-described racial/ethnic background	Country of birth	First language	Disability, physical difference, or chronic illness	Sexual identity
Tamara	38	South Asian, Guyanese, Canadian	Guyana	English	Heart attack, heart problems, rheumatoid arthritis in early adolescence	Heterosexual
Tara	24	Canadian with Irish and French roots	Canada	English	Asthma in childhood	Heterosexual
Venita	20	South Asian Canadian, Hindu	Canada	English	Undiagnosed menstrual pain	Uncertain
Vera	24	Asian, Vietnamese, Australian, Canadian	Canada	English	Rheumatoid arthritis from adolescence	Heterosexual
Yolanda	23	Dutch, Indonesian	Canada	English		Heterosexual
Yvonna	30	Polish	Canada	English	Celiac disease from adolescence	Heterosexual
Zoë	29	West Indian, Canadian	Jamaica	English		Heterosexual

Education	Class background	Current income (limited under $30,000)	Self-identified size	Self-described puberty experience
High school	Immigrant, working class	Working class, clerk	Fluctuates, identified as thin in childhood, overweight in adulthood	Early developer, felt overdeveloped, breasts too large in adolescence, had a breast reduction later in life
College	Upper middle class	Limited	Fluctuates, identified as too thin in childhood, worried about weight since adolescence (age 15 or 16)	Was a late developer, but wanted to delay development as long as possible because she felt fat
University	Immigrant, working class	Student, social worker	Identified as too thin since adolescence	Felt too small, late bloomer, underdeveloped in adolescence, heavy painful, periods, flat chested, "butch"
University	Immigrant, working class	Limited, office worker	Average, identified as too thin since adolescence	Late bloomer, experienced breasts as too small. body as having no curves, felt underdeveloped
University	Middle class	Middle, editor	Identified as overweight since adolescence (grade 4 or 5)	Early developer, breasts and body size too big
University	Middle class	Middle, teacher	Identified as too thin in childhood and adolescence	On-time puberty but felt she had no curves, small breasts, and a too tall body
University	Immigrant, working class	Middle, mother, health care manager	Fluctuates, worried about weight since late adolescence	Early developer, felt overdeveloped, hips and butt too big in adolescence

Appendix B: Interview Guide and Advertising Flyer

Body Image across the Life Span Interview Guide

Why did you decide to be interviewed? What made you respond to the advertisement?
What is it about this topic that struck a chord for you? Is it important to you? How?

Tell me about the history of your body in childhood

What is an early or perhaps one of your earliest memories of your body?
What are your recollections of your appearance and physical abilities as a child?
How did you feel about your body/looks when you were a child?
What, if anything, did your family tell you about your body? Looks? Abilities?
What, if anything, did other people, adults and kids, tell you about your body? Abilities?
Did you ever look at your reflection and think you were different from other kids? How did you learn this?
Were you ever teased because of the way you looked? The way your body moved or worked?
When did you become aware of your ethnicity or racial identity? How did you learn this? What did others (family, friends, school, pop culture) tell you about this?
When were you aware of having a disability and/or physical difference? How did you learn this? What did others tell you about this?

What, if anything, did you learn about your body in medical systems?
What were the effects of these experiences on your sense of body?
Your sense of self?
What do you remember about grooming in your childhood? (Hair
care rituals? Clothing? Other grooming practices?) Who took care of
you and what messages did you receive through these experiences?
What toys, books, films, and TV did you like? What activities were
you interested in?
How would you describe your gender? What did tomboy or girly girl
mean to you?
Were there any key moments/memories/images when you learned
something new about your body or your feelings about your body
changed? Tell me about them.

Tell me about your experiences of your body in adolescence

Tell me about puberty (your period, breasts, body fat, any other
changes or occurrences).
Did puberty change your feelings about or consciousness of your
body? If so, how?
When were you first aware of sex, sexuality? What words were used
to describe body parts in your family, among your peers, in your community?
Tell me about others' responses to your changing body. Did you get
any messages about your body in your encounters at home and at
school? Elsewhere?
Did others look or comment on your body changes? What happened?
What were the effects of these experiences on your sense of body?
Your sense of self?
What messages about your body, if any, did you get from the medical
system?
How do you think your mother, sisters, and other girls related to your
body? How did you feel about and relate to their bodies as a child and
adolescent?
How do you think your father, brothers, and boys felt about and related to your body? How did you feel about and relate to their bodies
as a child and adolescent?
Was clothing, make-up, hair, etc. important to you when you were an
adolescent? Why or why not? Was your family able to afford the clothing you wanted? Dental work? Skin care? Assistive devices?

What kinds of media did you like? What were you interested in reading, watching, doing?

Did your first sexual experiences affect your feelings about your body? If so how?

To what extent did you feel like a girl? A woman? How and when did you feel this way?

Were there any key moments/memories/images when your feelings about your body/appearance changed? Tell me about them.

Tell me about your experiences of your body in your adult years

Have you ever altered or wanted to alter your body through surgery? If so, describe.

Do you have children? Has this affected your body image? If yes, how?

Have any major life events impacted on your body image/awareness? (losses, transitions)

Have you had any injuries/illnesses/physical conditions in your adulthood? Have they affected your feelings about/experiences of your body? How?

Have health professionals/doctors influenced your experiences of your body? How?

Are there any other adult experiences that have affected your experiences of your body?

When, if at all, do you feel like a woman? When, if at all, do you not feel like a woman?

Are there times when you feel more South Asian, African Caribbean, and Asian or how you define your racial identity?

Are there times when you feel more disabled/different than other times? When and how?

Were there any key events/memories that changed your feelings about your body?

Do you or have you experienced pleasure through changing your body/appearance? Pain?

Are there people, events, or time periods that have made you feel good about your body? How? Are there people, events, or periods of time that have made you feel bad about your body? How?

When have you felt best about your body? When have you felt worst about your body?

Have you experienced pain or pleasure (emotional and/or physical)

because of your appearance/ abilities? Explain.
Have you ever felt trapped by your body? Have you ever felt liberated by your body?

Current beliefs and feelings about your body and appearance

What is your body ideal? Is there an ideal that you strive towards? When and how?
What are your current feelings about your body? What do you currently do to alter/improve your appearance? Physical abilities?
Do you believe social factors affect your image? Tell me about your views on this. Does your understanding of the "larger picture" affect your feelings toward your body? How you modify your body? If so, how?
Do you see a connection between your body and self-image? If so, what is it?
Is your appearance connected to your identity? If so, how?
Is the physical self you present to the world congruent with your inner self? If so how? If not, what would make them more congruent?
Is there anything else that you would like to add about this topic?

Advertising Flyer

Do you want to talk about beauty, physical ability, and your body?
Do you identify as a South Asian, Asian Canadian, African Canadian, or multi-racial woman?
Are you between the ages of 20 and 45?

You may be interested in participating in a research project on women and their bodies conducted at Women's College Hospital. If you identify as a South Asian, Asian Canadian, African Canadian, or multi-racial woman and can talk about beauty and your body, you may be interested in this study. The interview focuses on:

• What you think of ideals of beauty, whether they have affected you
• Identity and body image
• How you feel about your body weight, size, or shape
• The effect of your period, your development, breast-feeding, pregnancy, child-bearing, or aging on your body image
• Sexuality and your body
• Hair colour, style, or texture, and what it means to you

- Different shades of beauty, how you feel about issues surrounding skin colour
- Wrinkles, aging, and changes in your body over the years
- What it's like to have a disability or a hidden or visible physical difference, and how your abilities affect body image
- Things that make you feel good about your body
- Any other topics you want to discuss

This is an anonymous, confidential interview. You will have the opportunity to discuss your feelings and experiences in a non-judgmental way. If you want to talk about your body and your looks and how you feel about them, please give me a call at:

References

$5M to bring back ParticipACTION exercise program. (2007). CBC News, Health. http://www.cbc.ca/health/story/2007/02/19/partici paction.html

Ad*Access On-Line Project. John W. Hartman Center for Sales, Advertising & Marketing History. Duke University Libraries. http://library.duke.edu/ digitalcollections/adaccess/

Adams Hillard, P.J. (2002). Menstruation in young girls: a clinical perspective. *Obstetrics and Gynecology, 99*(4), 655–662. http://dx.doi.org/10.1016/ S0029-7844(02)01660-5 Medline:12039130

Adelman, L. (Executive producer), Cheng, J. (Producer & writer), & Shim, I. (Associate producer & writer). (2003). *Race: The power of an illusion* [Television series]. San Francisco: California Newsreel.

Adrian, B. (2003). *Framing the bride: Globalizing beauty and romance in Taiwan's bridal industry.* Berkeley: University of California Press.

Ahmed, M.L., Ong, K.K., & Dunger, D.B. (2009). Childhood obesity and the timing of puberty. *Trends in Endocrinology and Metabolism, 20*(5), 237–242. http://dx.doi.org/10.1016/j.tem.2009.02.004 Medline:19541497

Ahmed, S. (1998). Animated borders: Skin, colour and tanning. In M. Shildrick & J. Price (Eds.), *Vital signs: Feminist reconfigurations of the bio/logical body* (pp. 45–65). Edinburgh, Scotland: Edinburgh University Press.

Aksglaede, L., Juul, A., Leffers, H., Skakkebaek, N.E., & Andersson, A.M. (2006). The sensitivity of the child to sex steroids: Possible impact of exogenous estrogens. *Human Reproduction Update, 12*(4), 341–349. http://dx.doi. org/10.1093/humupd/dml018 Medline:16672247

Alaimo, S., & Hekman, S. (2008). Introduction: Emerging models of materiality in feminist theory. In S. Alaimo & S. Hekman (Eds.), *Material feminisms* (pp. 1–19). Bloomington: Indiana University Press.

Allan, J. (2005). Encounters with exclusion through disability arts. *Journal of Research in Special Educational Needs, 5*(1), 31–36. http://dx.doi.org/10.1111/j.1471-3802.2005.00036.x

Allan, J. (2010). The sociology of disability and the struggle for inclusive education. *British Journal of Sociology of Education, 31*(5), 603–619. http://dx.doi.org/10.1080/01425692.2010.500093

Alsaker, F.D. (1995). Is puberty a critical period for socialization? *Journal of Adolescence, 18*(4), 427–444. http://dx.doi.org/10.1006/jado.1995.1031

Altabe, M.N. (1996). Issues in the assessment and treatment of body image disturbance in culturally diverse populations. In J.K. Thompson (Ed.), *Body image, eating disorders and obesity: An integrative guide* (pp. 129–147). Washington, DC: American Psychological Association.

Always & Tampax (with Ontario Physical and Health Education Association). (2008). *Always changing: Student guide.* Rochester, NY: Procter & Gamble.

American Academy of Cosmetic Surgery (2009). AACS 2009 consumer survey patients' openness full report. http://www.cosmeticsurgery.org/media/position.cfm

American Association of University Women (1991). *Shortchanging girls, short-changing America: A nationwide poll to assess self esteem, educational experiences, interest in math and science, and career aspirations of girls and boys ages 9–15.* Washington: Author.

American Psychiatric Association. (2000). *Diagnostic and statistical manual of mental disorders* (4th ed., text rev.). Washington: Author.

American Psychological Association, Task Force on the Sexualization of Girls (2007). *Report of the APA task force on the sexualization of girls.* Washington: American Psychological Association. http://www.apa.org/pi/women/programs/girls/report.aspx

American Society for Aesthetic Plastic Surgery (2011). Demand for plastic surgery rebounds by almost 9%. *Statistics, surveys & trends.* http://www.surgery.org/media/news-releases/demand-for-plastic-surgery-rebounds-by-almost-9%

American Society of Plastic Surgeons (2011). *Report of the 2010 plastic surgery statistics: 2010 cosmetic demographics.* http://www.plasticsurgery.org/

Amnesty International USA. (2005). *Stonewalled: Police abuse and misconduct against lesbian, gay, bisexual and transgender people in the USA.* New York: Amnesty International USA.

Anderson, K. (2000). *A recognition of being: Reconstructing native womanhood.* Toronto: Sumach Press.

Anderson, S.E., Dallal, G.E., & Must, A. (2003). Relative weight and race influence average age at menarche: Results from two nationally representative surveys of US girls studied 25 years apart. *Pediatrics, 111*(4), 844–850. http://dx.doi.org/10.1542/peds.111.4.844 Medline:12671122

Angier, N. (1999). *Woman: An intimate geography*. Boston: Houghton Mifflin.

Anthias, F., & Yuval-Davis, N. (1992). *Racialized boundaries: Race, nation, gender, colour, and class and the anti-racist struggle*. London, Eng.: Routledge.

Aristotle. (2007). *On the generation of animals* (A. Platt, Trans.). eBooks@ Adelaide. http://ebooks.adelaide.edu.au/a/aristotle/generation/

Aristotle, & Peck, A.L. (1943). *Generation of animals*. London, Eng.: W. Heinemann.

Asberg, C., & Birke, L. (2010). Biology is a feminist issue: Interview with Lynda Birke. *European Journal of Women's Studies, 17*(4), 413–423. http://dx.doi.org/10.1177/1350506810377696

Atencio, M., & Wright, J. (2009). "Ballet it's too whitey": Discursive hierarchies of high school dance spaces and the constitution of embodied feminine subjectivities. *Gender and Education, 21*(1), 31–46. http://dx.doi.org/10.1080/09540250802213123

Attfield, J. (1996). Barbie and Action Man: Adult toys for girls and boys. In P. Kirkham (Ed.), *The gendered object* (pp. 80–89). Manchester, Eng.: Manchester University Press.

Auerbach, J.D. (1999). From the SWS president: Gender as proxy. *Gender & Society, 13*(6), 701–703. http://dx.doi.org/10.1177/089124399013006001

Azzarito, L. (2009). The rise of the corporate curriculum: Fatness, fitness, and whiteness. In J. Wright & V. Harwood (Eds.), *Biopolitics and the "obesity epidemic": Governing bodies* (pp. 183–198). New York: Routledge.

Azziz, R., Carmina, E., & Sawaya, M.E. (2000). Idiopathic hirsutism. *Endocrine Reviews, 21*(4), 347–362. http://dx.doi.org/10.1210/er.21.4.347 Medline:10950156

Bae, M. (2011). Interrogating girl power: Girlhood, popular media and post-feminism. *Visual Arts Research, 37*(2), 28–40. http://dx.doi.org/10.5406/visuartsrese.37.2.0028

Barad, K. (1998). Getting real: Technoscientific practices and the materialization of reality. *Differences: A Journal of Feminist Cultural Studies, 10*(2), 87–128.

Barad, K. (2003). Posthumanist performativity: Toward an understanding of how matter comes to matter. *Signs* (Chicago), *28*(3), 801–831. http://dx.doi.org/10.1086/345321

Barden, N. (2001). The development of gender identity. In S. Izzard & N. Barden (Eds.), *Rethinking gender and therapy: The changing realities of women* (pp. 6–29). Philadelphia: Open University Press.

Barker, E.T., & Galambos, N.L. (2003). Body dissatisfaction of adolescent girls and boys: Risk and resource factors. *Journal of Early Adolescence, 23*(2), 141–165. http://dx.doi.org/10.1177/0272431603023002002

Barnett, A., & Smith, Z. (2005). Toxic creams for sale as thousands seek whiter skin. *The Observer*. http://www.guardian.co.uk

Bartky, S. (1990). *Femininity and domination: Studies in the phenomenology of oppression*. New York: Routledge.

Basow, S.A. (1991). The hairless ideal: Women and their body hair. *Psychology of Women Quarterly, 15*(1), 83–96. http://dx.doi.org/10.1111/j.1471-6402.1991.tb00479.x

Basow, S.A., & Braman, A.C. (1998). Women and body hair: Social perceptions and attitudes. *Psychology of Women Quarterly, 22*(4), 637–645. http://dx.doi.org/10.1111/j.1471-6402.1998.tb00182.x

Battersby, C. (1998). *The phenomenal woman: Feminist metaphysics and the patterns of identity*. New York: Routledge.

Bauer, K.W., Yang, Y.W., & Austin, S.B. (2004). "How can we stay healthy when you're throwing all of this in front of us?" Findings from focus groups and interviews in middle schools on environmental influences on nutrition and physical activity. *Health Education & Behavior, 31*(1), 34–46. http://dx.doi.org/10.1177/1090198103255372 Medline:14768656

Beauboeuf-Lafontant, T. (2005). Keeping up appearances, getting fed up: The embodiment of strength among African American women. *Meridians, 5*(2), 104–123.

Beausoleil, N. (1994). Makeup in everyday life: An inquiry into the practices of urban American women of diverse backgrounds. In N. Sault (Ed.), *Many mirrors: Body image and social relations* (pp. 33–57). New Brunswick, NJ: Rutgers University Press.

Becker, A.E., Burwell, R.A., Gilman, S.E., Herzog, D.B., & Hamburg, P. (2002). Eating behaviours and attitudes following prolonged exposure to television among ethnic Fijian adolescent girls. *British Journal of Psychiatry, 180*(6), 509–514. http://dx.doi.org/10.1192/bjp.180.6.509 Medline:12042229

Bederman, G. (1996). *Manliness and civilization: A cultural history of gender and race in the United States, 1880–1917*. Chicago: University of Chicago Press.

Bélair, S., & Statistics Canada. (2007). *Participation and activity limitation survey 2006: Tables*. Ottawa, ON: Statistics Canada.

Belkin, L. (2000). The making of an 8-year-old woman. *New York Times Magazine*. http://www.nytimes.com

Bell, E.E., & Nkomo, S.M. (1998). Armoring: Learning to withstand racial oppression. *Journal of Comparative Family Studies, 29*(2), 285–295.

Bellis, M.A., Downing, J., & Ashton, J.R. (2006). Adults at 12? Trends in puberty and their public health consequences. *Journal of Epidemiology and Community Health, 60*(11), 910–911. http://dx.doi.org/10.1136/jech.2006.049379 Medline:17053275

Belsky, J., Steinberg, L., & Draper, P. (1991). Childhood experience, interpersonal development, and reproductive strategy: An evolutionary theory of socialization. *Child Development, 62*(4), 647–670. http://dx.doi.org/10.2307/1131166 Medline:1935336

Bennett, W., & Gurin, J. (1983). *The dieter's dilemma: Eating less and weighing more.* New York: Basic Books.

Berger, J. (1972). *Ways of seeing.* Harmondsworth, Eng.: Penguin Books.

Bernheimer, C. (1990). Introduction. In C. Bernheimer & C. Kahane (Eds.), *In Dora's case: Freud—hysteria—feminism* (pp. 1–18). New York: Columbia University Press.

Bernstein, B.B. (2001). From pedagogies to knowledges. In A. Morais, I. Neves, B. Davies, & H. Daniels (Eds.), *Towards a sociology of pedagogy: The contribution of Basil Bernstein to research* (pp. 363–368). New York: Peter Lang.

Bernstein, N. (1990). Objective bodily damage: Disfigurement and dignity. In T. F. Cash & T. Pruzinsky (Eds.), *Body images: Development, deviance and change* (pp. 131–148). New York: The Guilford Press.

Bhabha, H. (1994). *The location of culture.* New York: Routledge.

Bindel, J. (2010). Women: Embrace your facial hair! *The Guardian.* http://www.guardian.co.uk

Birke, L. (2000a). *Feminism and the biological body.* New Brunswick, NJ: Rutgers University Press.

Birke, L. (2000b). Sitting on the fence: Biology, feminism and gender-bending environments. *Women's Studies International Forum, 23*(5), 587–599. http://dx.doi.org/10.1016/S0277-5395(00)00127-8

Blackless, M., Charuvastra, A., Derryck, A., Fausto-Sterling, A., Lauzanne, K., & Lee, E. (2000). How sexually dimorphic are we? Review and synthesis. *American Journal of Human Biology, 12*(2), 151–166. http://dx.doi.org/10.1002/(SICI)1520-6300(200003/04)12:2<151::AID-AJHB1>3.0.CO;2-F Medline:11534012

Blaise, M. (2009). "What a girl wants, what a girl needs": Responding to sex, gender, and sexuality in the early childhood classroom. *Journal of Research in Childhood Education, 23*(4), 450–460. http://dx.doi.org/10.1080/02568540909594673

Block, S. (2010). *Ontario's growing gap: The role of race and gender.* Ottawa, ON: Canadian Centre for Policy Alternatives. http://www.policyalternatives.ca/sites/default/files/uploads/publications/reports/docs/The%20Role%20of%20Race%20Ontario%20Growing%20Gap.pdf

Blood, S.K. (2005). *Body work: The social construction of women's body image.* New York: Routledge.

Bloom, A. (2002). *Normal: Transsexual CEOs, cross-dressing cops, and hermaphrodites with attitude.* New York: Random House.

Blume, J. (1986). *Are you there God? It's me, Margaret.* New York: Yearling.

Bogaert, A.F. (2005). Age at puberty and father absence in a national probability sample. *Journal of Adolescence, 28*(4), 541–546. http://dx.doi. org/10.1016/j.adolescence.2004.10.008 Medline:16022888

Bombardieri, M. (2005). Summers' remarks on women draw fire. *Boston Globe.* http://www.boston.com/news/local/articles/2005/01/17/ summers_remarks_on_women_draw_fire/

Bonilla-Silva, E. (2002). We are all Americans! The Latin Americanization of racial stratification in the USA. *Race and Society, 5*(1), 3–16. http://dx.doi. org/10.1016/j.racsoc.2003.12.008

Bonilla-Silva, E., & Dietrich, D.R. (2009). The Latin Americanization of US race relations: A new pigmentocracy. In E.N. Glenn (Ed.), *Shades of difference: Why skin color matters* (pp. 40–60). Stanford, CA: Stanford University Press.

Bordo, S. (1993). *Unbearable weight: Feminism, Western culture and the body.* Los Angeles: University of California Press.

Bordo, S. (1999a). *The male body.* New York: Farrar, Straus and Giroux.

Bordo, S. (1999b). *Twilight zones: The hidden life of cultural images from Plato to O.J.* Berkeley: University of California Press.

Bordo, S. (2009). Not just "a white girl's thing": The changing face of food and body image problems. In H. Malson & M. Burns (Eds.), *Critical feminist approaches to eating dis/orders* (pp. 46–59). New York: Routledge.

Boutelle, K., Neumark-Sztainer, D., Story, M., & Resnick, M. (2002). Weight control behaviors among obese, overweight, and nonoverweight adolescents. *Journal of Pediatric Psychology, 27*(6), 531–540. http://dx.doi. org/10.1093/jpepsy/27.6.531 Medline:12177253

Boyce, W.F., King, M.A., & Roche, J. (2008). *Healthy settings for young people in Canada.* http://www.phac-aspc.gc.ca/hp-ps/dca-dea/publications/yjc/ pdf/youth-jeunes-eng.pdf

Braun, V. (2009). "The women are doing it for themselves": The rhetoric of choice and agency around female genital "cosmetic surgery." *Australian Feminist Studies, 24*(60), 233–249. http://dx.doi.org/10.1080/08164640902852449

Britzman, D.P. (1997). What is this thing called love? New discourses for understanding gay and lesbian youth. In S. de Castell & M. Bryson (Eds.), *Radical in<ter>ventions: Identity, politics, and difference/s in educational praxis* (pp. 183–207). Albany: State University of New York Press.

Brody, J. (1997). Girls and puberty: The crisis years. *New York Times.* Personal health. http://www.nytimes.com

Brooks-Gunn, J. (1984). The psychological significance of different pubertal events to young girls. *Journal of Early Adolescence, 4*(4), 315–327. http:// dx.doi.org/10.1177/0272431684044003

Brooks-Gunn, J., Warren, M.P., Rosso, J., & Gargiulo, J. (1987). Validity of self-report measures of girls' pubertal status. *Child Development, 58*(3), 829–841. http://dx.doi.org/10.2307/1130220 Medline:3608653

Brown, D.L. (2008). African American resiliency: Examining racial socialization and social support as protective factors. *Journal of Black Psychology, 34*(1), 32–48. http://dx.doi.org/10.1177/0095798407310538

Brown, L.M., & Gilligan, C. (1992). *Meeting at the crossroads: Women's psychology and girls' development*. Cambridge, MA: Harvard University Press.

Brown, S.L., Middleton, M.S., Berg, W.A., Soo, M.S., & Pennello, G. (2000). Prevalence of rupture of silicone gel breast implants revealed on MR imaging in a population of women in Birmingham, Alabama. *AJR (American Journal of Roentgenology), 175*(4), 1057–1064. http://dx.doi.org/10.2214/ajr.175.4.1751057 Medline:11000165

Brown, S.L., Pennello, G., Berg, W.A., Soo, M.S., & Middleton, M.S. (2001). Silicone gel breast implant rupture, extracapsular silicone, and health status in a population of women. *Journal of Rheumatology, 28*(5), 996–1003. Medline:11361228

Browne, J., & Messenger, S. (2003). Victorian spectacle: Julia Pastrana, the bearded and hairy female. *Endeavour, 27*(4), 155–159. http://dx.doi.org/10.1016/j.endeavour.2003.10.006 Medline:14652038

Brownell, K.D., & Horgen, K.B. (2004). *Food fight: The inside story of the food industry, America's obesity crisis, and what we can do about it*. Chicago: Contemporary Books.

Brownmiller, S. (1984). *Femininity*. New York: Linden Press / Simon & Schuster.

Bruch, H. (1974). *Eating disorders: Obesity, anorexia nervosa and the person within*. London: Routledge & Kegan Paul.

Bruch, H. (1978). *The golden cage: The enigma of anorexia nervosa*. Cambridge, MA: Harvard University Press.

Brumberg, J.J. (1997). *The body project: An intimate history of American girls*. New York: Vintage Books.

Buchan, W., & Buchan, A.P. (1813). *Domestic medicine, or, a treatise on the prevention and cure of diseases: With observations concerning sea-bathing, and on the use of the mineral waters; to which is annexed, a dispensatory for the use of private practitioners*. London, Eng.: Printed for T. Cadell and W. Davies [et. al.] and for W. Creech, at Edinburgh.

Buchanan, C.M., Eccles, J.S., & Becker, J.B. (1992). Are adolescents the victims of raging hormones: Evidence for activational effects of hormones on moods and behavior at adolescence. *Psychological Bulletin, 111*(1), 62–107. http://dx.doi.org/10.1037/0033-2909.111.1.62 Medline:1539089

Burman, E. (1997). Developmental psychology and its discontents. In D. Fox & I. Prilleltensky (Eds.), *Critical psychology: An introduction* (pp. 134–149). London: Sage.

Burman, E. (2008). *Developments: Child, image, nation.* New York: Routledge.

Burrows, A., & Cooper, M. (2002). Possible risk factors in the development of eating disorders in overweight pre-adolescent girls. *International Journal of Obesity and Related Metabolic Disorders, 26*(9), 1268–1273. http://dx.doi.org/10.1038/sj.ijo.0802033 Medline:12187406

Burrows, A., & Johnson, S. (2005). Girls' experiences of menarche and menstruation. *Journal of Reproductive and Infant Psychology, 23*(3), 235–249. http://dx.doi.org/10.1080/02646830500165846

Burrows, L. (2009). Pedagogizing families through obesity discourse. In J. Wright & V. Harwood (Eds.), *Biopolitics and the "obesity epidemic": Governing bodies* (pp. 127–140). New York: Routledge.

Burrows, L., Wright, J., & Jungersen-Smith, J. (2002). "Measure your belly": New Zealand children's constructions of health and fitness. *Journal of Teaching in Physical Education, 22,* 39–48.

Burton, L.M., Bonilla-Silva, E., Ray, V., Buckelew, R., & Hordge Freeman, E. (2010). Critical race theories, colorism, and the decade's research on families of color. *Journal of Marriage and the Family, 72*(3), 440–459. http://dx.doi.org/10.1111/j.1741-3737.2010.00712.x

Butler, J. (1988). Performative acts and gender constitution: An essay in phenomenology and feminist theory. *Theatre Journal, 40*(4), 519–531. http://dx.doi.org/10.2307/3207893

Butler, J. (1990). *Gender trouble: Feminism and the subversion of identity.* New York: Routledge.

Butler, J. (1993). *Bodies that matter: On the discursive limits of "sex."* New York: Routledge.

Butler, O.E. (2000). *Lilith's brood.* New York: Aspect/Warner Books.

Butts, S.F., & Seifer, D.B. (2010). Racial and ethnic differences in reproductive potential across the life cycle. *Fertility and Sterility, 93*(3), 681–690. http://dx.doi.org/10.1016/j.fertnstert.2009.10.047 Medline:19939362

Byrd, A.D., & Tharps, L.L. (2001). *Hair story: Untangling the roots of black hair in America.* New York: St Martin's Griffin.

Cadden, J. (1995). *Meanings of sex differences in the Middle Ages: Medicine, science and culture.* Cambridge, Eng.: Cambridge University Press.

Calgary radio station holds breast implant contest. (2011). CBC News. http://www.cbc.ca/news/canada/calgary/story/2011/06/14/calgary-breast-implant-contest-radio.html

Calogero, R.M., Tantleff-Dunn, S., & Thompson, J.K. (Eds.). (2011). *Self-objectification in women: Causes, consequences, and counteractions.* Washington: American Psychological Association. http://dx.doi.org/10.1037/12304-000

Cameron, C. (2007). Whose problem? Disability narratives and available identities. *Community Development Journal, 42*(4), 501–511. http://dx.doi.org/10.1093/cdj/bsm040

Campbell, S., Meynell, L., & Sherwin, S. (2009). *Embodiment and agency.* University Park: Pennsylvania State University Press.

Campos, P. (2004). *The obesity myth: Why America's obsession with weight is hazardous to your health.* New York: Gotham Books.

Canadian Race Relations Foundation (2000). *Racism in our schools: What to know about it; How to fight it.* http://www.crr.ca/divers-files/en/pub/faSh/ePubFaShRacScho.pdf

Canadian Research Institute for the Advancement of Women [CRIAW]. (2002). *Women's experience of racism: How race and gender interact.* http://criaw-icref.ca/WomensexperienceofracismHowraceandgenderinteract

Canadian Research Institute for the Advancement of Women. (2006). *Intersectional feminist frameworks: An emerging vision.* Ottawa, ON: Author.

CanWest News Service. (2006). Health Canada OKs silicone breast implants. *Canada.com.* http://www.canada.com/topics/news/national/story.html?id=637ceee1-3f4a-4844-8d05-f10ad76834f9&k=79318

Caplan, P., & Cosgrove, L. (Eds.). (2004). *Bias in psychiatric diagnosis.* Lanham, MD: Jason Aronson.

Carmichael, A.G., & Ratzan, R.M. (1991). *Medicine: A treasury of art and literature.* New York: Hugh Lauter Levin.

Carr, C.L. (2005). Tomboyism or lesbianism? Beyond sex/gender/sexual conflation. *Sex Roles, 53*(1–2), 119–131. http://dx.doi.org/10.1007/s11199-005-4286-5

Carr, C.L. (2007). Where have all the tomboys gone? Women's accounts of gender in adolescence. *Sex Roles, 56*(7–8), 439–448. http://dx.doi.org/10.1007/s11199-007-9183-7

Carroll, L. (2010). Growing up too soon? Puberty strikes 7-year-old girls. Msnbc.com, Health. http://www.msnbc.msn.com/id/38600414/ns/health-kids_and_parenting

Cash, T.F. & Smolak, L. (2011). Understanding body images: Historical and contemporary perspectives. T.F. Cash & L. Smolak (Eds.), *Body image: A handbook of science, practice and prevention* (pp. 3–11) Second ed. New York: The Guilford Press.

Castro, M., & Behrendt, T. (2009). Dora the explorer updates her look. Good Morning America. http://abcnews.go.com/GMA/Weekend/story?id=7033295&page=1

Centers for Disease Control and Prevention. (1997). Epidemiologic notes and reports, Toxic-shock syndrome – United States. *Morbidity and Mortality Weekly Report, 46*(22), 492–495. www.cdc.gov/mmwr/preview/mmwrhtml/00047818.htm

Chambers, S.A. (2007). "Sex" and the problem of the body: Reconstructing Judith Butler's theory of sex/gender. *Body & Society, 13*(4), 47–75. http://dx.doi.org/10.1177/1357034X07085537

Chandler, E., & Rice, C. (2013). Revisioning disability and difference. Paper presented for Project Re•Vision. Faculty of Health Sciences, University of Ontario Institute of Technology, Oshawa, ON.

Chase, C. (1998). Hermaphrodites with attitude: Mapping the emergence of intersex political activism. *GLQ: A Journal of Lesbian and Gay Studies, 4*, 189–211.

Chavasse, P.H. (1878). *Advice to a mother on the management of her children and on the treatment on the moment of some of their more pressing illnesses and accidents.* http://www.gutenberg.org/cache/epub/6595/pg6595.txt

Ciliska, D. (1990). *Beyond dieting: Psychoeducational interventions for chronically obese women: A non-dieting approach.* New York: Brunner/Mazel.

Clare, E. (2001). Stolen bodies, reclaimed bodies: Disability and queerness. *Public Culture, 13*(3), 359–366. http://dx.doi.org/10.1215/08992363-13-3-359

Clare, E. (2009). *Exile and pride: Disability, queerness and liberation.* Brooklyn, NY: South End Press.

Clarke, L.H., & Griffin, M. (2007). Becoming and being gendered through the body: Older women, their mothers and body image. *Ageing and Society, 27*(05), 701–718. http://dx.doi.org/10.1017/S0144686X0700623X

The clitoris needs more respect, doctor says. (2005). *Maclean's.* http://www2.macleans.ca/

Cogan, J.C., & Ernsberger, P. (1999). Dieting, weight, and health: Reconceptualizing research and policy. *Journal of Social Issues, 55*(2), 187–205. http://dx.doi.org/10.1111/0022-4537.00112

Cohen, E. (2004). The fine line between clinical and subclinical anorexia. In P. Caplan & L. Cosgrove (Eds.), *Bias in psychiatric diagnosis* (pp. 193–200). Lanham, MD: Jason Aronson.

Cole, E.R., & Zucker, A.N. (2007). Black and White women's perspectives on femininity. *Cultural Diversity & Ethnic Minority Psychology, 13*(1), 1–9. http://dx.doi.org/10.1037/1099-9809.13.1.1 Medline:17227171

Colebrook, C. (2006). Introduction. *Feminist Theory, 7*(2), 131–142. http://dx.doi.org/10.1177/1464700106064404

Coleman, R. (2008). The becoming of bodies: Girls, media effects, and body image. *Feminist Media Studies, 8*(2), 163–179. http://dx.doi.org/10.1080/14680770801980547

Coleman, R. (2009). *The becoming of bodies: Girls, images, experience.* Manchester, Eng.: Manchester University Press.

Coleman, R., & Figueroa, M. (2010). Past and future perfect? Beauty, affect and hope. *Journal for Cultural Research, 14*(4), 357–373. http://dx.doi.org/10.1080/14797581003765317

Collins, P.H. (2004). *Black sexual politics: African Americans, gender, and the new racism.* New York: Routledge. http://dx.doi.org/10.4324/9780203309506

Connell, R.W. (1987). *Gender and power: Society, the person, and sexual politics.* Stanford, CA: Stanford University Press.

Connell, R.W. (2002). *Gender.* Cambridge, Eng.: Polity Press.

Connors, C., & Stalker, K. (2007). Children's experiences of disability: Pointers to a social model of childhood disability. *Disability & Society, 22*(1), 19–33. http://dx.doi.org/10.1080/09687590601056162

Conrad, P., & Schneider, J.W. (1992). *Deviance and medicalization: From badness to sickness.* Philadelphia: Temple University Press.

Coole, D., & Frost, S. (2010). Introducing the new materialisms. In D. Coole & S. Frost (Eds.), *New materialisms: Ontology, agency and politics* (pp. 1–46). Durham, NC: Duke University Press.

Cooper, J.M. & Hutchinson, D.S. (Eds.). (1997). *Plato: Complete works.* Indianapolis: Hackett.

Cooper, S.C., & Koch, P.B. (2007). "Nobody told me nothin": Communication about menstruation among low-income African-American women. *Women & Health, 46*(1), 57–78. http://dx.doi.org/10.1300/J013v46n01_05 Medline:18032175

Cooter, R. (2008). Biocitizenship. *Lancet, 372*(9651), 1725. http://dx.doi.org/10.1016/S0140-6736(08)61719-5 Medline:19013311

Cosmetic surgery: Balancing risk. (2008). CBC News, In Depth: Health. http://www.cbc.ca/news/background/health/cosmetic-surgery.html

Costos, D., Ackerman, R., & Paradis, L. (2002). Recollections of menarche: Communication between mothers and daughters regarding menstruation. *Sex Roles, 46*(1/2), 49–59. http://dx.doi.org/10.1023/A:1016037618567

Covino, D.C. (2000). Abject criticism. *Genders Online Journal, 32.* http://www.genders.org/g32/g32_covino.html

Covino, D.C. (2004). *Amending the abject body: Aesthetic makeovers in medicine and culture.* New York: State University of New York Press.

Craig, M.L. (2002). *Ain't I a beauty queen?: Black women, beauty, and the politics of race*. New York: Oxford University Press. http://dx.doi.org/10.1093/acprof: oso/9780195152623.001.0001

Crawford, R. (2004). Risk ritual and the management of control and anxiety in medical culture. *Health, 8*(4), 505–528. http://dx.doi.org/10.1177/1363459304045701 Medline:15358901

Creed, B. (1993). *The monstrous feminine: Film, feminism, psychoanalysis*. New York: Routledge.

Crow, L. (1996). Including All of Our Lives: Renewing the social model of disability. In J. Morris, (Ed.), *Encounters with strangers: Feminism and disability* (pp. 206–227). London: The Women's Press.

Currie, D.H., Kelly, D.M., & Pomerantz, S. (2006). "The geeks shall inherit the earth": Girls' agency, subjectivity and empowerment. *Journal of Youth Studies, 9*(4), 419–436. http://dx.doi.org/10.1080/13676260600914416

Daane, S.P., & Rockwell, W.B. (1999). Breast reduction techniques and outcomes: A meta-analysis. *Aesthetic Surgery Journal, 19*(4), 293–303. http://dx.doi.org/10.1053/aq.1999.v19.100635001

Dann, T.C., & Roberts, D.F. (1973). End of the trend? A 12-year study of age at menarche. *British Medical Journal, 3*(5874), 265–267. http://dx.doi.org/10.1136/bmj.3.5874.265 Medline:4723465

Davies, B. (2003). *Frogs and snails and feminist tales: Preschool children and gender*. Cresskill, NJ: Hampton Press.

Davis, K. [Kathy]. (1995). *Reshaping the female body: The dilemma of cosmetic surgery*. New York: Routledge.

Davis, K. [Kiri]. (Director & writer). (2005). A *girl like me* [Motion picture]. http://www.youtube.com/watch?v=PAOZhuRb_Q8&feature=watch_response

Davis, L.J. [Lennard]. (1995). *Enforcing normalcy: Disability, deafness, and the body*. New York: Verso Press.

Davison, K.K., & Birch, L.L. (2002). Processes linking weight status and self-concept among girls from ages 5 to 7 years. *Developmental Psychology, 38*(5), 735–748. http://dx.doi.org/10.1037/0012-1649.38.5.735 Medline:12220051

Davison, K.K., Susman, E.J., & Birch, L.L. (2003). Percent body fat at age 5 predicts earlier pubertal development among girls at age 9. *Pediatrics, 111*(4), 815–821. http://dx.doi.org/10.1542/peds.111.4.815 Medline:12671118

De Beauvoir, S. (1974). *The second sex*. New York: Vintage Books.

De Lauretis, T. (1987). *Technologies of gender: Essays on theory, film, and fiction*. Bloomington: Indiana University Press.

Deutsch, C.H. (2007). A not-so-simple plan to keep African girls in school. *New York Times*. http://www.nytimes.com

Dion, S.D. (2005). Aboriginal people and stories of Canadian history: Investigating barriers and transforming relationships. In C.E. James (Ed.), *Possibilities and limitations: Multicultural policies and programs in Canada* (pp. 34–57). Halifax, NS: Fernwood.

Dion, S.D., Johnston, K., & Rice, C. (2010). *Decolonizing our schools: Aboriginal education in the Toronto District School Board*. Toronto: York University, Faculty of Education.

Diorio, J.A., & Munro, J. (2003). What does puberty mean to adolescents? Teaching and learning about bodily development. *Sex Education, 3*(2), 119–131. http://dx.doi.org/10.1080/14681810309040

Dixon, J.R., & Ahmed, S.F. (2007). Precocious puberty. *Paediatrics and Child Health, 17*(9), 343–348. http://dx.doi.org/10.1016/j.paed.2007.06.009

Dorn, L.D., & Rotenstein, D. (2004). Early puberty in girls: The case of premature adrenarche. *Women's Health Issues, 14*(6), 177–183. http://dx.doi.org/10.1016/j.whi.2004.08.008 Medline:15589767

Dorning, A.M. (2007). Black hair dos and don'ts. *ABC News*. http://abcnews.go.com/US/story?id=3710971&page=1

Douglas, S.J. (1994). *Where the girls are: Growing up female with the mass media*. New York: Times Books.

Dow, B.J. (2003). Feminism, Miss America and media mythology. *Rhetoric and Speech Affairs, 6*(1), 127–149. http://dx.doi.org/10.1353/rap.2003.0028

Dowling, M., & Dolan, L. (2001). Families with children with disabilities: Inequalities and the social model. *Disability & Society, 16*(1), 21–35. http://dx.doi.org/10.1080/713662027

Downing, J., & Bellis, M.A. (2009). Early pubertal onset and its relationship with sexual risk taking, substance use and anti-social behaviour: A preliminary cross-sectional study. *BMC Public Health, 9*(1), 446. http://dx.doi.org/10.1186/1471-2458-9-446 Medline:19958543

Drake, S. (2005). Dangerous times. Ragged Edge Online. http://www.ragged-edge-mag.com/reviews/drakemillionbaby.html.

Dreger, A.D. (1998). *Hermaphrodites and the medical invention of sex*. Cambridge, MA: Harvard University Press.

Driscoll, C. (2002). *Girls: Feminine adolescence in popular culture and cultural theory*. New York: Columbia University Press.

DuCille, A. (1994). Dyes and dolls: Multicultural Barbie. *Differences: A Journal of Feminist Cultural Studies, 6*, 46–68.

DuCille, A. (1996). *Skin trade*. Cambridge, MA: Harvard University Press.

Duden, B. (1991). *The woman beneath the skin: A doctor's patients in eighteenth-century Germany*. Cambridge, MA: Harvard University Press.

Duncan, P.D., Ritter, P.L., Dornbusch, S.M., Gross, R.T., & Merrill Carlsmith, J. (1985). The effects of pubertal timing on body image, school behavior, and deviance. *Journal of Youth and Adolescence, 14*(3), 227–235. http://dx.doi.org/10.1007/BF02090320

Durkin, S.J., & Paxton, S.J. (2002). Predictors of vulnerability to reduced body image satisfaction and psychological wellbeing in response to exposure to idealized female media images in adolescent girls. *Journal of Psychosomatic Research, 53*(5), 995–1005. http://dx.doi.org/10.1016/S0022-3999(02)00489-0 Medline:12445589

Dworkin, A. (1974). *Woman hating*. New York: Dutton.

Dwyer, C. (2000). Negotiating diasporic identities: Young British South Asian Muslim women. *Women's Studies International Forum, 23*(4), 475–486. http://dx.doi.org/10.1016/S0277-5395(00)00110-2

Dyer, R. (1997). *White: Essays on race and culture*. New York: Routledge.

Dykewomon, E. (2002). The body politic--meditations on identity. In G. Anzaldua & A. Keating, (Eds.), *The bridge we call home: Radical visions for transformation* (pp. 450–458). New York: Routledge.

Earls, F. J., Brooks-Gunn, J., Raudenbush, S. W., & Sampson, R. J. (N.d.). *Project on human development in Chicago neighborhoods (PHDCN): Physical Development Scale, Wave 3, 2000–2002* (ICPSR 13730). Ann Arbor, MI: Inter-university Consortium for Political and Social Research.

Edwards, K. (2008). Breast reduction surgery: This common procedure eases women's discomfort caused by large breasts; here's what you need to know about it. CBC News, Health. http://www.cbc.ca/news/health/story/2008/05/15/f-health-breastreductionsurgery.html

Egan, R.D., & Hawkes, G. (2007). Producing the prurient through the pedagogy of purity: Childhood sexuality and the social purity movement. *Journal of Historical Sociology, 20*(4), 443–461. http://dx.doi.org/10.1111/j.1467-6443.2007.00319.x

Egan, R.D., & Hawkes, G. (2008). Girls, sexuality and the strange carnalities of advertisements: Deconstructing the discourse of corporate paedophilia. *Australian Feminist Studies, 23*(57), 307–322. http://dx.doi.org/10.1080/08164640802233278

Ehrenreich, B. (2001). Stamping out a dread scourge. *Time Magazine*. http://www.time.com/time/magazine/article/0,9171,159040,00.html

Ehrenreich, B., & English, D. (2005). *For her own good: Two centuries of the experts' advice to women*. New York: Anchor Books.

Eisenberg, M.E., Neumark-Sztainer, D., & Story, M. (2003). Associations of weight-based teasing and emotional well-being among adolescents. *Archives of Pediatrics & Adolescent Medicine, 157*(8), 733–738. http://dx.doi.org/10.1001/archpedi.157.8.733 Medline:12912777

Eisner, R. (2001). More research needed on early puberty. ABCnews.com. http://abcnews.go.com/Health/story?id=117639&page=1

Ellis, B.J. (2004). Timing of pubertal maturation in girls: An integrated life history approach. *Psychological Bulletin, 130*(6), 920–958. http://dx.doi.org/10.1037/0033-2909.130.6.920 Medline:15535743

Ellis, B.J., & Garber, J. (2000). Psychosocial antecedents of variation in girls' pubertal timing: Maternal depression, stepfather presence, and marital and family stress. *Child Development, 71*(2), 485–501. http://dx.doi.org/10.1111/1467-8624.00159 Medline:10834479

Emirbayer, M., & Mische, A. (1998). What is agency? *American Journal of Sociology, 103*(4), 962–1023. http://dx.doi.org/10.1086/231294

Ende, M. (2004). Discriminating tastes, discriminating "boobs." Rabble.ca. http://www.rabble.ca/news/discriminating-tastes-discriminating-boobs

Erchull, M.J., Chrisler, J.C., Gorman, J.A., & Johnston-Robledo, I. (2002). Education and advertising: A content analysis of commercially produced booklets about menstruation. *Journal of Early Adolescence, 22*(4), 455–474. http://dx.doi.org/10.1177/027243102237192

Eriksen, S., & Goering, S. (2011). A test of the agency hypothesis in women's cosmetic surgery usage. *Sex Roles, 64*(11–12), 888–901. http://dx.doi.org/10.1007/s11199-011-9952-1

Ernsberger, P. (1987). NIH consensus conference on obesity: By whom and for what? *Journal of Nutrition, 117*(6), 1164–1166. Medline:3598729

Ernsberger, P., & Koletsky, R.J. (1999). Biomedical rationale for a wellness approach to obesity: An alternative to a focus on weight loss. *Journal of Social Issues, 55*(2), 221–260. http://dx.doi.org/10.1111/0022-4537.00114

Etcoff, N., Orbach, S., Scott, J., & D'Agostino, H. (2004). *The real truth about beauty: A global report. Findings of the global study on women, beauty and well-being.* Commissioned by Dove, Unilever Corporation. http://brandent.vo.msecnd.net/o9/beet01/dove_white_paper_final.pdf

Euling, S.Y., Selevan, S.G., Pescovitz, O.H., & Skakkebaek, N.E. (2005). Environmental factors and puberty timing: Summary of an expert panel workshop. *Toxicologist, 84*, S-1.

Evans, J., & Rich, E. (2011). Body policies and body pedagogies: Every child matters in totally pedagogised schools? *Journal of Education Policy, 26*(3), 361–379. http://dx.doi.org/10.1080/02680939.2010.500399

Evans, J., Rich, E., Allwood, R., & Davies, B. (2008). Body pedagogies, P/policy, health and gender. *British Educational Research Journal, 34*(3), 387–402. http://dx.doi.org/10.1080/01411920802042812

Faden, V.B., Ruffin, B., Newes-Adeyi, G., & Chen, C. (2010). The relationship among pubertal stage, age, and drinking in adolescent boys and girls.

Journal of Child & Adolescent Substance Abuse, 19(1), 1–15. http://dx.doi.
org/10.1080/10678280903185591

Fairburn, C.G., & Brownell, K.D. (Eds.). (2002). *Eating disorders and obesity:
A comprehensive handbook* (2nd ed.). New York: Guilford Press.

Fallon, P., Katzman, M., & Wooley, S. (Eds.). (1994). *Feminist perspectives on eating disorders*. New York: Guilford Press.

Farrell-Beck, J., & Gau, C. (2002). *Uplift: The bra in America*. Philadelphia: University of Pennsylvania Press.

Fat is "terror within," Surgeon General warns. (2006). *Los Angeles Times*.
http://articles.latimes.com/2006/mar/02/nation/na-briefs2.1

Fausto-Sterling, A. (2000). *Sexing the body: Gender politics and the construction of
sexuality*. New York: Basic Books.

Federation of Feminist Women's Health Centers. (1981). A *new view of a
woman's body*. New York: Simon & Schuster.

Felski, R. (2006). "Because it is beautiful": New feminist perspectives on beauty.
Feminist Theory, 7(2), 273–282. http://dx.doi.org/10.1177/1464700106064424

Feminine hygiene products market to reach 13 billion dollars by 2010, according to new report by Global Industry Analysts, Inc. (2008). Medical News
Today. http://www.medicalnewstoday.com/articles/104288.php

Ferguson, A.A. (2001). *Bad boys: Public schools in the making of black masculinity*.
Ann Arbor: University of Michigan Press.

Ferrante, J. (1988). Biomedical versus cultural constructions of abnormality: The case of idiopathic hirsutism in the United States. *Culture, Medicine
and Psychiatry, 12*(2), 219–238. http://dx.doi.org/10.1007/BF00116859
Medline:3044697

Fine, M., & McClelland, S.I. (2006). Sexuality education and desire: Still missing after all these years. *Harvard Educational Review, 76*, 297–338.

Fingerson, L. (2005). Agency and the body in adolescent menstrual talk. *Childhood, 12*(1), 91–110. http://dx.doi.org/10.1177/0907568205049894

1st Canadian Summit on Weight Bias and Discrimination a Success. (2011).
Canadian Obesity Network [Press Release]. Retrieved from http://www.
obesitynetwork.ca/page.aspx?page=2483&app=182&cat1=
457&tp=12&lk=no&menu=37

Fisher, S. (1990). The evolution of psychological concepts about the body. In
T. Cash & T. Pruzinsky (Eds.), *Body images: Development, deviance, and change*
(pp. 3–20). New York: The Guilford Press.

Foege, W.H., & Centers for Disease Control and Prevention (CDC). (2006).
CDC's 60th anniversary: Director's perspective – William H. Foege,
M.D., M.P.H., 1977–1983. *Morbidity and Mortality Weekly Report, 55*(39),
1071–1074. www.cdc.gov/mmwr/preview/mmwrhtml/mm5539a4.htm
Medline:17021593

Foucault, M. (1979). *Discipline and punish: The birth of the prison*. New York: Vintage Books.

Foucault, M. (1980). *The history of sexuality* (R. Hurley, Trans.). New York: Vintage Books.

Foucault, M. (1994). *The birth of the clinic: An archaeology of medical perception*. New York: Vintage Books.

Foucault, M., & Gordon, C. (1980). *Power/knowledge: Selected interviews and other writings 1972–1977*. New York: Pantheon Books.

Foucault, M., Marchetti, V., Salomoni, A., & Davidson, A.I. (2003). *Abnormal: Lectures at the Collège de France, 1974–1975*. New York: Picador.

Frank, G. (2000). *Venus on wheels: Two decades of dialogue on disability, biography, and being female in America*. Berkeley: University of California Press.

Frankenberg, R. (2001). The mirage of an unmarked whiteness. In B.B. Rasmussen, E. Klinenberg, I.J. Nexica, & M. Wray (Eds.), *The making and unmaking of whiteness* (pp. 72–96). Durham, NC: Duke University Press.

Fredrickson, B.L., & Harrison, K. (2005). Throwing like a girl: Self-objectification predicts adolescent girls' motor performance. *Journal of Sport and Social Issues, 29*(1), 79–101. http://dx.doi.org/10.1177/0193723504269878

Fredrickson, B.L., & Roberts, T.A. (1997). Objectification theory: Toward understanding women's lived experiences and mental health risks. *Psychology of Women Quarterly, 21*(2), 173–206. http://dx.doi.org/10.1111/j.1471-6402.1997.tb00108.x

Freedman, E. (2002). *No turning back: The history of feminism and the future of women*. New York: Ballantine Books.

Freeman, J.G., King, M.A., & Pickett, W. (with Craig, W., Elgar, F., Janssen, I., & Klinger, D.). (2011). *The health of Canada's young people: A mental health focus*. Ottawa, ON: Public Health Agency of Canada. http://dx.doi.org/10.1037/e614952012-001

Frost, L. (2001). *Young women and the body: A feminist sociology*. New York: Palgrave. http://dx.doi.org/10.1057/9780333985410

Frueh, J. (2001). *Monster/beauty: Building the body of love*. Berkeley: University of California Press. http://dx.doi.org/10.2307/1358957

Fullagar, S. (2009). Governing healthy family lifestyles through discourses of risk and responsibility. In J. Wright & V. Harwood (Eds.), *Biopolitics and the "obesity epidemic": Governing bodies* (pp. 108–126). New York: Routledge.

Galen, & May, M.T. (1968). *Galen on the usefulness of the parts of the body*. Ithaca, NY: Cornell University Press.

Gallagher, C.A. (2003). Color-blind privilege: The social and political functions of erasing the color line in post race America. *Race, Gender & Class, 10*(4), 22–37.

Gard, M., & Wright, J. (2005). *Obesity epidemic: Science, morality and ideology*. New York: Taylor & Francis.

Garfinkel, P. E., & Garner, D. M. (1982). *Anorexia nervosa: A multidimensional perspective*. New York: Brunner/Mazel.

Garland-Thomson, R. (1997). *Extraordinary bodies: Figuring physical disability in American culture and literature*. New York: Columbia University Press.

Garland-Thomson, R. (2007). Shape structures story: Fresh and feisty stories about disability. *Narrative, 15*(1), 113–123. http://dx.doi.org/10.1353/nar.2007.0005

Garland-Thomson, R. (2009). *Staring: How we look*. Toronto: Oxford University Press.

Ge, X., Conger, R.D., & Elder, G.H., Jr. (1996). Coming of age too early: Pubertal influences on girls' vulnerability to psychological distress. *Child Development, 67*(6), 3386–3400. http://dx.doi.org/10.2307/1131784 Medline:9071784

George, L. (2005). The end of the period. *Maclean's*. http://www.macleans.ca/article.jsp?content=20051213_117621_117621

Gill, R. (2007a). Critical respect: The difficulties and dilemmas of agency and "choice" for feminism: A reply to Duits and van Zoonen. *European Journal of Women's Studies, 14*(1), 69–80. http://dx.doi.org/10.1177/13505068070 72318

Gill, R. (2007b). Postfeminist media culture: Elements of a sensibility. *European Journal of Cultural Studies, 10*(2), 147–166. http://dx.doi.org/10.1177/136754 9407075898

Gill, R. (2008). Empowerment/sexism: Figuring female sexual agency in contemporary advertising. *Feminism & Psychology, 18*(1), 35–60. http://dx.doi.org/10.1177/0959353507084950

Gill, R. (2009). Beyond the "sexualization of culture" thesis: An intersectional analysis of "sixpacks," "midriffs" and "hot lesbians" in advertising. *Sexualities, 12*(2), 137–160. http://dx.doi.org/10.1177/1363460708100916

Gillen, M., & Lefkowitz, E.S. (2011). Body size perceptions in racially/ethnically diverse men and women: Implications for body image and self-esteem. *North American Journal of Psychology, 13*(3) 447-468.

Gillespie-Sells, K., Hill, M., & Robbins, B. (1998). *She dances to different drums: Research into disabled women's sexuality*. London, Eng.: King's Fund.

Gilligan, C. (1982). *In a different voice: Psychological theory and women's development*. Cambridge, MA: Harvard University Press.

Gilman, S.L. (1989). *Sexuality: An illustrated history. Representing the sexual in medicine and culture from the Middle Ages to the age of AIDS*. New York: Wiley.

Gimlin, D. (2006). The absent body project: Cosmetic surgery as a response to bodily dys-appearance. *Sociology, 40*(4), 699–716. http://dx.doi.org/10.1177/0038038506065156

Gimlin, D.L. (2002). *Body work: Beauty and self-image in American culture*. Berkeley: University of California Press.

Glenn, E.N. (Ed.). (2009). *Shades of difference: Why skin color matters*. Palo Alto, CA: Stanford University Press.

Gluckman, P.D., & Hanson, M.A. (2006). Evolution, development and timing of puberty. *Trends in Endocrinology and Metabolism, 17*(1), 7–12. http://dx.doi.org/10.1016/j.tem.2005.11.006 Medline:16311040

Goffman, E. (1963). *Stigma: Notes on the management of spoiled identity*. Englewood Cliffs, NJ: Prentice Hall.

Golub, M.S., Collman, G.W., Foster, P.M., Kimmel, C.A., Rajpert-De Meyts, E., Reiter, E.O., et al. (2008). Public health implications of altered puberty timing. *Pediatrics, 121*(Suppl 3), S218–S230. http://dx.doi.org/10.1542/peds.2007-1813G Medline:18245514

Gonick, M. (2006). Sugar and spice and something more than nice? Queer girls and transformations of social exclusion. In Y. Jiwani, C. Steenbergen, & C. Mitchell (Eds.), *Girlhood: Redefining the limits* (pp. 122–137). Montreal: Black Rose Books.

Gonzalez, M.C. (2010). *Gender now coloring book: A learning adventure for children and adults*. San Francisco: Reflection Press.

Goodley, D., & Lawthom, R. (2006). Disability studies and psychology: New allies? In D. Goodley & R. Lawthom (Eds.), *Disability and psychology: Critical introductions and reflections* (pp. 1–6). New York: Palgrave Macmillan.

Goodley, D., & Runswick-Cole, K. (2011). Something in the air? Creativity, culture and community. *RiDE: The Journal of Applied Theatre and Performance, 16*, 75–91.

Goodley, D., & Tregaskis, C. (2006). Storying disability and impairment: Retrospective accounts of disabled family life. *Qualitative Health Research, 16*(5), 630–646. http://dx.doi.org/10.1177/1049732305285840 Medline:16611969

Gould, S.J. (1992). *The panda's thumb: More reflections in natural history*. New York: W.W. Norton.

Gould, S.J. (1993). *The mismeasure of man*. New York: Norton.

Graaf, R., & Officinâ Hackiana. (1672). *Regneri de Graaf de mulierum organis generationi inservientibus tractatus novus: Demonstrans tam homines & animalia caetera omnia: quae vivipara dicuntur, haud minus quàm ovipara ab ovo originem ducere: ad Cosmum III, magnum Etruriae ducem*. Lugduni Batav: Ex Officinâ Hackiana.

Graber, J.A., Brooks-Gunn, J., & Warren, M.P. (1995). The antecedents of menarcheal age: Heredity, family environment, and stressful life events. *Child Development, 66*(2), 346–359. http://dx.doi.org/10.2307/1131582 Medline:7750370

Graber, J.A., Brooks-Gunn, J., & Warren, M.P. (2006). Pubertal effects on adjustment in girls: Moving from demonstrating effects to identifying pathways. *Journal of Youth and Adolescence, 35*(3), 391–401. http://dx.doi.org/10.1007/s10964-006-9049-2

Graber, J.A., Lewinsohn, P.M., Seeley, J.R., & Brooks-Gunn, J. (1997). Is psychopathology associated with the timing of pubertal development? *Journal of the American Academy of Child and Adolescent Psychiatry, 36*(12), 1768–1776. http://dx.doi.org/10.1097/00004583-199712000-00026 Medline:9401339

Greene, S. (2003). *The psychological development of girls and women: Rethinking change in time.* New York: Routlege.

Greer, G. (1972). *The female eunuch.* London, Eng.: Paladin.

Gremillion, H. (2003). *Feeding anorexia: Gender and power at a treatment center.* Durham, NC: Duke University Press.

Grogan, S. (2008). *Body image: Understanding body dissatisfaction in men, women, and children.* New York: Routledge.

Grosz, E.A. (1994). *Volatile bodies: Toward a corporeal feminism.* Bloomington: Indiana University Press.

Grosz, E.A. (1999). Becoming ... an introduction. In E.A. Grosz (Ed.), *Becomings: Explorations in time, memory, and futures* (pp. 1–11). Ithaca, NY: Cornell University Press.

Grosz, E.A. (2008). Darwin and feminism: Preliminary investigations for a possible alliance. In S. Alaimo & S. Hekman (Eds.), *Material feminisms* (pp. 23–51). Bloomington: Indiana University Press.

Grumbach, M.M., & Styne, D.M. (2003). Puberty: Ontogeny, neuroendocrinology, physiology, and disorders. In P.R. Larsen, H.M. Kronenberg, S. Melmed, & K.S. Polonsky (Eds.), *Williams textbook of endocrinology* (pp. 1115–1286). Philadelphia: Saunders.

Guerrero, L. (2009). Can the subaltern shop? The commodification of difference in the Bratz dolls. *Cultural Studies ↔ Critical Methodologies, 9*(2), 186–196. http://dx.doi.org/10.1177/1532708608325939

Gunther, D. F., & Diekema, D. S. (2006). Attenuating growth in children with profound developmental disability: A new approach to an old dilemma. *Archives of Pediatrics & Adolescent Medicine, 160*(10), 1013.

Gurian, M. (1996). *The wonder of boys: What parents, mentors and educators can do to shape boys into exceptional men.* New York: Jeremy Tarcher / Putman.

Haiken, E. (1997). *Venus envy: A history of cosmetic surgery.* Baltimore, MD: Johns Hopkins University Press.

Halberstam, J. (1998). *Female masculinity.* Durham, NC: Duke University Press.

Hall, G.S. (1904). *Youth: Its education, regimen, and hygiene* [Project Gutenberg version]. http://www.gutenberg.org/ebooks/9173

Hall, K. (2011). *Feminist disability studies*. Bloomington: Indiana University Press.

Hall, S. (Ed.). (2002). *Representation: Cultural representations and signifying practices*. London, Eng.: Sage.

Halse, C. (2009). Bio-citizenship: Virtue discourses and the birth of the bio-citizen. In J. Wright & V. Harwood (Eds.), *Biopolitics and the "obesity epidemic": Governing bodies* (pp. 45–59). New York: Routledge.

Hammonds, E.M. (1999). Toward a genealogy of Black female sexuality: The problematic of silence. In J. Price & M. Shildrick (Eds.), *Feminist theory and the body: A reader* (pp. 93–104). New York: Routledge.

Hammonds, E.M. (2001). Black (w)holes and the geometry of Black female sexuality. In K.-K. Bhavnani (Ed.), *Feminism and "race"* (pp. 379–393). New York: Oxford University Press.

Handa, A. (2003). *Of silk saris and mini-skirts: South Asian girls walk the tightrope of culture*. Toronto: Women's Press.

Harding, K. (2008). The illustrated BMI categories project [Web log post]. http://kateharding.net/bmi-illustrated/

Harris-Perry, M. (2009). Bad Black mothers [Web log post]. *The Nation*. http://www.thenation.com/blog/bad-black-mothers.

Harrison, M.S., & Thomas, K.M. (2009). The hidden prejudice in selection: A research investigation on skin color bias. *Journal of Applied Social Psychology, 39*(1), 134–168. http://dx.doi.org/10.1111/j.1559-1816.2008.00433.x

Harwood, V. (2009). Theorizing biopedagogies. In J. Wright & V. Harwood (Eds.), *Biopolitics and the "obesity epidemic": Governing bodies* (pp. 16–30). New York: Routledge.

Hassouneh-Phillips, D., McNeff, E., Powers, L., & Curry, M.A. (2005). Invalidation: A central process underlying maltreatment of women with disabilities. *Women & Health, 41*(1), 33–50. http://dx.doi.org/10.1300/J013v41n01_03 Medline:16048867

Health Canada. (2002). *A report on mental illnesses in Canada*. Ottawa, ON: Author.

Hearn, A. (2007). Shake yo' tail feathers: Watching and performing gender. Women's Studies 100: An Introduction to Women's Studies. Lecture conducted from Trent University, Peterborough, ON.

Heinberg, L. J. (1996). Theories of body image disturbance. In J. K. Thompson (Ed.), *Body image, eating disorders and obesity: An integrative guide* (pp. 27–48).Washington, DC: American Psychological Association.

Heiss, S.N. (2011). Locating the bodies of women and disability in definitions of beauty: An analysis of Dove's Campaign for Real Beauty. *Disability Studies Quarterly, 31*(1). http://dsq-sds.org/article/view/1367/1497

Herman-Giddens, M.E., Slora, E.J., Wasserman, R.C., Bourdony, C.J., Bhapkar, M.V., Koch, G.G., & Hasemeier, C.M. (1997). Secondary sexual characteristics and menses in young girls seen in office practice: A study from the Pediatric Research in Office Settings network. *Pediatrics, 99*(4), 505–512. http://dx.doi.org/10.1542/peds.99.4.505 Medline:9093289

Herzig, R.M. (2000). The woman beneath the hair: Treating hypertrichosis, 1870–1930. *NWSA Journal, 12*(3), 50–66. http://dx.doi.org/10.2979/NWS.2000.12.3.50 Medline:19530370

Hesse-Biber, S., Leavy, P., Quinn, C.E., & Zoino, J. (2006). The mass marketing of disordered eating and eating disorders: The social psychology of women, thinness and culture. *Women's Studies International Forum, 29*(2), 208–224. http://dx.doi.org/10.1016/j.wsif.2006.03.007

Heyes, C.J., & Jones, M. (2009). Cosmetic surgery in the age of gender. In C.J. Heyes & M. Jones (Eds.), *Cosmetic surgery: A feminist primer* (pp. 1–17). Farnham, Eng.: Ashgate.

Hill, M.E. (2002). Skin color and the perceptions of attractiveness among African Americans: Does gender make a difference? *Social Psychology Quarterly, 65*(1), 77–91. http://dx.doi.org/10.2307/3090169

Hill, M.S. (2010). Gazing at objectification theory through a social constructionist lens. In J.D. Raskin, S.K. Bridges, & R.A. Neimeyer (Eds.), *Studies in meaning 4: Constructivist perspectives on theory, practice, and social justice* (pp. 205–226). New York: Pace University Press.

Hird, M.J. (2003a). New feminist sociological directions. *Canadian Journal of Sociology, 28*(4), 447–462. http://dx.doi.org/10.2307/3341837

Hird, M.J. (2003b). Thinking about "sex" in education. *Sex Education, 3*(3), 187–200. http://dx.doi.org/10.1080/1468181032000119087

Hird, M.J. (2004). *Sex, gender and science*. New York: Palgrave Macmillan. http://dx.doi.org/10.1057/9780230510715

Hird, M.J. (2006). Animal transex. *Australian Feminist Studies, 21*(49), 35–50. http://dx.doi.org/10.1080/08164640500470636

Hirsch, H.J., Gillis, D., Strich, D., Chertin, B., Farkas, A., Lindenberg, T., Gelber, H., & Spitz, I.M. (2005). The histrelin implant: A novel treatment for central precocious puberty. *Pediatrics, 116*(6), e798–e802. http://dx.doi.org/10.1542/peds.2005-0538 Medline:16322137

Hirsute. (N.d.). In *Collins English Dictionary* (10th ed.). http://dictionary.reference.com/browse/hirsute

Hiscott, G. (2004). Bratz the new queen of the fashion-doll world as Barbie is toppled. *The Independent*. http://www.independent.co.uk

Hitchcock, C.L., & Prior, J.C. (2003). *Menstrual Suppression*. Panel delivered at the Fifteenth Biennial Meeting of the Society for Menstrual Cycle Research, Pittsburgh, PA. http://menstruationresearch.org

Hitchcock, C.L., & Prior, J.C. (2004). Evidence about extending the duration of oral contraceptive use to suppress menstruation. *Women's Health*

Issues, 14(6), 201–211. http://dx.doi.org/10.1016/j.whi.2004.08.005 Medline:15589770

Hobson, J. (2005). *Venus in the dark: Blackness and beauty in popular culture.* New York: Routledge.

Hogan, M.I. (2006). Making contact: Teaching, bodies, and the ethics of multiculturalism. *Review of Education, Pedagogy & Cultural Studies, 28*(3–4), 355–366. http://dx.doi.org/10.1080/10714410600873241

Hohle, R. (2009). The body and citizenship in social movement research: Embodied performances and the deracialized self in the Black civil rights movement 1961–1965. *Sociological Quarterly, 50*(2), 283–307. http://dx.doi.org/10.1111/j.1533-8525.2009.01141.x

Holliday, R., & Sanchez Taylor, J. (2006). Aesthetic surgery as false beauty. *Feminist Theory, 7*(2), 179–195. http://dx.doi.org/10.1177/1464700106064418

Hope, C. (1982). Caucasian female body hair and American culture. *Journal of American Culture, 5*(1), 93–99. http://dx.doi.org/10.1111/j.1542-734X.1982.0501_93.x

Hossain, A. (2008). The color complex: Is the fixation really fair? Sapna Magazine. http://sapnamagazine.com

Hotchkiss, A.K., Rider, C.V., Blystone, C.R., Wilson, V.S., Hartig, P.C., Ankley, G.T., Foster, P.M., Gray, C.L., & Gray, L.E. (2008). Fifteen years after "Wingspread" – environmental endocrine disrupters and human and wildlife health: Where we are today and where we need to go. *Toxicological Sciences, 105*(2), 235–259. http://dx.doi.org/10.1093/toxsci/kfn030 Medline:18281716

Houppert, K. (1999). *The curse. Confronting the last unmentionable taboo: Menstruation.* New York: Farrar, Straus and Giroux.

Howze, J. (2005). Miss education. *The Guardian.* http://www.guardian.co.uk

Hoyt, A., & Andrist, L. (2003). *Menstrual suppression.* Panel delivered at the Fifteenth Biennial Meeting of the Society for Menstrual Cycle Research, Pittsburgh, PA. http://menstruationresearch.org

Hubbard, R. (1990). *The politics of women's biology.* New Brunswick, NJ: Rutgers University Press.

Hughes, C. (2012). Seeing blindness in children's picturebooks. *Journal of Literary & Cultural Disability Studies, 6*(1), 35–51. http://dx.doi.org/10.3828/jlcds.2012.3

Hughes, D. (2003). Correlates of African American and Latino parents' messages to children about ethnicity and race: A comparative study of racial socialization. *American Journal of Community Psychology, 31*(1–2), 15–33. http://dx.doi.org/10.1023/A:1023066418688 Medline:12741687

Hughes, M., & Hertel, B.R. (1990). The significance of color remains: A study of life chances, mate selection, and ethnic consciousness among Black Americans. *Social Forces, 68*, 1105–1120.

Hunter, M.L. (1998). Colorstruck: Skin color stratification in the lives of African American women. *Sociological Inquiry, 68*(4), 517–535. http://dx.doi.org/10.1111/j.1475-682X.1998.tb00483.x

Hunter, M.L. (2002). "If you're light you're alright": Light skin color as social capital for women of color. *Gender & Society, 16*, 175–193.

Hunter, M.L. (2005). *Race, gender, and the politics of skin tone.* New York: Routledge.

Hunter, M.L. (2007). The persistent problem of colorism: Skin tone, status, and inequality. *Social Compass, 1*(1), 237–254. http://dx.doi.org/10.1111/j.1751-9020.2007.00006.x

Hyde, J.S., & McKinley, N.M. (1997). Gender differences in cognition: Results from meta-analyses. In P.J. Caplan, M. Crawford, J.S. Hyde, & J.T. Richardson (Eds.), *Gender differences in human cognition* (pp. 30–51). New York: Oxford University Press. http://dx.doi.org/10.1093/acprof:oso/9780195112917.003.0002

Hyde, J.S., Rosenberg, B.G., & Behrman, J.A. (1977). Tomboyism. *Psychology of Women Quarterly, 2*(1), 73–75. http://dx.doi.org/10.1111/j.1471-6402.1977.tb00574.x

Iannantuono, A.C., & Tylka, T.L. (2012). Interpersonal and intrapersonal links to body appreciation in college women: An exploratory model. *Body Image, 9*(2), 227–235. http://dx.doi.org/10.1016/j.bodyim.2012.01.004 Medline:22401976

Ibáñez, L., Ong, K., Valls, C., Marcos, M.V., Dunger, D.B., & de Zegher, F. (2006). Metformin treatment to prevent early puberty in girls with precocious pubarche. *Journal of Clinical Endocrinology and Metabolism, 91*(8), 2888–2891. http://dx.doi.org/10.1210/jc.2006-0336 Medline:16684823

Ibanga, I. (2009). Obama's choice to bare arms causes uproar. Good Morning America. http://abcnews.go.com/GMA/story?id=6986019&page=1

Ikeda, J.P., Crawford, P.B., & Woodward-Lopez, G. (2006). BMI screening in schools: Helpful or harmful. *Health Education Research, 21*(6), 761–769. http://dx.doi.org/10.1093/her/cyl144 Medline:17093140

International Society of Aesthetic Plastic Surgery. (2010). *Biennial global survey. ISAPS international survey on aesthetic/cosmetic procedures performed in 2009.* www.yourplasticsurgeryguide.com/trends/2010-isaps-biennial-study.htm

Irvine, J.M. (1994). Cultural differences and adolescent sexualities. In J.M. Irvine (Ed.), *Sexual cultures and the construction of adolescent identities* (pp. 3–28). Philadelphia: Temple University Press.

Irvine, J.M. (2002). *Talk about sex: The battles over sex education in the United States.* Berkeley: University of California Press.

Irving, L.M. (2000). Promoting size acceptance in elementary school children: The EDAP puppet program. *Eating Disorders, 8*(3), 221–232. http://dx.doi.org/10.1080/10640260008251229

Ittyerah, M., & Kumar, N. (2007). The actual and ideal self-concept in disabled children, adolescents and adults. *Psychology and Developing Societies 19*(1), 81–112.

Jacobson, S.H., & McLay, L.A. (2006). The economic impact of obesity on automobile fuel consumption. *Engineering Economist, 51*(4), 307–323. http://dx.doi.org/10.1080/00137910600987586

James, A. (1995). On being a child: The self, the group, and the category. In A. Cohen & N. Rapport (Eds.), *Questions of consciousness* (pp. 60–76). London: Routledge. http://dx.doi.org/10.4324/9780203449486_chapter_3

James, A. (2000). Embodied being(s): Understanding the self and the body in childhood. In A. Prout (Ed.), *The body, childhood, and society* (pp. 19–37). Basingstoke, Eng.: Palgrave Macmillan.

James, C.E., & Wood, M. (2005). Multicultural education in Canada. In C.E. James (Ed.), *Possibilities and limitations: Multicultural policies and programs in Canada* (pp. 93–107). Halifax, NS: Fernwood.

Jansen, C. (2005). Canadian multiculturalism. In C.E. James (Ed.), *Possibilities and limitations: Multicultural policies and programs in Canada* (pp. 21–33). Halifax, NS: Fernwood.

Jeffreys, S. (2005). *Beauty and misogyny: Harmful cultural practices in the West.* New York: Routledge.

Jenkins, R. (1996). *Social identity.* London, Eng.: Routledge.

Jhally, S. (2009). Codes of gender [Online lecture]. http://www.sutjhally.com/courses/comm387/clickheretogotothe/

Jiwani, Y. (2006). Racialized violence and girls and young women of colour. In Y. Jiwani, C. Steenbergen, & C. Mitchell (Eds.), *Girlhood: Redefining the limits* (pp. 70–88). Montreal: Black Rose Books.

Johnson, D.B., Gerstein, D.E., Evans, A.E., & Woodward-Lopez, G. (2006). Preventing obesity: A life cycle perspective. *Journal of the American Dietetic Association, 106*(1), 97–102. http://dx.doi.org/10.1016/j.jada.2005.09.048 Medline:16390672

Johnston, J., & Taylor, J. (2008). Feminist consumerism and fat activists: A comparative study of grassroots activism and the Dove Real Beauty Campaign. *Signs, 33*(4), 941–966. http://dx.doi.org/10.1086/528849

Johnston-Robledo, I., & Barnack, J. (2003). *Menstrual suppression.* Panel delivered at the Fifteenth Biennial Meeting of the Society for Menstrual Cycle Research, Pittsburgh, PA. http://menstruationresearch.org

Jones, J.M., Bennett, S., Olmsted, M.P., Lawson, M.L., & Rodin, G. (2001). Disordered eating attitudes and behaviours in teenaged girls: A school-based study. *Canadian Medical Association Journal, 165*(5), 547–552. Medline:11563206

Jones, T. (2000). Shades of brown: The law of skin color. *Duke Law Journal, 49*(6), 1487–1557. http://dx.doi.org/10.2307/1373052

Jordan, J. (2010). *Relational-cultural therapy.* Washington: American Psychological Association.

Jutel, A. (2006). The emergence of overweight as a disease entity: Measuring up normality. *Social Science & Medicine, 63*(9), 2268–2276. http://dx.doi.org/10.1016/j.socscimed.2006.05.028 Medline:16846671

Jutel, A. (2009). Doctor's orders: Diagnosis, medical authority and the exploitation of the fat body. In J. Wright & V. Harwood (Eds.), *Biopolitics and the "obesity epidemic": Governing bodies* (pp. 60–77). New York: Routledge.

Juul, A., Teilmann, G., Scheike, T., Hertel, N.T., Holm, K., Laursen, E.M., Main, K.M., & Skakkebaek, N.E. (2006). Pubertal development in Danish children: Comparison of recent European and US data. *International Journal of Andrology, 29*(1), 247–255; discussion 286–290. http://dx.doi.org/10.1111/j.1365-2605.2005.00556.x Medline:16466546

Kafer, A. (2013). *Feminist, queer, crip.* Bloomington, IN: Indiana University Press.

Kantor, J. (2009). Michelle Obama goes sleeveless, again [Web log post]. *New York Times.* http://thecaucus.blogs.nytimes.com/2009/02/25/michelle-obama-goes-sleeveless-again/

Kaplan, K. (2007). FDA approves first pill to stop periods: The birth-control drug halts menstruation, but breakthrough bleeding occurred in trials. *Los Angeles Times.* http://articles.latimes.com/2007/may/23/science/sci-pill23

Kaplowitz, P.B. (2006). Pubertal development in girls: Secular trends. *Current Opinion in Obstetrics & Gynecology, 18*(5), 487–491. http://dx.doi.org/10.1097/01.gco.0000242949.02373.09 Medline:16932041

Kaplowitz, P.B., Slora, E.J., Wasserman, R.C., Pedlow, S.E., & Herman-Giddens, M.E. (2001). Earlier onset of puberty in girls: Relation to increased body mass index and race. *Pediatrics, 108*(2), 347–353. http://dx.doi.org/10.1542/peds.108.2.347 Medline:11483799

Kaspin, D.D. (2002). Conclusion: Signifying power in Africa. In P.S. Landau & D.D. Kaspin (Eds.), *Images and empire: Visuality in colonial and postcolonial Africa* (pp. 320–336). Berkeley: University of California Press.

Keith, L. (1996). Encounters with strangers: The public's responses to disabled women and how this affects our sense of self. In J. Morris (Ed.), *Encounters with strangers: Feminism and disability* (pp. 69–88). London, Eng.: Women's Press.

Keith, V.M., & Herring, C. (1991). Skin tone stratification in the Black community. *American Journal of Sociology, 97*(3), 760–778. http://dx.doi.org/10.1086/229819

Kelly, J. (1997). *Under the gaze: Learning to be Black in white society.* Halifax, NS: Fernwood.

Kennedy, M. (1996). Sexual abuse and disabled children. In J. Morris (Ed.), *Encounters with strangers: Feminism and disability* (pp. 116–134). London, Eng.: Women's Press.

Kenny, L.D. (2000). Doing my homework: The autoethnography of a white teenage girl. In F.W. Twine & J.W. Warren (Eds.), *Racing research, researching race: Methodological dilemmas in critical race studies* (pp. 111–134). New York: New York University Press.

Kessler, S.J., & McKenna, W. (2000). Gender construction in everyday life: Transsexualism. *Feminism & Psychology, 10*(1), 11–29. http://dx.doi.org/10.1177/0959353500010001003

Kimmel, M.S. (2004). *The gendered society.* New York: Oxford University Press.

Kissling, E.A. (2002). On the rag on screen: Menarche in film and television. *Sex Roles, 46*(1/2), 5–12. http://dx.doi.org/10.1023/A:1016029416750

Kissling, E.A. (2006). *Capitalizing on the curse: The business of menstruation.* Boulder, CO: Lynne Rienner.

Kittay, E.F. (2011). Forever small: The strange case of Ashley X. *Hypatia, 26*(3), 610–631.

Knauss, C., Paxton, S.J., & Alsaker, F.D. (2008). Body dissatisfaction in adolescent boys and girls: Objectified body consciousness, internalization of the media body ideal and perceived pressure from media. *Sex Roles, 59*(9–10), 633–643. http://dx.doi.org/10.1007/s11199-008-9474-7

Koggel, C. (2004). Concepts of beauty: A feminist philosopher thinks about paradigms and consequences. Beauty Symposium. http://serendip.bryn mawr.edu/local/scisoc/beauty/koggeldoc.html

Krane, V., Choi, P., Baird, S., Aimar, C., & Kauer, K. (2004). Living the paradox: Female athletes negotiate femininity and muscularity. *Sex Roles, 50*(5/6), 315–329.

Kretsedemas, P. (2010). "But she's not Black!" Viewer interpretations of "Angry Black women" on prime time TV. *Journal of African American Studies, 14*(2), 149–170. http://dx.doi.org/10.1007/s12111-009-9116-3

Kristeva, J. (1982). *Powers of horror: An essay on abjection.* New York: Columbia University Press.

Kudlick, C.J. (2005). Disability history, power, and rethinking the idea of "the other." *Publications of the Modern Language Association, 120*, 557–561.

Kunz, G.J., Klein, K.O., Clemons, R.D., Gottschalk, M.E., & Jones, K.L. (2004). Virilization of young children after topical androgen use by their parents. *Pediatrics, 114*(1), 282–284. http://dx.doi.org/10.1542/peds.114.1.282 Medline:15231947

Kurien, P. (1999). Gendered ethnicity: Creating a Hindu Indian identity in the United States. *American Behavioral Scientist, 42*(4), 648–670. http://dx.doi. org/10.1177/00027649921954408

Labre, M. P. (2002). The Brazilian wax: New hairlessness norm for women? *Journal of Communication Inquiry, 26*(2), 113-132.

Lalonde, R.N., Jones, J.M., & Stroink, M.L. (2008). Racial identity, racial attitudes, and race socialization among Black Canadian parents. *Canadian Journal of Behavioural Science, 40*(3), 129–139. http://dx.doi.org/10.1037/0008-400X.40.3.129

Lane, R. (2009). Trans as bodily becoming: Rethinking the biological as diversity, not dichotomy. *Hypatia, 24*(3), 136–157. http://dx.doi.org/10.1111/j.1527-2001.2009.01049.x

Lanza, S.T., & Collins, L.M. (2002). Pubertal timing and the onset of substance use in females during early adolescence. *Prevention Science, 3*(1), 69–82. http://dx.doi.org/10.1023/A:1014675410947 Medline:12002560

Laqueur, T.W. (1990). *Making sex: Body and gender from the Greeks to Freud.* Cambridge, MA: Harvard University Press.

Larkin, J., & Rice, C. (2005). Beyond "healthy eating" and "healthy weights": Harassment and the health curriculum in middle schools. *Body Image, 2*(3), 219–232. http://dx.doi.org/10.1016/j.bodyim.2005.07.001 Medline:18089190

Latner, J.D., & Wilson, R.E. (2011). Obesity and body image in adulthood. In T.F. Cash & L. Smolak (Eds.), *Body image: A handbook of science, practice and prevention* (pp. 189–197). Second ed. New York: The Guilford Press.

Lau, D.C., & Obesity Canada Clinical Practice Guidelines Steering Committee and Expert Panel. (2007). Synopsis of the 2006 Canadian clinical practice guidelines on the management and prevention of obesity in adults and children. *Canadian Medical Association Journal, 176*(8), 1103–1106. http://dx.doi. org/10.1503/cmaj.070306 Medline:17420493

Lawrence, R.G. (2004). Framing obesity: The evolution of news discourse on a public health issue. *Harvard International Journal of Press/Politics, 9*(3), 56–75. http://dx.doi.org/10.1177/1081180X04266581

Lawrence, J.W. & Fauerbach, J.A. (2011). Body image issues associated with burn injuries. In T.F. Cash & L. Smolak (Eds.), *Body image: A handbook of science, practice and prevention* (pp. 358–365). Second ed. New York: The Guilford Press.

Leahy, D. (2009). Disgusting pedagogies. In J. Wright & V. Harwood (Eds.), *Biopolitics and the "obesity epidemic": Governing bodies* (pp. 172–182). New York: Routledge.

LeBesco, K. (2004). *Revolting bodies? The struggle to redefine fat identity*. Boston: University of Massachusetts Press.

Lee, J. [Janet]. (1994). Menarche and the (hetero)sexualization of the female body. *Gender & Society, 8*(3), 343–362. http://dx.doi.org/10.1177/089124394008003004

Lee, J. [Janet]. (1997). Never innocent: Breasted experiences in women's bodily narratives of puberty. *Feminism & Psychology, 7*(4), 453–474. http://dx.doi.org/10.1177/0959353597074002

Lee, J. [Janet]. (2008). "A Kotex and a smile": Mothers and daughters at menarche. *Journal of Family Issues, 29*(10), 1325–1347. http://dx.doi.org/10.1177/0192513X08316117

Lee, J. [Janet]. (2009). Bodies at menarche: Stories of shame, concealment, and sexual maturation. *Sex Roles, 60*(9–10), 615–627. http://dx.doi.org/10.1007/s11199-008-9569-1

Lee, J. [Janet], & Sasser-Coen, J. (1996). *Blood stories: Menarche and the politics of the female body in contemporary U.S. society*. New York: Routledge.

Lee, J.M., Appugliese, D., Kaciroti, N., Corwyn, R.F., Bradley, R.H., & Lumeng, J.C. (2007). Weight status in young girls and the onset of puberty. *Pediatrics, 119*(3), e624–e630. http://dx.doi.org/10.1542/peds.2006-2188 Medline:17332182

Leininger, M., Dyches, T.T., Prater, M.A., & Heath, M.A. (2010). Newbery Award winning books 1975–2009: How do they portray disabilities? *Education and training in autism and developmental disabilities, 45*(4), 583–596.

Leistikow, N. (2003). Indian women criticize "Fair and Lovely" ideal. We news. http://www.womensenews.org/story/the-world/030428/indian-women-criticize-fair-and-lovely-ideal

Lemonick, M.D. (2000). Teens before their time. *Time Magazine*. (U.S.) http://www.time.com/time/magazine/article/0,9171,998347-7,00.html

Lerum, K., & Dworkin, S.L. (2009). "Bad girls rule": an interdisciplinary feminist commentary on the report of the APA Task Force on the Sexualization of Girls. *Journal of Sex Research, 46*(4), 250–263. http://dx.doi.org/10.1080/00224490903079542 Medline:19657944

Lesko, N. (1996). Denaturalizing adolescence: The politics of contemporary representations. *Youth & Society, 28*(2), 139–161. http://dx.doi.org/10.1177/0044118X96028002001

Levy, A. (2006). *Female chauvinist pigs: Women and the rise of raunch culture*. New York: Free Press.

Lewis, A. (2003). *Race in the schoolyard: Negotiating the color line in classrooms and communities*. New Brunswick, NJ: Rutgers University Press.

Liao, L.M., Missenden, K., Hallam, R.S., & Conway, G.S. (2005). Experience of early pubertal development: A preliminary analysis. *Journal of Reproductive and Infant Psychology, 23*(3), 219–233. http://dx.doi.org/10.1080/0264683050 0165804

Liao, S., Savulescu, J., & Sheehan, M. (2007). The Ashley Treatment: Best interests, convenience, and parental decision-making. *Hastings Center Report, 37*(2), 16-20.

Liimakka, S. (2008). The influence of cultural images and other people on young women's embodied agency. *Young: Nordic Journal of Youth Research, 16*, 131–152.

Liimakka, S. (2011). Cartesian and corporeal agency: Women's studies students' reflections on body experience. *Gender and Education, 23*(7), 811–823. http://dx.doi.org/10.1080/09540253.2010.536144

Lim, L. (2009). Mattel hopes Shanghai is a Barbie world. *NPR.* http://www.npr.org/

Linn, S. (2009). A royal juggernaut: The Disney princesses and other commercialized threats to creative play and the path to self-realization for young girls. In S. Olfman (Ed.), *The sexualization of childhood* (pp. 33–50). Westport, CT: Praeger.

Linton, S. (2006). *My body politic: A memoir*. Ann Arbor: University of Michigan Press.

Lintott, S. (2010). Feminist aesthetics and the neglect of natural beauty. *Environmental Values, 19*(3), 315–333. http://dx.doi.org/10.3197/096327110X519853

Loprete, M. (1992). Double take: Behind every "Pretty Woman" stands a prettier woman, a superfit body double to the stars. CBS Money Watch. http://findarticles.com/p/articles/mi_m0675/is_n4_v10/ai_12448376/

Loshny, H. (2005). From birth control to menstrual control: The launch of the extended oral contraceptive, Seasonale. *Canadian Woman Studies/Les cahiers de la femme, 24*(1), 63–67.

Love, S.M. (with Lindsey, K.). (2005). *Dr. Susan Love's breast book*. Cambridge, MA: Da Capo Press.

Lutz, B.J., & Bowers, B.J. (2005). Disability in everyday life. *Qualitative Health Research, 15*(8), 1037–1054. http://dx.doi.org/10.1177/104973230527 8631 Medline:16221878

Macdonald, D., Wright, J., & Abbott, R. (2010). Anxieties and aspirations: The making of active, informed citizens. In J. Wright & D. Macdonald (Eds.), *Young people, physical activity and the everyday* (pp. 121–135). London, Eng.: Routledge.

MacDonald, G. (2001). Girls under the knife. *Globe and Mail*, pp. R1, R25.

MacIntosh, P. (1989). White privilege: Unpacking the invisible knapsack. *Peace and Freedom Magazine*, 10–12.

MacNeill, M. (1999). Social marketing, gender, and the science of fitness: A case study of ParticipACTION campaigns. In P. White & K. Young (Eds.), *Sport and gender in Canada* (pp. 215–231). Toronto: Oxford University Press.

MacNeill, M., & Rail, G. (2010). The visions, voices and moves of young "Canadians": Exploring diversity, subjectivity and cultural constructions of fitness and health. In J. Wright & D. Macdonald (Eds.), *Young people, physical activity and the everyday* (pp. 175–194). London, Eng.: Routledge.

Magnan, M. (2007). New pill specifically designed to limit periods to four times a year [Final edition]. *Calgary Herald*, p. C10.

Maher, J.K., Herbst, K.C., Childs, N.M., & Finn, S. (2008). Racial stereotypes in children's television commercials. *Journal of Advertising Research, 48*(1), 80–93. http://dx.doi.org/10.2501/S0021849908080100

Malacrida, C. (2005). Discipline and dehumanization in a total institution: Institutional survivors' descriptions of Time-Out Rooms. *Disability & Society, 20*, 523–537. http://dx.doi.org/10.1080/09687590500156238

Malcom, N.L. (2003). Constructing female athleticism: A study of girls' recreational softball. *American Behavioral Scientist, 46*(10), 1387–1404. http://dx.doi.org/10.1177/0002764203046010007

Malson, H. (2009). Appearing to disappear: Postmodern femininities and self-starved subjectivities. In H. Malson & M. Burns (Eds.), *Critical feminist approaches to eating dis/orders* (pp. 135–145). New York: Routledge.

Malson, H., & Burns, M. (Eds.). (2009). *Critical feminist approaches to eating dis/orders*. New York: Routledge.

Mama, A. (1995). *Beyond the masks: Race, gender and subjectivity*. London, Eng.: Routledge. http://dx.doi.org/10.4324/9780203405499

Marchessault, G. (2000). One mother and daughter's approach to resisting weight preoccupation. In B. Miedema, J.M. Stoppard, & V. Anderson (Eds.), *Women's bodies, women's lives* (pp. 203–226). Toronto: Sumach Press.

Marecek, J. (2001). After the facts: Psychology and the study of gender. *Canadian Psychology / Psychologie Canadienne, 42*(4), 254–267. http://dx.doi.org/10.1037/h0086894

Markey, C.N., & Markey, P.M. (2010). A correlational and experimental examination of reality television viewing and interest in cosmetic surgery. *Body Image, 7*(2), 165–171. http://dx.doi.org/10.1016/j.bodyim.2009.10.006 Medline:20089464

Markula, P., Burns, M., & Riley, S. (2008). Introducing critical bodies: Representations, identities and practices of weight management. In S. Riley, M. Burns, H. Frith, S. Wiggins, & P. Markula (Eds.), *Critical bodies: Representations, identities and practices of weight management* (pp. 1–22). New York: Palgrave Macmillan.

Marshall, W.A., & Tanner, J.M. (1969). Variations in pattern of pubertal changes in girls. *Archives of Disease in Childhood, 44*(235), 291–303. http://dx.doi.org/10.1136/adc.44.235.291 Medline:5785179

Marshall, W.A., & Tanner, J.M. (1970). Variations in the pattern of pubertal changes in boys. *Archives of Disease in Childhood, 45*(239), 13–23. http://dx.doi.org/10.1136/adc.45.239.13 Medline:5440182

Martin, E. (1992). *The woman in the body: A cultural analysis of reproduction.* Boston: Beacon Press Books.

Martin, K.A. (1996). *Puberty, sexuality and the self: Girls and boys at adolescence.* New York: Routledge.

Mattel Inc. (2009). Barbie launches new line of Black dolls called So In Style [Press release]. http://www.barbiemedia.com/?page=21&story=40

Mattel introduces Black Barbies, gets mixed reviews. (2009). Fox News website. http://www.foxnews.com/story/0,2933,562706,00.html#ixzz1C58UZYFc

Mattel says it erred: Teen talk Barbie turns silent on math. (1992). *New York Times.* http://www.nytimes.com/

Mazzarella, S.R. (2008). *A growing concern: U.S. newspaper coverage of "early puberty" in girls.* Paper presented at the 58th annual International Communications Association Conference, Montreal.

McCann, F. (2010). Keep your hair on – it's only a bit of leg fuzz. *Irish Times.* http://www.irishtimes.com/news/keep-your-hair-on-it-s-only-a-bit-of-leg-fuzz-1.1272318

McClelland, S.I., & Fine, M. (2008). Writing on cellophane: Studying teen women's sexual desires, inventing methodological release points. In K. Gallagher (Ed.), *The methodological dilemma: Creative, critical and collaborative approaches to qualitative research* (pp. 232–255). London, Eng.: Routledge.

McClintock, A. (1995). *Imperial leather: Race, gender and sexuality in the colonial contest.* New York: Routledge.

McCloskey, J. C. (1976). How to make the most of body image theory in nursing practice. *Nursing, 6*(5), 68–73.

McKeever, P., & Miller, K.L. (2004). Mothering children who have disabilities: A Bourdieusian interpretation of maternal practices. *Social Science &*

Medicine, 59(6), 1177–1191. http://dx.doi.org/10.1016/j.socscimed. 2003.12.023 Medline:15210090

McKinley, N.M. (1998). Gender differences in undergraduates' body esteem: The mediating effect of objectified body consciousness and actual/ideal weight discrepancy. *Sex Roles, 39*(1–2), 113–123. http://dx.doi.org/10.1023/A:1018834001203

McKinley, N.M. (1999a). Ideal weight/ideal women: Society constructs the female. In J. Sobal & D. Maurer (Eds.), *Weighty issues: Fatness and thinness as social problems* (pp. 97–105). New York: Aldine De Gruyter.

McKinley, N.M. (1999b). Women and objectified body consciousness: Mothers' and daughters' body experience in cultural, developmental, and familial context. *Developmental Psychology, 35*(3), 760–769. http://dx.doi.org/10.1037/0012-1649.35.3.760 Medline:10380866

McKinley, N.M. (2011). Feminist perspectives on body image. In T. F. Cash & L. Smolak (Eds.), *Body image: A handbook of science, practice and prevention* (pp. 48–55). Second ed. New York: Guilford Press.

McLaren, A. (1990). *Our own master race: Eugenics in Canada, 1885–1945*. Toronto: McClelland & Stewart.

McLaughlin, J., & Goodley, D. (2008). Seeking and rejecting certainty: Exposing the sophisticated lifeworlds of parents of disabled babies. *Sociology, 42*(2), 317–335. http://dx.doi.org/10.1177/0038038507087356

McNay, L. (2010). Feminism and post-identity politics: The problem of agency. *Constellations, 17*(4), 512–525. http://dx.doi.org/10.1111/j.1467-8675.2010.00611.x

McVey, G.L., Pepler, D., Davis, R., Flett, G.L., & Abdolell, M. (2002). Risk and protective factors associated with disordered eating during early adolescence. *Journal of Early Adolescence, 22*(1), 75–95. http://dx.doi.org/10.1177/0272431602022001004

Meekosha, H. (2011). Decolonising disability: Thinking and acting globally. *Disability & Society, 26*(6), 667–682. http://dx.doi.org/10.1080/09687599.2011.602860

Melchior-Bonnet, S. (2001). *The mirror: A history*. New York: Routledge.

Mellin, A.E., Neumark-Sztainer, D., Story, M., Ireland, M., & Resnick, M.D. (2002). Unhealthy behaviors and psychosocial difficulties among overweight adolescents: the potential impact of familial factors. *Journal of Adolescent Health, 31*(2), 145–153. http://dx.doi.org/10.1016/S1054-139X(01)00396-2 Medline:12127384

Mello, A.A., Domingos, N.A., & Miyazaki, M.C. (2010). Improvement in quality of life and self-esteem after breast reduction surgery. *Aesthetic*

Plastic Surgery, 34(1), 59–64. http://dx.doi.org/10.1007/s00266-009-9409-x Medline:19768493

Melwani, L. (2007). The white complex: What's behind the Indian prejudice for fair skin? *Little India.* www.littleindia.com/nri/1828-the-white-complex.html

Merleau-Ponty, M. (1962). *Phemomenology of perception.* London, Eng.: Routledge.

Merskin, D. (1999). Adolescence, advertising, and the ideology of menstruation. *Sex Roles, 40*(11–12), 941–957. http://dx.doi.org/10.1023/A:1018881206965

Metzl, J.M., & Poirier, S. (2004). Difference and identity in medicine. *Literature and Medicine, 23*(1), vi–xii. http://dx.di.org/10.1353/lm.2004.0008

Meyerowitz, J. (2002). *How sex changed: A history of transsexuality in the United States.* Cambridge, MA: Harvard University Press.

Miles, A.E. (1974). Julia Pastrana: The bearded lady. *Proceedings of the Royal Society of Medicine, 67*(2), 160–164. Medline:4595237

Miller, J.B. (1976). *Toward a new psychology of women.* Boston: Beacon Press.

Miller, W.C. (1999). Fitness and fatness in relation to health: Implications for a paradigm shift. *Journal of Social Issues, 55*(2), 207–219. http://dx.doi.org/10.1111/0022-4537.00113

Millman, M. (1980). *Such a pretty face: Being fat in America.* New York: Norton.

Mintel (2008). Shaving and hair removal products in the United States 2008. Research and Markets. http://www.researchandmarkets.com/research/68409a/shaving_and_hair_r

Mire, A. (2005). The emerging skin-whitening industry. CounterPunch. http://www.counterpunch.org/2005/07/28/the-emerging-skin-whitening-industry/

Mitchell, A., Rundle, L., & Karaian, L. (Eds.). (2001). *Turbo chicks: Talking young feminisms.* Toronto: Sumach Press.

Mitchell, C. & Reid-Walsh, J. (Eds.). (2005). *Seven going on seventeen: Tween studies in the culture of girlhood.* New York: Peter Lang.

Mitchell, D.T., & Snyder, S.L. (2001). Re-engaging the body: Disability studies and the resistance to embodiment. *Public Culture, 13*(3), 367–390. http://dx.doi.org/10.1215/08992363-13-3-367

Mitchinson, W. (1987). Medical perceptions of healthy women: The case of late nineteenth century Canada. *Canadian Woman Studies / Les cahiers de la femme, 8*(4), 42–43.

Moffitt, T.E., Caspi, A., Belsky, J., & Silva, P.A. (1992). Childhood experience and the onset of menarche: A test of a sociobiological model. *Child Development, 63*(1), 47–58. http://dx.doi.org/10.2307/1130900 Medline:1551329

Moi, T. (1999). *What is a woman? And other essays*. Oxford, Eng.: Oxford University Press.

Moore, R.B. (1976/2006). Racism in the English language. In J. O'Brien (Ed.), *The production of reality: Essays and readings on social interaction* (pp. 119–126). Thousand Oaks, CA: Pine Forge Press.

Morgan, K.P. (1991/2009). Women and the knife: Cosmetic surgery and the colonization of women's bodies. In C.J. Heyes & M. Jones (Eds.), *Cosmetic surgery: A feminist primer* (pp. 49–77). Farnham, Eng.: Ashgate.

Morimura, Y. (2008). Yasumasa Morimura: Self-portrait as art history. http://www.assemblylanguage.com/images/Morimura.html.

Mulvey, L. (1975). Visual pleasure and narrative cinema. *Screen, 16*(3), 6–18. http://dx.doi.org/10.1093/screen/16.3.6

Murguia, E., & Telles, E.E. (1996). Phenotype and schooling among Mexican Americans. *Sociology of Education, 69*(4), 276–289. http://dx.doi.org/10.2307/2112715

Murnen, S.K., & Smolak, L. (2009). Are feminist women protected from body image problems? A meta-analytic review of relevant research. *Sex Roles, 60*(3–4), 186–197. http://dx.doi.org/10.1007/s11199-008-9523-2

Murphy, T. (2009). Technology, tools and toxic expectations: Post-publication notes on *New Technologies and Human Rights Law, Innovation and Technology, 1*, 181–202.

Mutua, N.K. (2001). The semiotics of accessibility and the cultural construction of disability. In L.J. Rogers & B.B. Swadener (Eds.), *Semiotics and dis/ability: Interrogating categories of difference* (pp. 103–116). Albany: State University of New York Press.

Nabi, R.L. (2009). Cosmetic surgery makeover programs and intentions to undergo cosmetic enhancements: A consideration of three models of media effects. *Human Communication Research, 35*(1), 1–27. http://dx.doi.org/10.1111/j.1468-2958.2008.01336.x

Nadeem, E., & Graham, S. (2005). Early puberty, peer victimization, and internalizing symptoms in ethnic minority adolescents. *Journal of Early Adolescence, 25*(2), 197–222. http://dx.doi.org/10.1177/0272431604274177

Namaste, V. (2000). *Invisible lives: The erasure of transsexual and transgendered people*. Chicago: University of Chicago Press.

Napheys, G.H. (1889). *The physical life of woman: Advice to the maiden, wife and mother*. http://www.gutenberg.org/files/24001/24001-h/24001-h.htm

Narayan, U. (2000). Undoing the "package picture" of cultures. *Signs, 25*(4), 1083–1086. http://dx.doi.org/10.1086/495524

Nasser, M., & Malson, H. (2009). Beyond western dis/orders: Thinness and self-starvation in other-ed women. In H. Malson & M. Burns (Eds.), *Critical feminist approaches to eating dis/orders* (pp. 74–86). New York: Routledge.

Naugler, D. (2009). Crossing the cosmetic/reconstructive divide: The instructive situation of breast reduction surgery. In C.J. Heyes & M. Jones (Eds.), *Cosmetic surgery: A feminist primer* (pp. 225–237). Farnham, Eng.: Ashgate.

Neblett, E.W., Jr., White, R.L., Ford, K.R., Philip, C.L., Nguyên, H.X., & Sellers, R.M. (2008). Patterns of racial socialization and psychological adjustment: Can parental communications about race reduce the impact of racial discrimination? *Journal of Research on Adolescence, 18*(3), 477–515. http://dx.doi.org/10.1111/j.1532-7795.2008.00568.x

Nelson, E., & Jordan, M. (2000). Seeking new markets for tampons, Procter & Gamble tries "bonding sessions" and school slide shows to win sales in Mexico. *Wall Street Journal.* http://www.stayfreemagazine.org/public/wsj_tampons.html

Nelson, R. (2007). Little women. *American Journal of Nursing, 107*(12), 25–26. http://dx.doi.org/10.1097/01.NAJ.0000301009.03630.f7 Medline: 18049052

Neumark-Sztainer, D., Story, M., & Faibisch, L. (1998). Perceived stigmatization among overweight African-American and Caucasian adolescent girls. *Journal of Adolescent Health, 23*(5), 264–270. http://dx.doi.org/10.1016/S1054-139X(98)00044-5 Medline:9814386

Neumark-Sztainer, D., Story, M., Hannan, P.J., Perry, C.L., & Irving, L.M. (2002). Weight-related concerns and behaviors among overweight and nonoverweight adolescents: Implications for preventing weight-related disorders. *Archives of Pediatrics & Adolescent Medicine, 156*(2), 171–178. http://dx.doi.org/10.1001/archpedi.156.2.171 Medline:11814380

Neumark-Sztainer, D. (2011). Obesity and body image in youth. In T.F. Cash & L. Smolak (Eds.), *Body image: A handbook of science, practice and prevention* (pp. 180–188). Second ed. New York: The Guilford Press.

Newell, R. (2000). *Body image and disfigurement care.* London: Routledge.

Newman, A.A. (2007). Depilatory market moves far beyond the short-shorts wearers. *New York Times.* http://www.nytimes.com/

O'Brien, S., & Szeman, I. (2004). *Popular culture: A user's guide.* Toronto: Nelson.

O'Dea, J.A., & Caputi, P. (2001). Association between socioeconomic status, weight, age and gender, and the body image and weight control practices of 6- to 19-year-old children and adolescents. *Health Education Research, 16*(5), 521–532. http://dx.doi.org/10.1093/her/16.5.521 Medline:11675800

O'Grady, L. (1992/2003). Olympia's maid: Reclaiming Black female subjectivity. In A. Jones (Ed.), *The feminism and visual culture reader* (pp. 174–186). New York: Routledge.

Oliver, K.L., & Lalik, R. (2004a). "The Beauty Walk": Interrogating whiteness as the norm for beauty within one school's hidden curriculum. In J. Evans, B. Davies, & J. Wright (Eds.), *Body Knowledge and Control: Studies in the Sociology of Education and Health* (pp. 115–129). New York: Routledge.

Oliver, K.L., & Lalik, R. (2004b). Critical inquiry on the body in girls' physical education classes: A critical poststructural perspective. *Journal of Teaching in Physical Education, 2*(2), 162–195.

Oliver, M. (1990). *Understanding disability, from theory to practice.* London, Eng.: Macmillan.

Ontario. (2004). *2004 Chief Medical Officer of Health report: Healthy weights, healthy lives.* Toronto: Chief Medical Officer of Health.

Orbach, S. (1979). *Fat is a feminist issue: The anti-diet guide to permanent weight loss.* New York: Berkley Books.

Orbach, S. (1993). *Hunger strike: The anorectic's struggle as a metaphor for our age* (2nd ed.). London, Eng.: Penguin.

Orenstein, P. (1994). *Schoolgirls: Young women, self-esteem, and the confidence gap.* New York: Anchor Books.

Orenstein, P. (2011). *Cinderella ate my daughter: Dispatches from the front lines of the new girlie-girl culture.* New York: HarperCollins.

Oster, E., & Thornton, R. (2011). Menstruation, sanitary products, and school attendance: Evidence from a randomized evaluation. *American Economic Journal: Applied Economics, 3*(1), 91–100. http://dx.doi.org/10.1257/app.3.1.91

Oudshoorn, N. (1994). *Beyond the natural body: An archaeology of sex hormones.* London, Eng.: Routledge. http://dx.doi.org/10.4324/9780203421529

Paechter, C., & Clark, S. (2007). Who are tomboys and how do we recognise them? *Women's Studies International Forum, 30*(4), 342–354. http://dx.doi.org/10.1016/j.wsif.2007.05.005

Park, D.C., & Radford, J.P. (1998). From the case files: Reconstructing a history of involuntary sterilisation. *Disability & Society, 13*(3), 317–342. http://dx.doi.org/10.1080/09687599826669 Medline:11660707

Peiss, K.L. (1999). *Hope in a jar: The making of America's beauty culture.* New York: Henry Holt.

Pesa, J.A., Syre, T.R., & Jones, E. (2000). Psychosocial differences associated with body weight among female adolescents: The importance of body image. *Journal of Adolescent Health, 26*(5), 330–337. http://dx.doi.org/10.1016/S1054-139X(99)00118-4 Medline:10775825

Petersen, A.C., Tobin-Richards, M., & Boxer, A. (1983). Puberty: Its measurement and its meaning. *Journal of Early Adolescence, 3*(1–2), 47–62. http:// dx.doi.org/10.1177/027243168331005

Peterson, M.J. (2008). Precocious puberty in the Victorian medical gaze. *Special issue, Nineteenth-Century Gender Studies, 4*(2). http://ncgsjournal.com/issue42/peterson.htm

Peterson, R.D., Grippo, K.P., & Tantleff-Dunn, S. (2008). Empowerment and powerlessness: A closer look at the relationship between feminism, body image and eating disturbance. *Sex Roles, 58*(9–10), 639–648. http://dx.doi. org/10.1007/s11199-007-9377-z

Peterson, R.D., Tantleff-Dunn, S., & Bedwell, J.S. (2006). The effects of exposure to feminist ideology on women's body image. *Body Image, 3*(3), 237–246. http://dx.doi.org/10.1016/j.bodyim.2006.05.004 Medline:18089226

Pilgrim, D. (2000). Jim Crow Museum of Racist Memorabilia. Ferris State University. http://www.ferris.edu/jimcrow/mammies/

Pinto, K. (2007). Growing up young: The relationship between childhood stress and coping with early puberty. *Journal of Early Adolescence, 27*(4), 509–544. http://dx.doi.org/10.1177/0272431607302936

Pinto, P. (2008). Women, disability and the right to health. In P. Armstrong & J. Dreadman, (Eds.), *Women's health: Intersections of policy, research, and practice* (pp. 119–133). Toronto: Women's Press.

Pipher, M.B. (1994). *Reviving Ophelia: Saving the selves of adolescent girls.* New York: Putnam.

Piran, N., Carter, W., Thompson, S., & Pajouhandeh, P. (2002). Powerful girls: A contradiction in terms? Young women speak about their experiences of growing up in a girl's body. In S. Abbey (Ed.), *ASPP* (pp. 206–210). Welland, ON: Soleil.

Popenoe, R. (2004). *Feeding desire: Fatness, beauty, and sexuality among a Saharan people.* New York: Routledge.

Poran, M.A. (2002). Denying diversity: Perceptions of beauty and social comparison processes among Latina, Black and white women. *Sex Roles, 47*(1–2), 65–81. http://dx.doi.org/10.1023/A:1020683720636

Posner, R.B. (2006). Early menarche: A review of research on trends in timing, racial differences, etiology and psychosocial consequences. *Sex Roles, 54*(5–6), 315–322. http://dx.doi.org/10.1007/s11199-006-9003-5

Pozner, J.L. (2010). *Reality bites back: The troubling truth about guilty pleasure TV.* Berkeley, CA: Seal Press.

Priestley, M. (1998). Childhood disability and disabled childhoods: Agendas for research. *Childhood, 5*(2), 207–223. http://dx.doi.org/10.1177/090756829 8005002007

Pruzinsky, T. (1990). Psychopathology of bodily experience: Expanded perspectives. In T. Cash & T. Pruzinsky (Eds.), *Body images: Development, deviance, and change* (pp. 170–189). New York: The Guilford Press.

Quibell, R. (2005). *The living history project: Exploring the lived experiences of living with disability 1981–2002*. Paper presented at the International Conference on Engaging Communities, Brisbane, Australia. www.engaging communities2005.org/abstracts/Quibell-Ruth-final.pdf

Rabinor, J.R. (2004). The "eating disordered" patient. In P. Caplan & L. Cosgrove (Eds.), *Bias in psychiatric diagnosis* (pp. 189–192). Lanham, MD: Jason Aronson.

Rail, G., & Lafrance, M. (2009). Confessions of the flesh and biopedagogies: Discursive constructions of obesity on *Nip/Tuck*. *Medical Humanities, 35*(2), 76–79. http://dx.doi.org/10.1136/jmh.2009.001610

Raine, K.D. (2004). *Overweight and obesity in Canada: A population health perspective*. Ottawa, ON: Canadian Institute for Health Information.

Rapp, R., & Ginsburg, F. (2001). Enabling disability: Rewriting kinship, reimagining citizenship. *Public Culture, 13*(3), 533–556. http://dx.doi.org/10.1215/08992363-13-3-533

Ray, C.C. (2010). Bras and cancer. *New York Times*. http://www.nytimes.com/

Reardon, R., & Grogan, S. (2011). Women's reasons for seeking breast reduction: A qualitative investigation. *Journal of Health Psychology, 16*(1), 31–41. http://dx.doi.org/10.1177/1359105310367531 Medline:20656768

Reay, D. (2001). "Spice girls," "nice girls," "girlies," and "tomboys": Gender discourses, girls' cultures and femininities in the primary classroom. *Gender and Education, 13*(2), 153–166. http://dx.doi.org/10.1080/09540250120051178

Rebick, J. (2005). *Ten thousand roses: The making of a feminist revolution*. Toronto: Penguin Canada.

Recently released market study: Toys and games – North America (NAFTA) industry guide. (2010). PR-inside.com www.live-pr.com/en/toys-games-north-america-r1049248397.htm

Reel, J.J., & Bucciere R.A. (2010). Ableism and body image: Conceptualizing how individuals are marginalized. *Women in Sport and Physical Activity Journal 19*(1), 91-97.

Reid-Brinkley, S.R. (2007). The essence of res(ex)pectability Black women's negotiation of Black femininity in rap music and music video. *Meridians, 8*(1), 236–260. http://dx.doi.org/10.2979/MER.2007.8.1.236

Renold, E. (2006). "They won't let us play ... unless you're going out with one of them": Girls, boys and Butler's "heterosexual matrix" in the primary

years. *British Journal of Sociology of Education, 27*(4), 489–509. http://dx.doi.
org/10.1080/01425690600803111

Renold, E. (2008). Tomboy. In C. Mitchell & J. Reid-Walsh (Eds.), *Girl culture:
An encyclopedia* (vol. 2, pp. 578–580). Westport, CT: Greenwood Press.

Repeating "feminazi" comment, Limbaugh reprises familiar theme. (2006).
Media Matters for America. http://mediamatters.org/mmtv/200601
060006

Ricciardelli, L.A., & McCabe, M.P. (2001). Children's body image concerns
and eating disturbance: A review of the literature. *Clinical Psychology
Review, 21*(3), 325–344. http://dx.doi.org/10.1016/S0272-7358(99)00051-3
Medline:11288604

Rice, C. (1996). Trauma and eating problems: Expanding the debate. *Eating
Disorders, 4*(3), 197–237. http://dx.doi.org/10.1080/10640269608251177

Rice, C. (1997). Body image: A key to eating disorders. *Chatelaine Magazine*, p.
50.

Rice, C. (2003). *Becoming women: Body image, identity, and difference in the passage
to womanhood* (Doctoral thesis, York University, Toronto, Canada).

Rice, C. (2007). Becoming "the fat girl": Acquisition of an unfit identity. *Wom-
en's Studies International Forum, 30*(2), 158–174. http://dx.doi.org/10.1016/j.
wsif.2007.01.001

Rice, C. (2009a). Exacting beauty: Exploring women's body projects and problems in the 21st century. In N. Mandell (Ed.), Feminist issues: Race, class
and sexuality (pp. 131–160). Toronto: Pearson Canada.

Rice, C. (2009b). How big girls become fat girls: The cultural production of
problem eating and physical inactivity. In H. Malson & M. Burns (Eds.),
Critical feminist approaches to eating dis/orders (pp. 97–109). New York:
Routledge.

Rice, C. (2009c). Imagining the other? Ethical challenges of researching and
writing women's embodied lives. *Feminism & Psychology, 19*(2), 245–266.
http://dx.doi.org/10.1177/0959353509102222

Rice, C., & Langdon, L. (1991). The use and misuse of diagnostic labels. *NEDIC
Bulletin, 6*(1), 1–4.

Rice, C., Renooy, L., & Odette, F. (2008). Talking about body image, identity,
and difference. Workshop and paper presented for the Envisioning New
Meanings of Disability and Difference Project. York Institute for Health
Research. York University, Toronto, ON.

Rice, C., Renooy, L., Zitzlesberger, H., Aubin, A., & Odette, F. (2003). *Talking about body image, identity, disability, and difference: A facilitator's manual*.
Toronto: AboutFace International.

Rice, C., & Russell, V. (2002). *Embodying equity: Body image as an equity issue.* Toronto: Green Dragon Press.

Rice, C., Zitzelsberger, H., Porch, W., & Ignagni, E. (2005a). Creating community across disability and difference. *Canadian Woman Studies / Les cahiers de la femme, 24* (1), 187–193.

Rice, C., Zitzelsberger, H., Porch, W., & Ignagni, E. (2005b). Envisioning new meanings of disability and difference. *International Journal of Narrative Therapy and Community Work, 3 & 4,* 119–130.

Rich, E. (2010). Obesity assemblages and surveillance in schools. *International Journal of Qualitative Studies in Education, 23*(7), 803–821. http://dx.doi.org/10.1080/09518398.2010.529474

Rich, E. (2011). "I see her being obesed!": Public pedagogy, reality media and the obesity crisis. *Health, 15*(1), 3–21. http://dx.doi.org/10.1177/1363459309358127 Medline:21212111

Riddell, L., Varto, H., & Hodgson, Z.G. (2010). Smooth talking: The phenomenon of pubic hair removal in women. *Canadian Journal of Human Sexuality, 19,* 121–130.

Roberts, C. (2002). "A matter of embodied fact": Sex hormones and the history of bodies. *Feminist Theory, 3*(1), 7–26. http://dx.doi.org/10.1177/1460012002003001063

Roberts, D. (1997). *Killing Black body: Race, reproduction and the meaning of liberty.* New York: Pantheon.

Roberts, T.A. (2004). Female trouble: The menstrual self-evaluation scale and women's self-objectification. *Psychology of Women Quarterly, 28*(1), 22–26. http://dx.doi.org/10.1111/j.1471-6402.2004.00119.x

Rodin, J., Silberstein, L., & Striegel-Moore, R. (1984). Women and weight: a normative discontent. In *Nebraska symposium on motivation.* University of Nebraska Press.

Rogers, L.J. & Swadener, B.B. (Eds.). (2001). *Semiotics and dis/ability: Interrogating categories of difference.* Albany: State University of New York Press.

Roman, L.G. (2009a). Disability arts and culture as public pedagogy. *International Journal of Inclusive Education, 13*(7), 667–675. http://dx.doi.org/10.1080/13603110903041912

Roman, L.G. (2009b). Go figure! Public pedagogies, invisible impairments and the performative paradoxes of visibility as veracity. *International Journal of Inclusive Education, 13*(7), 677–698. http://dx.doi.org/10.1080/13603110903041920

Romans, S.E., Martin, J.M., Gendall, K., & Herbison, G.P. (2003). Age of menarche: the role of some psychosocial factors. *Psychological Medicine, 33*(5),

933–939. http://dx.doi.org/10.1017/S0033291703007530 Medline: 12877408

Rooks, N.M. (1996). *Hair raising: Beauty, culture, and African American women.* New Brunswick, NJ: Rutgers University Press.

Rooks, N.M. (2001). Wearing your race wrong: Hair, drama, and a politics of representation for African American women at play on a battlefield. In M. Bennett & V.D. Dickerson (Eds.), *Recovering the Black female body: Self-representations by African American women* (pp. 279–295). New Brunswick, NJ: Rutgers University Press.

Rootman, I., & Edwards, P. (2004). The best laid schemes of mice and men ... ParticipACTION's legacy and the future of physical activity promotion in Canada. *Canadian Journal of Public Health, 95*(Suppl 2), S37–S42. Medline:15250605

Rose, N., & Novas, C. (2005). Biological citizenship. In A. Ong & S.J. Collier (Eds.), *Global assemblages: Technology, politics, and ethics as anthropological problems* (pp. 439–463). Oxford, Eng.: Blackwell Publishing.

Rosen, J.C. (1990). Body image disturbances in eating disorders. In T. Cash & T. Pruzinsky (Eds.), *Body images: Development, deviance, and change* (pp. 190–214). New York: The Guilford Press.

Ross, B. (2005). *Fat or fiction: Weighing the obesity epidemic.* New York: Taylor & Francis.

Ross, S.D., & Lester, P.M. (Eds.). (2011). *Images that injure: Pictorial stereotypes in the media.* Santa Barbara, CA: Praeger.

Rossini, E. (2009). Because every little Chinese girl dreams of being a blond haired, blue-eyed shopaholic [Web log post]. The Illusionists. http://theillusionists.org/?p=385

Rubenstein, J. (2010). After a year of scrutiny, Caster Semenya can compete as a woman. Change.org. http://gayrights.change.org/blog/view/after_a_year_of_scrutiny_caster_semenya_can_compete_as_a_woman

Rubin, G. (1975). The traffic in women: Notes on the "political economy" of sex. In R. Reiter (Ed.), *Toward an anthropology of women* (pp. 157–210). New York: Monthly Review Press.

Rubin, L.R., Nemeroff, C.J., & Russo, N.F. (2004). Exploring feminist women's body consciousness. *Psychology of Women Quarterly, 28*(1), 27–37. http://dx.doi.org/10.1111/j.1471-6402.2004.00120.x

Rumsey, N. & Harcourt, D. (2011). Body image and congenital conditions resulting in visible difference. In T. F. Cash & L. Smolak (Eds.), *Body image: A handbook of science, practice and prevention* (pp. 253–260). Second ed. New York: The Guilford Press.

Russell, K., Wilson, M., & Hall, R. (1992). *The color complex: The politics of skin color among African Americans*. New York: Anchor Books.

Sahay, S., & Piran, N. (1997). Skin-color preferences and body satisfaction among South Asian-Canadian and European-Canadian female university students. *Journal of Social Psychology, 137*(2), 161–171. http://dx.doi.org/10.1080/00224549709595427 Medline:9140216

Sax, L. (2005). *Why gender matters: What parents and teachers need to know about the emerging science of sex differences*. New York: Broadway Books.

Schering Corporation. (1934). *Magic and medicine in menstruation*. http://www.mum.org/scher1.htm

Schick, V.R., Rima, B.N., & Calabrese, S.K. (2011). Evulvalution: the portrayal of women's external genitalia and physique across time and the current barbie doll ideals. *Journal of Sex Research, 48*(1), 74–81. http://dx.doi.org/10.1080/00224490903308404 Medline:19916105

Schiebinger, L.L. (1993). *Nature's body: Gender and the making of modern science*. Boston: Beacon Press.

Schiebinger, L.L. (2000). Introduction. In L.L. Schiebinger (Ed.), *Feminism and the body* (pp. 1–21). New York: Oxford.

Schippers, M. (2007). Recovering the feminine other: Masculinity, femininity, and gender hegemony. *Theory and Society, 36*(1), 85–102. http://dx.doi.org/10.1007/s11186-007-9022-4

Schoenfielder, L., & Wieser, B. (Eds.). (1983). *Shadow on a tightrope: Writings by women on fat oppression*. Iowa City, IA: Aunt Lute Books.

Schor, J. (2004). *Born to buy: The commercialized child and the new consumer culture*. New York: Scribner.

Schreck, C.J., Burek, M.W., Stewart, E.A., & Miller, J.M. (2007). Distress and violent victimization among young adolescents: Early puberty and the social interactionist explanation. *Journal of Research in Crime and Delinquency, 44*(4), 381–405. http://dx.doi.org/10.1177/0022427807305851

Schrock, D., Reid, L., & Boyd, E.M. (2005). Transsexuals' embodiment of womanhood. *Gender & Society, 19*(3), 317–335. http://dx.doi.org/10.1177/0891243204273496

Schwartz, H. (1986). *Never satisfied: A cultural history of diets, fantasies, and fat*. New York: Free Press.

Scott, L. (2005). *Fresh lipstick: Redressing fashion and feminism*. New York: Palgrave.

Seasonique™ now available in Canada, the next generation extended cycle pill designed to provide 4 menstrual periods per year. (2011). Digital Journal. http://www.digitaljournal.com/pr/281270#ixzz1KdwdkhLB

Shane, S.H. (2008). Reaching puberty early. *Colorlines, 11*(4), 26–30.

Sheldon, A.P., Renwich, R., & Yoshida, K.K. (2011). Exploring body image and self-concept of men with acquired spinal cord injuries. *American Journal of Men's Health 5*(4), 306–317.

Sherwin, A. (2006). Reality TV puts disabled women in beauty show. *The Times*. http://www.timesonline.co.uk/tol/news/world/europe/article1068730.ece

Shildrick, M. (1997). *Leaky bodies and boundaries: Feminism, postmodernism and (bio)ethics*. London, Eng.: Routledge.

Shildrick, M. (2007). Dangerous discourses: Anxiety, desire, and disability. *Studies in Gender and Sexuality, 8*(3), 221–244. http://dx.doi.org/10.1080/15240650701226490

Shontz, F.C. (1990). Body image and physical disability. In T. Cash & T. Pruzinsky (Eds.), *Body images: Development, deviance, and change* (pp. 146–169). New York: The Guilford Press.

Siddiqi, S.U., Van Dyke, D.C., Donohoue, P., & McBrien, D.M. (1999). Premature sexual development in individuals with neurodevelopmental disabilities. *Developmental Medicine and Child Neurology, 41*(6), 392–395. http://dx.doi.org/10.1017/S0012162299000857 Medline:10400173

Siegel, J.M., Yancey, A.K., Aneshensel, C.S., & Schuler, R. (1999). Body image, perceived pubertal timing, and adolescent mental health. *Journal of Adolescent Health, 25*(2), 155–165. http://dx.doi.org/10.1016/S1054-139X(98)00160-8 Medline:10447043

Silbereisen, R.K., Petersen, A.C., Albrecht, H.T., & Kracke, B. (1989). Maturational timing and the development of problem behavior: Longitudinal studies in adolescence. *Journal of Early Adolescence, 9*(3), 247–268. http://dx.doi.org/10.1177/0272431689093005

Singer, N. (2008). Do my breast implants have a warranty? *New York Times*. http://www.nytimes.com/2008/01/17/fashion/17SKIN.html?_r=1&oref=slogin

Skeggs, B. (2002). Ambivalent femininities. In S. Jackson & S. Scott (Eds.), *Gender: A sociological reader* (pp. 311–325). New York: Routledge.

Slater, A., & Tiggemann, M. (2010). Body image and disordered eating in adolescent girls and boys: A test of objectification theory. *Sex Roles, 63*(1–2), 42–49. http://dx.doi.org/10.1007/s11199-010-9794-2

Slyper, A.H. (2006). The pubertal timing controversy in the USA, and a review of possible causative factors for the advance in timing of onset of puberty. *Clinical Endocrinology, 65*(1), 1–8. http://dx.doi.org/10.1111/j.1365-2265.2006.02539.x Medline:16817811

Smolak, L., & Cash, T.F. (2011). Future challenges for body image science, practice and prevention. In T.F. Cash & L. Smolak (Eds.), *Body image:*

A handbook of science, practice and prevention (pp. 471–478). Second ed. New York: The Guilford Press.

Smolak, L., Levine, M.P., & Gralen, S. (1993). The impact of puberty and dating on eating problems among middle school girls. *Journal of Youth and Adolescence, 22*(4), 355–368. http://dx.doi.org/10.1007/BF01537718

Smolak, L. & Thompson J. K. (2009). Body Image, eating disorders, and obesity in children and adolescents: Introduction to the second edition. In L. Smolak & J. K. Thompson (Eds.), *Body image, eating disorders and obesity in youth: Assessment, prevention and treatment* (pp. 3–14). Second ed. Washington DC: American Psychological Association.

Snyder, S.L., & Mitchell, D.T. (2001). Re-engaging the Body: Disability studies and the resistance to embodiment. *Public Culture, 13*(3), 367–389.

Snyder, S.L., & Mitchell, D.T. (2006). *Cultural locations of disability.* Chicago: University of Chicago Press. http://dx.doi.org/10.7208/chicago/9780226767307.001.0001

Society for Menstrual Cycle Research. (2003). *Menstrual Suppression* [Position statement]. Developed at the Menstrual Suppression Panel at the Fifteenth Biennial Meeting of the Society for Menstrual Cycle Research, Pittsburgh, PA. http://menstruationresearch.org

Spade, J.Z., & Valentine, C.G. (2011). *The kaleidoscope of gender: Prisms, patterns, and possibilities.* Thousand Oaks, CA: Sage.

Spence, J. (1988). *Putting myself in the picture: A political, personal and photographic autobiography.* Seattle, WA: Real Comet Press.

Staiger, A.D. (2006). *Learning difference: Race and schooling in the multiracial metropolis.* Stanford, CA: Stanford University Press.

Stanley, A. (2009). Disabled, and seeking acceptance in fashion. *New York Times.* www.nytimes.com/2009/12/01/arts/television/01model.html

Statistics Canada. (2003). *Visible minority groups and sex for population, for Canada, provinces, territories, census metropolitan areas and census agglomerations, 2001 Census* (Statistics Canada catalogue no. 97F0010XIE2001002). http://www.statcan.gc.ca/bsolc/olc-cel/olc-cel?catno=97F0010XIE2001002&lang=eng

Stearns, P.N. (1997). *Fat history: Bodies and beauty in the modern West.* New York: New York University Press.

Steinem, G. (1978/2004). If men could menstruate – a political fantasy. In N. Worcester & M.H. Whatley (Eds.), *Women's health: Readings on social, economic, and political issues* (pp. 195–196). Dubuque, IA: Kendall/Hunt Publishing.

Steiner-Adair, C. (1990). The body politic: Normal female adolescent development and the development of eating disorders. In C. Gilligan, N.P. Lyons, &

T.J. Hammer (Eds.), *Making connections: The relational worlds of adolescent girls at Emma Willard School* (pp. 162–182). Cambridge, MA: Harvard University Press.

Steingraber, S. (2007). *The falling age of puberty in U.S. girls: What we know, what we need to know*. San Francisco: Breast Cancer Fund.

Stoller, R.J. (1968). *Sex and gender: On the development of masculinity and femininity*. New York: Science House.

Stotzer, R.L. (2009). Violence against transgender people: A review of United States data. *Aggression and Violent Behavior, 14*(3), 170–179. http://dx.doi.org/10.1016/j.avb.2009.01.006

Stuart, A., & Donaghue, N. (2011). Choosing to conform: The discursive complexities of choice in relation to feminine beauty practices. *Feminism & Psychology, 22*(1), 98–121. http://dx.doi.org/10.1177/0959353511424362

Sullivan, D.A. (2001). *Cosmetic surgery: The cutting edge of commercial medicine in America*. New Brunswick, NJ: Rutgers University Press.

Summers, L.H. (2005). Remarks at NBER Conference on Diversifying the Science & Engineering Workforce, Cambridge, MA. http://web.archive.org/web/20080130023006/http://www.president.harvard.edu/speeches/2005/nber.html

Summers-Effler, E. (2004). Little girls in women's bodies: Social interaction and the strategizing of early breast development. *Sex Roles, 51*(1–2), 29–44. http://dx.doi.org/10.1023/B:SERS.0000032307.16204.ec

Swee, W., Klontz, K.C., & Lambert, L.A. (2000). A nationwide outbreak of alopecia associated with the use of a hair-relaxing formulation. *Archives of Dermatology, 136*(9), 1104–1108. http://dx.doi.org/10.1001/archderm.136.9.1104 Medline:10987865

Székely, E.A. (1988). *Never too thin*. Toronto: The Women's Press.

Talbot, M. (2006). Little hotties: Barbie's new rivals. *The New Yorker.* http://www.newamerica.net/publications/articles/2006/little_hotties_4487

Talpade, M. (2004). Nutritional differences as a function of early sexual maturation among African American girls. *North American Journal of Psychology, 6*, 383–392.

Talpade, M. (2006). African American child-women: Nutrition theory revisited. *Adolescence, 41*(161), 91–102. Medline:16689443

Tambrands Canada. (1993). *The inside story teacher's resource: A supplementary resource on puberty for ages 10–14.* Palmer, MA: Author.

Tanner, J.M. (1962). *Growth at adolescence, with a general consideration of the effects of hereditary and environmental factors upon growth and maturation from birth to maturity.* Oxford, Eng.: Blackwell Scientific Publications.

Taylor, C., & Peter, T. (with McMinn, T.L., Schachter, K., Beldom, S., Ferry, A., Gross , Z., Paquin, S.). (2011). *Every class in every school: The first national climate survey on homophobia, biphobia, and transphobia in Canadian schools. Final report.* Toronto: Egale Canada Human Rights Trust.

Taylor, D. (1998). A savage performance: Guillermo Gomez-Pena and Coco Fusco's "Couple in the cage." *Drama Review, 42*(2), 160–180. http://dx.doi.org/10.1162/dram.1998.42.2.160

Teitelman, A.M. (2004). Adolescent girls' perspectives of family interactions related to menarche and sexual health. *Qualitative Health Research, 14*(9), 1292–1308. http://dx.doi.org/10.1177/1049732304268794 Medline:15448301

Telzer, E.H., & Vazquez Garcia, H. (2009). Skin color and self-perceptions of immigrant and U.S.-born Latinas: The moderating role of racial socialization and ethnic identity. *Hispanic Journal of Behavioral Sciences, 31*(3), 357–374. http://dx.doi.org/10.1177/0739986309336913

Thomas, A.J., Speight, S.L., & Witherspoon, K.M. (2010). Racial socialization, racial identity, and race-related stress of African American parents. *Family Journal, 18*(4), 407–412. http://dx.doi.org/10.1177/1066480710372913

Thomas, C. (1999). *Female forms: Experiencing and understanding disability.* Buckingham, Eng.: Open University Press.

Thomas Fisher Rare Book Library, Landon, R., Oldfield, P., & Associated Medical Services, Inc. (2006). *Ars medica: Medical illustration through the ages. An exhibition to commemorate the seventieth anniversary of the founding of Associated Medical Services. Exhibition and catalogue.* Toronto: Thomas Fisher Rare Book Library.

Thompson, B.W. (1994). *A hunger so wide and so deep: American women speak out on eating problems.* Minneapolis: University of Minnesota Press.

Thompson, J.K. (1990). *Body image disturbance: Assessment and treatment.* Elmsford, NY: Pergamon Press.

Thompson, J.K., Heinberg, L.J., Altabe, M., & Tantleff-Dunn, S. (1999). *Exacting beauty: Theory, assessment, and treatment of body image disturbance.* Washington, DC: American Psychological Association.

Thompson, J.K., Penner, L.A., & Altabe, M.N. (1990). Procedures, problems, and progress in the assessment of body images. In T. Cash & T. Pruzinsky (Eds.), *Body images: Development, deviance, and change* (pp. 21–49). New York: The Guilford Press.

Thompson, M.S., & Keith, V.M. (2001). The blacker the berry: Gender, skin tone, self-esteem, and self-efficacy. *Gender & Society, 15*(3), 336–357. http://dx.doi.org/10.1177/089124301015003002

Thorne, B. (1993). *Gender play: Girls and boys in school.* New Brunswick, NJ: Rutgers University Press.

Tiggemann, M., & Hodgson, S. (2008). The hairlessness norm extended: Reasons for and predictors of women's body hair removal at different body sites. *Sex Roles, 59*(11–12), 889–897. http://dx.doi.org/10.1007/s11199-008-9494-3

Timmons, H. (2007). Telling India's modern women they have power, even over their skin tone. *New York Times.* http://www.nytimes.com/2007/05/30/business/media/30adco.html?ex=1181620800&en=201&_r=1&

Titchkosky, T. (2001). Disability: A rose by any other name? "People-first" language in Canadian society. *Canadian Review of Sociology / Revue canadienne de sociologie, 38*(2), 125–140. http://dx.doi.org/10.1111/j.1755-618X.2001.tb00967.x

Titchkosky, T. (2007). *Reading and writing disability differently: The textured life of embodiment.* Toronto: University of Toronto Press.

Tither, J.M., & Ellis, B.J. (2008). Impact of fathers on daughters' age at menarche: A genetically and environmentally controlled sibling study. *Developmental Psychology, 44*(5), 1409–1420. http://dx.doi.org/10.1037/a0001 3065 Medline:18793072

Toerien, M., & Wilkinson, S. (2003). Gender and body hair: Constructing the feminine woman. *Women's Studies International Forum, 26*(4), 333–344. http://dx.doi.org/10.1016/S0277-5395(03)00078-5

Tolman, D.L. (2002). *Dilemmas of desire: Teenage girls talk about sexuality.* Cambridge, MA: Harvard University Press.

Townsend, T.G. (2008). Protecting our daughters: Intersection of race, class and gender in African American mothers' socialization of their daughters' heterosexuality. *Sex Roles, 59*(5–6), 429–442. http://dx.doi.org/10.1007/s11199-008-9409-3

Trebay, G. (2008). He's pregnant. You're speechless. *New York Times.* http://www.nytimes.com/2008/06/22/fashion/22pregnant.html

Tregaskis, C. (2002). Social model theory: The story so far. *Disability & Society, 17*(4), 457–470. http://dx.doi.org/10.1080/09687590220140377

Tremblay, M.S., Katzmarzyk, P.T., & Willms, J.D. (2002). Temporal trends in overweight and obesity in Canada, 1981–1996. *International Journal of Obesity, 26*(4), 538–543. http://dx.doi.org/10.1038/sj.ijo.0801923 Medline:12075581

Turner, L. (1999). Column inches. *The Independent.* http://www.independent.co.uk/life-style/column-inches-1091081.html

Tweed, A. (2003). *Health care utilization among women who have undergone breast implant surgery.* Vancouver: British Columbia Centre of Excellence for Women's Health.

Unger, R.K. (1979). Toward a Redefinition of Sex and Gender. *American Psychologist, 34*(11), 1085–1094. http://dx.doi.org/10.1037/0003-066X.34.11.1085

University of Iowa Hospitals and Clinics (2006). *Precocious puberty in girls.* www.uihealthcare.org/Adam/?/HIE Multimedia/1/001168

UPIAS. (1976). *Fundamental principles of disability.* London: The Union of the Physically Impaired Against Segregation.

Uskul, A.K. (2004). Women's menarche stories from a multicultural sample. *Social Science & Medicine, 59*(4), 667–679. http://dx.doi.org/10.1016/j.socscimed.2003.11.031 Medline:15177826

Ussher, J.M. (1989). *The psychology of the female body.* London, Eng.: Routledge.

Ussher, J.M. (1997). *Fantasies of femininity: Reframing the boundaries of sex.* New Brunswick, NJ: Rutgers University Press.

Valeras, A.B. (2010). "We don't have a box": Understanding hidden disability identity utilizing narrative research methodology. *Disability Studies Quarterly, 30*(3–4). http://dsq-sds.org/article/view/1267/1297

van Jaarsveld, C.H., Fidler, J.A., Simon, A.E., & Wardle, J. (2007). Persistent impact of pubertal timing on trends in smoking, food choice, activity, and stress in adolescence. *Psychosomatic Medicine, 69*(8), 798–806. http://dx.doi.org/10.1097/PSY.0b013e3181576106 Medline:17942841

Van Marsh, A. (2007). UK's skin bleaching trade exposed. CNN.com, Health. http://edition.cnn.com/2007/HEALTH/11/26/vanmarsh.skinbleaching/index.html

Vander Wal, J.S. (2004). Eating and body image concerns among average-weight and obese African American and Hispanic girls. *Eating Behaviors, 5*(2), 181–187. http://dx.doi.org/10.1016/j.eatbeh.2004.01.007 Medline:15093787

Vanwesenbeeck, I. (2009). The risks and rights of sexualization: An appreciative commentary on Lerum and Dworkin's "bad girls rule". *Journal of Sex Research, 46*(4), 268–273. http://dx.doi.org/10.1080/00224490903082694 Medline:19657946

Veet® survey reveals groomed bikini lines more important to women than toned bodies. (2011). PR Web. http://www.prweb.com/releases/2011/5/prweb8415224.htm

Veninga, C. (2009). Fitting in: The embodied politics of race in Seattle's desegregated schools. *Social & Cultural Geography, 10*(2), 107–129. http://dx.doi.org/10.1080/14649360802652103

Vesalius, A. (1543). *De humani corporis fabrica* (On the fabric of the human body). http://vesalius.northwestern.edu/

Viglione, J., Hannon, L., & DeFina, R. (2011). The impact of light skin on prison time for Black female offenders. *Social Science Journal, 48*(1), 250–258. http://dx.doi.org/10.1016/j.soscij.2010.08.003

Vonarburg, E. (1992). *The Maerlande chronicles.* Victoria, BC: Tesseract Books.

Wagner-Ott, A. (2002). Analysis of gender identity through doll and action figure politics in art education. *Studies in Art Education, 43*(3), 246–263. http://dx.doi.org/10.2307/1321088

Wallace-Sanders, K. (2008). *Mammy: A century of race, gender, and southern memory.* Ann Arbor: University of Michigan Press.

Walters, T., & Griffis, L. (n.d.). *Imagery, individual identity and independent living: Addressing oppression through positive imagery.* Independent Living Canada. http://www.ilcanada.ca/article/imagery-and-disability--248.asp

Wang, Y. (2002). Is obesity associated with early sexual maturation? A comparison of the association in American boys versus girls. *Pediatrics, 110*(5), 903–910. http://dx.doi.org/10.1542/peds.110.5.903 Medline:12415028

Warburton, S. (2011). Global lingerie market sees uplifting forecast. Global Intimate Wear. http://www.globalintimatewear.com/news/content.aspx?ns_id=2901

Ward, J.V. (1996). Raising resisters: The role of truth telling in the psychological development of African American Girls. In B.J. Ross Leadbeater & N. Way (Eds.), *Urban girls: Resisting stereotypes, creating identities* (pp. 85–99). New York: New York University Press.

Weber, B.R. (2007). Makeover as takeover: Scenes of affective domination on makeover TV. *Configurations, 15*(1), 77–99. http://dx.doi.org/10.1353/con.0.0020

Weiss, G. (1999). *Body images: Embodiment as intercorporeality.* New York: Routledge.

Welch, D. (2007). Zoo trapped in own cage. *Sydney Morning Herald.* http://www.smh.com.au/articles/2007/08/14/1186857485649.html

Wellesley College & American Association of University Women. (1992). *How schools shortchange girls: The AAUW report. A study of major findings on girls and education.* Washington: AAUW Educational Foundation.

Wendell, S. (1996). *The rejected body: Feminist philosophical reflections on disability.* New York: Routledge.

Wendell, S. (2008). Notes from bed: Learning from chronic illness. In D. Driedger & M. Owen (Eds.), *Dissonant disabilities: Women with chronic illnesses explore their lives* (pp. 209–217). Toronto: Women's Press.

West, C., & Zimmerman, D.H. (1987). Doing gender. *Gender & Society, 1*(2), 125–151. http://dx.doi.org/10.1177/0891243287001002002

White authority in the media. (2010). Media Awareness Network. http://www.media-awareness.ca/english/issues/stereotyping/whiteness_and_privilege/whiteness_authority.cfm

Wilchins, R.A. (2004). *Queer theory, gender theory: An instant primer*. Los Angeles: Alyson Books.

Wilder, J., & Cain, C. (2011). Teaching and learning color consciousness in Black families: Exploring family processes and women's experiences with colorism. *Journal of Family Issues, 32*(5), 577–604. http://dx.doi.org/10.1177/0192513X10390858

Williams, C. (2002). Naked, neutered, or noble: The Black female body in America and the problem of photographic history. In K. Wallace-Sanders (Ed.), *Skin-deep, spirit strong: The Black female body in American culture* (pp. 182–200). Ann Arbor: University of Michigan Press.

Williams, L.S. (2002). Trying on gender, gender regimes, and the process of becoming women. *Gender & Society, 16*(1), 29–52. http://dx.doi.org/10.1177/0891243202016001003

Williams, L.S. (2009). Doing culture with girls like me: Why trying on gender and intersectionality matters. *Social Compass, 3*(2), 217–233. http://dx.doi.org/10.1111/j.1751-9020.2009.00197.x

Wilson, D., & Macdonald, D. (2010). *The income gap between Aboriginal peoples and the rest of Canada*. Ottawa, ON: Canadian Centre for Policy Alternatives. http://www.policyalternatives.ca/sites/default/files/uploads/publica tions/reports/docs/Aboriginal%20Income%20Gap.pdf

"Win a boob-job" advert is rapped. (2005). *BBC News*. http://www.bbc.co.uk/news/

Wolf, N. (1992). *The beauty myth: How images of beauty are used against women*. New York: Anchor Books.

Wood-Barcalow, N.L., Tylka, T.L., & Augustus-Horvath, C.L. (2010). "But I Like My Body": Positive body image characteristics and a holistic model for young-adult women. *Body Image, 7*(2), 106–116. http://dx.doi.org/10.1016/j.bodyim.2010.01.001 Medline:20153990

Woodside, D.B., Garfinkel, P.E., Lin, E., Goering, P., Kaplan, A.S., Goldbloom, D.S., & Kennedy, S.H. (2001). Comparisons of men with full or partial eating disorders, men without eating disorders, and women with eating disorders in the community. *American Journal of Psychiatry, 158*(4), 570–574. http://dx.doi.org/10.1176/appi.ajp.158.4.570 Medline:11282690

World Health Organization. (2000). *Obesity: Preventing and managing the global epidemic*. Geneva, Switzerland: Author.

World Health Organization. (n.d.). *Controlling the global obesity epidemic*. http://www.who.int/nutrition/topics/obesity/en/index.html

World shaving products market to exceed US$25.7 billion by 2010. (2008). PR Web. http://www.prweb.com/releases/shaving_products/razors_shavers_lotions/prweb741274.htm

Wright, J. (2009). Biopower, biopedagogies and the obesity epidemic. In J. Wright & V. Harwood (Eds.), *Biopolitics and the "obesity epidemic": Governing bodies* (pp. 1–14). New York: Routledge.

Yates, A. (1989). Current perspectives on the eating disorders: I. History, psychological and biological aspects. *Journal of the American Academy of Child and Adolescent Psychiatry 28*(6), 813–828.

Yeoman, F., Asome, C., & Keeley, G. (2006). Skinniest models are banned from catwalk. *The Times.* www.thetimes.co.uk/tto/news/world/europe/article2599996.ece

Yildiz, B. O., Bolour, S., Woods, K., Moore, A., & Azziz, R. (2010). Visually scoring hirsutism. *Human reproduction update, 16*(1), 51-64.

Young, I.M. (1990). *Throwing like a girl and other essays in feminist philosophy and social theory.* Bloomington: Indiana University Press.

Yun, A.J., Bazar, K.A., & Lee, P.Y. (2004). Pineal attrition, loss of cognitive plasticity, and onset of puberty during the teen years: Is it a modern maladaptation exposed by evolutionary displacement? *Medical Hypotheses, 63*(6), 939–950. http://dx.doi.org/10.1016/j.mehy.2004.07.027 Medline:15504560

Zehr, J.L., Culbert, K.M., Sisk, C.L., & Klump, K.L. (2007). An association of early puberty with disordered eating and anxiety in a population of undergraduate women and men. *Hormones and Behavior, 52*(4), 427–435. http://dx.doi.org/10.1016/j.yhbeh.2007.06.005 Medline:17707381

Zitzelsberger, H., Rice, C., Whittington-Walsh, F., Odette, F., & Aubin, A. (2002). *Building bridges across difference and disability: A resource guide for health providers.* Toronto: Building Bridges.

Zitzelsberger, H.M. (2005). (In)visibility: Accounts of embodiment of women with physical disabilities and differences. *Disability & Society, 20*(4), 389–403. http://dx.doi.org/10.1080/09687590500086492

Zitzelsberger, H.M. (2010). Sylvie: A reflection on embodiments and transformations. *Radical Psychology, 8*(1). http://radicalpsychology.org/vol8-1/zitzelsberger.html

Index